Los Angeles &
the Future of Urban Cultures

Los Angeles & the Future of Urban Cultures

A Special Issue of *American Quarterly*

Edited by

Raúl Homero Villa
& George J. Sánchez

The Johns Hopkins University Press
Baltimore & London

© 2005 American Studies Association
All rights reserved. Published 2005
Printed in the United States of America on acid-free paper
9 8 7 6 5 4 3 2 1

The Johns Hopkins University Press
2715 North Charles Street
Baltimore, Maryland 21218-4363
www.press.jhu.edu

ISBN 0-8018-8208-7 (pbk.)

Library of Congress Control Number: 2004116626

A catalog record for this book is available from the British Library.

Book design by William Longhauser

For more information about *American Quarterly*, please see:
www.press.jhu.edu/journals/american_quarterly/

Contents

Preface   *vii*
    Marita Sturken

Introduction:
Los Angeles Studies and the Future of Urban Cultures / 1
    Raúl Homero Villa and George J. Sánchez

Best MTA Bus Line: The Number 18, yes, let's take a trip down
Whittier Boulevard / 9
    Marisela Norte

Learning from Los Angeles: Another One Rides the Bus / 13
    George Lipsitz

Los Angeles and American Studies in a Pacific World of Migrations / 33
    Henry Yu

Border City: Race and Social Distance in Los Angeles / 47
    Greg Hise

The Figure of the Neighbor: Los Angeles Past and Future / 61
    Dana Cuff

Straight into Compton: American Dreams, Urban Nightmares,
and the Metamorphosis of a Black Suburb / 85
    Josh Sides

L.A. Race Woman: Charlotta Bass and the Complexities of Black Political
Development in Los Angeles / 109
    Regina Freer

"What's Good for Boyle Heights Is Good for the Jews":
Creating Multiracialism on the Eastside during the 1950s / 135
    George J. Sánchez

The Art of the City: Modernism, Censorship, and the Emergence of
Los Angeles's Postwar Art Scene / 165
    Sarah Schrank

Bringing Music to the People: Race, Urban Culture, and Municipal Politics in
Postwar Los Angeles / 195
    Anthony Macías

The Battle of Los Angeles: The Cultural Politics of Chicana/o Music in the Greater
Eastside / 221
    Victor Hugo Viesca

What Is an MC If He Can't Rap to Banda?
Making Music in Nuevo L.A. / 243
    Josh Kun

Fools Banished from the Kingdom: Remapping Geographies of Gang Violence
between the Americas (Los Angeles and San Salvador) / 261
    Elana Zilberg

Borders and Social Distinction in the Global Suburb / 283
    Kristen Hill Maher

Nuestra Los Angeles / 309
    Michael Nevin Willard

Contributors   347
Index   351

Preface

Thuis volume is the first special issue of *American Quarterly* to be published in book form. It is the aim of these special issues to bring together innovative and timely scholarship in the interdisciplinary field of American studies that intersects with other academic disciplines and fields of study. *Los Angeles and the Future of Urban Cultures* thus presents a range of scholarship and artistic production that demonstrates the dialogue between American studies and urban studies. It brings together the work of Los Angeles artists and American studies scholars working in urban history, cultural theory, ethnic studies, political science, anthropology, English, art history, and architecture, to examine what the city of Los Angeles can tell us about urban culture, diasporic communities, racial and ethnic identities, urban cultural production, social justice and injustice, and the postindustrial, global cities of the twenty-first century.

This book is the result of a collective effort by *American Quarterly* editors, guest editors, and staff members. *American Quarterly* is the journal of the American Studies Association, and we are grateful to ASA executive director John Stephens and former ASA president Amy Kaplan for their support. In addition to guest editors Raúl Villa, who worked tirelessly on this issue and shaped it in important ways, and George Sánchez, who originally conceived the idea of celebrating the move of *American Quarterly* to the West Coast by focusing on Los Angeles, this book benefited from the steady and valuable editorial labor of *American Quarterly* associate editors Barry Shank and Katherine Kinney and managing board members Shelley Streeby and Eric Avila, and from the enthusiastic support of the rest of the managing board: Mary Dudziak, Judith Jackson Fossett, Carla Kaplan, Fred Moten, Bruce Robertson, John Carlos Rowe, Helena M. Wall, and Henry Yu. *American Quarterly* managing editor Hillary Jenks was crucial to keeping this editing process well coordinated, and *American Quarterly* staff members Cynthia Willis, Melissa Anderson, Ariella Horwitz, Stephanie Kolberg, Cynthia Maram, Mark Okuhata, and Leon James Snodgrass provided invaluable support labor. Stacey Lynn was our skilled and steady copy editor. Many of these essays were originally presented at a conference that was generously hosted by the Huntington Library. We are grateful for the funding support that we have received from the College of Letters, Arts and Sciences, the Provost's Office, and the Annenberg School for Communication at the University of Southern California, and the James Irvine Foundation. At the Johns Hopkins University Press, this project has been expertly shepherded by William Breichner, Lynn Logan, and Claire McCabe. Finally, we thank William Longhauser, whose wonderful design helped us to make this book a reflection of the vibrant visual world that is L.A.

—Marita Sturken, Editor, *American Quarterly*

Los Angeles &
the Future of Urban Cultures

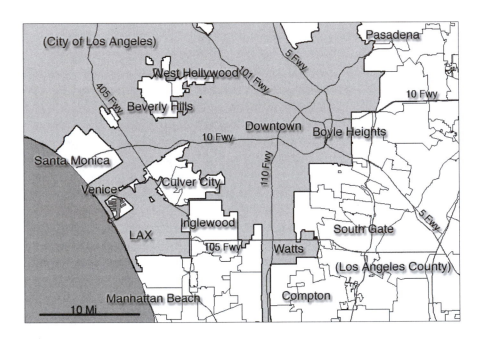

Introduction:
Los Angeles Studies and the Future of Urban Cultures

This special issue of *American Quarterly* focuses on Los Angeles as an emblematic site through which the scholarship of American studies can be examined at its most innovative—as a city in which the local is deployed in complex practices of identity and community formation within the broader networks of globalization that continue to define and redefine what constitutes America. This issue was initiated by the fact that *American Quarterly* is now housed, for the first time in its history, on the West Coast of the United States. Yet, while we do want to acknowledge the symbolic import of *AQ*'s much belated acceptance of Horace Greeley's famous directive to "go west," our "local" focus on Los Angeles is intended to draw attention to the current practices and strategies of the field of American studies more broadly.

Our localized attention to Los Angeles thus aims to examine the city not as an exceptional site, but, rather, as one that is indicative of the key issues that define contemporary American studies. To this end, the essays collected here follow upon, but do not fully subscribe to, the macro-perspectives of the "L.A. School" of urban studies, which defines the greater Los Angeles metropolitan region as preeminently, perhaps singularly, exemplary of the tendential urban processes at work in all "world cities," if not all major cities across the globe. By extension, the paradigmatic qualities of metro Los Angeles allow for predictive and generalizable conclusions to be drawn from its past and present urban processes. In this vein, Mike Davis, who is something of an outlaw cousin to the L.A. School proper, ascribes just such a prophetic quality to the study of Los Angeles in the title and method of his well-known book *City of Quartz: Excavating the Future in Los Angeles*. In titling this issue "Los Angeles and the Future of Urban Cultures," we want to call attention to the tension between those two broad positions: the paradigmatic singularity and prognostic quality of metropolitan Los Angeles. The opportunity of a special issue to gather essays focused on related concerns, in this case the forms and meanings of urban culture in a globally inflected but locally distinctive metropolis, may allow us to

Figure 1.
Map of City of Los Angeles and Adjacent Municipalities, courtesy of Philip J. Ethington.

consider how American studies as a field, like Los Angeles as a subject, calls for a particular kind of *situated* intellectual practice. As a city shaped successively by eighteenth-century European colonization, nineteenth-century U.S. territorial expansion, and twentieth-century migration from across the nation and the world, Los Angeles has come to embody both the hopes and fears of Americans looking to the future of the nation and the world. At the same time, these rich and troubled historical precedents ask us to be deeply attentive to the importance of place and location (in all their implications) if we hope to understand our own historical moment and best prepare for our evolving future.

The opportunity of a special issue also allows us to focus attention on several artists whose work is similarly situated in metropolitan Los Angeles, yet who connect to wider practices of identity and community formation within broad networks of globalization. The cover of this issue features the work of artist Alma Lopez, who speaks to the present and future of Los Angeles: representations of the hope and despair, the promises and boundaries that such a global city exemplifies. Robbert Flick's photography of streetscapes along the boulevards of the region emphasizes spatial mobility while pushing us to see the future of world cities reshaped by human migration, global capital, and cultural exchange. The milieu of the urban bus rider is vividly introduced to us through the poetry of Marisela Norte, who directly interacts with this global, yet quite local, world on a daily basis, marking the changes to the Los Angeles landscape over both time and geography.

George Lipsitz's essay, "Learning from Los Angeles: Another One Rides the Bus," asks us to "learn from Los Angeles," not necessarily because it is special or unique, but because it has much to tell us about living in places that constitute a crossroads for so many different networks of peoples and cultures. He rightfully notes that if we are to envision the democratic and egalitarian cultural spaces of our possible future we must learn from the past of Los Angeles, and other places like it, both inside and outside the United States. Knowing where we stand, both in physical place and state of mind, matters tremendously, as it informs the actions we take, individually and collectively, to realize our visions in the future.

Henry Yu's essay, "Los Angeles and American Studies in a Pacific World of Migration," and Greg Hise's essay, "Border City: Race and Social Distance in Los Angeles," extend the consideration of Los Angeles as a social and spatial nexus, but take it in very different directions. Yu reflects on the many global routes and forces that have brought people to this crossroads. In this account, he asks us to view migration as central to American studies scholarship, thus escaping the parochial nationalism that has often defined the field and that of immigration studies. By emphasizing the long-standing role of transnational migration in linking local places across space, he calls on us to interrogate the various spatial practices and ideologies that have constructed both national-ism and regional distinctiveness as particular acts of imagination. Rather than emphasize movement and fluidity, Hise reveals the border-making processes that have long defined the city's concrete social geography. In his analysis, these urban practices of social distinction are organizing tropes of Los Angeles's modernity, as it was imagined and enacted by the white men who would come to control this particular outpost of empire. The rigid ethnic binaries that structured the developing metropolis were not only mapped onto particular racialized bodies, but were built into physical form on the landscape, giving imagined difference a topography that would be repeatedly reenacted in the history of the region.

The varied perspectives of these opening essays point us toward distinct strategies for understanding the broad shaping patterns and forces at play in the Los Angeles region. In light of such intellectual variety, how could any single publication pretend to fairly represent the state of this metropolis and the methods necessary to understand it? How, in other words, can we best know this place called Los Angeles? The very expansiveness of this urban ob-ject famously mocked as "sixty suburbs in search of a city," demanded a par-ticular sort of specificity in our approach. So, taking a cue from our lived experience of the city (and those of the many authors who inhabit it with us), we felt that understanding Los Angeles required close historical, material, and conceptual attention to its variegated neighborhood formations. It is in these distinct and localized community geographies that the everyday problems and promises of urban life are played out. By attending to various case-specific investigations in the subsequent essays, we hoped to construct a cumulative, but necessarily approximate and partial sense of what the amorphous entity "Los Angeles" was and is, and how to understand it in the present moment.

To this end, Dana Cuff's essay, "The Figure of the Neighbor: Los Angeles Past and Future," takes the neighborhood as a conceptual and interpretive point of departure. Cuff analyzes the politics of neighbor relations and broader civic participation produced differently in five distinct residential areas, which traverse both historical time and regional space, as they are subjected to and respond to changing urban conditions. The practiced ideologies of neighbor relations, embodied in the "figure of the neighbor," are critical in shaping the relationship between individual households and the larger urban culture. This relationship may take the form of casual neighborhood support structures or may fan out to include more formally organized neighborhood associations and public political mobilization. Josh Sides's essay, "Straight into Compton:

American Dreams, Urban Nightmares, and the Metamorphosis of a Black Suburb," reveals the specific and shifting conditions of life and status in the urban imagination of a single neighborhood across time. Compton has been a neighborhood in transition from its first incarnation as a white-only city guarding against integration to a relatively stable African American–dominated suburb in which black home owners were able to approximate the American Dream and organize their own civic leadership and institutions. That the place name "Compton" became a mass-media symbol for racial despair in the wake of economic restructuring, labor market disintegration, and gang violence suggests how the discursive ability of an individual neighborhood to represent its own sense of political, economic, and cultural identity is severely compromised and vulnerable in our age of globalized media saturation. Complementing Sides's analysis, Regina Freer's essay, "L.A. Race Woman: Charlotta Bass and the Complexities of Black Political Development in Los Angeles," reveals how African Americans' political ideology and actions were shaped by the unique circumstances of their neighborhoods in the pre– and post–World War II period. The relatively open housing options and distance from overt racial violence in the prewar period distinguished Los Angeles for blacks, who moved to Los Angeles in order to own homes and escape the confines of the East Coast and the American South. Even as increased segregation after the war exacerbated racial conditions and constrained black residential spaces, the still relatively small size of the community within a larger multiethnic population compelled cross-class solidarity and cross-ethnic coalitions beyond its emerging borders. Bass's political life as a "race woman" was defined by these evolving contours of Los Angeles's black community, for whom she advocated in her journalistic and organizational activism.

In many metropolitan areas, the demographic, economic, and physical transformations set in motion during and after World War II would profoundly reorient urban and civil society toward its present conditions. In Los Angeles, the struggle over the form and meaning of urban culture was dramatically enacted in and across its neighborhoods during the 1950s. The next group of essays reflect the resurgence of scholarly interest in this period of supposed cultural repression and conformity. They highlight a battle of civic wills as government bureaucrats and political elites tried to impose their ideals on specific neighborhoods and communities, often under the guise of anticommunism, while specific community alliances pushed for more creative expression and social justice.

In his essay, "'What's Good for Boyle Heights Is Good for the Jews': Creating Multiracialism on the Eastside during the 1950s," George Sánchez looks at the Eastside neighborhood of Boyle Heights, where a liberal and leftist

Jewish community attempted to create a multiracial progressive constituency that would stand as an "example of democratic progress" for the rest of the city. The avant-garde and modernist communities of artists treated in Sarah Schrank's essay, "The Art of the City: Modernism, Censorship, and the Emergence of Los Angeles's Postwar Art Scene," attempted to establish neighborhoods of alternative lifestyles and free artistic expression both in Venice and near the Ferus Gallery in West Los Angeles. However, these places of creative identity and experimentation fell victim to the cannibalizing power of entrepreneurial capitalism and the harassment of local police authority. In both Sanchez's and Schrank's essays, the cultural politics of specific Los Angeles communities are framed by questions of racial equality and public surveillance, with claims of "communist inspiration" being used to limit the range of urban civility and expression. The complexities of postwar music explored in Anthony Macías's essay, "Bringing Music to the People: Race, Urban Culture, and Municipal Politics in Postwar Los Angeles," were also played out across the social geography and political boundaries of Southern California and in a social arena of conflicting ideas about the form and nature of civic culture. On one side of this contested terrain, a multiracial community of musicians and entrepreneurs created a rich rhythm-and-blues scene in the company of a loyal and growing fan base drawn from nearly all the region's neighborhoods. Enabled by a resourceful infrastructure and the mobility of young people seeking expressive venues across the region, these early scenesters refused to settle for what civic elites and police considered proper cultural and leisure pursuits. This dialectical antagonism of cultural taste and practices created "competing visions of Los Angeles." The competition would play itself out well beyond the period treated by Macías, as music became a recurring flash point for subsequent generations of expressive identity politics.

Victor Viesca's essay, "The Battle of Los Angeles: The Cultural Politics of Chicana/o Music in the Greater Eastside," and Josh Kun's essay, "What Is an MC If He Can't Rap to Banda? Making Music in Nuevo L.A.," suggest the continuing vitality and symbolic urgency of music in late-twentieth- and early-twenty-first-century Los Angeles. Both authors point to the florescence of cultural ingenuity and hybridity in the music of the "Greater Eastside," that growing megaregion of predominantly Mexican neighborhoods in eastern and southern Los Angeles County, in the wake of urban restructuring, economic deindustrialization, and massive circular migration across the U.S.–Mexico border. Viesca uncovers musical and cultural expressive practices that draw upon the "traveling cultures" of Asian, Latin American, and African diasporas in the multiracial communities of this Mexican-dominated region. These creative practices also expand the meaning of a "Chicana/o" cultural politics to include ethnic multiplicity, greater gender equity, and actively politicized community orientations. Like Viesca, Kun analyzes the emergent cultural politics of a city in which whites are a demographic (if not yet political) minority, but focuses on the borrowings across black and Latino cultural scenes that combine U.S. "urban" and Mexican "regional" music into new configurations of transnational, hybrid cultural expression. Both authors see the music scene in Los Angeles at the beginning of this century as having deep historical roots and resonances, while pointing toward emergent cultural ideologies and practices that transgress previously bounded elements of genre, language, and style. As Kun notes, the sound of "Nuevo L.A." produces recombinant forms of civic-cultural identity in which musical producers and consumers are no longer asked "to choose one world over the other but allow[ed] . . . to flow between both."

And yet, even as globalization and new demographic circumstances have enabled emergent forms of creativity to transcend bounded cultural categories, these same conditions have produced other social and spatial constraints characteristic of "Nuevo L.A." Both Elana Zilberg and Kristen Hill Maher deal with specific and distinct neighborhoods in the region that have experienced the negative repercussions of global migration, transnational subjectivities, and cultural flows. With ethnographic research spanning two nations, Zilberg's essay, "Fools Banished from the Kingdom: Remapping Geographies of Gang Violence between the Americas (Los Angeles and San Salvador)," describes the "forced transnationality" of deported Salvadoran youth from Los Angeles's immigrant barrio neighborhoods, often through the collaboration of local police departments and the federal Immigration and Naturalization Service. Deported Salvadoran immigrant gang youth are banished from the United States and "returned" to a "home" they do not remember, creating new geographies of belonging, exclusion, and violence that intertwine the barrio landscape of Los Angeles with its paired barrios in San Salvador. In "Borders and Social Distinction in the Global Suburb," Maher also investigates the role of globalization in Southern California, but in the radically different milieu of suburban Orange County. In her ethnographic study, globalization has eviscerated the absolute physical segregation that used to secure suburban communities like predominantly white Irvine from the perceived urban ills of greater Los Angeles. In response, white suburbanites have created new typologies and everyday practices of cultural distinction to keep residents of nearby Santa Ana, with its Latino immigrant majority, at a safe social, if not absolute spatial, distance. Maher makes clear the irony that the very benefits accruing to Irvine residents through a globalized economy also create the conditions that bring "urban" minorities regularly to their neighborhood for service labor. This pattern forces new regimes of social regulation to emerge and define the borders of a global suburb. In this analysis, we can see that the formative practices and ideologies that constructed the early "modern" metropolis of Los Angeles at the turn of the twentieth century, as noted by Greg Hise, are still at work, with new spatial twists, in the postmodern megalopolis of Southern California.

As the essays collected here take up the complexities of Los Angeles's social geography across time, and particularly since World War II, they mirror the exciting proliferation of cultural studies perspectives that have come to characterize the field of American studies over the last decade and a half. For example, the cultivation of truly diverse perspectives and topics by the selection committees of the annual meetings of the American Studies Association since the early 1990s highlights a welcome and necessary commitment to the value of intellectual diversity. Michael Willard's bibliographic review essay, "Nuestra Los Angeles," which concludes this collection, offers us another vantage point for considering the real and valuable expansion of Los Angeles studies by way of the many recent works that coincide with this substantive diversification of American studies. Willard situates contemporary Los Angeles scholarship in relation to the precursory groundwork laid out by Carey McWilliams in the 1940s, and provides a map of the succeeding generation of Los Angeles studies scholars who are filling in the details of that broad L.A. School perspective, with particular attention to its many constituent cultural and community landscapes. This current and proliferating generation of scholarship mirrors the diversification of subjects and conceptual tool kits in the current scholarly practices of American studies more broadly. This is no accident, of course, as many of these authors have received specific academic training in and maintain institutional affiliations with American studies programs. We hope that the readers of this volume will appreciate the synergistic possibilities we are indicating in the intersection of current Los Angeles studies and American studies generally.

This publication is the result of a collective process, involving significant input from an extended editorial group and the administrative staff at *American Quarterly*. For their invaluable contributions to this cause, we would like to thank *American Quarterly* editors Marita Sturken, Katherine Kinney, and Barry Shank, *AQ* managing board members Eric Avila and Shelley Streeby, *AQ* editorial staff members Hillary Jenks and Cynthia Willis, and our colleague Bill Deverell.

—Raúl Homero Villa and George J. Sánchez

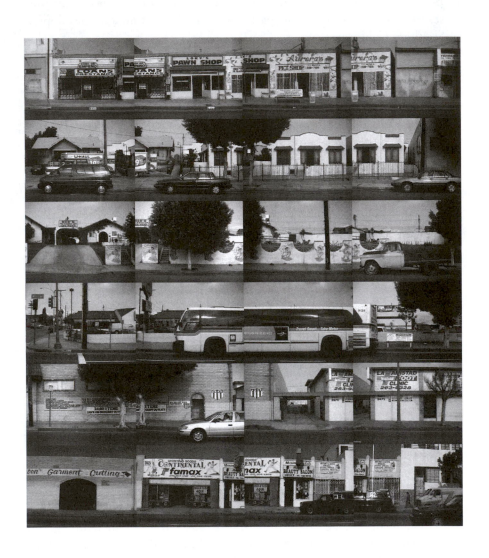

Best MTA Bus Line:
The Number 18, yes, let's take a trip down Whittier Boulevard

Marisela Norte

"So Moms, lemme ask you something. How old was I when you first took me on a bus ride down Whittier Boulevard?" "You were almost 3," she says. "I was still holding you in my arms."

There is just a slight wistfulness in her tone. For the past 44 years, the town where I live, my East Los Angeles, still holds me in its arms. And for those 44 years I have opted for that No. 18 bus as my sole means of transport, of navigating through that very same Thomas Brothers Guide (Orange County pages included) tucked underneath the seat of your car. I purchased my first Thomas Brothers Guide in Chinatown from a guy named Manny, who was having an "Everything Must Go Thomas Brothers Guide Closeout Sale" from the trunk of his burgundy '69 Riviera. Let the record so state, straight up and with a twist.

With all due respect to Joan Didion, I like to sit next to someone I don't know (and may never see again) better than I like sitting behind the wheel of a car (most likely alone). Los Angeles doesn't need another driver out on the streets. And call me superstitious, but I learned how to drive in a green '71 Pinto in the Biba-lipped, T. Rex–meets–Al Green teenage Summer of '72. I ask myself, just how would I maneuver gearshifts, gas pedals, while adjusting seamed stockings and rear views of Whittier Boulevard as a miniature pine-tree air freshener sways back and forth in sleep-inducing arcs? Why have me behind the wheel, when, through a bus window darkly on the Number 18, I am able to take poetic leaps and transport myself through the language of street corners and memory, imagined lives and my dreams of East L.A. Days and Fellini Nights?

Figure 1.
Photographs of Whittier Boulevard by Robbert Flick.

A man across town I know smiles whenever I mention my discovery of the midtown street named Fedora. He has a love connection to that street, and we banter like Phyllis Diedrichson and Walter Neff in *Double Indemnity*. So then, let me lay claim to Record Avenue and Baby Junior's legendary collection of vintage 45s, to Ford Boulevard School's Room 6 Class of '66: Lizze G. and

Frances C., this one goes out to you. From the nuts at the Nut Wagon to the Calvary Cemetery, DGamboa, I walk with you always.

My neighborhood—framed by Yum Yum Donuts, a Fotomat, and just down the street a storefront with a hand-painted sign that reads *Neuroticos Anonimos*—why have I yet to check in? When I close my eyes, I can still see a solid gold cow on the roof of the dairy on the Boulevard. A couple of doors down I still imagine a blond woman in an aquamarine dress sitting next to a tuxedoed man with patent-leather hair. They are sitting in a green room, nervously holding hands, their eyes fixed on the red flashing ON THE AIR sign in a corner. I imagined this couple as the bus went past a small sign for Rafu Television. As a kid, I thought for sure it was a bigtime television studio. My imaginary couple never suspected once that dusty stacks of television sets waited to be repaired.

It's 1968, and I am boarding the then-No. 72 bus on Whittier and Arizona, deliriously happy because I suspect that this particular bus will be filled with the cool guys from Garfield. Back in the day, you could check out the storefronts on the Boulevard and the likes of Dottie Dean, Kurly's, the Record Inn and Victor's Men's Wear, where a sign still reads, "Where you shop in taste, not in haste." Nowadays, Whittier Boulevard offers the best stretch of 99-, 98-, 97- and 89-cent stores around. If your taste runs to knockoff Hello Kitty backpacks and Kellogg's Corn Flakes imported from Israel, the Boulevard really shouldn't be missed.

It's 1979, and I am boarding the bus once again at the corner of Whittier Boulevard and Soto. Years from now, the sign at Carnitas Michoacan will read, "Over 5 Zillion Sold." This is the same sign I will one day alter to read, "Over 5 Zillion Still Ignored." Anyway, it's the late '70s, and I am busing downtown to transfer to the Number 10, which eventually will make its way toward Melrose Avenue and my first of many waitress gigs to come. Later that year, I will meet a rich young Hollywood producer and fall in love. He will go on to MTV Video Award fame. I will go on to MTA fame, when my words make their way inside buses throughout Los Angeles County as part of the Poetry in Motion project.

It's 1984, and I am crossing the bridge that links Whittier Boulevard to downtown Los Angeles. This is probably one of my favorite views of the city. Judging from the *Blade Runner*–esque black eye makeup I wear, I am on my way to meet my chums at Clifton's on Seventh and Broadway before we work our way through gallery party after gallery party. This is when artists could still afford the cheap rents around Rose and Traction, and it was just like that scene out of *La Dolce Vita* where partygoers held candelabra, and we made our way through stairwells up to rooftops and another view of our city. Back then, there was never any question about how and when I would be getting home. These days, I make sure to take that last sip before another Unhappy Hour comes to a close.

It's 2003, and I'm still cruising the Boulevard. There's a makeshift taqueria sandwiched between an eye clinic and a notary public on Whittier Boulevard where families gather nightly to watch *El Privilegio de Amar* and *Velo de Novia* on a small TV sitting on the hood of the owner's pickup truck. On several occasions, I've gotten off the bus to enjoy a couple of tacos and watch another long-suffering telenovela heroine weep through her waterproof mascara. The kids are all doing their homework. I stand at the corner of Whittier and Lorena and catch a glimpse of the downtown skyline. There's a comfort in knowing that the green sign on the skyscraper to the left brings back memories to East Angelenos. I like to think that there's a kid riding on a bus somewhere who also thinks of it as the Emerald City. Maybe he or she will be moved to pick up a pen and someday write a poem.

Sir Lonely puts his shades on. His Imperials pierce the moon, and so a page from the Puppet Zone falls over the blue night. Baby Loca carries 45s and checks out all the guys. Impalas slide around the corner in dangerous love as three stars hang heavy over the East.

Me drive? I don't think so.

Learning from Los Angeles: Another One Rides the Bus

George Lipsitz

The movement of the editorial offices of the *American Quarterly* from its historic home at eastern colleges, universities, and cultural institutions to Los Angeles and the University of Southern California presents us with cause for celebration.[1] This is not a declaration of coastal chauvinism or of local pride. It is certainly not a judgment about any of us as individuals in relation to our professional colleagues elsewhere. The particularities of place and the specificities of social relations require us to hope that *all* precincts are heard from, that we learn how life is lived everywhere in its full plurality and diversity. No place is innately superior to anyplace else; all places are intersections, crossroads, and nodes in larger spatial networks, but the people putting out the *American Quarterly* now live here, no place else. We have an opportunity to learn from Los Angeles and to pass on what we learn to a wider world.

The journal's conversations about American studies and what we call "American culture" take place today at a critical time. The most powerful people and the most entrenched institutions in our society are now waging a careful, calculated, and comprehensive cultural campaign about the meaning of America and American culture. Politicians and public relations specialists, marketers and military leaders, advertisers and entertainers speak to us with virtually one voice about what it means to be American. At this moment of danger it is incumbent on us to speak with precision and presence of mind about this abstraction called America.

The optic on "America" that Los Angeles offers presents us with extraordinary opportunities and solemn responsibilities. What can be seen from this particular standpoint might tell us a great deal about the abstraction called "America" and its cultures, if we succeed in opening our eyes and our ears, our minds and our hearts. This is a place populated by migrants from all over the nation and all over the globe. It is a place that is the home of powerful cultural industries, of mythmakers who magnify both the strengths and weaknesses of the local society to a wider world. This place is a site of struggle and servitude, imagination and affluence, gluttonous greed and punitive poverty. It is a place where people secure unpredictable pleasures and a place where people endure unbearable pain.

Learning from Los Angeles means hearing its voices and deciphering its signs and symbols. Fortunately for us, we are surrounded by expert listeners, interpreters, and analysts. Marisela Norte, Los Angeles's brilliant spoken word artist and singular cultural treasure, is one of the people who can teach us how to read the writing on the walls and to hear the words being spoken in so many different languages in this city. Every weekday, Norte rides the Number 18 bus from her home in East Los Angeles to her job downtown. She writes poems about the people, places, and things that she sees from her vantage point on the bus. For many years she let the length of the bus ride determine the length of her poems. When she reached her stop, the poem was over. Of course, given the unpredictable pace of bus service in Los Angeles, this meant that all forms of poetry remained possible, from the haiku to the epic.

Many people think of the bus as the transportation mode of last resort, as the crowded, messy, dirty, noisy nightmare lampooned in Los Angeles's own Weird Al Yankovic's parody of Queen's "Another One Bites the Dust": "Another One Rides the Bus." Yet for aggrieved populations the bus is more a necessity than a nightmare. Moira Rachel Kenney reveals in her history of gay and lesbian Los Angeles how important it has been for people judged nonnormative and criminal because of their sexuality to create "a mobility of daily life," noting that bars near the Greyhound bus station downtown emerged as the center of gay and lesbian life in the 1940s because they provided spaces in the city where people could interact with strangers without suspicion.[2]

Norte knows that a perfect bus never comes along. If you want to go somewhere, you hop on the first one that comes and take your chances. She became known as the "bus poet of Los Angeles" because of her powerful pieces delineating *las vidas de ellas*—the lives of working women in Los Angeles—women compelled by their limited incomes to ride public transportation in a city organized around automobile travel, women who shop at thrift stores in the glamour capital of the universe for bargain clothes with the labels cut out, women who struggle for dignity and respect in the face of the whistles, catcalls, sexist billboards, and even worse forms of harassment they risk as women negotiating public space in the city. Norte recognizes the bus as simultaneously a site of containment *and* connection, of incarceration *and* affiliation, of solitude *and* sociality.

As soon as I heard about Norte's writing, her work piqued my interest. Perhaps I thought I would profit from meeting the "bus poet" because my own writing has so often been described as "pedestrian." But as I got to know

Norte and her work, I saw that there was another, much more important, reason. Like so many other Los Angeles artists, intellectuals, and activists, Norte helps us see the part of the future that is already here in the present, the possibilities produced by the very problems that plague us.

Norte's Los Angeles is the Los Angeles of the late Gil Cuadros, who titled his collection of short stories about the metropolis *The City of God*, ironically mocking Saint Augustine's teleological vision, contrasting the writer's own AIDS-wracked body with the metropolitan body politic suffering from its own deleterious divisions and diseases.[3]

Norte's Los Angeles is the Los Angeles of former Black Panther Michael Zinzun, who received a brutal beating from police officers, causing him to lose his sight in one eye. In an imaginative reversal, he took the money he won suing the police department to establish the Coalition Against Police Abuse, an organization created to keep an "eye" on the police, in the process giving new meaning to the biblical phrase "an eye for an eye."

Norte's Los Angeles is the Los Angeles where warring gangs came together to sign a truce, placing the welfare of the entire community above the prestige of their own "sets." Recording under the name Makavelli (not Machiavelli), Tupac Shakur lauded the truce, advising that you can "love your hood" but still remember "that it's all good."

Norte's Los Angeles is the Los Angeles where Korean American, Japanese American, and Latina women professionals working at the Japanese American National Museum collaborated in 2002 with Chicano scholar George Sanchez to stage an exhibit and a series of programs remembering the multicultural history of the Boyle Heights neighborhood—now a Latino/a *barrio*, but once home to a mixed population of Japanese Americans, Latinos, Russian Molokans, blacks, and Jews. Through the educational activities of this Boyle Heights Project, Latino/a students at Roosevelt High School discovered that an empty spot on their school campus had been planned as a rock garden in the 1940s by Japanese American students who never completed the project because they and their families were placed in internment camps. As a tribute and as a statement of protest against the injustice of the internment, the Latino/a students completed the rock garden and dedicated it to those Roosevelt High School students who had been interned.[4]

The democratic and generative cultural imaginary of Los Angeles appears in brilliant relief in *Songs of the Unsung*, the posthumously published autobiography of jazz musician and cultural visionary Horace Tapscott. The book begins with an unusual turn of phrase, as Tapscott relates that he was born in 1934 in a hospital named Jefferson Davis in segregated Houston, Texas. From that moment on, he asserts, "I was locked here on this earth."[5] Mentioned immediately after "Jefferson Davis" and "segregated Houston, Texas," the phase "locked on this earth" connotes containment and incarceration, linking the life of a supremely successful contemporary African American musician to the lives of his slave ancestors and to the lives of the hundreds of thousands of black youths and adults presently locked up in the prisons of the United States.

Tapscott's memoir presents story after story of spatial and cultural confinement, of housing segregation, employment discrimination, police surveillance, and the marginalization and devaluation of black cultural creators and creations. Yet the book tells another story as well. "To lock on" also means to locate and follow a moving target. Tapscott's account reveals how he was "locked on this earth" in that sense as well, methodically "moving," literally and figuratively, to achieve his goals despite the shackles and bonds designed to keep him contained and immobile.

Tapscott writes lyrically about moving with his family to Los Angeles as a child, about the vibrant street life in the city's black neighborhoods, and about the many different kinds of teachers he encountered at "Sidewalk University." Even walking down the street provided inspiration for him. "To walk down Central," he remembers, "by the time you got to the end of the block, you'd have heard a whole new melody, because so many things were happening."[6]

Not everyone walked down Central. Buddy Collette and Charles Mingus lived along the Avenue, twelve blocks from each other in Watts. When they started getting musical jobs downtown, they would get on the Pacific Electric Interurban Streetcar (the Red Car) at the 103rd Street stop. Collette recalls that Mingus would unzip the cover of his bass and start to play. Collette would take out his alto saxophone and they would jam all the way downtown. "The conductor and the motorman would wave," Collette claims. "They didn't mind."[7]

The skills Tapscott learned from high school music teachers, relatives, friends, and fellow musicians enabled him to secure an opportunity to join the Lionel Hampton Band and see the world. But playing with the Hampton ensemble one evening, Tapscott came to feel that his victory had been a hollow one, that in the context of the commercial music industry, his playing had lost its meaning. He decided to come home to south central Los Angeles, to return to the neighborhood he left, to set up a center "to preserve and teach and show and perform the music of black Americans and Pan-African music, to preserve it by playing it and writing it and taking it to the community."[8]

Tapscott's book is a brilliant study in how far one can go simply by staying home. With no financial support from philanthropic foundations, social movements, or the state, Tapscott relied on the creativity and goodwill of his neighbors. They established an orchestra made up of musicians who enjoyed the opportunity to play outside the confines of commercial recording studios and nightclubs. The music attracted dancers and dance teachers, actors, playwrights, painters, and poets. Shakespearean actor William Marshall appeared one day to teach acting to neighborhood children. Saxophonist and multi-instrument virtuoso Rahsaan Roland Kirk, famous for his trick of playing two saxophones at the same time during performances, came to the group to give music lessons to children because, as he explained to Tapscott, "before I leave here, every black kid in the neighborhood is going to be playing two horns at once. I'm gonna see to that. That's my role, Horace."[9]

Actor (and later television star) Marla Gibbs set up a women's group, while political activists from around the world came to the site to start holding discussions about current events. One way to secure admission to the group's performances was to bring a can of food. After performing, the artists would deliver the food personally to needy people. In an illuminating anecdote, Tapscott reveals the love of the local that enabled his project to thrive. He relates that he knew his project was a success one day when his band members canceled their regularly scheduled rehearsal. Tapscott went for a walk on the street and an inebriated street person stopped him to ask, "Where's our band?" He said "*our* band," Tapscott notes, not "*your* band," and that was enough to let the musician know he had achieved his goal.[10]

It was not just that Tapscott's "Arkestra" received no support from the city's cultural, political, and economic institutions, but rather that the group succeeded despite massive opposition and repression. Police surveillance and harassment plagued the group constantly, yet Tapscott and his collaborators created a democratic, egalitarian, and visionary cultural space, the kind of space that should now be of special concern to the *American Quarterly* and its readers.

At this moment, the plural, egalitarian, democratic, and intercultural "America" envisioned and enacted by artists, intellectuals, and activists in Los Angeles and so many other places is in jeopardy. In the name of fighting a war against terrorism, the leaders of the nation are waging a calculated cultural campaign designed to give a particular and parochial meaning to America. Their America is a country, not a continent, a nation that proves itself through military power, not by keeping its political promises. They believe that the story of America is one unified narrative told from one point of view. In the name of unity, they seek unanimity. In their America, the Constitution is a convenience to be discarded in times of crisis, not a solemn guarantee against tyranny. They want a land where we dance to their tune, not our land of a thousand dances.

In the name of America, our leaders seek to turn the United States into a permanent warfare state, to abrogate fundamental constitutional rights, to funnel public money in perpetuity to private firms whose executives preach the sanctity of competition while enjoying unearned profits from no-bid contracts secured through insider connections. They seek to incite through fear what they cannot inspire through faith. When they cannot lead us, they lie to us. They portray criticism of them and their plans as criticism of the country. In the process they endanger and destroy the very nation they purport to protect.

Enormous anguish, pain, and suffering were provoked on September 11, 2001, by the criminal acts of fundamentalist fascists steeped in their own falsehoods about military masculinity and the redemptive powers of violence. Desires for retribution and revenge are understandable. But the social warrant that is emerging in the wake of September 11 does not honor or avenge the victims of September 11. Instead, it exploits their suffering to advance a cruel, calculated, cynical, and sadistic campaign on behalf of narrow economic ends and selfish political purposes.

When the attacks first occurred, our leaders told us "everything had changed." But they then displayed a giddy enthusiasm, advancing their own interests in a time of national emergency, proving that very little had actually changed for them. Terrorism became the excuse for drilling for oil in the Alaskan wilderness, for eliminating the inheritance tax, for supporting the employers' lockout of the International Longshore and Warehouse Union, for checking up on the immigration status of workers on strike against a meat packing firm in Worthington, Minnesota, and for undermining the first, fourth, and fourteenth amendments to the Constitution. At a moment when leaders of the United States could have generated unprecedented unity and a shared sense of sacrifice, advancing their own narrow agenda appealed to them more.

Our leaders stoke our fears to provoke the kind of unbridled passion that will assure them of unchecked power. We see no serious rethinking of the U.S. policies that channeled three billion dollars into Afghanistan during the 1980s to arm, train, and sustain the very people who have now emerged as our enemies. We see no foresight about what it means to use the war in Iraq as an opportunity to test programs for privatization of postal services, military supply, prisons, and policing. Subcontractors hired by the executive branch receive vast sums of money and employ some ten to twenty thousand mercenaries, but remain unaccountable to Congress. The machine-gun toting guards who protect the ruler of Afghanistan and the U.S. chief administrator in Iraq are private security guards, not U.S. military personnel. From protecting missile defense sites to feeding troops to delivering mail to repairing damaged oil rigs, these companies secure windfall profits but can keep their exact duties, expenditures, and activities secret. They can funnel the money they make back into political campaigns to support politicians whose policies offer them even greater opportunities for economic gain.

This privatization is not a by-product of the war against terror; it is one of its main aims. It is no accident that instead of allocating funds to capture actual terrorists, the "war on terror" funded the Defense Advanced Research Projects Agency (DARPA) plan for online traders to win money by speculating on the likelihood of terrorist acts. The same commitment to privatization led to the misconceived "Terrorism Information and Prevention System" (TIPS) program, which invited completely untrained civilians to engage in unrestrained racial profiling by asking them to report "anything suspicious" to the government. The TIPS program was so poorly planned as a means for fighting terrorism that when it provoked a wave of completely unverified and unverifiable "tips" from frightened citizens, Pentagon officials confessed that they had no way to process this information. But in keeping with the spirit of privatization, military officials suggested that the callers contact the Fox Television Network program staff of *America's Most Wanted* and give *them* their "information."[11] When White House Chief of Staff Andrew Card was asked why the administration began pressing for war in Iraq in September 2002 rather than earlier, he replied that everyone knows that September, not August, is the appropriate time for launching new products.[12]

The commercialization and trivialization of the war appeared in dramatic form when the San Diego Padres baseball team took the field in 2002 wearing uniforms splattered with military camouflage, apparently concerned that the Cincinnati "Reds" had more than baseball on their minds. Wearing camouflage uniforms in a town filled with military personnel was a way of turning a national tragedy into a marketing opportunity, an attempt to link a product sold for profit to the public interest. Dressing up baseball players in camouflage uniforms is a far different kind of gesture than observing a moment of silence for the soldiers and civilians killed in the war, wearing black arm bands to mourn the dead, or donating a portion of gate receipts to pay the costs of medical care for all those in agony in military and civilian hospitals.

Moreover, the camouflage did not even work. Despite their uniforms, the Padres' players were clearly visible—even from the upper deck. If they could be seen from that far away how could they expect to fool the other team?[13] But while it is possible to laugh at this conflation of greed and narcissistic grandiosity, it is really no laughing matter. Part of the project of the War on Terrorism has been to have the lust of the spectator take center stage and eclipse the responsibilities of the citizen. We experience a war waged without solemnity, without sorrow, without sadness, without civilian soldiers or shared sacrifice. Instead, images of masculinist military heroism and patriarchal power are performed for us as spectacle and sensation. They appeal alternately to sadism and sentimentality.

The policies conjured up in the wake of the war do not seem to require analysis, argument, or even evidence. They appear to be true because they have been validated on the terrain of culture long before they emerged as part of a political program. Rehearsed for us over and over again in countless cultural performances, they are being played out now on a larger stage with consequences that extend far beyond the realm of culture.

We might imagine places like Los Angeles to be the innocent victims of this privileging of spectatorship over citizenship, marketing over moral suasion, self-interest and avarice over shared social purpose. But as the home of Hollywood films, the capital of commercial television, and the frontline of fashion, Los Angeles has been one of the primary generators of these ways of thinking and being, not just the recipient. The forms of citizenship, subjectivity, and social membership central to the America being orchestrated by the nation's elites are grounded firmly in the ideals and aspirations learned and legitimated in the apparatuses of commercial culture.[14]

Moreover, the centrality of military spending to the prosperity of the Los Angeles region in the second half of the twentieth century served as the cornerstone of the national policies that make warfare remunerative and rewarding for key segments of the population.[15] This defensive localism, which is premised upon hoarding resources for one's own community while displacing costs and burdens onto others, took root in homeowner politics and antibusing mobilizations in Los Angeles long before they became the dominant framework for national politics at home and overseas.[16] Thus, the core cultural and economic institutions of Los Angeles bear no small measure of responsibility for the America being authored in the midst of the war on terror, a war that produces glee rather than grief, celebration rather than sorrow, unlimited self-righteousness but very little actual righteousness.

American studies scholars know much about the origins of this America. David W. Noble's brilliant book *Death of a Nation* explains how Puritan interpretations of the writings of Machiavelli (not Makavelli) led them to view American space as a potential refuge from the corruptions of European time. As a result, seventeenth- and eighteenth-century wars of conquest and extermination (and the subsequent European settlement of the continent) were guided by "the metaphor of two worlds"—by the belief in America as an island of innocence and virtue in a global sea of corruption. Noble shows how this image requires a powerful discourse of countersubversion, initially because indigenous peoples held beliefs antithetical to European notions of freedom, but later because whenever America is shown to be not pure, not innocent, not virtuous, the blame must be projected onto impure outsiders or subversive disloyal insiders. Moreover, because the United States is now a bounded nation that seeks boundless markets, boundless sources of labor, and boundless access to raw materials, it is impossible for the nation to remain isolated from the world. If the world impinges on the putative purity of America, then the world must be made to be like America, or in the case of the war in Iraq, the world must be made to be like the privatized America envisioned by our leaders, not even like the "impure" America that actually exists.[17]

The metaphor of two worlds continues to guide social policy today in cities like Los Angeles. Blaming troubles on "alien" outsiders such as immigrants, undocumented workers, and foreign competitors, and on "subversive" insiders such as gays and lesbians, welfare mothers, gang members, feminists, and teachers has fueled a series of moral panics in Los Angeles and California since the 1970s. The antibusing movement, militarization of the border patrol and the police, the property tax revolt institutionalized in California's Proposition 13, the anti-immigrant hysteria promoted by Proposition 187, the criminalization of bilingual education, the repeal of affirmative action, and the massive efforts to incarcerate rather than educate the state's youths have in concert combined to hide the structural inequalities and irrationalities of the state's economy by scapegoating society's most vulnerable populations to advance the interests of the wealthy.

Richard Slotkin, Susan Jeffords, H. Bruce Franklin, and Ward Churchill have helped us see the role that culture plays in these processes at both the local and national levels. Their scholarship shows how stories about the innocent suffering of helpless captives have been used to stoke desires for retribution and revenge.[18] Churchill notes that the Hollywood western always depicts civilized settlers surrounded by superior numbers of "savage" Indians. The settlers are always surrounded, Churchill explains, yet somehow they wind up with the whole country. Sandra Gunning's work on the history of lynching helps us see the inner logic and cultural dynamics of spectacular violence enacted in the name of retribution and revenge. She argues that the sensational titillations of lynching became ends in themselves for nineteenth- and twentieth-century white vigilantes. It was not so much that interracial rape of white women offended them so much that it drove communities to lynch, she argues, as that the lure of lynching was so great that interracial rape was invented as the ultimate excuse legitimating the violence they wanted to commit anyway.[19]

The metaphor of two worlds with its countersubversive social warrant permeates the approach that Attorney General John Ashcroft takes in response to citizens who protest the Justice Department's severe and repeated violations of civil liberties under the guise of fighting terrorism. In a representative moment, testifying before the Judiciary Committee of the United States Senate Ashcroft warned, "To those who scare peace-loving people with phantoms of lost liberty, my message is this: your tactics only aid terrorists, for they erode our national unity and diminish our resolve. They give ammunition to America's enemies and pause to America's friends."[20]

Although it is disturbing that the attorney general of the United States views "lost liberty" so lightly, it is not surprising. Ashcroft represents the present-day manifestation of a very old "America," the America of white male Protestant propertied privilege. This is the America that looks back fondly to the days before the Civil War, the time before what W. E. B. Du Bois called "abolition democracy" and the enactment of the Fourteenth Amendment with its promises of equal protection of the law for all.[21] The America of abolition democracy is a product of what Robin Kelley calls the "freedom dreams" of black people and their practical and pragmatic moves to procure citizenship and full social membership in a country whose core institutions were predicated on their exclusion.[22] While never fully implemented, the Fourteenth Amendment, produced by the activism of free blacks who had once been slaves, helped many more people than African Americans. It eventually opened doors for immigrants and their children; changed the status of Catholics, Jews, Latinos, and Asian Americans; and provided the basis for barriers against discrimination against women, workers, gays and lesbians, and people with disabilities. For most of us, the Fourteenth Amendment is an abiding and nourishing presence in our lives. Knowingly or unknowingly, we drink from that well every day.

For John Ashcroft, however, and for the regime of white male propertied power and Anglo-Protestant hegemony he represents, the Fourteenth Amendment is a major problem. In a 1998 interview with *Southern Partisan*, an openly white supremacist publication, then Missouri senator John Ashcroft took a different tone about treason and subversion, defending as honorable the leaders of the slaveholding confederacy who took up arms against the government of the United States. Ashcroft condemned revisionist historians who, he charged, portrayed the leaders of the Confederacy as pursuing "some perverted agenda."[23] In a revealing Freudian slip, Ashcroft praised Jefferson Davis and the other leaders of the Confederate States of America for risking their lives and "subscribing their sacred fortunes and their honor" for their cause. He probably meant to say "their lives, their fortunes, and their sacred honor," echoing the term used by the leaders of the thirteen colonies when they committed themselves to the war of independence in 1776. But by moving the modifier "sacred" away from "honor" and attaching it instead to "fortunes," Ashcroft unwittingly revealed not only the true identity of what he finds sacred, but also the stakes of the debate over the Confederacy—the past and present material benefits that accrue to whites from what I have termed elsewhere "the possessive investment in whiteness."[24]

Ashcroft's support for the Confederacy and his contempt for the liberties secured by the Constitution is not simply rhetorical, as we can see from another story about the bus—not the Number 18 bus enshrined in the poetry of Marisela Norte, but rather to the school buses that John Ashcroft obstructed as attorney general and governor of Missouri. Ashcroft's political success as a politician has hinged on his efforts to resist a federal court order mandating desegregation of the St. Louis public schools. Because actions by city, county, state, and federal government bodies worked in concert to maintain an illegally segregated school system, the courts had to step in and respond to complaints by Mrs. Minnie Liddell and other black parents in St. Louis that their children's constitutional rights had been violated. The judiciary ordered a voluntary cross-district busing program that included the establishment of new magnet schools in the city of St. Louis. The state of Missouri was expressly ordered to encourage local governments to enforce fair housing laws and to promote integrated housing.

Ashcroft fought desegregation at every turn. He delayed the implementation of court orders, appealing even minor rulings to higher courts. He opposed every single magnet school proposal. As attorney general and later as governor, he argued that the state had no responsibility for the harm done to black children by the illegally segregated school system that the state helped to create and sustain. Ashcroft lied repeatedly to the people of his state, claiming that Missouri had never been found guilty of any wrongdoing in the St. Louis school desegregation case, when in fact, the state was obligated to pay most of the costs of the desegregation program precisely because the courts found that it deliberately and repeatedly violated the constitutional rights of black children.

Although propelled by the long fetch of history that stands behind racial oppression and suppression in the St. Louis area, as well as the national legacy emanating from the betrayal of Reconstruction and abolition democracy,

Ashcroft's massive resistance to school busing also displayed traces of learning from the sinister side of Los Angeles.

More than forty years ago, antibusing activists in the Los Angeles suburb of South Gate contended that the then mostly white South Gate High School could not be merged with the then mostly black Jordan High School in Watts less than one mile away because such a merger would compel students to cross the "dangerous" Alameda Street thoroughfare, even while the segregated setup required black children to cross the equally busy and "dangerous" Firestone Boulevard.[25] Disavowing any intention of preserving white privilege, these parents invoked their rights as property owners to resist sending their children to the schools they decided were plenty good enough for blacks, while refusing to allow black children to take advantage of the educational opportunities and amenities available to their children. Their resistance helped spark the statewide repeal of fair housing law in California in 1964 as well as the passage of a ballot initiative and ultimately an amendment to the state Constitution banning the integration plan ordered by the courts in the Crawford Case to desegregate Los Angeles schools. Subsequent organizations like Busstop in the San Fernando Valley and Bus-Bloc in Orange County helped make the Los Angeles region a model for the enemies of the Fourteenth Amendment—like John Ashcroft in Missouri.[26]

Under Ashcroft's guidance, the state of Missouri spent more than four million dollars to fight against school desegregation in St. Louis. The Missouri Housing Development Corporation under his supervision refused to take even the token step of enforcing fair housing laws, as it had been ordered to do by the federal courts. Even worse, the agency acquiesced to local resistance to new housing that might be integrated, allowing local governments to get away with ignoring the existing fair housing laws already on the books and designated "the highest national priority" by Congress. It should not be surprising that someone who admires the leaders of the Old Confederacy for acting on behalf of their "sacred fortunes" a century ago, would consider defense of the propertied interests of white people today a cause that outweighs the mandates of the Fourteenth Amendment. It is surprising, however, and appalling, that such a man could be appointed to a position as the nation's top law enforcement officer when part of his duties entail enforcement of the civil and constitutional rights of all citizens.[27]

The buses taking black children in St. Louis to those better schools that Ashcroft worked so hard to delay, to obstruct, and to minimize have not been the only vehicles taken out of service to the detriment of Fourteenth Amendment America. We need only return to Los Angeles and get back on the bus or, in this case, the streetcar. The music scene that nurtured Horace Tapscott and his fellow musicians thrived during the period when the Red Car "V" line trolleys ran from downtown to Watts. Public transportation made it possible for jazz and blues clubs along Central Avenue to attract clientele from different parts of the metropolis. At a time when racially exclusionary policies prevented blacks from entering clubs on the west side like the Swanee Inn on Westwood Boulevard where black musician Art Tatum played, Central Avenue became one of the few areas where whites and blacks could mix socially.[28] But the termination of the trolley lines and the mass migration of whites to new suburban subdivisions destroyed the social world of Central Avenue.

Automobile traffic and the concomitant need for parking spaces made buses and streetcar service less efficient, while a host of federal policies from the home owner's mortgage deduction to the dedication of gasoline taxes for new highway construction subsidized white flight to the suburbs. In 1951 alone, 126 Los Angeles motion picture theaters went out of business while the number of television sets in use reached 900,000.[29] As federal highway building, housing, and home loan policies favored development in suburban over urban locations, department stores lured customers away from downtowns by constructing branch stores with free parking in outlying areas. Suburbanization also helped undermine public mass transit, exacerbating traffic jams and creating a chronic shortage of parking spaces, which combined to make "public" sites in the city less accessible. Migration to the suburbs pulled customers away from traditional sites of public entertainment and encouraged the growth of home-based entertainments like the television set and the high-fidelity phonograph.[30]

Johnny Otis recalls how local authorities tried to ban rock-and-roll dances in the city of Los Angeles, and how police officers would enforce long-forgotten ordinances against someone under sixteen dancing with someone over sixteen as a way of disrupting perfectly peaceful gatherings. "They see black kids and Hispanic kids and Asian kids, and they don't like it. They just didn't want to see that. If it were all Asian and Hispanic and black they wouldn't care, but there were whites there, and they're mixing with the blacks."[31] But in this case, harassment backfired. Prohibitions within the city of Los Angeles forced Otis and other promoters to move dances farther out into unincorporated areas of Los Angeles County that had large Chicano populations. Coupled with continued television exposure, this change increased rather than decreased racial interactions. Herman "Sonny" Chaney, the lead singer of the Jaguars remembers, "We used to play a lot at the El Monte Legion Stadium, and the audiences were a good cross section of whites, Chicanos, and blacks . . . I don't think kids today even think in those terms; it's common to see racially mixed groups now. . . . But that was the beginning of rock'n'roll and they were all into the music, so they didn't care" (that the group and audience was mixed).[32]

Matt Garcia's splendid history of Los Angeles's citrus suburbs singles out the musical subculture at El Monte Legion Stadium as an important moment in the city's history, as a time when blacks from Compton mingled with whites from Beverly Hills and with Latinos and Asian Americans from East Los Angeles and the San Gabriel Valley. The social interactions and music of that era have been immortalized by Cleve Duncan and the Penguins in the song "Memories of El Monte," a nostalgic ballad written by Frank Zappa about the 1950s during the 1960s. For a brief period of time it was possible for young people to come to El Monte Legion Stadium or nearby Rainbow Gardens in Pomona and see for themselves the patterns of migration that link Los Angeles to a larger world, that connect spaces in L.A. to spaces in Mexico, Mississippi, and Manila, in Korea, Kansas City, and County Cork. Yet it did not take long before familiar patterns of residential segregation, mortgage discrimination, freeway building, and environmental racism once again resegregated the diverse population that came together briefly in El Monte during the 1950s.[33]

Yet all these patterns of segregation and suburbanization did not destroy the possibilities of the city bus. During the 1990s, an activist organization, the Labor Community Strategy Center (LCSC) started to organize the customers for public transportation into the Bus Riders Union. Recognizing that the new economy of Los Angeles included a great increase in service jobs and a decrease in industrial employment, the LCSC's strategists reasoned that one place where a large mass of workers could be found was on the bus. Workers traveling to many different jobs where they worked side by side with only a few others might seem like poor targets for "union" membership, but the cumulative total of janitors, maids, child care personnel, food service workers, clerks, secretaries, and day laborers riding the buses of Los Angeles on any given day produced the kind of critical mass that formerly existed only in factories and fields.

Organizers of the Bus Riders Union noticed that while inner-city bus riders provided the metropolitan transit system with its largest profits, they received the worst service and contended with the oldest and most poorly maintained buses with the worst-kept schedules. While revenues from suburban train riders provided the district with constant deficits, they received the best vehicles and the best services.

The union mobilized around these issues under the slogan "fight transit racism." Organizers maintained that inner-city bus riders received second-class service because they were people of color—or because they were white people who suffered from the neighborhood race effects of the poor services given to minority communities. They argued that the fight for lower bus fares, better services, and the adoption of nonpolluting vehicles was a fight against racism. At the same time, they insisted that the city could not have cleaner air or better bus services unless it came to grips with the role of racism in legitimating an unclean, unsafe, and inefficient transportation system.

The Bus Riders Union mobilized its members in support of lower fares, better service, and capital investment in the bus system to purchase "clean" compressed natural gas buses. They galvanized a mass constituency of low-income, transit-dependent workers, 50 percent of whom were Latino, 25 percent black, 20 percent white, and 5 percent Asian. The center recognized that the segmentation of the labor market and the stratification of bus service in Los Angeles gave new meanings to race and racism, creating a multiracial bus ridership with common grievances despite their racial, national, linguistic, and gender differences. [34]

Organizers for the Bus Riders Union used the slow pace of the buses through Los Angeles to their advantage by turning the buses into moving seminars on transit racism, as sites for reaching, convincing, and signing up new members. Their efforts drew forth a dynamic group of working-class leaders whose dazzling multilingual and intercultural skills reflect the diversity of the community brought together through membership in the union. Through mass action and a civil rights suit in federal court, the Bus Riders Union secured tremendous victories: a fare reduction that saved riders $25 million per year, a commitment to reduce crowding on inner-city bus routes by increasing service, and a pledge signed by city officials promising to purchase 233 compressed natural gas buses immediately and to exercise an option for an additional 55 more—for a total of 278 clean fuel buses for an expenditure of $89 million. The BRU stressed that this victory meant more than better air and better transportation; it entailed a transfer of wealth and resources from rich to poor, from middle-management suburban commuters to inner-city low-wage workers, and from subsidies for private auto dealers and suburban rail contractors and builders to direct expenditures on safe, efficient, and ecologically sound services for office workers, janitors, teachers' aides, and other unskilled workers.[35]

Although members of every racial group participated in the Bus Riders Union, the slogan of fighting transit racism and the politics behind it meant that more than identity was at stake. The Bus Riders Union victory showed that direct appeals to redress racial injuries could play a central role in community struggles while winning victories for a coalitional constituency. By presenting antiracism as a project about fairness *and* better public services, and by winning a victory that actually improved people's daily lives, the LCSC demonstrated how the organic solidarity that comes from race-based appeals need not inhibit the development of connecting ideologies required for transformative social change.

Perhaps most important, the Labor Community Strategy Center's organizing enacts what it envisions. Pamphlets printed in English, Spanish, and Korean demonstrate a commitment to inclusiveness that is very conspicuous in a divided city like Los Angeles. When passengers on a bus see black and Anglo organizers who speak Spanish or Latino organizers who can hand them a pamphlet in Korean, the group makes a powerful statement about what life in Los Angeles could be like. The organizers who have emerged from the rank and file of the Bus Riders Union may appear to some observers to be only low-wage workers performing menial tasks, people who are belittled and patronized at work. At union meetings, press conferences, city government hearings, and in demonstrations, however, the things they have learned from their lives as workers, immigrants, and community members come into sharp relief as they design effective strategies in a shared struggle for resources, opportunities, and human dignity. The organizational learning that takes place in the course of struggle in an interethnic, antiracist group like the Bus Riders Union not only advances the present struggle, but also prepares participants for the future.

As protests against the World Trade Organization became a focal point for grass roots challenges to neoliberalism in the late 1990s, the LCSC drew upon the expertise of its multinational membership to craft positions on global issues. The organization sent delegates to the World Congress Against Racism in South Africa, and embraced the demands made there by diasporic Africans for reckoning with slavery as a historical crime that requires contrition, repentance, and restitution before there can be true reconciliation. After September 11, 2001, the group engaged in intensive discussions about hate crimes at home and the costs of militarism around the world.

Bus Riders Union members might look like dispossessed and desperate immigrants from the Third World to others, but the LCSC recognizes that its members are also valuable "witnesses to empire," veterans of trade union and anti-imperialist struggles around the world. At a time when all too many U.S. organizations and institutions across the political spectrum continue to view the world from a narrow, parochial, and provincial national and (often) nationalist perspective, the LCSC recognizes that it is composed of people whose economic, social, and political survival depends on transnational networks rooted in understandings of "globalism" from below. LCSC members come from many countries and classes. They represent diverse interests and identity groups. They do not shed their differences once they join the organization, but rather make productive use of them to generate multiple epistemologies and ontologies rooted in complex and sometimes contradictory experiences, archives, and imaginaries. They produce a rare space for political discussions that are not shaped by the national chauvinism of an exclusive focus on the United States.

We need to listen to the Bus Riders Union, to Marisela Norte, to the Penguins, to Horace Tapscott. We might draw guidance in that endeavor from Michael Eric Dyson, who compares the work of socially conscious academics to a Trojan horse. We go through life and meet people who never get to voice their views or air their experiences in print, on television, or on the radio, people who conform to Horace Tapscott's definition of the members of his Arkestra—"people who had a lot to say and didn't have anyplace to say it."[36] Dyson says we should remember these people and carry them inside us. When we get a chance to write or speak, when we are welcomed in institutions where they are not allowed to enter, we can open ourselves up and let all those other people out.

We live in a time when the noblest words are being invoked for the most ignoble purposes. As scholars, teachers, and cultural workers, our tendency is to respond with noble words of our own. But noble words come easier than noble deeds. We might be well rewarded for producing ever more eloquent descriptions of human suffering, without really doing anything to ease that suffering. Yet what we choose to do with the platforms open to us will make a difference. We can speak only for ourselves, or we can use our situated knowledge to share the stage with artists, activists, and intellectuals who do not have the status in society to be regarded as intellectuals. We can go a long way, but we have to hop on the bus to do it.

The transfer of the offices of the *American Quarterly* to Los Angeles poses a challenge and an opportunity. We live in a place of success and sorrow, of possibility and pessimism, of hatred and healing. We cannot allow ourselves to become parochial and narrow in our vision. We cannot abdicate our responsibilities to think about how the spaces we inhabit relate to a wider world. But we can start from the particularities of place that are proximate to us. As Toni Morrison's narrator writes in *Song of Solomon*, "We live here. On this planet, in this nation, in this country right here. *No*where else! We got a home in this rock, don't you see!"[37]

Notes

1. I am grateful to Marita Sturken and George Sánchez for comments on an earlier draft of this piece which were extremely helpful in guiding my revisions. As always, our shared conversations are the most precious things that scholars possess.
2. Moira Rachel Kenney, *Mapping Gay L.A.* (Philadelphia: Temple University Press, 2001), 23.
3. Gil Cuadros, *City of God* (San Francisco: City Lights, 1994). I thank Rafael Perez Torres for alerting me to the importance of Cuadros and his work.
4. George Sánchez, "Working at the Crossroads: American Studies for the 21st Century: Presidential Address to the American Studies Association," *American Quarterly* 54.1, 1–23.
5. Horace Tapscott, *Songs of the Unsung: The Musical and Social Journey of Horace Tapscott* (Durham: Duke University Press, 2001), 1.
6. Ibid., 44.
7. Robert Gordon, *Jazz West Coast* (London: Quartet Books, 1986), 38.
8. Tapscott, *Songs of the Unsung*, 80.
9. Ibid., 143.
10. Ibid., 89.
11. Anthony D. Romero, "Living in Fear: How the U.S. Government's War on Terror Impacts American Lives," in *Lost Liberties: Ashcroft and the Assault on Personal Freedom,* ed. Cynthia Brown (New York: New Press, 2003), 119.
12. Elisabeth Bumiller, "Traces of Terror: The Strategy; Bush Aides Set Strategy to Sell Policy on Iraq," *New York Times,* September 7, 2002, Sec. A, 1.
13. Perhaps the camouflage uniforms were the idea of the Padres outfielders to cover up their ineptitude in recent years. What better excuse could an outfielder have for missing the "cut-off man" with their throws than "I couldn't see him; he was camouflaged"? Thanks to John Bloom for this insight.
14. Michael Rogin, *Ronald Reagan, the Movie: And Other Stories in Political Demonology* (Berkeley: University of California Press), 1987; Lynda Boose, "Techno-Muscularity and the 'Boy Eternal': From the Quagmire to the Gulf," in *The Cultures of U.S. Imperialism,* ed. Donald Pease and Amy Kaplan (Durham, N.C.: Duke University Press, 1994), 589–602; Susan Jeffords, *The Remasculinization of America: Gender and the Vietnam War* (Bloomington: Indiana University Press, 1989).
15. Roger W. Lotchin, *Fortress California 1910–1961: From Warfare to Welfare* (New York: Oxford, 1992); Edward Soja, *Postmodern Geographies* (London: Verso, 1989).
16. Clarence Lo, *Small Property versus Big Government: Social Origins of the Property Tax Revolt* (Berkeley: University of California Press, 1990); Lisa McGirr, *Suburban Warriors: The Origins of the New American Right* (Princeton: Princeton University Press, 2001); Catherine Jurca, *White Diaspora: The Suburb and the Twentieth-Century American Novel* (Princeton: Princeton University Press, 2001).
17. David W. Noble, *Death of a Nation* (Minneapolis: University of Minnesota, 2002), xxxv.
18. Richard Slotkin, *Regeneration through Violence: The Mythology of the American Frontier, 1600–1860* (New York: Harper Perennial, 1996); Jeffords, *The Remasculinization of America;* Ward Churchill, *Fantasies of the Master Race: Literature, Cinema, and the Colonization of American Indians* (San Francisco: City Lights, 1998); H. Bruce Franklin, *M.I.A. or Mythmaking in America* (Brooklyn: Hill Books, 1992).
19. Sandra Gunning, *Race, Rape, and Lynching: The Red Record of American Literature, 1890–1912* (New York: Oxford University Press, 1996).
20. Quoted in Aryeh Neier, "Introduction," in *Lost Liberties: Ashcroft and the Assault on Personal Freedom,* ed. Cynthia Brown (New York: The New Press, 2003), 8.
21. W. E. B. Du Bois, *Black Reconstruction in America* (New York: Russell and Russell, 1956).
22. Robin D. G. Kelley, *Freedom Dreams* (Boston: Beacon, 2002).
23. Ray Hartmann, "Is John Ashcroft a Racist or Does He Just Play One on TV?" *Riverfront Times,* October 13, 1999.
24. George Lipsitz, *The Possessive Investment in Whiteness: How White People Profit from Identity Politics* (Philadelphia: Temple University Press, 1998).
25. Becky M. Nicolaides, *My Blue Heaven: Life and Politics in the Working Class Suburbs of Los Angeles, 1920–1965* (Chicago: University of Chicago Press, 2002), 301–2.
26. McGirr, *Suburban Warriors,* 239–40.
27. Amy Stuart Wells and Robert L. Crain, *Stepping over the Color Line: African American Students in White Suburban Schools* (New Haven: Yale University Press, 1997), 312; Dennis R. Judd, "The Role of Government Policies in Promoting Residential Segregation in the St. Louis Metropolitan Area," *Journal of Negro Education* 66.3 (1997), 217.

28. Gary Marmonstein, "Central Avenue Jazz: Los Angeles Black Music of the Forties," *Southern California Quarterly* 70 (1988), 418–19.

29. Milton MacKaye, "The Big Brawl: Hollywood vs. Television," *Saturday Evening Post*, January 19, 1952, 17–18.

30. Lynn Spigel, "Installing the Television Set: Popular Discourses on Television and Domestic Space, 1948–1955," *Camera Obscura* 16 (1988), 20; MacKaye, "The Big Brawl," 71.

31. Interview with Johnny Otis, Altadena, California, December 14, 1986.

32. "PopBeat," *Los Angeles Times*, February 4, 1989, Part V, 6.

33. Matt Garcia, *A World of Its Own: Race, Labor, and Citrus in the Making of Greater Los Angeles, 1900–1970* (Chapel Hill: University of North Carolina Press, 2001), 189–214. By the 1990s El Monte became a site of segregation and low wage labor. In 1995, the State Labor Commission raided a sweat-shop in the suburb and discovered Thai and other immigrant workers held captive performing labor under slavelike conditions. An interethnic coalition from the Thai Community Development Center, Korean Immigrant Worker Advocates, and the Pilipino Workers' Center united to attend to the work-ers' survival needs to fight deportation and win back wages and punitive damages as well as to campaign for retailer accountability in the garment industry. The resulting publicity alerted a group of twenty-four Latino/a workers to their rights. They contacted the Korean Immigrant Worker Advocates to file a lawsuit on their behalf. See Miriam Ching Yoon Louie, *Sweatshop Warriors: Immigrant Women Workers Take on the Global Factory* (Boston: South End, 2001), 229–30.

34. Strategy Center News Analysis, October 10, 1997, 1.

35. Jeffrey L. Rabin and Richard Simon, "Court Order Spurs Plan to Buy 278 Buses," *Los Angeles Times*, September 26, 1997, Sec. B, 1.

36. Tapscott, *Songs of the Unsung*, 106.

37. Toni Morrison, *Song of Solomon* (New York; Penguin, 1997), 235. In the novel, this hope is frustrated by white vigilante violence, but Macon Dead's problem nonetheless remains our problem. I am grateful to Farah Jasmine Griffin for highlighting this part of the novel in her wonderful book *Who Set You Flowin'?* (New York: Oxford University Press, 1995), 41.

Los Angeles and American Studies in a Pacific World of Migrations

Henry Yu

If, as George Lipsitz suggests in his essay, Los Angeles is a street corner, taking a trip along the streets that lead to and from this intersection might trace a larger world in which it, and this place called "America," is embedded. Like many before, I have come to Los Angeles from elsewhere and now call it home, but instead of seeing myself at the end of a one-way journey that has ended in Los Angeles, a migrant to this place from somewhere else, I think of Los Angeles as an intersection on a larger grid. In this world, migration is a process without end, comings and goings rather than the singular leaving of one place and arriving at another by which we mythically understand the immigrant's story. Los Angeles is one street corner, one intersecting node for many journeys, and if we follow the roads outward we find ourselves navigating the well-worn paths of a much larger world, where people riding buses and buggies (and planes and trains and automobiles), or finding passage in the holds of trans-Pacific ocean liners, or hidden in the back of a pickup truck, come to and from and through Los Angeles. Each of us in Los Angeles is tied in long links to other people in other places, drawing a map dense with the scrawling lines of our journeys.

Is Anybody in L.A. Actually from Here?

The strange thing about Los Angeles in its incarnation as the entertainment capital of the world is that the celebrities so powerfully associated with Los Angeles are usually not from here, fueling an impression that nobody is ever actually from Los Angeles. Of course, Los Angeles, like any place, can claim plenty of people who were born and raised here, but its image is strong as a city in which everybody is from somewhere else. What if we were to export this particularly Los Angelean sense of imagined spatial belonging to the rest of the world? Rather than talk about how rooted the citizens of Los Angeles are to the physical space of the city, we could instead talk about how other metropolitan sites in the United States, North America, and perhaps around the world are actually more like Los Angeles in this aspect. Los Angeles, in other words, might not be the exception but the rule if we understand the history of the last two centuries as dominated by migration. First of all, we need to think about how we narrate migration. The actual movement of human bodies from one point to another has no inherent meaning, but is given meaning through the classifications of those movements. We imagine that going to work each day is one kind of movement, whether we walk two blocks to work or get on an airplane and fly across the continent. But if we get on a plane and "immigrate" to another country, even for job-related purposes, then this is a different kind of movement. My purpose is not to erase all distinctions between different forms of movement and migration, but to highlight how we categorize such differences. We should give more thought to the origins of our categories, and whether we should reclassify movements to achieve other political purposes. One of the most important benefits for American studies in placing migration to and from the Americas at the center of our scholarship, it seems to me, is to escape nationalism as our rationale.

So much of social scientific scholarship on migration for the last century has concentrated on "immigration," the influx of human bodies defined as foreign in origin to a nation. As Andreas Wimmer and Nina Glick Schiller have argued, this "methodological nationalism" has created generations of scholarship that have assumed the political interests of nation-states as the reason for the study of migration. Consequently, the question of assimilation into the host society dominated immigration scholarship from the earliest studies of the University of Chicago's sociology department, the foundational school for training social scientists in the United States.[1] Scholarship centered on national concerns has subsequently emphasized the crossing of national borders as the essential definition of what counted as immigration. The distance traveled or the existential experience of migration rarely determined the importance of migration. Michael Williams has labeled this a "border guard perspective," mocking how the study of migration so often took security and the control and incorporation of bodies as fundamental questions.[2]

There were many migrants at the turn of the twentieth century whose movements into the United States, for instance, provoked little concern: white, English-speaking Protestants from Canada were of little interest to most immigration scholars. Instead, immigration studies focused on groups that came to be defined as being a "problem" to the nation. Migrants from Asia, Latin America, and Southern and Eastern Europe needed to be studied and their movements observed. By the mid-twentieth century, the prevailing scholarship moved from a focus on these migrant groups as a problem to a study of their distinctive "cultures," shifting the question away from their desirability as foreigners to examinations of their lingering ethnicity within America. As exclusionary laws such as the 1882 Chinese Exclusion Act and the 1924 Reed-Johnson Act created categories of "illegal" immigrants, many migrants also assumed a "legal" identity defined by ever-changing legislation on citizenship and national status.[3]

Against this legacy of misapprehending migration, how should we instead understand it, and what might American studies learn from how Los Angeles has been shaped by migration? Following the authors of *Nations Unbound*, many scholars turned to the point of view of the migrants themselves to understand how the experience of migration is often a transnational process that ties together local places in more than one nation. Additionally, scholars traced the historical effects of colonialism in creating these linkages, recognizing how national belonging is no longer synonymous with residence in the geographic territory of the nation-state.[4] Other scholars have focused on the often circular networks created by labor migrants, with multidirectional flows that support national imaginings and nationalist political movements far away from "home" countries.[5]

The decentering of the nation within migration studies has helped release scholarship from the holding cells of the border guard perspective but can we go farther? There has been a tendency in studies of Chinese migration to Southeast Asia, for instance, to analytically blur the distinction between the "internal migration" within the Chinese nation-state and the "external" migration of Overseas Chinese, emphasizing how the phenomenon of a laborer moving from an agricultural village to a nearby market town to find work is linked to the out-migration of the same kinds of laborers to Southeast Asia and across the Pacific to the Americas. The distinction of internal versus external migration is thus shown to obscure how the two rely on the same migration networks.[6] How are we to study migration in the nineteenth and twentieth centuries, periods marked by the expanding power of nation-states and of their control of migrating bodies, without assuming the analytical centrality of the very borders that such nation-states created? The distinctions between internal and external migration, between plain old moving around and immigration/emigration, between legal migration and illegal smuggling, have also been the product of the border guard perspective. While they have powerfully shaped migration patterns, we should avoid seeing migration exclusively through these categories.

What if we considered not just the migration of human bodies across national boundaries, but the movement of bodies throughout space as the basis of our studies? If we thought, for instance, of Los Angeles and Vancouver, British Columbia (two local sites in which I am particularly interested), as two nodal intersections, two street corners in a larger set of crisscrossing paths, we would see how these places connect with each other and with myriad other sites around the Pacific and the Americas. There would be some nodes that would be denser than others, cities and ports and gathering places, busy intersections with people coming and leaving and going through. "Illegal migration," rather than a category that extends outward from the moment of border crossing, infecting the way we understand the whole experience of the migrant, would become only one of the ways that migration has been shaped in the last two centuries. We would see how it intersects with other processes. For instance, after the Chinese Exclusion Act of 1882, Chinese workers shifted to Canada, Australia, and Mexico as destinations. They also continued to come into the United States, but the process had been changed—curtailed and constrained, driven into illegality. Their movements, however, remained embedded in larger networks of migration that continued to exist and in which the United States was only one location.

If we saw the world through the eyes of my great-grandmother, how different would it look? Lee Choi Yee was in her eighties when she left China in 1965. She had already been entwined in a network of family labor migration that had connected her home village in Guangdong province with Sydney, Australia, and Honolulu, Hawai'i, and all up and down the west coast of North America for almost a century. Generations of young males had left similar rural villages in Guangdong province to labor in distant places, sending money back to support families and occasionally returning home to find wives and sire children. If they were lucky, they retired wealthy men. My great-grandmother's husband spent his entire adult life in Australia, and although he had asked for her to join him and the Aboriginal second wife he had married in Sydney, she never did. He spent two extended trips to China with her, once between 1908 and 1911, and another between 1918 and 1919, each time fathering a daughter. After he left the second time, she would never see him again. Replicating her own married life, my great-grandmother would marry her youngest daughter off to another overseas laborer in 1937, this one in North America, who, along with his brothers had looked for their fortunes in the Pacific Northwest borderlands that straddled the U.S.–Canada boundary.

To see the world through my great-grandmother's eyes is to see a world both intimate and local—a farm, a village, your children and husband's relatives around you—as well as vast and linked to far-flung places. For years, her husband would send back, along with regular monetary remittances, fresh apples and oranges from his grocery in Australia. Her daughter married in anticipation of similar remittances from her own husband, who worked for much of his life as a butcher on an Alaskan cruise ship. When my great-grandmother mortgaged some of the family farmland to pay the passage for her brother to Trinidad, she continued the practices of borrowing and lending that girded a family economy of migration. His voyage was an investment, to be repaid with returns in long years of labor on plantations and then in a corner store. Well before my great-grandmother crossed the ocean to join her relatives in the Americas, she had been linked by migrant chains that anchored her existence there. When she went with my mother and my grandmother to join my grandfather in 1965, she traveled a route that was well worn, albeit traced across water. For generations her relatives had traveled trans-Pacific shipping lines; she flew in an airplane.

In the decades before her death, she continued to live in a world whose mental geography spanned great distances, celebrating grandchildren's birthdays in the United States, in Canada, in China and Hong Kong. My brother was the first to travel to Los Angeles, as an architecture student at UCLA and then an architect based in L.A., creating an initial space in my great-grandmother's imagination for "Loh Sung" as she called it, so that my decade here can trace its genealogy back through his presence and mine and tie her whole long history of migration to a place she has never been. Of course, Los Angeles has a history of Chinese migration, going back to its origins as an urban settlement. The original Los Angles Chinatown was populated by people very much like my great-grandmother, peasants from rural areas of southern China near Hong Kong and Macau. More recently, just as in Vancouver, waves of migrants to Monterey Park and the San Gabriel Valley east of downtown L.A. have created new settlements that connect Los Angeles with Hong Kong, Shanghai, and Taiwan. The Chinese of Los Angeles are now linked with the migratory networks of people who have come from other areas in the United States and with places all through the Americas and Europe and around the Pacific and Asia.[7]

What lessons can we learn from such a life? Was my great-grandmother typical or not? Certainly she was representative of many women embedded in the migratory labor networks that tied the developing economies of the Americas to places of origin all around the Atlantic and the Pacific. The western coast of North America was not exceptional in this regard, attracting opportunistic migrants and laborers just as Argentina, Australia, South Africa, and the eastern United States had in the late nineteenth and early twentieth centuries. This period was marked by global flows of migration, and the chains of migration that linked disparate sites in Europe, Asia, Africa, and the Americas. Today, as my grandfather did decades ago, young Indonesian and Filipino cooks and waiters on Alaskan cruise ships spend long years away from their families, sending home remittances and connecting the places they visit to women and children in rural villages outside Jakarta and Manila. In Queens and Flushing, New York, workers from Fujian province in China mingle with those from Mexico, Pakistan, India, the Dominican Republic, El Salvador, and Guatemala, just as they do in downtown Los Angeles.

My great-grandmother's life was both typical and not, but the historical context of the migration networks in which she lived was and is a widespread phenomenon. Increasingly by the late nineteenth century, nation-states expressed their sovereignty by marking the bodies of those who crossed their borders. The Chinese Exclusion Act of 1882 necessitated a whole new bureaucracy to issue identification papers and control the movements of this newly created set of unwelcome migrants. Thus began a long process of differentiation between citizens and a class of perpetual foreigners that invested some bodies with privileges of national belonging while denying them to others defined as "aliens" and "ineligible to citizenship."[8] This process of national marking, with its demonization of some migrants as undesirable and the cementing of others into a common citizenry, paralleled similar processes in Canada, Australia, and New Zealand. Practices of white supremacy and new techniques of racialization helped legislate the uneven contours of national belonging around the globe.

In the United States, many of those who were defined by legislation as "aliens"—Chinese, Japanese, Filipino, East Indian, Mexican—found themselves, in the words of Mae Ngai, in the position of being "impossible subjects." However, we should be careful not to diminish the richness of these migrants' lives by seeing them only through the categories of their exclusion. They struggled despite the harshness of laws, defining in their own ways lives only partially encompassed by the category of "illegal" migrant. From the point of view of border guards, they were engaged in smuggling and deception, telling lies in order to cross national boundaries. For those who saw immigration laws as unjust and discriminatory, breaking such laws involved no moral evasion, and the fictions they created became a part of the everyday fabric of their lives. Because of quirks in the exclusion laws, some Chinese were allowed to migrate even after 1882: merchants and scholars could still enter and leave, and those born in the United States were accorded citizenry and the privileges of border crossing. Acquiring the paperwork of a "legal" migrant became a route to the United States, and a lively trade in identity papers developed. The man my great-grandmother chose as her daughter's husband bought a fictive identity to enter the United States. For the rest of his life, his official name in English would be Low. The first time his real name, Yeung, appeared in English was on his headstone.

The granting of instant citizenship to those born within the geographic borders of the United States has had a tremendous effect on static conceptions of spatial belonging. For the first half of U.S. history, the possession of U.S. citizenship bore little relationship to the privileges of traveling across its borders—almost anyone was allowed in, and so citizenship was superfluous. As Erika Lee argues, excluding the Chinese forced the development and expansion of federal immigration law, so that what began as legislation aimed at restricting the border crossings of a specific group became entangled with definitions of national citizenry. In the Supreme Court case *U.S. v. Wong Kim Ark* in 1898, national belonging through nativity became automatic for everyone, even the Chinese. American-born Chinese possessed rights as citizens, including the privileges of border crossing, that were more important than their legal identity as a race "ineligible" for citizenship.

This automatic citizenry through nativity has reinforced birthplace as the most basic legal form of spatial identity, but it has also informed spatial identity in general. Native-born Angelenos, that seemingly rare breed, have staked a claim to belonging over those who have moved to Los Angeles. Being "raised" in a place is a secondary form of belonging, one that can be measured in multiple ways, from an emphasis on schooling and youth as formative stages, to others that mark the passage of time—how many years of living in a place does it take before you can call yourself a native? What if you never do? Sometimes claims of belonging are produced by longing and desire, a need to feel at home here, or a feeling of exile that longs for a home elsewhere. Spatial belonging can even be against someone's wishes, propelled by the need of others (or of nation-states) to claim someone even if he or she never felt at home, or to exclude someone despite that person's desire to belong.

If we move away from categories of belonging that emphasize static definitions of place and legal regimes of citizenry, we can see spaces not as geographically bounded (mirroring the territorial claims of nation-states), but connected in fascinating ways by the movements of human bodies. And if we follow the bodies, Los Angeles as a site of intersection leads us away from the East Coast, Atlantic-centered perspective of so much U.S. scholarship. We would see the United States embedded in a world in which the Americas are a part of both Pacific and Atlantic migrations.

Los Angeles and Regional Migrations

If we begin with Los Angeles, we will see how regional distinctions are so powerfully the consequence of regional migration networks. For instance, patterns of racialization and white supremacy are almost directly tied to regional migration flows. The vast bulk of scholarly work on racialization in the United States has been focused on the historical creation and mainte-nance of the dichotomy between black and white. However, if we understand migration flows as regional, we see that the American South might be better understood as a southeast region connected to the slaveholding societies of the Caribbean and the trans-Atlantic flows of enslaved Africans that populat-ed the region. In the Northeast, a region dominated by large-scale European migration, the demonization of blacks helped mold together a diverse array of European migrants through the promised benefits of white supremacy. This was despite the fact that migrant flows of African Americans northward were relatively small until the twentieth century, but antiblack practices served a different purpose than in slaveholding regions in the Southeast. Understanding the dynamic of racialization in the Northeast as an outgrowth of the particular challenges of its migration history is crucial. Anti-Semitism and anti-Catholic practices dominated the region in the late nineteenth and early twentieth centuries, and the expansion of a generic Judeo-Christian whiteness to embrace Jews and Catholics was accompanied by a heightening of the racial divide between white and black, not its lessening.

The rise of ethnicity as a category was rooted in the migration patterns of the northeastern United States. Ostensibly, when W. Lloyd Warner and Leo Srole used the concept of ethnicity for the first time in the 1940s, it was to claim that racial groups were just one form of ethnicity. But the irony of the rise of the term *ethnicity* was that it came to describe migrant groups such as Irish, Italians, Slavs, and Jews that so recently had been vilified in the Northeast as inferior races. In separating out the intractable problem of African Americans as the primary remaining "racial" problem, Warner and Srole unwittingly recognized the process under way by which race as a con-cept was shifting in meaning in the Northeast; the expansion of white supremacy in the mid-twentieth century now allowed those willing and able to embrace it to erase problematic origins. Changes in clothing and manners, the adoption of English, the erasure of overt "ethnicity"—all created the illusion that ethnicity was somehow a choice, leaving behind those who could not pass for white in the dark cellar of a newly constricted category of race.

That this process was primarily focused in a northeastern region tied to trans-Atlantic flows of European migrants is quickly apparent when we compare it to the Northwest and the Southwest. These two regions were tied to trans-Pacific migrations and the conquest of formerly Spanish and American Indian territories. In the Southwest, the westward migration of European colonizers and the enslaved Africans brought along by the expansion of slavery crossed paths with Native Americans and the northern settlers of Spanish America. Most important, for much of the history of both the Northwest and the Southwest, Native American genocide and the labor politics of anti-Asian agitation, not antiblack practices, dominated processes of racialization. Early African American migrants who came to the western United States saw that another set of migrants was considered the primary problem, and before large numbers of African Americans arrived during World War II, it was the "Oriental problem" that dominated the racial politics of western cities such as Los Angeles, San Francisco, and Seattle. By the mid-twentieth century, Mexican labor migrations had come to replace the supply of Chinese, Japanese, Korean, Punjabi, and Filipinos cut off by exclusionary policies, and the racialization of Mexicans as eternal foreigners and cheap labor grafted onto similar representations of earlier Asian migrants.[9] In similar ways that antiblack politics helped amalgamate various Europeans into a common white supremacy, anti-Asian and anti-Mexican politics achieved a parallel result. Without an understanding of the consequences of regional networks of migration that brought migrants from Asia, Europe, Latin America, and the eastern United States to the Pacific coast, the very different patterns of regional racialization in the United States do not make sense.

More recently, scholarship focusing on imperialism and territorial expansion has placed areas such as the Southwest and overseas colonies such as Hawai'i and the Philippines at the center of U.S. history, in particular for the fifty years before and after the crucial date of 1898. The question of empire, it seems, has placed the West and the Pacific on the map.[10] The current scholarship of Vicente Diaz, Amy Stillman, and Damon Salesas at the University of Michigan, for instance, has the potential of reimagining the way that the United States has been engaged in the imperial contests of the region. Pacific studies scholars offer us a way of seeing the United States on the eastern edge of a world that has its own history, not autonomous and separate from the United States, but integral and intersecting, blending local and global connections.[11]

Most acutely, a century of recurring U.S. wars in Asia, from the conquest of the Philippines and Hawai'i through the conflict with Japan, with China in Korea, in Southeast Asia, and again in Central Asia now, has created a vicious dehumanization that sees in recurring cycles an Asian face of the enemy. We rarely consider military personnel migrants, but they are akin to the missionaries and civil servants who accompanied empire and in their own descriptions often described their travels in ways that any traveler going to a new land might. It is not surprising that the militarized migration of Americans into the Pacific created the mass tourism that would dominate sites such as Hawai'i, Bangkok, and Manila. Military expansion has been a particularly gendered form of migration, spawning a violent masculinity and accompanied by a sexual tourism replete with alluring images of Asian women as willing commodities. Between 1945 and 1965, when anti-Asian exclusion kept the borders of the Untied States closed to most Asian migrants, it was U.S. wars in Asia that were the direct source for many of those who did come: refugees and orphans from the Korean conflict or war brides of military personnel stationed in Japan and South Korea.

Differential migrations, in a sense, created the distinctiveness of the major regions of the United States by tying them into regional flows of human bodies. By following migrants as they move, we discover the local worlds in which they lived and see these sites of intersection as particularly generative places, with the capacity to create encounters and ideas and forms of social life that are bewildering in their complexity. Migrants create geographic space. Spatial imaginings are the product of movement, not of the static relationship between a body and the ground where it appears to root. Settlers are migrants who fantasize about stopping and making an organic tie between themselves and the land they occupy. A region is an act of imagination, an organizing and categorizing of a smaller subset of the ideas generated at these nodes of intersection, reflecting the density of migration routes and the pattern of connection between places. We might think of racial ideologies as one set of ideas generated at such sites, and nationalism as one particularly powerful mobilization of such regional cognition, produced by some migrants attempting to create and institute a shared sense of community with each other. In the historical case of the United States and other settler colonies, this often comes at the expense of other migrants or of aboriginal peoples. If we were to envision the Americas as a collection of intersecting nodes, connected with others around the world, we could reimagine this historical construct called "America" as the product of a limited number of these dense intersections.

Seeing American studies through the lens of migratory processes, then, foregrounds both the experience of individual migrants and the networks in which they are embedded. It also allows us to see how the ideas of "America" have migrated along these routes. If the question of "what is America" has been at the heart of American studies since its inception, here is a way that we can escape the parochial exceptionalism of too constrained a focus. If we see this imagined nation, and the border practices by which it is enacted, as the creation of the migratory networks that embed the Americas in a larger world, then the United States as a subject will not drive our scholarship like the administration of a citizenship oath. We can follow its travels, its appropriation and its reimagining, and recognize that it is just one of many ideas created out of the dense interactions that have occurred at nodal intersections. It might be one way by which we can truly forsake the political interests of nation building as the narrow rationale for scholarship.

"Life Differs from Death in the Matter of Movement"[12]

I will end by getting back to the places I live. After my great-grandmother migrated from her natal village to her husband's village in Zhongshan county, then to Shanghai, where her daughter worked in a textile factory, then across the Pacific to Canada, she embedded herself in her backyard garden in Vancouver. In this garden, she grew the vegetables of a time and place far away, offering them with friendly gestures to new neighbors who spoke English (or not) with Italian and Romanian and Punjabi accents. Afterward, she would watch wrestling on TV and mutter in frustration at the underhanded tactics of the bad guys (even in another language the simple dichotomies of professional wrestling are clear). Sometimes, after eating her daily dinner of salted fish, vegetables, and a bowl of rice, she would sit in her room patiently folding paper money festooned with bright gold and silver paint. She would fold paper for an hour here and an hour there, filling giant empty Pampers boxes that she had asked my mother to keep from the grocery store we ran. One day, in her late nineties, she decided to learn English. Day after day she repeated simple phrases such as "Good day" and "How are you?" When asked why she was trying so hard to learn a new language at her age, she replied that if she was going to be buried here, she wanted to know how to speak to her neighbors, just in case they did not speak Chinese. After she passed away, we opened up the dozens of densely packed Pampers boxes and burned all the hand-folded paper, sending to her the special ceremonial money that had value only in the afterworld.

We live here, in this world, but at any moment we don't know if this street corner that we call home will be the place we stop. There are roads that lead to other places, and people come and people go. We make friends and meet neighbors, and try to make our little corner a better place to live. All we can ask is that those who follow us remember the journeys we took, the people we knew, the places we were, and, if you're my great-grandmother, to send her some money at the end of the road so she can go hang out with her neighbors. Perhaps if historians followed these struggles and built their histories out of them rather than out of the abstraction called America, we might see a history of lives lived well and stories worth telling.

Notes

My thanks to Katherine Kinney, George Sanchez, Marita Sturken, Raul Villa, and other readers at *American Quarterly* for their editorial suggestions, as well as special gratitude to Brandy Lien Worrall for a close reading and major revisions. Thanks also to Hokulani Aikau, Rainer Buschmann, Vince Diaz, Madeline Hsu, Adria Imada, Masumi Izumi, Kehaulani Kauanui, Erika Lee, Davianna MacGregor, Adam McKeown, Mae Ngai, Gary Okihiro, JoAnna Poblete, Robert Chao Romero, Damon Salesas, Christen Sasaki, Paul Spickard, Amy Stillman, Edgar Wickberg, and Michael Williams for conversations about mutual interests in this essay's themes.

1. Andreas Wimmer and Nina Glick Schiller, "Methodological Nationalism, the Social Sciences, and the Study of Migration: An Essay in Historical Epistemology," in a special issue on "Transnational Migration: International Perspectives," ed. Peggy Levitt, Josh DeWind, and Steven Vertovec, *International Migration Review* 37.3 (2003); an updated version of nation studies of incorporation, Richard Alba and Victor Nee, *Remaking the American Mainstream: Assimilation and Contemporary Immigration* (Cambridge: Harvard University Press, 2003); for Chicago sociology and migration, my *Thinking Orientals: Migration, Contact, and Exoticism in Modern America* (New York: Oxford University Press, 2001).

2. Michael Williams, "Destination Qiaoxiang: Pearl River Delta Villages and Pacific Ports, 1849–1949" (doctoral dissertation, University of Hong Kong, 2002).

3. For a number of works on immigration, in particular Chinese migrants, and exclusionary policies, see Lucy Salyer, *Laws Harsh as Tigers: Chinese Immigrants and the Shaping of Immigration Law* (Chapel Hill: University of North Carolina Press, 1995); Adam McKeown, "Ritualization of Regulation: The Enforcement of Chinese Exclusion in the United States and China, *American Historical Review* 108.2 (April 2003): 377–403; Erika Lee, *At America's Gates: Chinese Immigration and American Exclusion, 1882–1943* (Chapel Hill: University of North Carolina Press, 2003); Mae Ngai, *Impossible Subjects: Illegal Aliens and the making of Modern America* (Princeton: Princeton University Press, 2004). On the border patrol, see Kathleen Lytle-Hernandez, "Entangling Bodies and Borders: Racial Profiling and the U.S. Border Patrol, 1924–1955" (doctoral dissertation, University of California, Los Angeles, 2002).

4. Linda G. Basch, Nina Glick Schiller, and Cristina Szanton Blanc, *Nations Unbound: Transnational Projects, Postcolonial Predicaments, and Deterritorialized Nation-States* (Langhorne, Pa.: Gordon and Breach, 1994); also Linda G. Basch, Nina Glick Schiller, and Cristina Szanton Blanc, *Towards a Transnational Perspective on Migration: Race, Class, Ethnicity, and Nationalism Reconsidered* (New York: New York Academy of Sciences, 1992).

5. Donna R. Gabaccia, "Is Everywhere Nowhere? Nomads, Nations, and the Immigrant Paradigm of United States History," *Journal of American History* 86.3; Madeline Hsu, *Dreaming of Gold, Dreaming*

of Home (Stanford, Calif.: Stanford University Press, 2000); Adam McKeown, "From Opium Farmer to Astronaut: A Global History of Diasporic Chinese Business," *Diaspora* 9 (2000); "Conceptualizing Chinese Diasporas, 1842–1949," *The Journal of Asian Studies* 58.2 (May 1999): 306–37; and "Transnational Chinese Families and Chinese Exclusion, 1875–1943," *Journal of American Ethnic History* 18.2 (Winter 1999). On Chinese migrants in the border region of Southern California and northern Mexico, Robert Chao Romero, "The Dragon in Big Lusong: Chinese Immigration and Settlement in Mexico, 1882–1940" (doctoral dissertation, University of California, Los Angeles, 2003).

6. See the pioneering work of G. William Skinner on overseas Chinese in Southeast Asia, as well as that of Wang Gungwu, Anthony Reid, and Edgar Wickberg.

7. For the intersections between Asian Americans and Latinos in Monterey Park, see Leland Saito, *Race and Politics: Asian Americans, Latinos, and Whites in a Los Angeles Suburb* (Urbana: University of Illinois Press, 1998); for more on the "new" suburban Chinatowns, Wei Li, "Spatial Transformation of an Urban Ethnic Community: Chinatown to Chinese Ethnoburb in Los Angeles" (doctoral dissertation, University of Southern California, 1997); Laurence J. C. Ma and Carolyn Cartier, *The Chinese Diaspora: Space, Place, Mobility, and Identity* (Lanham, Md.: Rowman Littlefield, 2003).

8. Ngai, *Impossible Subjects*; Erika Lee, *At America's Gates*. See also John Torpey, *The Invention of the Passport: Surveillance, Citizenship, and the State* (Cambridge: Cambridge University Press, 2000).

9. Richard White, *It's Your Misfortune and None of My Own: A History of the American West* (Norman: University of Oklahoma Press, 1991); Patricia Limerick, *Legacies of Conquest: The Unbroken Past of the American West* (New York: Norton, 1987); and Donald Worster, *Rivers of Empire: Water, Aridity, and the Growth of the American West* (New York: Pantheon, 1985). For regional interpretations of race in the West, Tomás Almaguer, *Racial Fault Lines: The Historical Origins of White Supremacy in California* (Berkeley: University of California, 1994); Quintard Taylor, *In Search of the Racial Frontier* (New York: Norton, 1998).

10. Amy Kaplan and Donald Pease, eds., *Cultures of United States Imperialism* (Durham: Duke University Press, 1993); Lisbeth Haas, *Conquests and Historical Identities in California, 1769–1936* (Berkeley: University of California Press, 1995); John C. Rowe, ed., *Post-Nationalist American Studies* (Berkeley: University of California Press, 2000); Shelley Streeby, *American Sensations: Class, Empire, and the Production of Popular Culture* (Berkeley: University of California Press, 2002).

11. On Pacific Islander studies, Joanne Rondilla, Debbie Hippolyte Wright, and Paul Spickard, eds., *Pacific Diasporas* (Honolulu: University of Hawai'i Press, 2002). On oceans, Jerry Bentley, "Seas and Oceans as Frameworks of Historical Analysis," *The Geographical Review* 89.2 (1999): 215–24. See also Gary Okihiro's forthcoming book, which includes his unpublished essay "Towards a Pacific Civilization." For an interesting view on migration from the point of view of Pacific Island navigators, see Vicente M. Diaz, director/writer/coproducer, *Sacred Vessels: Navigating Tradition and Identity in Micronesia* (29 mins., 1997), a video documentary about the survival of traditional seafaring in Polowat, Central Carolines, and its revival in Guam and the Marianas.

12. Roderick McKenzie, "Movement and the Ability to Live," Proceedings of the Institute of International Relations, 1926, reprinted in McKenzie, *On Human Ecology*, edited and with an introduction by Amos Hawley (Chicago: University of Chicago Press, 1968), 134.

Border City:
Race and Social Distance in Los Angeles

Greg Hise

> The modern resident in the City of the Angels has seen in the past fifteen years the many and sweeping changes wrought by industry and capital and brains, which have transformed a sleepy little Spanish-Mexican pueblo into our modern, bustling and up-to-date metropolis. If a *Fundador* were to rise from his tomb, under the floor of the Mission . . . and take a *pasear* over [sic] the city, there would be few localities he would recognize. The church and the Plaza, and a part of what is now Chinatown, and old Sonoratown, and an occasional ruined adobe—these would be all.
>
> Mary E. Mooney, 1900[1]

It is fitting for the *American Quarterly* to inaugurate its move to USC with a special issue devoted to Los Angeles and the *future* of urban culture. Before the ink dried on the Treaty of Guadalupe Hidalgo, in truth before the United States expanded its national boundary through a land grab of Alta California and Mexico's northern territory, Yankee boosters and place promoters had begun sketching the outlines for a city of the future, a great modern metropolis rising on the site of a Spanish-Mexican pueblo. The future focus of those putative pioneers has informed subsequent analysis; scholarship on Los Angeles is steeped in place promotion; few consider an actual place.[2]

Whether looking north from New Spain, later Mexico, or west from Europe's North Atlantic colonies or Europe itself, the pueblo of Los Angeles and Alta California appeared to be on the edge of the world geographically and on the margins of world trade and of world history, the latter understood as the role those in California played in shaping global events. The received history of California is of a provincial backwater thrust onto the world stage with the discovery of gold in 1848, the territory then brought into the Union, the modern nation-state, solely for its mineral wealth. A second gold rush occurred during World War II when federal defense dollars jump-started the economy in a region that had remained an extractive colony for corporations and financiers based in Europe and on the East Coast. Most accounts of the post-WWII era focus on the suburb (presented as a qualitatively and functionally distinct component of urban growth), on metropolitan and regional expansion (often characterized simply as sprawl), and on Californians' propensity for innovations in popular culture and all forms of social experiments. In other words, Los Angeles and California remain a place apart. More recently Southern California has been cast as the prototype for a new epoch, postmodernity, a product of new regimes of capital, of economic restructuring, of the primacy of space over time, of an epistemological break.[3]

Although rarely, if ever, framed that succinctly, this abridged account captures the narrative arc of Los Angeles and California studies. Note, for example, the titles Carey McWilliams coined for his influential and popular histories: *Southern California: An Island on the Land* (1946) and *California: The Great Exception* (1949).[4] All such accounts of a preindustrial state, of its late and seemingly instantaneous entry into a modern era, of its role as an indicator and bellwether for the twenty-first century flatten complexity, downplay continuity, override the local, and ignore the drag history exerts on the present. Stated this way, we can begin to appreciate the degree to which first Europeans' and then Anglo-Americans' ideas about California, particularly the "southland," were in effect tropes of modernity. European myths of Queen Califia, the accounts of Spanish explorers and settlers, late-nineteenth-century booster rhetoric, chamber of commerce pronouncements from the 1920s and 1930s, each evoke a place apart, the site for a new, improved race, a paradise waiting only for the shaping hand of white men. Current pronouncements that "one can see urban trends more clearly in Los Angeles since they are less complicated by a longer history of urbanization" echo earlier discourse. As contrary as such claims are to our common sense, a perception that this city exists in an eternal present, a present that prefigures other cities' futures, is more commonly shared than historians and other scholars would care to believe.[5]

If the future has held an undue grip on our analysis, what might a contingent history, a history of place, as opposed to a history of place promotion, reveal? How might such a history be framed? Resurrecting the pueblo and the nineteenth-century American city, a provincial settlement contemporaries viewed as little more than a "cow town," reveals it to have been a borderland, a site, a locale where people, resources, and ideas originating in different societies and cultures across the globe came together. In coming together, Tongva, Spaniards, Mexicans, Yankees, Chinese, and others created a hybrid or metis city and culture, what Mechal Sobel, in a different context aptly described as a "world made together."[6] Los Angeles was then and remains a crossroads. That border city—with its specific location in and relation to the nation-state, with the particular nature and timing of its economic development, with its precise patterns of immigration and the particular constitution of its demographic diversity—fixed an imprint that we need to understand if we are to come to terms with the contemporary world city and plan adequately for the challenge of tomorrow's transnational megaregion. Nineteenth- and early-twentieth-century visitors and residents, workers and capitalists, immigrants and elected officials left records, and these sources speak in singular yet related ways about place-making, identity formation, and the conflicts and partial resolutions resulting from the overlay of American systems of property, law, and the like over the Mexican-era ciudad and the Spanish pueblo.

Symbols and Structures

During a 1929 meeting of the Los Angeles Area Chamber of Commerce, its president, William Lacy, addressed the board of directors regarding their interest in promoting preservation of the region's "romantic history, and of all things that will keep California, California." The latter included monuments like the "old Fremont headquarters at the Plaza." Lacy viewed "these old landmarks" as signs and symbols of a past that impeded, rather than enhanced, the future. The city he knew in 1875 "was just awakening then from its slumber of one hundred years" (so much for Yankee enterprise)

> and those old landmarks were here then and they haven't changed since except to get more dilapidated. Now all this talk about bringing back the Plaza to its early condition has never appealed to me because when I came here the Plaza was a little square open place as it is today and the streets surrounding it were about two or three feet deep in dust and dogs ran around in there and Mexicans and that sort of thing. Surrounding it were a few typical Mexican stores with sacks of beans sitting in the front and strings of chiles and garlic and Mexican sausage covered with flies. That is the condition in Los Angeles. I don't want those conditions brought back.[7]

Lacy imagined himself a realist. In fact, he was rehearsing a trope essential for the creation of a modern Los Angeles: Mexicans quiescently fading away, like the "old dilapidated landmarks," the adobe structures of Sonoratown. It is a trope both cultural and spatial. Lacy equated Mexicans with slumber, dust and dirt, flies and dogs, a crumbling past, and with a Plaza surrounded by shops and businesses catering to those other than Anglo. Anglos such as Lacy defined space so that Mexicans (and other "foreigners") who, of course, never did fade away, might be segregated into specific districts. Analyzing the means and methods they employed in defining, securing, and maintaining boundaries and zones within the city, their use of policy and regulation, of social reform initiatives, of myth and popular culture reveals how some Angelenos thought about space, territory, and place and the ways spatiality informed their understanding and their very conception of the city.

Lacy's contempt for the Mexican (a catch-all term Yankees who arrived after 1847 used for Mexican nationals, Mexican-origin citizens, and Californios) does not surprise us. We have now a deep literature exploring the ways race-based thinking has and continues to structure social relations and to define differing opportunities and life chances in American society. For California and Los Angeles, one thinks immediately of work by Alexander Saxton, Leonard Pitt, and Douglas Monroy.[8] The latter two have shown the significance of Los Angeles's founding as a colonial city for a later history of racism. Whether it was Spaniards striving to secure the border, convert the indigenous peoples, and impose their customs and beliefs or Americans striving toward the same ends after 1847, one aspect of the city's borderland status has been its role as an outpost of empire. In each case we find uncertainty, fear, and contempt for those who came before. Yankees arriving after 1847 chose either to convert Californios and Mexican nationals (Americanization), to ignore them, or to isolate them as a distinct group, a colony with its own space (Sonoratown) which Americans, whether resident or visitor, associated with a past that was static, hidebound, traditional, outside the course of history. In one sense, Anglos understood Sonoratown and its people (the "Mexican") to be a counter-space, everything their city was not. They also imagined it a counterweight against which they must hew and struggle to elevate Los Angeles into the future. In that sense, Sonoratown served as a marker against which Anglos could measure their progress.

But how did Angelenos define, secure, and maintain boundaries and zones within the city? What means and methods did they employ when assigning space to Mexicans, for example? Answering such questions requires study of the local state (policy and regulation) and the "soft" state (social reform initiatives), as well as popular culture and myth (cognitive space and mental maps). Folders in the USC Regional History Center labeled "Sonoratown" provide clues. Despite a seeming incongruity of designating the core section of the nascent American city as a place apart, a "little bit of Mexico," it is impressive to discover the speed at which adobe and the bricks made by mixing this clay soil with straw, assumed significance in the Anglo imaginary. Over time and through repeated use, Anglos endowed adobe (both the thing and the word) with considerable meaning. It served as a sign of the old and the antiquated and as shorthand for those who had formed the brick, built the walls, and lived and worked in adobe structures. When Anglos saw these structures "melting," they were looking at a natural event rather than an unfortunate and utterly preventable product of neglect (and perhaps despair). In that act Anglos read the passing of an earlier age. Yankees arriving in the second half of the nineteenth century found a culture whose most visible, most significant, most imposing artifacts were seemingly impermanent, were literally made of clay. The disappearing adobe, whether a dissipating ruin or lost to demolition, and the association of adobe with Sonoratown in the Anglo imagination, signaled a past giving way inextricably to the present and the prospect of a future built on a blank slate rather than on the foundation of a Spanish-Mexican past; for many Yankees history began today, or so it seemed.[9]

This figurative clearing away was a form of appropriation. It was also part of a process to superimpose one set of cultural markers with another. Anglos strove to overlay alternative boundary and property lines on an existing pattern of land held in common, under rights of use (usufruct), or outright grants. The wood or brick building, the orthogonal grid of uniformly dimensioned streets, the fifty-foot parcel or thirty-five-acre donation lot with a surveyor's monument and property lines fixed according to township coordinates are all markers. Each served to focus economic, social, and cultural practices, to establish political legitimacy, and to create conditions of hegemony. They are symbols, in other words, but they are also structures.[10]

Social segregation—the parsing of individuals and groups in space along lines defined by race-ethnicity; by income, status, and class; by gender—whether elective or imposed, formal or informal, legal or extralegal is a signature aspect of the modern city under industrial capitalism. Functional segregation, zoning space in cities according to activities and assigning these to discrete districts, is an equally powerful sign and structure for the modern city. Historians tend to consider social space (nearness and remoteness, us and them) independent of the space of practice (territory, land use, locality). They equate social relations with social segregation and nuisance with zoning. These equations imply a causal relationship, and causality is conceived to be directional (a concern with nuisance activities leads to zoning, for example). However, we know through experience and acknowledge in the abstract that causality is not unidirectional. Social segregation affects social relations; zoning regulations confer both monetary and symbolic value on land; the social and the spatial are intertwined. It will surprise no one to hear that race is a factor in land use decisions or that there are reasons why a zoning map registers so closely with a census map when one is overlaid on the other.[11]

We could examine this set of relations in any city. Indeed, the similarities between policy formulation, everyday practices, and perceptions of race and space in Los Angeles with that in, say, New York, Chicago, Atlanta, Seattle, or Miami ought to be apparent in the empirical sketches that follow. Though select and abbreviated, these cases are nevertheless illustrative of the ways and means nineteenth- and early-twentieth-century residents of and visitors to Los Angeles engaged in place-making and identity formation and of how they defined and enacted space in the city.

A Topography of Race

A perceived social distance and the actual designation of districts with people and activities were fundamental coordinates for Anglos' mental maps of turn-of-the-century Los Angeles. We find traces of individual and collective maps in citizen petitions to the city council, memoirs, institutional records and reports, and surveys of land and property. What emerges from the archival sources is a record of space defined through experience (a journey to work, sites of leisure, religion, or service) and through words and texts (stories, newspaper accounts, official reports and social surveys). As we might expect, it is a landscape composed of parts, the parts pieced together to create both an individual's city and a sense of a city shared with others. These sources also reveal what we might call a topography of place, a literal and figural annotation of the material city in three dimensions. On closer inspection, this appears to have been a topography of race.

A primary coordinate for Angelenos' topography of place was the customary vertical axis of up and down, a scale of relative position in space of the type people then and now associate with a social hierarchy of high and low (think of cultural anthropology or, more concretely, the almost universal social gradient of flatlanders and hill dwellers in contemporary Los Angeles). A related coordinate can be observed in the common use of "east" as a referent for the low. *Alcaldes* elected to the Spanish, then Mexican, *ayuntamiento* (civic council) drew distinctions between the west and east sides of the river (banishing both the Indian village and the dog pound to the east), and this dichotomy has been foundational for thinking about space, for the experience of place, for identity and meaning from that time forward. In Los Angeles, west and east have been markers of race-ethnicity, class, status, and prospect. West and east served then and serve now as a putative divide separating landscapes of leisure from landscapes of production and labor, separating those whose privilege flows from affluence and influence and those who aspire to attain the rights others assume are a birthright.

In the Spanish-Mexican era and well into the twentieth century (in some aspects up to the present day) land east of the Plaza, below the bluff, on the bottomland along the river, has been associated with base needs and uses. The river, like the *zanjas* that it fed and that distributed its water to fields and families throughout the pueblo and the city, provided residents a basic necessity. At the same time, the river and the *zanjas* served a second basic need; both carried off refuse and waste. *Ayuntamiento*, common council, and city council records are littered with proclamations, petitions, and ordinances intended to regulate residents' use of the watercourses for everything from bathing and washing to discarding carcasses and increasingly to control the discharge of chemicals, offal, and other by-products of manufacturing. Municipal agencies were, in fact, one of the leading offenders; the city leased land to industrialists, spread its sewerage across the bottomlands (as fertilizer), and maintained its dump along the banks of the river into the 1930s.[12]

The Plaza site is on a bluff above the river bottomlands. The area immediately north of the Plaza, the zone Angelenos designated Sonoratown in the 1850s and knew by that name and all it connoted for at least a century, is on an upward slope that runs to Elysian Park. Yet when the *Los Angeles Times* interviewed a resident of the district in 1885, it identified this "octogenarian" as someone residing "*down* in Sonoratown."[13] When a sociologist studied the "causes of delinquency among fifty negro boys" in 1923, he described Central Avenue, from Ninth to Eighteenth streets, then the residential and commercial center of African American life in Los Angeles, as "Black Broadway" a term he found in common use among the "colored folks of the East Side."[14] (Central Avenue is more than a mile *west* of the Los Angeles River.)

Angelenos held an ambiguous, perhaps conflicted, perception of the river and the low-lying land east of Alameda Street. Given this, there is little surprise that when decisions were made regarding where slaughterhouses ought to be located, where gasworks might best be sited, or where the plague was centered, elected officials, sanitarians, business leaders, and a majority of voters looked east, to the low-lying land along both sides of the river and toward East Los Angeles, the Heights, and Belvedere.

Defining Social Distance

Beginning in the first years of the twentieth century and extending into the 1930s, a cadre of settlement house workers, municipal officials, and students and faculty from USC's School of Social Work repeatedly surveyed and studied the house courts, remnant adobes, and box-car housing in the so-called congested districts between the Plaza and the river. Despite the fact that the number of Mexican nationals and Mexicans with citizenship constituted a simple majority in only a handful of blocks and districts, social reformers of all stripes saw this area as a Mexican village in the heart of an American city and viewed its putative problems as the "Mexican problem." Like their counterparts in New York, Chicago, Pittsburgh, and Boston, these reformers defined the problem as environmental. They sought progress, uplift, and improvement through better housing.[15]

These disparate reports share a thinly veiled subtext concerning the nature of the putative boundary separating those studied from those doing the research. Nora Sterry, a sociology student at USC, structured her study of the Macy Street district as an ecosystem made up of diverse, independent yet interrelated ecologies scaled from the individual (child, student, worker, Syrian, and so on) to the family, a race-ethnic group, a school district, a neighborhood, increasing in geographic reach and number to the city. The Macy Street School constituted one such unit. Sterry's description of the district and its "conditions" was Dickensian. It was a world unto itself. The streets were a "veritable maze," "littered with rubbish and filth," in some cases never seen by the street department. The district lay "along the old river bed," three feet below the Alameda Street grade along the base of a ten-foot rise to the Plaza (hence to the "east" and low).[16] There is a fear, vaguely articulated, that the line dividing this district from other districts might be porous (or perhaps not an actual boundary). Even if contained, mere proximity to Mexicans, Chinese, Russians, and the like might threaten social order and economic boundaries, as might the actual proximity of the immigrant districts to the city center. These lines convey fear: of borders drawn and breached, of districts invaded, of possible, even likely, social contagion.

In marking Sonoratown, Chinatown, the Macy Street district, and the like, social surveyors, public health officials, school administrators, and other quantifiers and definers of urban space worked to articulate social distance. Their metric appears to have been a measure near enough to allow a useful, manageable oversight of Mexicans (for example) yet sufficiently removed to isolate those other than the cipher group from the immediate presence of a Mexican as an individual, a person one might encounter as a subject rather than a member of an objective group. Stated differently, the unexpressed, perhaps unexamined, rationale for these projects was to locate a point, an ideal distance, from which Anglos might lose sight of an individual and that person would recede in space until they became a figure in a landscape, an unknown among the unknowable many who inhabited the city's "foreign districts." Whether intended or not, these surveys made visible the distance Angelenos maintained individually and as members of social groups.[17]

If we were to continue this account chronologically, our cases might include a 1924 epidemic when city officials mapped foreign bodies and assigned space to Mexicans, Italians, Chinese, and other race-ethnic groups following reports of a critically ill woman, referred to simply as a "Mexican patient," diagnosed with pneumonia (later confirmed as pneumonic plague). Fear spread as quickly as disease and faced fewer barriers in transmission. In response, physicians and officials from the California State Board of Health and the Health Department of the City of Los Angeles strove to define disease spatially, articulate its boundaries, and police the border.[18]

Or we might consider the 1931 La Fiesta, a commemoration marking the 150th anniversary of the pueblo founding, a weeklong celebration when Angelenos, visitors, and invited guests put history on parade. Opening day (September 4) began at city hall. Following a salute of "guns, church bells, and factory whistles," Governor Rolph paid homage to Felipe de Neve, the "George Washington of California." Revelers then left this site of political power and walked three-tenths of a mile to the Plaza. There a choir sang "ancient hymns" and four acolytes led a procession of soldiers, monks, and an actor playing de Neve in a reenactment of the pueblo founding.[19] From city hall to the Plaza, in the space of three blocks, one could contrast the old city with the new, the "curious customs" of those former residents in the "Adobe Age" with the infrastructure, governance, and culture of the modern city. Simply by walking from one site to the other, celebrants could in their minds' eyes experience a passage from the present (a present intimately connected to ideas of the future, a present that was all about a possible future) to a past that was known, final, in essence, dead. In memory, time had become place.

For the 1940s we could consult a study funded by the Haynes Foundation analyzing 185 places in the county. The authors ranked each place according to a metric of relative social standing. We find Belvedere, Vernon, Bandini, Chavez Ravine, and Bell Gardens in the bottom six slots trailed only by Terminal Island, a working-class district dominated by canneries, a district whose primarily Japanese-origin population would soon be interned under Executive Order 9102. Or we might consider an "ecological analysis" of a "natural area," Hollenbeck, a district east of the river spanning the flats and Boyle Heights. The author, Cloyd Gustafson, had served as pastor of the Euclid Heights Methodist Church. His table of contents reflects his training in sociology at USC with Emory Bogardus. Gustafson devoted chapters to deterioration, invasion, assimilation, racial attitudes, disorganization, disintegration, and the like. In essence, it is a study of groups defined by nationality and language and the degree to which members of each group have (or have not) assimilated. Of note for this account of how boundaries have been drawn is the author's correlation between distribution and assimilation (the greater the degree of distribution the more "advanced" the degree of assimilation) and between topography and a group's relative rank in the grid of organization or disorganization.[20]

Gustafson's overall assessment of Hollenbeck as a "pre-slum area," the product of past isolation, of an absence of restrictions (that is, zoning) and community planning, and of rapid growth and change is most damning. His conclusions correlate point by point with those we find in reports from the Los Angeles Housing Authority's surveys of "blighted" districts conducted during the 1930s in consultation with the Works Progress Administration, as well as the appraisals of surveyors who inventoried Boyle Heights and other "blighted districts" during the Depression under the auspices of the Home Owners Loan Corporation (HOLC). The HOLC appraisers' field observations and color-coded maps directed the flow of investment capital *into* districts with strict zoning controls, high relative rates of owner occupants, and high percentages of white residents and *away from* districts characterized as heterogeneous in terms of land use and demographics. In the immediate pre- and post-World War II years, engineers and transportation planners engaged in the design of restricted access roadways consulted the appraisers' maps and plotted lines that followed contours defined by the surveyors' social gradients.[21]

We might then turn our focus to another type of urban renewal, the razing and eventual rebuilding of entire districts. Bunker Hill, the State of California's first redevelopment project (CAL-1), initiated a fifty-year effort to bring affluent Angelenos "downtown." (Although the Community Redevelopment Agency's [CRA] "downtown" sits atop Bunker Hill, newspapers, magazines, and other popular media routinely refer to downtown as part of the city's "Eastside.") Next the CRA removed long-term, primarily Latino residents from Chavez Ravine. The ensuing battle over public subsidies for housing was a critical factor in the recall of Mayor Bowron and eviscerated support for municipal, state, and federal programs designed to house low-income residents in decent dwellings within existing communities. More recently faith-based organizations have taken up this struggle within a framework of neighborhood councils, the product of recent reform to the city's charter.[22]

The implications of these and similar events have been partially obscured through attention to space as either physical or social when it is both. Ideas and actions reformers, planners, and other agents of the local state imagined as a helpful strategy, or at the very least an innocuous divvying up of land and assigning property, have led to concentrations of like people and, more invidious, a concentration of inequities in wealth; in housing; in access to capital, education, health care, and other services; in prospects and aspirations. All manner of metrics underscore the simple fact that space matters; where you live, which school district, which council district you call home, which hospital an ambulance takes you to, all these lines on the map structure the odds you will graduate high school (much less attend a university) or whether you will survive a heart attack.

Globalism on the Ground

Los Angeles has been a border city since its founding. It has been and remains a site where people, artifacts, and ideas from around the globe converge, a place where residents and newcomers, Californios and Yankees, Chinese and Molokans, African Americans and Filipinos created a hybrid or metis culture and city. We can trace the arc, pattern, and implications of this process over time through attention to the creation and re-creation of particular landscapes. Attention to site, locality, and place allows us to see globalism on the ground. The Laws of the Indies, the precept for laying out Spanish pueblos, codified a hybrid of Spanish-European ideals with indigenous New World settlements. We find a similar metis architecture or metis landscape in the sequent occupation of the Plaza area, the subsequent reuse and repurposing of nineteenth-century structures like the Lugo adobe, which émigré merchants from China adapted for commerce as they and other immigrants carved out a place of least resistance on the east side of the Plaza.

More recently, journalists, design professionals, and scholars have called attention to the ways first- and second-generation immigrants have transformed areas such as Boyle Heights, Huntington Park, and Montebello. Residents and businesses in these districts have adopted and adapted the relatively dense, small lot, cottage housing, and boulevard commercial strips put in place by prior émigrés (from Russia, eastern Europe, Mexico, and Japan), a built landscape that Jews who moved west from Boyle Heights, working-class whites moving east from Huntington Park and South Gate to Downey, and upwardly mobile Mexican Americans moving to Pico Rivera and Whittier left behind. The presence of street vendors, murals, and shrines, the use of fences, front yards, and front porches as semipublic spaces (what James Rojas calls an "enacted environment")—these alterations and activities have been read as signs of cultural retention, as everyday acts of resistance against a putatively hegemonic national culture and a global, corporate, consumer culture.[23]

Districts like Boyle Heights have been transformed as macrolevel factors such as economic restructuring, demographic dynamism, and national policy inflect with local or microlevel factors such as investment and disinvestment, access to housing, and codes and regulations. Interpreting these events requires theory that accounts for the local in a world where capital is global, culture is recombinant, and citizenship is increasingly flexible and transnational. This is not a call for new theory, rather for theory informed by history. The world has been in Southern California for more than 150 years. Urban historians and cultural geographers who study the region have much to learn from social historians such as George Sanchez and sociologists such as Gaspar Rivera-Salgado, scholars who follow people back and forth across national borders and who analyze the ways this circulation of people and ideas continually shape and reshape society and culture on both sides of a border.[24] Comparative studies of urbanization and of race and place in Los Angeles and Mexico City or Santa Ana (Orange County) and Guadalajara would undoubtedly reveal these networks and flows of people and an international trade in ideas, capital, and culture. A more challenging and, I suspect, ultimately more indicative type of study might begin with the premise of transnational citizenship and consider how these processes are transforming the use and meaning of urban space in cities on both sides of national borders.

In Los Angeles, the repeated surveys and the habitual surveillance of Mexicans and foreigners, the marking of the Plaza and its surrounding areas as Sonoratown (with subunits of Chinatown, Macy Street, and the like), the very use of the term *Sonora* remind us that the construction of race and identity in and through space is a process and that this process takes place at multiple scales, from an individual body (with its psychological and sensory perception of internal and external and of bodily boundaries), to an urban district, to the nation-state and its boundaries with other nations. Certainly Los Angeles's proximity to the international border, as well as the history of border crossing by Mexicans and Central Americans, has been critical in the creation of a border city and in the formation of individual and collective racial identity in California.

Notes

1. "Side-Lights on Old Los Angeles," *Publications of the Historical Society of Southern California*, vol. 5, 1900–02, 43.

2. Well known and representative studies are Robert Fogelson, *The Fragmented Metropolis: Los Angeles, 1850–1930* (Berkeley: University of California Press, 1967/1993), and Mike Davis, *City of Quartz: Excavating the Future in Los Angeles* (London: Verso, 1990), though a similar framework can be found on one hand in the antiquarian and analytic accounts the Historical Society published in its Annals and on the other in current publications associated with a Los Angeles "School," an introduction to which can be found in Allen J. Scott and Edward W. Soja, eds., *The City: Los Angeles and Urban Theory at the End of the Twentieth Century* (Berkeley: University of California Press, 1996).

3. An introduction to this literature would include essays collected in Michael J. Dear, ed., *From Chicago to L.A.: Making Sense of Urban Theory* (Thousand Oaks, Calif.: Sage, 2002); Scott and Soja, eds. *The City*; Roger Waldinger and Mehdi Bozorgmeir, eds., *Ethnic Los Angeles* (New York: Russell Sage, 1996); Norman M. Klein, *The History of Forgetting: Los Angeles and the Erasure of Memory* (London: Verso, 1997); David Reid, ed., *Sex, Death, and God in L.A.* (New York: Pantheon, 1992). For a critical assessment of this scholarship, see the reviews of Soja and Scott, *The City*, collected as "Historicizing the City of Angels," in *American Historical Review* 105.5 (Dec. 2000): 1667–91, and Philip J. Ethington, "Waiting for the L.A. School," *Southern California Quarterly* 80.3 (fall 1998): 349–62.

4. Carey McWilliams, *Southern California: An Island on the Land* (Salt Lake City: Peregrine Smith, 1946/1990), and Carey McWilliams, *California: The Great Exception* (Berkeley: University of California Press, 1949/1999).

5. Quote from Renia Ehrenfeucht, "The New Regionalism: A Conversation with Edward Soja," *Critical Planning* 9 (summer 2002), 5–12.

6. Mechal Sobel, *The World They Made Together: Black and White Values in Eighteenth-Century Virginia* (Princeton: Princeton University Press, 1987). Many cities are "hybrid" in this sense. Acknowledging Los Angeles's typicality might be a first step toward new interpretive insights.

7. Los Angeles Area Chamber of Commerce, "Minutes," Jan. 17, 1929, 1–5, Regional History Collection, Specialized Libraries and Archival Collections, University of Southern California.

8. Alexander Saxton, *The Indispensable Enemy: Labor and the Anti-Chinese Movement in California* (Berkeley, University of California Press, 1971); Leonard Pitt, *The Decline of the Californios: A Social History of the Spanish-Speaking Californians, 1846–1890* (Berkeley: University of California Press, 1966); Douglas Monroy, *Thrown Among Strangers: The Making of Mexican Culture in Frontier California* (Berkeley: University of California Press, 1990).

9. See for example "Melting Away," *Los Angeles Times* (hereafter *LAT*), July 28, 1882, and Jackson Graves, *My Seventy Years in California* (Los Angeles: Times-Mirror Press, 1927), especially chapter 17: "The Passing of the Dominant Race." See William Deverell, *Whitewashed Adobe: The Rise of Los Angeles and the Remaking of Its Mexican Past* (Berkeley: University of California Press, 2004), for an account of Anglos appropriating the Mexican-Spanish past to promote the future.

10. I have borrowed the formulation "symbols and structures" from Laura A. Benton, *Law and Colonial Cultures: Legal Regimes in World History, 1400-1900* (New York: Cambridge University Press, 2002), 2.

11. On spatial types, see Henri Lefebvre, *The Production of Space* (Oxford: Basil Blackwell, 1991).

12. City Council records, Los Angeles City Archives.

13. *LAT*, July 18, 1885. In a similar vein, see Rev. Eugene Sugranes, "Early Days in Los Angeles," *The Tidings*, February 20, 1914, reprinted in Monsignor Francis J. Weber, *The Old Plaza Church: Nuestra Senora de Los Angeles* (Los Angeles: s.n., 1980), 154–57.

14. Homer K. Watson, "A Study of the Causes of Delinquency Among Fifty Negro Boys Assigned to the Special Schools in Los Angeles" (master's thesis, Department of Sociology, University of Southern California, 1923), 10.

15. Sociologists at the University of Chicago developed "social distance" as a conceptual framework and theory, and a Chicago graduate, Emory S. Bogardus, further developed it as a method in his work on race and culture in Los Angeles. Emory Bogardus, *Introduction to Social Research: A Text and Reference Study* (Los Angeles: Suttonhouse Ltd., 1936). The California Commission of Immigration and Housing, "A Community Survey Made in Los Angeles City" (San Francisco: The Commission, 1919), records a Mexican plurality in four of eleven districts and an American plurality in five.

Elizabeth Fuller, "The Mexican Housing Problem in Los Angeles," *Studies in Sociology* 17.1 (Nov. 1920): 1–11, quote: 2; Gladys Patric, *A Study of Housing and Social Conditions in the Ann Street District of Los Angeles, California* (Los Angeles: Los Angeles Society for the Study and Prevention of Tuberculosis, c. 1917).

16. Nora Sterry, "The Sociological Basis for the Re-Organization of the Macy Street School" (master's thesis, Department of Sociology, University of Southern California, 1924). District conditions are in chapter two: "Social and Educational Needs Revealed by a Community Survey," quotes: 37, 29, 12.

17. See, for example, Dana W. Bartlett, *The Better City: A Sociological Study of a Modern City* (Los Angeles: Neuner Company Press, 1907); John E. Kienle, "Housing Conditions among the Mexican Population of Los Angeles" (master's thesis, Department of Sociology, University of Southern California, 1912); Emory Bogardus, "The House-Court Problem," *American Journal of Sociology* 22 (Nov. 1919): 391–99.

18. Deverell, *Whitewashed Adobe*, chap. 5. See California State Board of Health, "Report of Plague Eradicative Measures for Nov. 1924 through June 1925," Huntington Library, San Marino, California.

19. "Story of City's Century and Half of Existence Unfolds in Glittering Four-Flag Pageant," *LAT*, September 5, 1931; "History Repeats Itself," *LAT*, September 8, 1931; "Los Angeles Opens Fiesta Marking 150th Year Since Founding," *San Francisco Chronicle*, September 5, 1931; Historical Society of Southern California, *Annual Publications* 15 (1931), a special issue devoted to La Fiesta.

20. Eshref Shevky and Marilyn Williams, *The Social Areas of Los Angeles: Analysis and Typology* (Los Angeles: The Haynes Foundation, 1949); Cloyd V. Gustafson, "An Ecological Analysis of the Hollenbeck Area of Los Angeles" (master's thesis, Department of Sociology, University of Southern California, 1940), quotations: 40, 69, 73.

21. United States Works Progress Administration (Calif.), *Housing Survey Covering Portions of the City of Los Angeles, California. Conducted under the Supervision of the Housing Authority of the City of Los Angeles, California, WPA project no. 65-1-07-70* (Los Angeles, Housing Authority, 1940). HOLC property survey, University of Southern California digital archive *http://cwis.usc.edu/dept/LAS/history/historylab/HOLC/*.

22. Don Parsons, "This Modern Marvel: Bunker Hill, Chavez Ravine, and the Politics of Modernism in Los Angeles," *Southern California Quarterly* 75.3–4 (fall/winter 1993); Dana Cuff, *The Provisional City: Los Angeles Stories of Architecture and Urbanism* (Cambridge, Mass.: MIT Press, 2000).

23. James Rojas, "The Enacted Environment: Examining the Streets and Yards of East Los Angeles," in *Everyday America: Cultural Landscape Studies after J. B. Jackson*, ed. Chris Wilson and Paul Groth (Berkeley: University of California Press, 2003).

24. George Sanchez, *Becoming Mexican-American: Ethnicity, Culture and Identity in Chicano Los Angeles, 1900–1945* (New York: Oxford University Press, 1993); Gaspar Rivera-Salgado, "Cross-Border Grassroots Organizations and the Indigenous Migrant Experience," in *Cross-Border Dialogues: U.S.–Mexican Social Movement Networking*, ed. David Brooks and Jonathan Fox (La Jolla: Center for U.S.-Mexican Studies, University of California, San Diego, 2002).

The Figure of the Neighbor: Los Angeles Past and Future

Dana Cuff

When Alexis de Tocqueville traveled across America in the early nineteenth century, he noted that widespread, voluntary participation in government improved not only the individual's character, but it developed a commitment to the common good and produced a sense of ownership with its commensurate responsibilities. Without participation, the citizen becomes "indifferent to the fate of the spot which he inhabits, . . . and the condition of his village, the police of his street, the repairs of the church or parsonage" will not personally matter.[1] Throughout *Democracy in America*, Tocqueville offers examples of citizen participation centered upon local physical spaces: streets, schools, churches, villages. Both local place and the participation itself are at the root of civil society in Tocqueville's analysis. While Tocqueville is usually read for notions of democracy and democratic procedure, we can extend Tocqueville. Where he concludes that participation inspired character and public responsibility, I argue that the fate of the spot we inhabit, the village, street, or church, induces citizens' voluntary participation in political life. My own research into Los Angeles communities and into what I will call the figure of the neighbor reiterates the power of local place.

Neighbor Form

Los Angeles is a patchwork of neighborhoods, politically institutionalized through neighborhood councils, publicly marked by municipal signage, and subjectively identified by their residents. Besides giving different territories their individual identities, the neighborhood and its material form offer terrain for significant social relations. Porches, stoops, apartment house lobbies, and picture windows establish a transition between the private and public spheres, bridging the household and the neighborhood. Side yards, party walls, and fences mediate between neighbors. The political signs and holiday decorations placed in a window communicate the occupant's identity. Sidewalks, streets, and parks, while technically public, belong to the neighborhood, and trespassers are noted. Local cafes, elementary schools, and neighborhood markets extend the living room to act as community rooms where residents interact on relatively neutral ground. The American residential landscape, be it urban or suburban, frames a range of dynamic, potent relationships. Those relationships of interest here are situated between the house and the city, in the zone between domestic privacy and the public realm. Settings in that zone embody what can be called the figure of the neighbor. It is in this sense that I wish to discuss the neighbor within Los Angeles, and within urban cultures at large.[2]

The construct of the figure of the neighbor is multifaceted. It not only implies material figures such as windows on the street, but embodies conceptions of self, stranger, other, friend, enemy. Intrinsically, the neighbor is an intersubjective mediation between self and the other: one must be one to have one. In a form of reciprocal spatial identity, subject and object are mutually dependent; self and other are intrinsically bound. In this formulation, the neighbor is inherently and conceptually the link between the individual and the social context. This is visible in the physical form of the neighborhood. The image of Levittown portrayed the mass middle class, a silent majority, more poignantly than did any sociological investigation of postwar society.[3] The repetitious massing of isolated building blocks, unembellished facades, intimate separations between dwellings, formal distance from the public street, and lack of public space evinced a disregard for the collective and a pinning of all hope on social reproduction within the nuclear family.

My analysis does not assume a causal relationship between neighborhood design and the sociopolitical relations therein, but instead operates on the assumption that sociality is differentially enabled by particular environments. When groups of dwellings are planned, they embody a figure of the neighbor that can be discerned, an intended figure that stands in relation to the practiced figure. Thus, with Los Angeles as the subject field, an historical examination of neighborhoods and their sociality might reveal the various figures of the neighbor that design and development have assumed in the twentieth century. This historical study can simultaneously inform architects, planners, and urban designers as they imagine future dwellings. The latter is particularly relevant, since data suggest suburban expansion is slowing, instigating new forms of housing development within urban neighborhoods.[4] Because the figure of the neighbor is rigidly inscribed in suburban housing patterns, architecture and planning have played a limited role there. Infill housing within cities, however, requires innovative design that can refigure the neighbor.

Los Angeles has much to teach us about urban social relations, particularly if we look at its most provisional neighborhoods—those that have undergone vast transformation.[5] Through the demolition of older neighborhoods, along with the construction of large new communities over the past century, Los Angeles has continuously remade sizable sections of its domestic terrain. Across the United States, such demolition was instigated through slum clearance and urban renewal programs. Los Angeles's "slums" were unlike those of other major cities in that they comprised primarily low-rise, detached housing. The domestic spaces of the city where residents have the most invested in symbolic, temporal, financial, and social terms, viscerally present to the observer the meeting point of private and public lives. The neighborhood, in Los Angeles and elsewhere, sits at the intersection of space and politics. It follows then that the neighbor, the link between self and society, is the basic unit of a democratic politics of the city.[6]

While observers from Bachelard to Vidler have read the house as a representation of some form of the individuated self, it is possible to read the flip side of the domestic setting as a representation of the collective other.[7] Rather than standing as a manifestation of the individual, the house and its context are imbued with sociological implication. Since only a few of us have the means to express ourselves by choosing a house as we might choose our clothing on any given day, we take what we can get and make of it what we can. In opposition to the established idea that the house is a "symbol of self," the contemporary middle-class house is more likely to be a symbol of everyone else.[8] The scale of investment, coupled with high rates of mobility, means that we purchase and remodel for resale. That speculative house is a reflection less of the owner than of the owner's conception of all prospective buyers—a collective, generalized other.

Beyond this expression of the other in the house itself are the spaces situated between the house and the city, between the apartment and the street. These shared, even neighborly areas link individuals visually, physically, or proprietarily. Those that are intentionally designed represent a low level of variety in terms of type, regulation, and form. In contrast to this limited infrastructure of neighbor forms, residents find myriad ad hoc ways to establish connections between private and public, deployed differently by different cultural and ethnic communities. These are the places—outside the private realm of our own homes, and shy of the public realm of the city itself—where an intimate politics of the local, a civil relation among strangers, might be situated.

Interwar L.A.: Brief Excursions to Provisional Neighborhoods

To understand figures of the neighbor for future urban cultures, we should first scan several key moments in the past century when urban development took dramatically novel turns. At each turn, we can evaluate the material presence and the sociopolitical practices in light of the neighbor.

Every new residential plan, every new urban design, embodies implicit notions about relationships among the house, the neighborhood, and the citizen. To capture some understanding of this sociophysical phenomenon, I offer snapshots of four Los Angeles neighborhoods. The snapshots are taken at a moment when each neighborhood was threatened, because such moments call for collective, political action. Under threat, some neighborhoods coalesce with a strong defense while others splinter and give way. While there can be no definitive conclusions from these cases, they do allow us to examine the range of factors that have produced the figure of the neighbor in Los Angeles.[9]

The first and second cases are intimately tied by being located on the same site: homes and businesses in the Boyle Heights Flats were demolished to make way for 802 units of public housing at Aliso Village in the early 1940s. Originally laid out with modernist, utopian goals, Aliso Village persisted for more than fifty years before it too was demolished. The neighborhoods in this area, strikingly opposed in form but alike in their segregation from the rest of Los Angeles, were destroyed despite varying neighbor practices. The third case, temporary veteran's housing built in Quonset huts, demonstrates that even when residents are not particularly attached to their dwellings, they can organize to retain a shared resource. The last case tracks a typical suburban area that is situated adjacent to wetlands slated for development. Here, the model of private individualism is contradicted and simultaneously reinforced by resident associations that actively engaged in planning the neighboring property. From these cases a number of core issues emerge:

1) the role played by boundaries, segregation, and distinctions between inside and outside;
2) the significance of residential choice; and
3) the relationship between civil society and publicly-directed neighborhood action.

Together, these four examples lead to speculation about Los Angeles versions of the neighborhood, and about ways neighborhoods spawn broader urban public interest. I conclude with a final example: an experiment to strengthen an existing community by establishing new figures of the neighbor from within.

Figure 1.
Composite of Las Vegas
Street in the Flats, 1940.
Composite, Dana Cuff,
from HACLA appraisal
images.

The Flats

In Los Angeles at the turn of the twentieth century, recent immigrants of Italian, Irish, Mexican, Greek, and Russian descent, along with African Americans and Mexican Americans, were spatially and socially segregated by the white Anglo-Saxons who dominated political structures at all levels. This translated into an urban mosaic of segregation and residential restrictions. The Flats, that part of Boyle Heights located just east of the Los Angeles River, was home at that time to a predominantly ethnic-Mexican population, along with recently emigrated Molokan Russians. The neighborhood became a primary focus of the first housing commission in 1906 and the first housing ordinance in 1907, which concerned what were called house courts.[10] This ordinance, unlike those that followed, was not intended to rid the city of these high-density, poorly built units, but to improve them, especially their shared facilities, such as the common water source and exterior bathrooms. Health, but also neighborhood moral standards, reformers believed, could be improved by more stringent sanitation guidelines.

House courts comprised one- or two-room units with a common walkway down the center of the lot where a water faucet was located and with shared toilets located at the back. Sometimes these courts were built as private rental property, sometimes by employers as worker housing. These substreets created a shared domestic realm for laundry, child care, and socializing. Later, this model was usurped by multiple units built behind a primary house on the street, reflecting the transformation of immigrants who became landholders with their own tenants. The collective space of neighbors was diminished on the lot and pushed back out to the public street.

Still, these residents shared a particular social and physical figure of the neighbor. The elementary school, as well as the river, functioned as local infrastructure to give shape to the community. Residents' descriptions of life in the Flats concerned their common geographic plights (flooding by the L.A. River or eradication sweeps for bubonic plague), immigration status (Americanization programs and evening language school), or day-to-day existence (the rag man, the vegetable vendor, and the evening work whistle from the Cudahy meat-packing plant). Propinquity governed all these social networks and was productive of what appears to have been a high degree of civility. When the time came to tear down these early "slums," there was no apparent resistance to demolition, although various documents indicate that residents did not want to move.[11]

From the outside, the Flats, like other central urban neighborhoods in L.A., was a de facto site of otherness, where recent immigrants and poor people of color were permitted, or restricted, to live by the powers that be. While residents there constructed an internal community of civility and neighborliness, much remained determined by outside forces, such as flood control, the housing commission, and later the housing authority. Ideologically, a contagion model of neighbors was imposed there by outsiders, be they reformers or government agents. Disease, vagrancy, immorality—these would spread like a virus from house to house, and then beyond the borders into the next neighborhood unless contained.[12] Urban blight was the physical correlate of this pathology, where run-down houses were portrayed by housing advocates, lending institutions, and city officials alike as dragging down their neighbors.

Aliso Village

To counteract the contagion, in 1942 the Flats were destroyed with municipal and federal funds and Aliso Village public housing was built in its place.[13] For about twenty years, from the mid-1930s to the mid-1950s, Los Angeles, along with other American cities, tried to radically restructure urban neighborhoods through federally subsidized housing construction programs. Called "modern housing" by housing activists, low-rise, planned developments were the prevailing utopian neighborhood model.[14] Local agencies like the Housing Authority of the City of Los Angeles built primarily garden apartments in contrast to the high-rise towers that stigmatized public housing programs nationwide.

Reflecting progressive ideals, public housing was to be temporary shelter for an upwardly mobile, working poor and was intended to Americanize the growing population of immigrants, now neighbors. It is ironic that this project of cultural domination was undertaken in what was in fact highly un-American housing. Socialist in terms of image and provision, public housing was originally advocated for the same reasons it would later be viciously attacked by critics in the McCarthy era. Modern housing stood in contrast to Ameri-

Figure 2.
Demolition of Aliso Village, 2000. Photograph by Dana Cuff.

can housing practices: it was built with federal subsidy from housing policy established in the New Deal era. To critics, this smacked of socialism, as did its physical image. At Aliso Village, dwelling units expressed no individual property boundaries, and all the resources beyond the front door were shared: splash pools, pedestrian walks, clotheslines, and playgrounds. Such housing was utopian in the comprehensiveness of its sociopolitical goals to produce better citizens, boost economic mobility, and create shared social networks. In a word, public housing was expected to eradicate the problems of the "slums" they had just buried.

Modern housing—public housing—embodied a radical notion of neighborhoods. These were to be collective developments that emphasized the whole over the individual household.[15] Their planning and site organization portrayed this communitarian agenda, creating veritable islands of new housing amid remnants of the slums they overran. While Aliso Village was characterized by a stripped-down, modernist architecture, its garden apartments were particularly well planned, with natural ventilation and light, modern plumbing conveniences, and shared community amenities such as recreational areas, meeting rooms, and laundry facilities. The Aliso Village site plan was particularly well designed, creating smaller groupings of apartments around courtyards, separating traffic from children's play, and organizing the entire development like a pinwheel around the school. The most significant neighborhood institution, the Utah Elementary School, was the only building left standing when all the Flats had been razed. The school stood, and indeed still stands, as an anchor for the neighborhood, symbolizing a measure of persistence in the face of convulsive change.

Modern public housing comprised holistically planned, autonomous neighborhoods with definitive boundaries that contained its residents spatially, managerially, and economically. More than eight hundred households in Aliso Village all had one landlord: the Housing Authority of the City of Los Angeles. Deterioration due to inadequate operating budgets set in almost immediately, encouraging households that could leave to do so.[16] The social networks that had formed were not strong enough to overcome problems that seemed equally bounded by the utopian rational plan, such as gangs, deteriorating housing, and lack of security. By the time the neighboring public housing project, Pico-Aliso was demolished in 1997, only a small but ineffective political protest was mustered for a neighborhood that hardly seemed worth fighting for anymore, even by its own occupants.

Utopian planning requires large-scale undertakings in order to reshape broad swaths of everyday life. A form of domestic colonization, such planning also demands authority and obsequiousness. These qualities were implicit in the housing authority's governance of residents. When residents finally confronted untenable circumstances, moving seemed like their only option and another convulsive transformation began. By 2003, Aliso Village had been replaced by Pueblo del Sol, a new mixed-income housing development, once again planned around the school.[17] This housing, consistent with the principles of traditional neighborhood districts and new urbanism, has located once again an extensive, shared realm for social interaction within the site.

Neighbor Practices

Several conclusions can be drawn from the Flats and Aliso Village in terms of the figure of the neighbor. In the Flats, neighboring practices were located on the street, in settings such as front-yard gardens, porches, a neighborhood school, and the local businesses interspersed throughout the neighborhood. The form of Aliso Village could not have been more different. Individual gardens and porches were replaced by collective yards for laundry and children's play. Instead of providing small-scale mediation between private and public, Aliso Village's outdoor space was entirely semipublic and shared among residents. Individual dwelling units bore little relation to the street, oriented instead toward the courtyard. The school, still at the heart of the neighborhood, continued to function as a magnet of sociality.

Both the Flats and Aliso Village, however different, evidenced clear figures of the neighbor. In terms of social relations, the Flats described an informal relationship between individuals, while Aliso Village cast the individual as part of a formal collective. With regard to boundary definition, the Flats had loose edges that segregated recent immigrants and poor Mexican American residents from the rest of Los Angeles. In contrast, Aliso Village was contained unambiguously, its interior defined by a singular architecture as well as by public ownership that stood in direct contrast to the city beyond is borders.

Residents of the Flats and Aliso Village did not actively resist demolition, though a small protest was mounted in the latter case. The explanation for this muted resistance is multifaceted. The fact that residents were steered into both neighborhoods by racial discrimination, the physical problems with the housing stock, and the social problems experienced by community members (such as harassment by the city, local gangs, etc.), may have cumulatively made neighbors "indifferent to the spot [they] inhabit" in Tocqueville's words. Moreover, civic indifference, if not outright antagonism toward the communities in question, cast justifiable doubt among neighbors upon the potential effectiveness of their protests. That indifference was registered in a decaying physical environment, particularly in the public housing, where maintenance was supposed to be a municipal responsibility. The school, however, stands apart. Central to both neighborhoods, it was retained and persists today, playing the same function for the recently built replacement housing.

Both the Flats and Aliso Village are examples of community formation based in part on otherness—forces outside the boundaries determined to a large extent who would live inside the boundaries. Spatially repressed, these neighborhoods organized internally but were unable to fend off external threats that eventually brought about their demise. In these contexts the figure of the neighbor could be locally cooperative without expanding into political activism. This can be described as internal civility, characterized by collective operation within the neighborhood (for example, running a cooperative preschool) without publicly directed or civic activism.

These cases add nuance to the general idea that the neighbor stands at the intersection of space and politics. In theory, the neighbor is both strange and proximate, involving a nearness that is arbitrary, accidental, and transient. There, where we live, without choice as to who lives next to us, we engage community without intentionality. The sociologist and planner Mel Webber in 1963 identified the peculiar phenomenon of "community without propinquity"—a form of community among those who live at a distance, based on common interest established across space (as with work groups). Webber's community without propinquity was contrasted with communities of place, which depend upon proximity within a locality.[18] My focus here is upon locality, but without the traditional associations that the terms *community* and even *place* suggest. Neighborhood is a territory shared by residents without implying internal civility or that residents share interests, backgrounds, or histories. These are the residents of noir suburban literature and contemporary gated communities.[19] Those neighborhoods evince stereotypes of paranoia and alienation among residents who flee the city to wall themselves off from xenophobic uncertainties. This figure of the neighbor is the shadow of a hyper-romanticized community of friends. These dialectic projections reverberate on the neighborhood's conceptually neutral ground.

If, in theory, the figure of the neighbor begins as a blank slate, there are many indicators that in practice the neighbor is increasingly complex and civil. In the United States, the portent of low formal political participation is coupled with the rise of neighborhood politics. According to Berger and Neuhaus, civil society is gaining momentum in the neighborhood. "The neighborhood," they contend, "should be seen as the key mediating structure in the reordering of our national life."[20] They make a distinction between two types of neighborhoods: those of social cohesion and neighborhoods of elective choice. While my work corroborates the increasing significance of neighborhoods, it offers different typological distinctions. First, literature since the *Levittowners* challenges the notion of cohesion, and second, current housing markets challenge the notion of choice. Instead, neighborhoods are selected by default and reflect conceptions of identity and difference both externally and from within.

In terms of internal cohesion, the external pressures brought to bear on occupants of the Flats and Aliso Village steered them toward a limited set of neighborhoods. Economics, racial segregation, social stigmatization, and the Home Owners' Loan Corporation's red-lining constructed an invisible wall around the Flats as effective as those of Orange County's gated communities. Exclusion of the other at least as much as, if not more than, inclusion of sameness governed neighborhood formation. As for choice, location options for most households are highly restricted by the factors of cost, availability, proximity to jobs and schools, and access. Instead, most people, but especially those of limited means, live in what can be called "default neighborhoods," those that best meet their basic needs: compared to elsewhere, it is more affordable, it has housing available to them, and it is nearer where they work and/or where their kids go to school. Such neighborhoods are chosen, but under severely restricted opportunities for choice.

Under these conditions, default neighborhoods hardly create coherence among residents. This unfamiliarity among those living in close proximity can threaten social isolation, but can also promise political hope. While residents' only common interest may be geographic, it is a strong bond: that interest is persistent (the terrain does not disappear), shared (everyone is connected by common geography), and nontrivial (we care where we live). And thus is readied the petri dish of a neighborhood politics, where an argument between two neighbors over a car that too often blocks the driveway turns into a street's worth of households informally discussing crowded parking conditions, which ends up at the planning commission, where neighbors formally debate the merits of permit parking. The internal civility generated enables neighbors to organize politically with greater effectiveness on subsequent issues—say, when an unwanted commercial development is proposed nearby.

The neighbor, then, is the last unavoidable front of spatial politics where civility and contention may emerge, where abstractions of the other are met, literally face-to-face, and sustained over extended periods of time. The figure of the neighbor, however, remains a *potential* for socio-spatial action, realized in some, but by no means all, cases. We read too often after natural disasters like the Northridge earthquake of 1994 that people have met their long-term neighbors for the first time. Moreover, neighbor relations are not always as trivial as the proverbial cup of sugar would indicate, nor as friendly. From German Jews remembering the Holocaust to Muslims in northern India today, stories from war-torn cities describe neighbors who murdered neighbors, as well as those who rescued them.

It may be that "default neighborhoods" hold greater potential for civility than the idealized neighborhoods of cohesion due to the presumed levels of difference and identity, respectively. Under conditions where residents perceive relative homogeneity in their neighborhood, they may be less prepared to cope with inevitable disagreement compared to residents who recognize their heterogeneity.

Sociologists and political theorists have paid special attention to neighborhood associations because they are unlike other types of group formation where membership is voluntary and based on common interest. Neighborhood associations are based on proxemics, open to all residing within a given area, and in some instances, membership is even mandatory.[21] Among home-owner associations there is some indication that important differences in operating styles exist. One study found two distinct styles of neighboring: a private, friendship form and a public, group-interdependence form. Those associations based on friendship-like bonds were less effective in overcoming schisms and accommodating differences than those that followed a more public style of association. In the first of the two styles, neighbors emphasize the individual freedom associated with the home and private life, seeking compatible others whose interests and circumstances form the basis for a discretionary relationship. In the second form, neighbors are obligated to one another prior to any personal relationship, recognizing their interdependence regardless of their diversity. The public neighborhood group is inclusive and open to the participation of all residents, while the private neighborhood group is based on compatibility. The latter then runs the risk of implosion when disagreements are strong, since it has no ideological framework for reconciling differences.

Silverman's distinction between public and private neighbor styles is useful for examining forms of political association and their relative effectiveness. Two very different residential developments in Los Angeles offer some clues about the effects of residential choice on social homogeneity among neighbors, and loosely upon resultant neighbor styles. Coupled with an analysis of the two different physical places, the concept of civil society can be examined in the context of Los Angeles neighborhoods.

Rodger Young Village

At Rodger Young Village, rather unloved but much needed housing in the form of 1,500 units in 750 Quonset huts was built in 1946 on a former airfield at the edge of Griffith Park as temporary shelter for returning veterans and their families. The severity of the L.A. housing shortage left people living in their cars, on the streets, in garages, and doubled up. When Rodger Young Village opened, thousands of veterans of all races, colors, and creeds hoped to move in—a default neighborhood if ever there was one.

Rodger Young's Quonset huts were compactly laid out with no concern for shared space. Residents, confronted with such unmediated close quarters, took matters into their own hands. The ends of the huts' vaults were converted into virtual garden porches by their tenants, with wooden lattice, shading devices, planting, and fences. Residents formed committees to solve neighborhood problems, both physical and social, creating a high degree of internal civility. Accustomed to turning adverse circumstances to their own ends through ad hoc means, the veterans and their wives organized to gain telephone service, increase community services, protest civil rights abuses, and ultimately resist demolition and displacement. Though they saw the Quonset huts as temporarily serving their own needs, Rodger Young's residents wanted to preserve the huts for future families needing low-rent housing. Their actions, founded on effective neighborhood organization to serve local needs, extended to the public interest.

Figure 3.
Setting up connections at Rodger Young Village, 1946. Photograph by Leonard Nadel, courtesy of Evie Nadel.

Though the largest school in that part of Los Angeles was in the Village, it was the Village Shopping Center that dominated Rodger Young's ad hoc figure of the neighbor. Old airport hangars adjacent to the housing were converted to grocery store, shops, and services. This center mirrored the emergence of strong, spontaneous social organizations. Their style was explicitly public and not based on friendship per se, since the only presumed commonality among participants was war service. Strong social and political alignments soon formed within Rodger Young Village. Conservative interests were represented by the Knights of Columbus while progressives, some of whom

were members of a local communist cell, organized most of the political activity in the Village. Effective neighborhood practices and activism built a way for the unfamiliar to grow familiar, in which blacks, Latinos, and whites, communists and noncommunists, veterans and their wives, shaped a new social order. Although Rodger Young Village was originally planned for closure in 1949, just three years after it was constructed, residents' actions delayed demolition for five more years, but eventually their Quonset huts were dismantled and residents were dispersed across the city.

Westchester

It is useful to contrast Rodger Young Village, the ultimate default neighborhood, with Westchester, Los Angeles's own version of Levittown. There, elective choice (still, among few options) produced a relatively cohesive social setting in terms of class and ethnicity. Across the United States, white families moved into middle-class status after the war, settling in suburbs like Westchester. Wrapped in the mythos of the American Dream, Westchester represented the suburban free market ideal. Construction began in 1940 with defense worker housing, and by 1948 some twenty-five thousand people had taken up residence in Westchester's many neighborhoods, all of which followed the typical physical pattern of the suburbs. Its general planning strategies lend insight into the figure of the neighbor. The unit of building was not the house, but the ten-to fifty-acre tract of land where somewhere between fifty and three hundred houses would be located along new streets with new infrastructure, created by "community builders."[22] These so-called communities were created by an efficient plotting of the land and by traffic management guidelines. Broad arterials for through traffic created superblocks, while residential areas turned their backs on these boulevards to focus on an internal network of smaller streets. These blocks contained almost no shared spaces besides the streets themselves, since developers in Westchester made decidedly inadequate plans for schools, parks, or other neighborhood institutions. There was but one large-scale commercial zone, designed not for neighborhood foot traffic as at Rodger Young, but for shoppers arriving by car. Thus, the house itself was the de facto figure of the neighbor, with the nuclear family isolated inside.

Driven by cost, price caps set by the government, and the vastly inadequate supply of housing, the Los Angeles builders included only economically beneficial components in their planning. These inadequacies were quickly recognized by Westchester's early residents, who organized to provide for library and school facilities. More recently, home-owner associations developed effec-

Figure 4.
An original 1940s Westchester house today. Photograph by Dana Cuff.

tive means to voice their interests in the adjacent Playa Vista project. Just below Westchester's bluffs, a thousand acres of coastal wetlands and fields were planned for an immense new town of housing, office, and retail establishments. In response, Westchester residents rallied against high-rise towers, and for wetlands preservation, joining a broad range of interest groups from across the west side of L.A. Their concern for the wetlands can be viewed as both a local good (nearby accessible open space) and a public good (environmental preservation). While I do not have adequate data that pairs a neighborhood's physical qualities and activist resident associations, it appears that the public interest activity began in homes along the bluffs which would be most directly impacted by the new development. Through meetings in their homes, neighbors organized friendship-based associations that in some cases converted to public styles of self-governance.

Civility in the Neighborhood

One indicator of the social bonds in an area is its residents' effectiveness at organizing for neighborhood action in response to impending change. Rodger Young Village and Westchester suggest that both default and elective neighborhoods can be productive of internal civility. Both Rodger Young Village and Westchester mustered strong organizations to negotiate imposed transformations to their neighborhoods. In both cases, residents believed that unique and much-needed resources would be destroyed without their political activism. In both cases, resident efforts went beyond internal civility to exercise external or public civility. While their actions had locally positive benefit, they were also based on broader concerns about civil rights, the need for low-rent housing for families of color,[23] and for environmental protection. In both cases, political efforts were only partially successful, for although demolition was delayed at Rodger Young Village, the Quonset huts were eventually torn down. And at Westchester, Playa Vista's developers expanded the wetlands preserve but did not significantly reduce overall development goals. In the suburban tract homes and the Quonset huts alike, a public style of resident association was built in which friendships were not the basis but a side effect of the organizing. In this sense, the figure of the neighbor in these two areas does not fit stereotypical notions of the sugar-bearing, stoop-sitting, gossip-sharing individuals.

If the figure of the neighbor is the smallest political seed of larger civil society, if not liberal democracy, then neighbor relations would further congruent habits such as cooperation, tolerance, and fairness. In practice, neighbor relations frequently are not very "neighborly." According to Freud, the ideal of a civilized society governed by the injunction to love the neighbor is strangely unreasonable. Love should discriminate among people and be given to those who deserve it. "Not only is this stranger [the neighbor] in general unworthy of my love; I must honestly confess that he has more claim to my hostility and even my hatred."[24] Some researchers have found neighbor relations are fundamentally antagonistic. And when neighborhood groups organize to resist change as characterizes NIMBY (not in my backyard) actions, self-interest can overwhelm public good. The Los Angeles case studies were selected because they demonstrated practices distinct from NIMBY stereotypes, offering examples of neighbor politics that address larger public interests. Political scientist Nancy Rosenblum debates the common assumption that voluntary associations, such as neighborhood groups, are the kernel of larger, civil society because they perform "as inhibitors of unrestrained majoritarianism, and as training grounds for participation and leadership."[25] Rosenblum argues that it is naive to think voluntary associations directly mimic and thus serve liberal public culture.[26] But, these L.A. cases suggest that neighborhood-based voluntary associations can serve local, internal interests as well as broader public interests of civil society. Thus, the figure of the neighbor can assume civil and political form under certain circumstances. If we examine the contemporary urban environment, we might see new avenues to encourage a more civil society. There are at least three changes in the context of the American residential scene that precipitate a revision of our understanding of the neighbor: reurbanization, urban splintering, and dynamic spatial politics.

First, the decade of the 1990s was marked by widespread urban growth: 72 percent of cities gained residents, averaging 8 percent in overall population growth. There was also a "downtown rebound": nearly 70 percent of the top cities studied showed an increase in their central business district population.[27] While the suburbs continued to grow at a faster rate than the modest growth of urban neighborhoods, the latter marks a significant trend. The figure of the neighbor in urban neighborhoods will necessarily differ from the neighbor of the suburbs, and the form of urban neighborhoods must differ as well. Los Angeles captures glimpses of the new era that is in store, particularly in the southwest but not restricted there, for cities that have grown via suburban sprawl past the point of reasonable limits.[28] In the coming decades, new housing developments will be built in smaller increments, on less land, in existing neighborhoods, where populations and housing stock are more diverse, closer in, utilizing existing infrastructure.

Second, urban politics are increasingly fragmented, from the wide array of groups lobbying for their particular interests to the initiative process promoting single issues. This general phenomenon has become a cliché in the analyses of identity politics, the fragmentation of the left, and the rise of American individualism.[29] In terms of the neighborhood, this century has witnessed the privatization of domestic life via gated residential streets and governance through various forms of mandatory home-owner associations. The latter are part and parcel of planned unit development, condominiums, and co-op apartments. The rise of common-interest housing developments and a privatized public sphere have presaged a problematic era in civic governance and civil society more generally. In Los Angeles, existing neighborhoods are politically represented by neighborhood councils that legitimate a civic role for spatially based community groups. While such councils insure local representation, they simultaneously reinforce urban splintering.

Finally, a related but less studied trend comprises the dynamic spatial politics attending this fragmentation: increasing mobility and nomadism, the privatization of public space, and the abandonment of the public sphere. Legal battles between neighbors, NIMBY groups that deny services to the homeless, city planning boards overrun by special interests—these characterize local politics around the country. Some parts of Los Angeles function as extensions of homelands further south for recent immigrants who stay just long enough in one neighborhood to find footing in another part of the city. For a brief time in the post–Rodney King period, the area known as South Central shifted from a series of local struggles to an L.A.–wide concern. The dynamic populations and politics of cities create complications for the growth of civility as groups vie to make their own local, episodic needs known. Competitive representation stands in where regional cooperation is needed, and communities isolate themselves from their surrounding environs. Under these circumstances, it is important to seek ways to move between local and regional interests, to expand and refigure the neighbor. In L.A. and elsewhere, reurbanization, splintered urbanism, and dynamic spatial politics compel us to rethink the figure of the neighbor both conceptually and in terms of the physical environment.

Architecture and Urban Design

To begin to build a more civil society within urban cultures, neighborhood form cannot be set by exclusionary tactics of segregation or boundary definition. Rather than walled domains of seeming similarity, a local catalyst constellates the figure of the neighbor around something worth saving to the community. In this regard, neighborhood plans should accommodate more than private, individual interests. Individual residential units, while requiring careful design, cannot be the focus of such plans. Instead attention needs to be directed toward common interests identified with the group and interstitial spaces located between group members. A more complex elaboration of semi-private and semipublic spaces is called for. Beyond balconies and apartment laundry rooms to side yards and parklands, the figure of the neighbor needs space for its embodiment. Lastly, while socioeconomic and ethnic heterogeneity cannot be designed into a neighborhood by architects and planners, at least designers can help to avoid implied homogeneity. This does not mean that the design must have formal variety, but that the settings—their program, scale, context, and functions—are varied. A single architectural approach could produce, for example, large and small dwelling units that give out onto a range of shared spaces in various ways, enhancing the potential for neighborhood formation.

Encouraging new neighborhoods to contribute to civil society, toward constructive political action, requires some shared physical infrastructure to protect or improve, in contrast to more abstract common goods such as property value or security. This can include affordable housing (as at Rodger Young Village), parks (or the wetlands for Westchester), schools, or parking—resources that benefit residents collectively and are thus worth fighting for. When residents can literally see the consequences of community action, they are better able to construct neighbor organizations. This may explain why acting to prevent change seems stronger than acting on behalf of improvement: the improvements are not visible until after they have been constructed. Hannah Arendt understood this when she argued that "our feeling for reality depends utterly upon appearance and therefore upon the existence of a public realm into which things can appear out of the darkness of sheltered existence."[30] The material form of community, the apparent shape of a neighborhood, is the fundamental stuff of a local public realm and the local basis of civil society.

From the Garden City of Ebenezer Howard to the neotraditional development by Robert Stern and Disney Corporation at Celebration, from the 1914 communist colony at Llano del Rio northeast of L.A. to Park La Brea still standing midcity, architects have sought to encourage more utopian, civic, and engaged neighborhood life. Yet the form and scale of these efforts has paid little attention to the growth of civil society. Indeed, utopian schemes, from public housing's modernist socialism to New Urbanism's retro-village of individualists, have mirrored the gated community model in which exclusionary practices predominate. My own research suggests that such communities will be less likely to exhibit public civility—a concern for the public good of the city outside their own boundaries.

The next wave of urban infill residential development must grapple with another figure of the neighbor and new spaces of civility. A projective reading of the case studies indicates that the timing and scale of residential development are influential in ways that are counterintuitive. Large-scale "new towns" built from scratch characterize most quasi-utopian undertakings, but regardless of their goals, such projects will not be as successful as infill developments in establishing a diverse, public figure of the neighbor. But what is the infill to be developed? Of course, more and varied housing must be built, but the first development mandate is the neighborhood sphere of semipublic space. The rigid, speculative house and interior can be contrasted with an intrinsically vague, ill-defined figure of the neighbor. We should encourage design invention within the residential sphere situated between households—in the shared spaces, in the site plan, in neighborhood institutions.

I would like to demonstrate through one final contemporary example that a new figure of the neighbor in Los Angeles can arise in concert with architectural innovation. Can the next figure of the neighbor be designed to make more possible not just local but public civility? This case serves as a conclusion and points a positive course, one that involves citizens, architects, activists, and residents together. It also fits within this study's style of argument in which the figure of the neighbor is revealed through cultural production of programs, buildings, and political practices.

Pueblo Nuevo: A Conclusion and a Beginning

The MacArthur Park neighborhood gets its name because it includes one of L.A.'s great public open spaces. One of the densest and poorest communities in the city, its residents are primarily recent immigrants from Central America. They move to the MacArthur Park area as a first stopping ground, doubling or tripling up in apartments with other families from their towns of origin. Language and immigration status discourage public life within institutions like the local schools, but the greatest barrier is school overcrowding. MacArthur Park children are bussed as far as an hour away from their homes, limiting the families' opportunities to be part of their children's education and removing from the neighborhood one of its most significant semipublic spheres.[31]

From the late 1990s to the present there rose a series of building rehabilitations on Burlington Avenue, between Wilshire Boulevard and 7th Street in

Figure 5.
Dedication of Camino Nuevo Charter Academy elementary school, 2000. Photograph by Tom Bonner courtesy of Daly, Genik Architects.

the MacArthur Park community. Warehouses, abandoned buildings, and parking lots have been converted into schools and playgrounds. In contrast to prevailing models of public housing, gated communities, and Westchester, at MacArthur Park the core is being strengthened for a neighborhood whose boundaries are unknown. An Episcopal priest, Philip Lance, initiated the process when he opened Pueblo Nuevo thrift store and cooperatively owned janitorial service. Seeing that locally based jobs were only one part of combating problems in the neighborhood, he investigated the possibilities of a charter school. Together with Daly, Genik Architects, my firm of Community Design Associates gathered information at group meetings, in interviews, and by observing nearby elementary schools. Community members who were connected to other Pueblo Nuevo efforts, as well as local teachers and prospective school parents, contributed to the school planning. That effort gave birth to Camino Nuevo Charter Academy, an elementary school that opened in 2000, where test scores show steady improvement and which won the prestigious Rudy Bruner Award for Urban Excellence in 2003—a national prize given to the project that best combines good community work, good design, and good programs.[32] A preschool and middle school were added in 2001, and a high school is set to open in fall 2004. The incremental projects of Pueblo Nuevo each give form to a part of a larger, long-term goal of stabilizing and improving neighbors' lives as well as their neighborhood. Together, programs and physical form have secured the street so that children are safe to get an intense, academically challenging experience.

The genius of Pueblo Nuevo resides in its emphasis on the figure of the neighbor, the support of the MacArthur Park area's collective identity rather than individual accommodation. Moreover, by building schools with a highly regarded curriculum and a design that has won much recognition, Camino

Nuevo gives residents institutions that are dignified and worth saving.[33] Unlike the modernist utopian plans of Aliso Village, these schools are intended to respect cultural identities of the neighborhood. Rather than employing iconic representations such as a Latin American architectural motif, the architecture reflects desired functions as well as cutting-edge school design. The provision of a protected, semipublic open space, a plaza of sorts, where the elementary school meets the street, was a solution built out of community input. In the highly public realm, as in MacArthur Park itself, those with insecure immigration status tend to maintain anonymity. This may not limit intimate neighbor relations, but it restricts more public, external civility. However, at the neighborhood scale, the public realm can be more local, more secure, and more participatory. At Camino Nuevo, parents and grandparents use the school as a community center. Evening classes are offered to teach computer skills and English language. Together, a strong figure of the neighbor, enacted through programs, institutions, and architecture, may help build stability in this otherwise fragile neighborhood. Pueblo Nuevo reinforces the notion that strong neighbor form fosters the development of neighborhood-scale civility.

Pueblo Nuevo's urban operations portray a new model that can be described as spatially integrated, incrementalist, and yet, paradoxically, utopian.[34] The embodiment of the neighbor may indeed reside in a fragmented utopia.[35] The modern figure of the neighbor in L.A. has assumed various shapes over the past century, from a reformist utopia to a single-family free market ideal. In each case, large-scale transformation of the urban fabric laid out an entirely new neighborhood. It is characteristic of such neighborhoods that they will find themselves vulnerable to convulsive change and threatened with annihilation. The case of Pueblo Nuevo Development puts forward an alternative strategy: to build within a residential area a new figure of the neighbor, in the form of neighborhood-scale institutions. If this strategy were indeed effective, we would soon see residents working to improve the new schools or increase social services in their neighborhood. In addition, those same residents might build a politics that extends beyond the MacArthur Park community, contributing their voices to the larger civil society of Los Angeles. This, indeed, would be a positive direction for the future of urban cultures.

Los Angeles is an excellent site for the study of the neighbor, since its modern residential environment is peppered with housing experiments. The continuous populations booms, the absence of a historic building fabric (for example, compared to Boston's Back Bay), and the uniquely strong home-building industry set L.A. up as a neighborhood laboratory. The city created from its many experiments a textured figure of the neighbor, while simultaneously establishing the grounds for its constant modification. New development pressures, particularly on the oldest suburbs of L.A. now inside the city and highly heterogeneous in social and physical terms, set the stage for contemporary explorations in the neighborhood. Because of their heterogeneity, these next neighborhoods hold a strong potential for local and public civility. With infill projects of schools, housing, and community services, new figures of the neighbor will be born.

Notes

1. Alexis de Tocqueville, *Democracy in America*, trans. P. B. Henry Reeve and Francis Bowen, vols. 1 and 2 (New York: Vintage Press, 1960 [1835, 1840]).
2. The author wishes to acknowledge the support of the Humanities Research Institute of the University of California and the fellowship program called "The Ethics of the Neighbor."
3. Herbert J. Gans, *The Levittowners: Ways of Life and Politics in a New Suburban Community* (New York: Vintage Books, 1967).
4. In an important study titled *Sprawl Hits the Wall: Confronting the Realities of Metropolitan Los Angeles* (Los Angeles and Washington, D.C.: The Southern California Studies Center of the University of Southern California and The Brookings Institution Center on Urban and Metropolitan Policy, 2001), Michael Dear demonstrates that suburban expansion in the outer L.A. basin has peaked, returning population and development pressure to the city.
5. This essay builds upon earlier research by the author published in the book *The Provisional City: Los Angeles Stories of Architecture and Urbanism* (Cambridge, Mass.: MIT Press, 2000). While my earlier work describes these communities extensively in terms of their development history, here I examine their physical form in relation to sociopolitical behavior.
6. The neighbor is formulated differently in philosophical discourse about the religious injunction to love the neighbor.
7. Gaston Bachelard, *The Poetics of Space*, trans. M. Jolas (Boston: Beacon Press, 1969); Anthony Vidler, *The Architectural Uncanny: Essays in the Modern Unhomely* (Cambridge, Mass.: MIT Press, 1992).
8. The house as symbol of self was articulated by Clare Cooper in *The House as Symbol of Self* (Berkeley: Institute of Urban and Regional Development, University of California, 1971).
9. While each of the case study neighborhoods were in some ways coherent, they should not be seen as homogeneous. The brief descriptions offered here cannot but allude to the internal diversity, particularly in social terms. Characterizations of the different neighborhoods are drawn from a wide range of sources that include archival materials, interviews with residents, and observations in neighborhoods where possible. Expanded description and analysis of the case studies can be found in Cuff, *The Provisional City*.
10. At the beginning of the twentieth century, a series of reports were written on housing conditions in Los Angeles. House courts are described in *Report of the Housing Commission of the City of Los Angeles 1906–1908* (Los Angeles: Housing Commission, 1909.)
11. When the entire neighborhood was threatened with demolition, it appears that the majority of Flats' residents spoke a common language, did not want to move, and shared numerous social ties. Documents such as diaries, maps for eminent domain proceedings, and interviews provide evidence to draw these conclusions.
12. These existing neighborhoods were appraised, purchased through eminent domain, and razed, leaving nothing in their wake. Their residents were scattered to other affordable neighborhoods around the city, and though they were promised units in the new housing, that promise was broken when rental priority was given to war workers and veterans at different points in time.
13. See Cuff, *The Provisional City*, for a full explanation of how Los Angeles neighborhoods came to be defined as slums for demolition.

14. See Catherine Bauer's seminal text, *Modern Housing* (Boston: Houghton Mifflin, 1934).
15. Although public housing was initially segregated, that is, each development's residents were to be a single race that mirrored the surrounding neighborhood, this plan was undermined by progressive housing activists like Frank Wilkinson and the Citizen's Housing Council in L.A.
16. Robert Fishman has completed new research about the problematic implications of inadequate operating budgets of local housing authorities, forthcoming in the journal *Places*. Paper presented at Princeton University Symposium, Housing and Public Policy, October 2003.
17. Pueblo del Sol is a HOPE VI project of the Department of Housing and Urban Development of the Federal Government. HOPE VI was the housing provision program that followed traditional public housing, intended to cure the latter's ills with mixed-income strategies. Pueblo del Sol includes a community center on the school site, with pools and exercise room, along with 470 units of housing. Since only a portion of the units are for very low income families, the loss of affordable housing is great. Approximately a hundred families of Aliso Village's original 802 units were relocated into Pueblo del Sol.
18. Webber first wrote about the concept of community without propinquity in 1963, but the most accessible source was published several years later in Melvin Webber's "Order in Diversity: Community Without Propinquity," in *Neighborhood, City, and Metropolis*, ed. R. Gutman and D. Popenoe (New York: Random House, 1970), 791–811.
19. On suburban literature, see Catherine Jurca's *White Diaspora: The Suburb and the Twentieth-Century American Novel* (Princeton: Princeton University Press, 2001). Setha Low's *Behind the Gates: Life, Security, and the Pursuit of Happiness in Fortress America* (New York: Routledge, 2003) is an informative text on the gated community.
20. Peter L. Berger and Richard John Neuhaus, "To Empower People: From State to Civil Society," in *The Essential Civil Society Reader*, ed. D. E. Eberly (Lanham, Md.: Rowman and Littlefield, 2000), 149.
21. See, for example, Evan McKenzie's *Privatopia: Homeowner Associations and the Rise of Residential Private Government* (New Haven: Yale University Press, 1994). On styles of neighboring, see the study by Carol J. Silverman and Stephen E. Barton, *Obligation Versus Friendship: The Effects of Neighboring Style on Neighborhood Organization* (Berkeley, Calif.: Institute of Urban and Regional Development, University of California, 1988).
22. This name was given to the newly organized home-building industry giants by Marc Weiss in his book *The Rise of the Community Builders* (New York: Columbia University Press, 1987).
23. Black and Latino families experienced the most severe housing shortage in postwar L.A., due at least in part to legally sanctioned racial restrictions across the city.
24. Sigmund Freud, *Civilization and Its Discontents*, trans. J. Strachey (New York: W. W. Norton, 1961 [1930]), 67.
25. For a discussion of both sides of this argument, see Nancy L. Rosenblum, *Membership and Morals: The Personal Uses of Pluralism in America* (Princeton: Princeton University Press, 1998), 3.
26. Rosenblum develops a series of case studies to demonstrate that groups serve many purposes for their members, including an informal support for political legitimacy and stability. She studies proprietary home-owners' associations as a particularly unusual form of social and political organization in America, because membership is not controlled by the group, nor voluntary, but is required upon purchase of a property. Neighborhood organizations, by comparison, require the group to admit any resident of some geographic area, but participation is voluntary. Whether formally organized or not, neighborhood-based interaction is based on the circumstances of spatial adjacency rather than ideology. No wonder then that neighborhoods have tried so hard, historically, to restrict residency to a chosen group. Unlike Rotarians or neo-Nazi skinheads, neighborhood groups have no ideological base outside the common interest they share in the proximate environment known as their neighborhood, and no means to deny any resident membership except social exclusion. See Rosenblum, *Membership and Morals*.
27. Alan Berube and Benjamin Forman, "Patchwork Cities: Patterns of Urban Population Growth in the 1990s," in *Redefining Urban and Suburban America*, ed. Bruce Katz and Robert E. Land (Washington, D.C.: Brookings Institution Press, 2003).
28. Various aspects of the end of sprawl are documented in Dear, *Sprawl Hits the Wall*.
29. For example, see James A. Vela-McConnell, *Who Is My Neighbor?* (Albany: State University of New York Press, 1999).
30. Hannah Arendt, *The Human Condition* (Chicago: University of Chicago, 1958), 51.
31. For an excellent description of the neighborhood, schools, and community, see the Bruner Foundation Web site at *http://www.brunerfoundation.org/p/2003_camino.html* and a forthcoming book by Jay

Farbstein titled *Creative Community Building: 2003 Rudy Bruner Award for Urban Excellence* (Cambridge, Mass.: Bruner Foundation, 2004). In the chapter on Camino Nuevo Charter Academy, MacArthur Park area's density is estimated at 145 persons per acre, compared to 14 persons per acre citywide.

32. See Farbstein, *Creative Community Building.*
33. The curriculum planning was done by Paul Cummins of New Visions in conjunction with education-management experts at ExEd (Excellent Education Development). Daly, Genik Architects' designs for the schools have been published widely and have won numerous architectural awards as well as the Rudy Bruner Gold Medal.
34. Utopian undertakings are characterized by their spatial efforts to separate themselves from the surrounding social context. In addition, social utopias are constructed as comprehensive plans that encompass the totality of the residents' existence. Thus, incremental and infill projects would not fit traditional utopian models.
35. Manfredo Tafuri, *Architecture and Utopia* (Cambridge, Mass.: MIT Press, 1976).

Straight into Compton: American Dreams, Urban Nightmares, and the Metamorphosis of a Black Suburb

Josh Sides

In few American suburbs have firearms played a more central role in civic destiny than they have in the city of Compton in Southern California. In 1953, a pair of Colt .45 pistols, wielded by black Korean War veteran Alfred Jackson and his wife, Luquella, served as tools of the last resort for African Americans integrating a hostile white suburb.[1] The Jacksons' determination to defend themselves against the churning white mob, which had assembled in front of the Jackson home just as their moving van arrived, had the intended effect: when Alfred's close friend stepped out of the house with a 12-gauge shotgun, the crowd dispersed. The Jacksons' victory in this unheralded "battle for Compton" precipitated a rapid recomposition of the population of this historically white suburb, allowing a relatively well employed segment of Southern California's black population to enjoy the benefits of the much-vaunted suburban California lifestyle of the 1950s and 1960s. Compton quickly became an anomalous beacon of hope, the pride of thousands of middle-class African Americans in Southern California through the 1970s.

Yet by the 1980s, Compton had become something else entirely: a metonym for the urban crisis. As the isolated street gang skirmishes of the late 1970s devolved into a brutal guerilla war for control of the lucrative crack cocaine trade in the 1980s, young Comptonites turned their guns upon themselves, spraying their own neighborhoods with bullets, riddling with lethal lead the very homes that had inspired such hope in the 1950s. During the late 1980s and early 1990s Hollywood's film and popular music industries exploited the growing regional notoriety of Compton, transforming the city into a national symbol of racialized blight and crime. In recent years the diffusion of "Compton" has even gone international: in the late 1990s Japanese teenagers eagerly ordered hats with the word "Compton" embroidered in gangster font on the brim from Japanese-language editions of Southern California's *Lowrider* magazine.[2] Ironically, Japanese competition in the automotive and steel industries in the early 1980s had been a significant source of economic decline in Compton, and by the 1990s, a cynical representation of the city had become one of its chief exports.

How Compton made this sweeping transition, from an exemplary African American suburb to an urban nightmare, is at once a story of social and economic historical transformation: de jure desegregation, shifting regional and global labor demand, declining retail sales, and changing municipal tax burdens. But it is also a story of perceptual change as well, about what Compton once represented, to both insiders and outsiders, and what it has come to represent. By the late 1980s, that perception of Compton arguably became more influential to the city's destiny than its own real history. That Compton ever represented anything other than what it now does seems inconceivable, a fact that makes the excavation of its historic meaning and representation all the more important.

Antediluvian Compton

Compton's contemporary notoriety belies its historic ordinariness: by the standards of 1920s' Los Angeles, it was an unexceptional city, typical, in fact, of a cluster of suburbs like Huntington Park, South Gate, Bell Gardens, Lynwood, Maywood, and Bell, that lay adjacent to and mostly east of Alameda Boulevard. These working-class suburbs, described so well in Becky Nicolaides's work, shared a common central-city geography and blue-collar composition that distinguished them from the more distant, affluent, and consumption-oriented suburbs of the post–World War II era.[3] The "Hub City's" boosters touted the affordability of houses in Compton and their proximity to the two adjacent poles of Los Angeles County's industrial core, the Eastside Industrial District and Central Manufacturing District.

The vision of Compton as "the ideal home city" and as a "residential center for industrial workers" appealed to thousands of California-bound migrants from the Midwest between the 1920s and the 1950s, who sought suburban tranquility amid ample blue-collar employment.[4] Equally enthusiastic were industrial employers in the region's automobile, steel, and food-processing plants, who benefited from a large supply of mortgage-conscious white workers in close proximity. Conditions in Compton, the Industrial Department of the Los Angeles Chamber of Commerce noted in its 1920s promotional literature, "were good, since workers may live close to their work in inexpensive homes of individuality, where flowers and gardens may be grown the year round. White help prevails."[5] Recognizing these "ideal" circumstances, the National Civic League awarded its prestigious 1952 All-American Cities Award to Compton, one of only eleven American cities to receive the coveted honor that year.

Central, of course, to Compton's "All-American" identity was the fierce maintenance of racial exclusion by the city's white home owners, real estate brokers, civic leaders, and law enforcement personnel, who, combined, constituted a virtual phalanx against racial integration. Unquestionably, white home owners were the advance guard, first instituting highly effective racially restrictive housing covenants in 1921.[6] Bolstering these covenants were real estate brokers, whose licenses could be revoked for integrating neighborhoods, and the FHA, which flatly denied loans in areas not covered by covenants as a matter of policy. And the Compton City Council sanctioned the maintenance of Compton's whiteness repeatedly, but most conspicuously in the early years of World War II, when it forcefully resisted the construction of a public housing complex in Compton because it was considered "Negro housing."[7] Finally, law enforcement agencies in Compton, and all of its adjacent working-class suburbs, vigorously defended the racialized boundaries of urban space by regularly harassing black motorists who dared to cross them.

Rallying behind the slogan "Keep the Negroes North of 130th Street," militant defenders of Compton's whiteness were incredibly successful.[8] As late as 1948, even as waves of African American migrants flooded Los Angeles, Compton's segregationists held the day: of a population of forty-five thousand, fewer than fifty were African Americans. The only exception to Compton's lily-white composition was the presence of a very small Mexican barrio on the northern tip of the city, immediately adjacent to the unincorporated areas of Willowbrook and Watts. Compton's whites successfully contained that small population of Mexicans by refusing to sell them homes outside of the barrio, or "pricing" Mexicans out by advocating civic improvements near the barrio.[9] But in Compton, as with the rest of Southern California and probably most of the Southwest, white hostility toward Mexicans was never as intense as the dread, fear, and hatred they felt toward blacks. Mexicans—by virtue of their lighter complexions, and their critical role in the labor market of the region—generally occupied a middling social status, somewhere between that of blacks and whites.[10] If many whites thought of Mexicans as a necessary evil, blacks were both unnecessary and evil.

But the late 1940s and early 1950s were dangerous years for Compton's segregationists. First, pressure from the west was rising rapidly. Southern California's great black migration—which was at high tide between World War II and the late 1960s—was rapidly transforming the adjacent city of Los Angeles. Neighborhoods like Watts, Willowbrook, and Avalon, which had been highly diverse, multiracial communities prior to World War II, were becoming steadily blacker and blacker, and after World War II, they approached 100 percent African American populations.[11] Second, many African Americans desired to leave the racial confines of South Central. A 1956 Urban League survey of 678 black families in Los Angeles revealed, in fact, that 84 percent would buy or rent in a "nonminority" neighborhood if they could.[12] Third, the landmark Supreme Court decisions *Shelley v. Kramer* and *Barrows v. Jackson*, handed down in 1948 and 1953 respectively, effectively abolished racially restrictive housing covenants, the most entrenched barrier to neighborhood integration. Finally, a growing proportion of African American families were now enjoying double incomes, quickly integrating both blue- and white-collar occupations in many sectors of the region's dynamic labor market. Recognizing that the overcrowded and disproportionately poor community of South Central could not sustain their vision of the American Dream, these families increasingly set their sights westerly and easterly, seeking middle-class stability in communities like West Adams, Crenshaw, and Compton.

As black ambition surged, so too did the vigilance of those whites determined to limit black residential mobility. Throughout the region, white home owners employed various techniques (at least twenty-six different ones, according to a 1947 study by the Los Angeles Urban League) to "scare off" prospective black home buyers, including vandalism, cross burnings, bombings, and death threats.[13] White resistance surfaced in the formerly white neighborhoods of South Central, in the more distant San Fernando Valley, and, most stridently, east of Alameda. A white home owner in Huntington Park, which lay to the north and east of Compton, complained to Governor Earl Warren, "In Southern States they have laws that keep the 'niggers' in their places, but unfortunately, for the white race in this state, there is nothing to control them . . . I think that there should be separate places for the Negroes to live instead of continually coming to white communities."[14] This renewed antiblack hostility made the racial integration of white suburbs by blacks an extremely unlikely prospect long after the legal victories of desegregation had been achieved.

Blacks and the American Dream in Compton

Ultimately, however, geography was destiny for Compton. Unlike its neighboring blue-collar suburbs, much of Compton lay to the west of Alameda, immediately adjacent to the areas of increased black concentration. In the 1940s, perhaps before the imminent threat of racial integration was perceived by the city council, Compton eagerly annexed large parcels of unincorporated space on its southwestern periphery with the hopes of boosting the city's already substantial tax base through new residential and industrial development. But after the legal scaffolding of de jure segregation fell with *Shelley* and *Barrows*, undeveloped parcels of that recently annexed land were exposed to housing developers who saw the great financial potential in building new, unrestricted housing, just east of the ghetto. Several developers, Davenport Builders chief among them, did just that, selling the first unrestricted homes in 1952 on a patch of land that had only recently been a cornfield.[15]

As the Davenport development suggests, the end of de jure segregation prompted a variety of responses from local whites in Compton. Although most whites abhorred and resisted integration, some recognized its market potential. Because African Americans seeking homes outside of South Central were generally willing to pay more for homes in Compton than whites were, some white home owners quickly sold to the aspiring black suburbanites, usually to the great consternation of their neighbors. Some whites in Compton likely tried to convince their white neighbors of the value of integration, to prevent wholesale white flight and potential property devaluation. (In Crenshaw, a group called Crenshaw Neighbors had some success in this vein through the 1970s, but I have found no evidence of a similar organization in Compton).[16] Finally, there were some reported incidents of liberal whites, genuinely sympathetic to black aspirations, buying houses in Compton so that they could quickly resell to blacks, without a profit.[17]

But the overwhelming response to black aspirations in Compton and elsewhere in Southern California was massive resistance by segregationists. Trouble began at Enterprise Middle School, an integrated Compton school between Central and Avalon on Compton Boulevard, where black and white students engaged in sporadic clashes in January of 1953. The next month, several white property owners were beaten and threatened for listing their properties with the South Los Angeles Realty Investment Company, which sold to both white and black buyers.[18] In the following months, shrewd Comptonites in a white home owners' association scoured the city codes in search of a way to punish real estate agents who sold to blacks, finally dredging up an obscure and never-enforced law prohibiting the "peddling" of real estate within Compton city limits and arresting five real estate agents.[19] In May, exasperated white home owners resorted to vandalism and picketing, staking out a spot in the Jacksons' driveway, before being driven off by the well-armed black family.

Sporadic acts of vandalism continued through the summer of 1953, but white residents increasingly recognized that the settlement of blacks in

Compton could not be stopped. Instead of attempting coexistence, many white Compton home owners decided to leave rather than risk a loss in property value. This reaction, common in transitional neighborhoods throughout Los Angeles County and the United States, was exacerbated in Compton by white and black real estate brokers who sought to stimulate a "panic selling" frenzy. Unscrupulous real estate agents of both races warned white home owners that unless they sold quickly, their property value would plummet. During the 1950s, panic selling and continued black in-migration dramatically reshaped Compton's racial composition. African Americans, who represented less than 5 percent of Compton's population in 1950, represented 40 percent of its population by 1960. In 1961 Loren Miller observed, with some ambivalence, Compton's rapid growth as a black suburb: "I doubt there are any other cities of Compton's size that can boast—if that's the word—a comparable percentage of Negroes."[20]

In striking contrast to the pattern of residential succession typical throughout the United States at the time, African Americans in Compton did not move into dilapidated homes in declining neighborhoods. "For once," one prominent African American observed of Compton's new black suburbanites, "the Negro did not move into slums; for once he came into good housing."[21] Indeed, the census of 1960 would reveal that 93 percent of Compton blacks lived in homes built since 1940 and more than half of those in homes built since 1950. Not only were Compton's homes new, but also big. Almost 75 percent of black households in Compton had four to five rooms.[22] In all except the skin color of a quickly rising proportion of its residents, Compton continued to look very much like the fabled American suburb of the 1950s, well into the late 1960s, and in some pockets, to the present (fig. 1).

Despite the persistence of racism in Compton, African Americans truly benefited from their suburban relocation. Indeed, the suburban dream of peace and comfort came true for the thousands of blue-collar African Americans who moved to Compton during the 1950s. When white journalist Richard Elman visited Compton in the 1960s, he was amazed by this new black suburbia. Compton's superior racially integrated schools, he observed, had created a much better crop of black students than one found in the ghettos of Watts or South Central: "Compton has become a city which sends its Negro high-school graduates to state colleges, to Berkeley and UCLA, and some even can afford to go as far away as Fisk."[23] Locally, black families increasingly sent their children to Compton Community College, considered at the time to be one of the state's best community colleges.

African Americans in Compton perceived themselves, and were perceived by many other African Americans, as thoroughly middle class. Compton's

Figure 1.
A far cry from the "ghetto" imagery of poverty, blight, and gang warfare increasingly associated with Compton by the 1980s, this photograph from 1982 suggests the resilience and vitality of the lower-middle-class dream in Compton. Photograph by Mike Mullen, *Herald Examiner* Collection, courtesy of the Los Angeles Public Library.

black residents were representative of that group of blacks who secured steady blue-collar employment along the industrial corridor. The material benefits of that employment, revealed in figures from the 1960 census, truly set them apart from their cohort west of the city. Most strikingly, unemployment in Compton was less than a third of that in Watts. A much higher proportion of men and women in Compton worked as full-time factory operatives than did those in Watts. Seventeen percent of black men in Compton were craftsmen and about one-third were operatives. Another 17 percent were professional and clerical workers. Twenty-four percent of Compton's black women were factory operatives, 20 percent were clerical workers, and 9 percent were professionals. Accordingly, median income of Compton residents was almost twice that of Watts residents.[24] Although contemporary observers and subsequent scholars viewed black migration to Compton as "ghetto sprawl," or an extension of the black ghetto, it clearly was not. For Compton's residents, the city was far from the ghetto. Even blacks forced to buy older homes in Compton felt a bit of the suburban dream. Mary Cuthbertson, an African

American migrant from North Carolina remembered how her late husband felt about owning a home in Compton: "It was a very old house, but being the first house he owned in his lifetime, it just meant a lot to him to *own your own house*."[25] In contrast to the physical deterioration of Watts, Compton's proud, black home owners had meticulously groomed gardens and, for the most part, well-maintained housing. A white resident of Compton candidly acknowledged that the new black neighbors "are stable; in our neighborhood they are of a good class; many buy their homes and take good care of them; we wouldn't exchange Compton for any other place."[26] A white businessman in Compton grudgingly admitted to a white reporter: "Of course they're [African Americans] moving into our city and there's nothing legal we can do to stop it. But you would be surprised—I'll take you through some of the streets they took over—clean as anything you want to see."[27] And a reporter for the *New York Times* marveled, in 1969, at the "life styles of Compton" where "nurses and small-business men take meticulous care of their small, frame houses and colorful flower gardens."[28] Although Compton was adjacent to Watts and Willowbrook, it was, for its residents, worlds away. The distinction often earned the scorn of blacks "left behind" in Watts. One complained that "our middle-class Negroes who move out to Compton . . . don't care about us."[29]

Deindustrialization, Death, and Taxes

On the eve of the infamous Watts riot of 1965, the maintenance of the American Dream for blacks in Compton was still conceivable, as was relative racial peace between the city's now equally divided populations. To be sure, whites still maintained a firm grip on power in the city, including a virtual racial monopoly in city politics, law enforcement, and the local newspaper, the *Compton Herald-American*. But blacks were making political progress, most conspicuously in 1963, a banner year for African Americans in Southern California. In Los Angeles, and after decades of frustration, blacks finally made political headway, gaining a remarkable three seats on the fifteen-seat Los Angeles City Council, one occupied by future black mayor Tom Bradley. But for black Comptonites the far more exciting victory that year was scored by local automobile sales manger Douglas Dollarhide, Compton's first black city councilman and, later, first black mayor.[30] Dollarhide's rise, and the subsequent elections of African Americans to positions in city government, established Compton as the "vanguard of black empowerment" in the United States, a fact not lost on proud Comptonites.[31]

Furthermore, while most whites throughout Southern California probably ignored the class dimensions of the August riot—perceiving it as a universal "black phenomenon"—there is evidence that at least some whites in Compton made far more subtle distinctions between those African Americans in the ghetto of Watts and those in Compton. For example, when rioters in Watts and Willowbrook moved toward Compton, they met with fierce resistance from whites *and* blacks, who collectively—if only temporarily—identified as home owners, rather than members of different racial groups. Leroy Conley, a black man who headed the Business Men's Association in Compton organized a group of black and white Comptonites armed with shotguns to repel the potential invaders. "We were all working together," Conley recalled. "There wasn't any black or white."[32]

But this peace under fire was short-lived. The far more enduring legacy of the Watts riot was its stimulation of wholesale white flight from Compton. As whites left Compton, they also abandoned their retail businesses, leaving Compton's Central Business district, which stretched along Compton Boulevard between Willowbrook and Alameda, virtually empty by the late 1960s (see figs. 2 and 3). Deprived of this crucial tax base, and lacking much significant industrial development, Compton compensated by raising property taxes to one of the highest levels in the county.[33] Additionally, under mayoralty of Dollarhide, Compton began its ongoing quest to expand its tax base through the annexation of unincorporated county land. In 1968, the city annexed five hundred acres of vacant land for an industrial park, but tenants were slow to move into the city, whose reputation, quite unfairly, was tarnished by the Watts riot (the remaining seventeen acres of this tract, appraised at $1.4 million, was sold, out of desperation, to a developer for $500,000 in 1982).[34] And, according to Mike Davis, when Dollarhide sought permits for greater annexation from the all-white County Local Area Formation Commission, Compton was systematically passed over for wealthier, white-majority communities like Long Beach, Carson, and Torrance.[35]

Simultaneously, Southern California's economy and labor market underwent a transformation that seriously undermined the pillars of black prosperity in Compton: a sharp decline in steady, unionized, blue-collar, manufacturing employment in, and immediately adjacent to, black Los Angeles. Although the 1965 Watts riot would certainly accelerate industrial flight from Los Angeles, that process was already well under way as early as 1963, when the out-migration of jobs in furniture, metal, electrical, textile, and oil refining machinery industries from South Central was first documented by researchers from UCLA's Institute of Industrial Relations. Following a trend set by the aircraft, aerospace, and electronics firms in prior decades, manufacturers increasingly sought to lower their tax burden, expand their plant size, and, it was hoped, connect to new markets by leaving the central city. Between mid-1963

Figure 2.
A typical street scene on Compton Boulevard, the main thoroughfare of Compton's thriving retail district, shortly before Christmas, 1954. From the *Herald Examiner* Collection, courtesy of the Los Angeles Public Library.

Figure 3.
Compton Boulevard, abandoned, 1982. The swift departure of white-owned businesses in the late 1960s and 1970s not only crippled the once-thriving retail district, but also erased a critical component of the city's tax base. Photograph by Mike Mullen, *Herald Examiner* Collection, courtesy of the Los Angeles Public Library.

and mid-1964, thirty-three industrial manufacturing firms left South Central and parts of East Los Angeles.[36] The pace of this process intensified through the 1970s as Chrysler, Goodrich, Uniroyal, U.S. Steel, Norris Industries, Ford Motors, Firestone, Goodyear, Bethlehem Steel, and General Motors all left the region, culminating in a devastating wave of plant closures between 1978 and 1982 that eliminated more than seventy thousand jobs in blue-collar occupations along the Alameda corridor.[37] Having climbed steadily for two decades, the proportion of the black male workforce working as operatives in manufacturing firms began to fall in the 1960s, and their absolute employment in manufacturing dropped in the early 1970s.

With more than a third of its population employed in manufacturing industries, Compton was probably affected more than any other black area in Southern California. Although the unemployment rate remained much lower than neighboring Watts and Willowbrook, it crept from 8.7 to 10 percent for black men between 1960 and 1970. One reporter from the *New York Times* observed that black "residents noticed changes: Stores are closing, the streets are dirtier, the merchandise is shoddier." Consequently, the children of Compton felt very differently about the city than their parents had when they moved there in the 1950s. One black teenager felt "the kids should have something they can be proud of. Now they just hang their heads when they mention Compton."[38]

Far more troublesome, however, than Compton teenagers' tendency to "hang their heads," was their propensity to join street gangs. Coinciding, and undoubtedly fueled by, the decline in legitimate employment opportunities was the explosive rise in black street gangs in Compton and throughout black Los Angeles during the early 1970s. Although the initial black gangs of the 1940s were largely defensive—protecting black youth from marauding gangs of white, segregationist teens—by the late 1960s, gang warfare had become a purely internecine affair, pitting black youth against black youth based simply on the neighborhoods in which they lived. Shortly after the 1969 founding of the Crips at Freemont High School in South Central, a group of black youth on Piru Street in Compton started the Bloods, adopting the red color of their local high school, Centennial High.[39] This territoriality intensified in the 1980s, as black gangs competed for control of the lucrative trade in "rock" cocaine (crack), a very affordable, easily distributable, and highly addictive drug.[40] Compton became the epicenter of gang violence and has consistently had the greatest number of gangs of any city in Los Angeles County other than Los Angeles itself. The disproportionate popularity of gangs in Compton relative to other black areas in Southern California can be explained partially by a

demographic anomaly: by 1969, Compton had one of the highest proportions of youth of any Southern California city, with almost half of the population under eighteen years of age.[41] But clearly, gang affiliation was also about
a renunciation of the "straight" life, an angry response to the failed promises
of this once-proud city.

Shortly after holding hearings in 1974 and early 1975, the Los Angeles
County Grand Jury published a grim inventory of rising gang violence, dys-
functional schools, corrupt civic administrators, inadequate public transportation, excessive taxation, poor law enforcement, and unusually high welfare
dependency. But the report also records the battle cry of Compton's aging,
and increasingly outnumbered, middle class. Longtime middle-class residents
excoriated the values, behavior, and goals of Compton's poorer newcomers,
fighting desperately to save the waning American Dream in Compton.[42]

That Compton, by the late 1970s, was in deep trouble was confirmed in a
careful and rigorous Rand study in 1982, "Troubled Suburbs: An Exploratory
Study." Prepared for the Department of Housing and Urban Development
(HUD), the report analyzed a number of variables—including education, income, crime, employment, and municipal fiscal health—and produced a list
of eighty-four "troubled" suburbs, fourteen of which were considered "disaster areas."[43] Not surprisingly, Compton made this later list. Yet what was far
more illuminating about the report was not that Compton was in "trouble,"
but rather that it was not *uniquely* troubled. In fact, the Rand report found
that the scarcely cited suburbs of Hoboken, New Jersey; Highland Park, Michigan; Chester, Pennsylvania; East St. Louis, Illinois; Camden, New Jersey; and
Alton, Illinois, were all considerably more "troubled" than Compton. Compton,
according to the clear-eyed report, was not *anomalous* (with the exception of
its uniquely large black population and its prevalent black leadership), but
rather *typical* of America's declining suburbs.

Representing Compton and Creating Metonymy

If Compton had already achieved some regional notoriety among whites by
the early 1960s, this fact was, apparently, not generally known outside of California. Ironically, it was this ignorance of the racial transition swiftly under-
foot in Compton that contributed to one of its most nuanced chronicles,
Richard M. Elman's *Ill at Ease in Compton*, published in 1967. A Jewish Brooklyn native and freelance writer, Elman was sent to Compton in 1964 at the
behest of the New York public television station to cover voter behavior prior
to the Goldwater-Johnson election. Selected cursorily by East Coast researchers as a "typical" American suburb, Compton defied Elman's expectations and

those of the news show's producers. After informing the producer that almost half of Compton's population was black, Elman and the cameramen were told to "shoot around some of these Negroes." According to Elman, the producer rejected the idea of including blacks in the news feature because "it just wouldn't be a typical American town. I asked for Main Street USA and you've given us Harlem." Ultimately, Compton's black population was "excised on the cutting room floor," leaving a public television report a decade behind the time: a Compton of 1954 perhaps, but not of 1964. "The educationalists," Elman recalled, "presented a portrait of the typical American voter that was as bland as it was boring and as boring as it was white."[44]

His curiosity about Compton piqued, Elman returned in 1967, two years after the Watts riot and shortly after finishing his first book, the *Poorhouse State: The American Way of Life on Public Assistance* (1966). The Compton that Elman encountered was still a thoroughly divided city, predominantly black west of Alameda and exclusively white to the east, and it was the destiny of this border that created the underlying tension in Elman's reportage. *Ill at Ease in Compton* depicts a Compton whose fate is not yet sealed, a Compton that is not necessarily destined to be either solidly black or predominantly poor, a Compton in which interracial coexistence is still conceivable, if greatly under attack. It is also a city whose black residents are "safely lower-middle-class" and live in neighborhoods where "motorboats and campers are parked with about the same profusion as in the white neighborhoods."[45] Despite the many signs that Compton still represented what it had a decade earlier—a refuge from ghetto life for middle-class African Americans—Elman was sensitive to the extent to which that vision depended on whites staying in Compton. The mounting flight of white home owners and businessmen undercut the very promise of that vision. "It is getting harder and harder," Elman wrote, "for the black man to aspire even to Compton when he looks around him and sees the way the white man's children feel about it."[46]

Had whites in Compton carefully read Elman's work—which they most assuredly did not—the future of the city might have been quite different. His interview with "Jewish housewife" Dahlia Gottlieb, for example, is a portrait of peaceful coexistence between whites and blacks. Far from regretting the arrival of blacks, Gottlieb derived a sense of satisfaction with the multiracial world she and her neighbors were creating, and evinced a strong sense of admiration for the strivings of lower-middle-class African Americans.[47] Harry Dolan, who reviewed *Ill at Ease in Compton* for the *New York Times* was sensitive to the potential for interracial coexistence in Compton, but also to its fragility. "Elman," he wrote, "has found that the new world of the Negro is something like the land promised by the old songs. For the first time many

Negro men work at jobs that lift them into the middle class." "But with this," he continued, "comes the built-in problem of troubled suburbia." What "remains to be seen," Dolan concluded, was whether the responses of blacks and whites to "modern American life will cause friction and racial tension, or be resolved on a new level of human cooperation."[48] The historic significance of *Ill at Ease in Compton* lies not in its literary splendor or its popularity (according to Pantheon's sales department, the book sold fewer than three thousand copies). Rather it was the last publicly known account of Compton that recognized the potential for the city's alternative future.

Between the publication of *Ill at Ease in Compton* and the 1980s, "Compton" began its dreary metamorphosis from place name to metonym. The 1969 mayoral election of Douglas Dollarhide drew nationwide attention, though of a highly ambiguous nature. The *Los Angeles Times* somewhat condescendingly regarded Dollarhide's mayoralty—and the near monopoly blacks now held in local politics—as "an experiment in Negro self-government." The *New York Times* quizzically examined the "woes" of this "test tube" city. Although the *New York Times* coverage of Compton was generally sympathetic, it clearly posed to readers the very question that Dollarhide anticipated: "People are saying we can't do it. They are saying that we can't govern ourselves."[49] The 1973 election of Doris Davis, one of the nation's first black women mayors, further intensified the curiosity about and scrutiny of Compton. And what this scrutiny turned up was almost always a story of decline. By 1973, for example, the *Los Angeles Times* unceremoniously described Compton as a "ghetto of poverty, crime, gang violence, unemployment and blight."[50] It is not, of course, that descriptions of Compton were wholly inaccurate. Rather it is that Compton was no more "troubled" than a number of other suburbs explored by Rand in 1982 and, in fact, far less troubled than several.

But if the material circumstances of Compton were typical of America's declining suburbs, its location was not; its geographic proximity to the heart of the nation's film and music industry further shaped Compton's transformation to metonym. If this transition had begun prior to the 1980s, it was greatly accelerated by the release of *Straight Outta Compton* (1988, Ruthless/Priority), by the rap group NWA (Niggas With Attitude). Banned from most radio stations—and more important, MTV—the album nonetheless became an instant hit, ultimately selling more than three million copies.[51] NWA's presumably autobiographical account of life in Compton portrayed an infinitely bleak social landscape, where "ruthless" gangsters got high, stole cars, "blasted" other gangsters, "slaughtered" police officers, and tricked "bitches" into having sex with them. The incendiary "F*** the Police"—in which a ferocious MC Ren portrays himself as a "sniper" determined to murder police officers—drew the censure of the Federal Bureau of Investigation and focused media attention on violence in rap. So inflammatory was NWA that the group was the subject of a feature in *Newsweek* in 1990. If *Newsweek's* national readership knew not of Compton before the article, they found out that the "appalling expressions of attitude" uttered by NWA came directly from the "sorry Los Angeles slum of Compton."[52] Setting aside the album's historic role in the long-standing debate over freedom of artistic expression in the United States, much of the significance of *Straight Outta Compton* lay in its definitional power, its role in creating a national, even global, perception of a place largely disconnected from its history.

The power of this role was not lost on the members of NWA, who were far more savvy than they professed to be on the tracks of *Straight Outta Compton*. "It's just an image," MC Ren later candidly told the *Los Angeles Times*. "We got to do something that would distinguish ourselves. We was just trying to be different."[53] That "hard" image—a staple of rap music since the 1980s—was indelibly linked to Compton by a group of African American youth who did not, themselves, always embody it. Easy-E (Eric Wright), despite his brief career as a drug dealer, was the product of a lower-middle-class home, the son of a U.S. postal worker; Ice Cube (O'Shea Jackson), the main voice of NWA, had to be lured back from Arizona—where he had gone to take advanced architecture courses—to record the album.[54]

But the fact that NWA manufactured, to a certain degree, their own "hardness" should not—and did not—distract listeners from the essentially honest and authentic reportage delivered on *Straight Outta Compton*. NWA did not invent images from the streets of Compton, but rather selectively filtered them in a way to deliver the most sensational and shocking impression to listeners. Of course, NWA's desire to locate Compton was not sociological but mostly commercial: part of NWA's place naming and claiming was a direct challenge to the hegemony of East Coast rappers, who'd long relied on Queens and the Bronx to communicate an urban sensibility.[55] A highly spacialized discourse, in fact, was increasingly typical of rap during this era, but NWA shifted that discourse to Los Angeles, and also upped the ante with gratuitous glorifications of violence. In this context, NWA (and subsequent performers Compton's Most Wanted and DJ Quick) was involved in an innocuous, competitive, and essentially playful contest between regions, not unlike professional athletes proclaiming the superiority of their own region or team. But on the streets that NWA described, place claiming and territoriality also had deadly consequences, informing the menacing gangster interrogatory, what you claim? vernacularly synonymous with, where you from? or, what gang are you in?

After NWA, "Compton" became a virtually irresistible, and imminently exploitable, metonym for rappers, and more influentially, filmmakers. In director John Singleton's powerful Oscar-nominated 1991 film, *Boyz in the 'Hood,* Compton makes a brief appearance as the most insidious and forsaken zone of greater South Central Los Angeles. In a central scene halfway through the film, Jason "Furious" Styles (Lawrence Fishburne)—a small businessman and perennial disciplinarian—coaxes his son, Tre Styles (Cuba Gooding Jr.), and his best friend, Ricky Baker (Morris Chesnut), to leave the relative gentility of their native South Central for a didactic excursion to Compton. As Tre and Ricky exit the car, they regard Compton warily, eyeing the gang-bangers and hustlers congregating in the littered yard of a ramshackle home. There Furious Styles delivers an impassioned monologue about the causes of deterioration in Compton. Relying on the viewer's popular perception of Compton (consider that the title of the film is drawn from the NWA song of the same name, featured on its first album, *NWA and the Posse*), Singleton casually reverses the general historic reality here. Determined to show the vitality and striving of lower-middle-class black Los Angeles, but unwilling to confound viewers accustomed to a particular vision of Compton, Singleton depicts a blighted Compton in contrast to the well-maintained homes and lawns of neighboring South Central.

The Hughes Brothers' 1993 *Menace II Society* presents a similarly cynical representation of Compton, though in a different way. The film is set exclusively in Watts, and primarily in and around its notorious Jordan Downs housing project. But Compton nonetheless plays an important role, not as a physical space, but as an idea. For example, when troubled thug Chauncy (Clifton Powell) angrily dismisses a white co-conspirator from his Watts house, he challenges him to find his way safely out of Watts on Compton Avenue.[56] This ominous send-off has the intended effect, sending the unnamed white character (one of only several in the film) scurrying nervously back to his car. If he understands the implication, so too do the viewers, and in this sense both the characters and the directors exploit the same vision of Compton. Similarly, the soundtrack is punctuated with well-timed and conspicuous references to Compton, when scenes require an added hint of infamy. For example, even as vengeful Caine "Kaydee" Lawson (Tyrin Turner) approaches a moment of clarity—contemplating his friends' invitation to leave Watts for Kansas—the relative calm is disrupted by DJ Quick's warning not to "fuck" with African Americans from Compton. An unyieldingly bleak film, *Menace II Society* served to further confirm the notoriety of Compton.

But popular culture, it should be remembered, has always been a two-way street, requiring not only production, but also willful consumption. The immediate popularity of NWA's early demo tapes among black youth in South Central suggests that the group was clearly tapping into imagery, sounds, and beats that reverberated locally. And for African Americans nationally, NWA did what most rap has done for African Americans: it conveyed—as Tricia Rose put it—the "pulse, pleasures, and problems of black urban life."[57] But mainstream success in the United States, by definition, requires the support of white consumers, and *Straight Outta Compton* was no exception. In fact, Priority Records estimated that 80 percent of its customers were white, male teenagers in suburbs. This figure is unverifiable and likely exaggerated, but it is roughly consistent with recent surveys by *Source* magazine showing that 70 percent of rap consumers are white.[58] Of course, white consumption of black popular culture has a long history in the United States, dating back, at least, to the jazz age of the 1920s.[59] But that process has arguably been more complex since NWA, as the one-upmanship of gangster rap has pushed the genre further into the realm of explicit violence and graphic sex. White consumers of rap music are now not only buying into an image of "coolness," but also often one of extreme narcissism, misogyny, and violence, perpetrated by African Americans. As Bill Yousman has effectively argued, this consumption reflects a simultaneous "blackophilia" and "blackophobia" among white consumers, allowing white consumers to "contain their fears and animosities towards Blacks through rituals . . . of adoration."[60]

Similarly, *Boyz in the 'Hood*, *Menace II Society*, and other "'hood" films of the early 1990s were widely viewed by both black and white audiences. Black films had long presented dark images of "the 'hood" to white viewers. Melvin Van Peebles' *Sweet Sweetback's Baadasss Song* (1971), for example, depicted the unnamed streets and boulevards of Los Angeles as a white-controlled maze, constraining the physical and sexual prowess of the badman protagonist, Sweetback. But the novelty of 'hood films of the 1990s was their naming and claiming of specific places, and in this sense the genre served as the visual counterpart to the hip-hop music of the era. These films also served as urban geography lessons—no matter how flawed—for white audiences both eager and fearful to know of the 'hood. Ironically, however, whatever nuanced messages of hope and humanity these films tried to assert were likely lost on theater-goers who found themselves participating in uneasy reenactments of the films' violence themes, as fights and shootings erupted at screenings of *Boyz* and *New Jack City* nationwide.

What's in a Name? The Elision of "Compton"

The naming of streets—as a number of scholars have explored—can be a powerful act, shaping regional memory and identification and reinforcing reigning political ideologies.[61] For African Americans in particular, the creation of a commemorative landscape through the naming of Martin Luther King Jr. Boulevards throughout the country has been an important place-claiming ritual. After much resistance and political wrangling, Los Angeles's own Santa Barbara Avenue was renamed Martin Luther King Jr. Boulevard in 1982. In Los Angeles and elsewhere, African Americans viewed this process not only as a victory for the memory of the slain civil rights leader, but also an official recognition and affirmation of the presence of African Americans in white-majority cities. But blacks in Compton discovered that the renaming of places could also be used as an unceremonious *renunciation* of their place in the larger metropolis. By the late 1980s, in fact, the word *Compton* had become so powerfully suggestive, so notorious, the city's surrounding suburbs successfully lobbied to literally erase Compton from their city maps.

The process of eliding Compton began in 1985, when the Dominguez Medical Center moved its mail room from one side of the hospital to the other in order to switch the mailing address from Compton to Long Beach. No sooner had the ink dried on this change than the city council of Paramount, lying to the east of Compton across the Los Angeles River voted to rename its two-mile stretch of Compton Boulevard, Somerset Boulevard. In an attempt to lure Southern California development moguls Kaufman & Broad to build a $14 million single-family home complex there, the heavily Latino city voted to change the name in 1986. Testament to Compton's transition to metonym, one Paramount businessman who supported the name change argued that "the word *Compton* does not paint a picture of a first-class residential community since the area is too well known for the slums and strife that existed there for the last 20 or so years." A Paramount real estate broker—apparently unaware of Paramount's shared status as a "disaster area" in the 1982 Rand report—stated, "It's good for the area. We are supporting it because they have a number of problems across the freeway (in Compton)."[62]

The renaming movement lay dormant for two years until late in 1988 (the same year NWA released *Straight Outta Compton*) when Compton's neighbor to the west, Gardena, voted to change its stretch of Compton Boulevard to Marine Avenue for "consistency" with Manhattan Beach. Within the next two years, Lawndale, Hawthorne, and finally Redondo Beach all changed their respective stretches of Compton Boulevard as well, and, in an instant, Compton

Boulevard was gone in all but the notorious city itself.[63] Compton's leadership recognized this move for what it was: an attempt to disassociate from the reputation of the predominantly black and crime-ridden suburb. Former Compton city councilman Robert Adams defended his city: "I've lived in Compton 39 years, and I think Compton is one of the nicest cities around. We got first-class citizens here, law-abiding citizens." "But," he continued, "the majority of those citizens are black, and you still have bigots out there."[64]

The final, and certainly most ironic, blow in the battle to erase Compton from the map actually came from Comptonites. In the summer of 1990, the unincorporated area known as East Compton furtively, and successfully, petitioned the county to change its name to East Rancho Dominguez. Initially shocked by the perceived betrayal, Comptonites soon recognized that the disassociation was an ironic boon for them. It was, in fact, East Compton that had disproportionately besmirched the name of Compton during the 1980s. Law enforcement agencies had long considered East Compton one of the most dangerous areas in Compton because its proximity to the 710 freeway made it the most coveted region in Compton's raging drug wars.[65] Evidently, for East Comptonites, the name "Compton" had become a more terrifying specter than the real crime and violence it had so long implied. One would be hard-pressed to find a more telling example of the practical triumph of *ideas* about places over the actual *histories* of places. This triumph would have been problematic for Compton during any era, but during the wave of urban disinvestment of the Reagan and Bush era, it had disastrous consequences.

Representing Contemporary Compton

If popular representations and perceptions of Compton have failed to reflect the complex history of Compton, they've also failed to accurately portray its contemporary demographic reality. Most conspicuously, Latinos are almost entirely absent from metonymic Compton. This is a glaring oversight given that Latinos already made up 42 percent of the city's population by 1990 and officially became a majority population in 2000.[66] Understanding the Latino presence is not merely a matter of inclusiveness; it is a matter of reinterpreting the meaning of Compton. Latinos in Compton, of course, have already been the subject of careful scholarly investigation and responsible media reporting, but the extent to which they become part of the popular notion of Compton remains to be seen.[67] Far more important to Compton's Latinos, however, is the extent to which they are represented *politically* in this longtime bastion of black political empowerment. As political scientist Regina Freer has demonstrated, Compton's black leaders have generally "viewed the assertion of Latino demands as a threat to not only their own individual power, but more broadly as threats to African American political empowerment."[68] In the early years of the new century, African American political leaders are waging what may be their final battle to claim and define Compton, under vastly different circumstances than those encountered by Alfred and Luquella Jackson in 1953.

In 1998, Catherine Borek, a teacher at Dominguez High School embarked on a daunting task: to produce the first dramatic play at the school in more than twenty years, the 1938 Thornton Wilder classic, *Our Town*. Chronicled in the independent 2002 documentary *OT: Our Town*, the production proceeds, against all odds, in a school best known for generating gang members and professional basketball players. In it, a remarkable group of black and Latino teenagers reinvent this all-American play about family life in Grover's Corners, New Hampshire, giving it a bit of local flavor, but, more important, challenging stereotypes about Compton's youth. After a successful opening night, the precocious stage manager, Ebony Starr Norwood-Brown, contemplates the meaning of the play. For her, it demonstrated "we're not that different" from people "even in Idaho," "but we're *way* different from what you think we are." Of course most Americans never will see this independent release, and that is a shame, because it has the potential to create a new perception of Compton, one worthy of the abiding character and ambition of a healthy proportion of the residents in this long-maligned city.

But the story of Compton is not just one of rectifying misrepresentations. There is a larger lesson here about the heavily freighted nature of geographic descriptors. Place names are rarely just that; in most cases we use them to refer to or imply a larger set of events, ideas, and developments in our personal and collective memories. Most of us recognize that when we say "Paris in the Springtime," we are referring to a whole collection of feelings and senses associated with a geographic location and place in time and not simply an exact spot during a particular month. Yet we are generally insensitive to the ways in which metonymy and other rhetorical devices have *political* as well as linguistic consequences. Compton is just one example of the dire consequences of metonymy misused, when a place name is employed as a condensed representation of a host of urban ills of which it is but a small part. We are extraordinarily sensitive to the consequences of stereotyping people, ethnicities, genders, and races, yet we remain insufficiently skeptical about what we imply when we think we are simply referring to a place.

Notes

1. "Full Compton Story Told in Eagle Series," *California Eagle,* May 14, 1953, 1, 2, 8.
2. John L. Mitchell, "Lowrider Cruising to Japanese Market," *Los Angeles Times,* July 14, 1996, 1.
3. Becky Nicolaides, "'Where the Working Man Is Welcomed': Working-Class Suburbs in Los Angeles, 1900–1940," *Pacific Historical Review* 68 (November 1999): 517–59; Becky Nicolaides, *My Blue Heaven: Life and Politics in the Working-Class Suburbs of Los Angeles, 1920–1965* (Chicago: University of Chicago Press, 2002). See also Greg Hise, "Industry and Imaginative Geographies," and Mike Davis, "Sunshine and the Open Shop: Ford and Darwin in 1920s Los Angeles," in *Metropolis in the Making: Los Angeles in the 1920s,* ed. Tom Sitton and William Deverall (Berkeley: University of California Press, 2001), 13–44, 97–122.
4. These booster descriptions appear in the Compton ephemera in folder 19, box 83, of the Don Meadows Collection, Special Collections, University of California, Irvine.
5. Davis, "Sunshine and Open Shop," 117.
6. Al Camarillo, "Black and Brown in Compton: Demographic Change, Suburban Decline, and Intergroup Relations in a South Central Los Angeles Community, 1950–2000," in *Not Just Black and White: Immigration, Race, and Ethnicity, Then and Now,* ed. George Frederickson and Nancy Foner (Los Angeles: Russell Sage Foundation, 2004), 364.
7. The proposed project was subsequently relocated to Watts. See "Testimony of Loren Miller," *Governor's Commission on the Los Angeles Riots, Transcripts,* vol. X, 6–10.
8. The slogan "Keep the Negroes North of 130th Street" appears in Loren Miller's discussion of race restrictions in the 1940s (cited above). In the *California Eagle* ("Compton Acquits All Five Realty Board Brokers," May 7, 1953, 1, 8), it appears as "Keep the Negroes North of 134th Street." This discrepancy reflects the fact that, as blacks continued to push southward, segregationists regularly issued updated rallying cries against further black encroachment, repeatedly defining and redefining a geography of exclusion.
9. See Alberto M. Camarillo, "Chicano Urban History: A Study of Compton's Barrio, 1936–1970," *Aztlan* 2 (spring 1970): 79–106; "Black and Brown in Compton," 358–76.
10. I elaborate on this regional racial dynamic in *L.A. City Limits: African American Los Angeles from the Great Depression to the Present* (Berkeley: University of California Press, 2004). See also Neil Foley, *White Scourge: Mexicans, Blacks, and Poor Whites in Texas Cotton Culture* (Berkeley: University of California Press, 1999).
11. U.S. Bureau of the Census, *Sixteenth Census of the United States: 1940, Population and Housing: Statistics for Census Tracts,* vol. 2 (Washington: GPO, 1942), 4–6; *Census of Population: 1950, Census Tract Statistics, Los Angeles, California and Adjacent Area* (Washington: GPO, 1952), 9–53; *Census of Population and Housing: 1960, Census Tracts, Los Angeles-Long Beach, Calif. Standard Metropolitan Statistical Area* (Washington: GPO, 1962), 25–161.
12. U.S. Commission on Civil Rights, *Hearings Held in Los Angeles and San Francisco, January 25–28, 1960* (Washington: Government Printing Office, 1960), 203.
13. *Hearings before the United States Commission on Civil Rights* 158–59.
14. William C. Ardery to Earl Warren, July 17, 1946, folder 3640:3677, Earl Warren Papers, California State Archives, Sacramento.
15. Sylvester Gibbs, interview with author, June 2, 1998, Los Angeles, California. Transcripts of this and other interviews were donated to the Southern California Library for Social Studies and Research, Los Angeles, where they can be viewed.
16. The activities of Crenshaw Neighbors are chronicled in the journal *The Integrator,* copies of which are available at the Southern California Library for Social Studies and Research, in Los Angeles.
17. Camarillo, "Black and Brown in Compton," 364.
18. "Vigilantes Brutally Beat Man over Sale to Negroes," *California Eagle,* February 19, 1953, 1–2.
19. "Compton Acquits All Five Realty Board Brokers," *California Eagle,* May 7, 1953, 1, 8.
20. In fact, Miller was right: according to the census of 1970, Compton had the largest proportion of blacks of any American suburb. See Judith Fernandez and John Pincus, *Troubled Suburbs: An Exploratory Study* (Rand: Santa Monica, 1982), 137.
21. Welfare Planning Council, *Compton: A Community in Transition; A Needs and Resources Study of the Compton Area,* (Los Angeles: 1962), 36.
22. *1960 Census Tracts,* 850.
23. Richard Elman, *Ill at Ease in Compton* (New York: Pantheon Books, 1967), 24.
24. *1960 Census Tracts,* 577.

25. Mary Cuthbertson, interview with author, July 20, 1998, Los Angeles, California.

26. *Compton: A Community in Transition*, 82.

27. Bob Ellis, "Compton Residents Agree: Negroes Can't Be Kept Out," *California Eagle*, June 18, 1953, 2.

28. Steven V. Roberts, "Compton, Calif., 65% Negro, Believes in Integration and in Peaceful Change," *New York Times*, June 8, 1969, 65.

29. *Watts Writers' Workshop, from the Ashes: Voices of Watts* (New York: New American Library, 1967), 8.

30. Roberts, "Compton, Calif., 65% Negro," 65.

31. Regina Freer, "Black Brown Cities: Black Urban Regimes and the Challenge of Changing Demographics," unpublished paper presented at the Western Political Science Association Annual Meeting, Denver, Colorado, March 27–29, 2003.

32. Gerald Horne, *Fire This Time: The Watts Uprising and the 1960s* (Charlottesville: University of Virginia Press, 1995), 119.

33. Ahmed Mohammed Widaatalla, "Effect of Racial Change on the Tax Base of the City of Compton" (doctoral dissertation, University of California, Los Angeles, 1970), 13, 37–40.

34. Frank Clifford, "Compton Development: Was Price Right?" *Los Angeles Times*, November 22, 1982, sec. 2, 1, 4.

35. Mike Davis, *Dead Cities: And Other Tales* (New York: New Press, 2002), 280.

36. Joel D. Leidner, "Major Factors in Industrial Location," appendix 7, in *Hard-Core Unemployment and Poverty in Los Angeles* (Los Angeles: Institute of Industrial Relations, University of California, Los Angeles, 1965).

37. Edward Soja, Rebecca Morales, and Goetz Wolff, "Urban Restructuring: An Analysis of Social and Spatial Change in Los Angeles," *Economic Geography* 59 (1983), 217; Donahoe, "Workers' Response to Plant Closures: The Cases of Steel and Auto in Southeast Los Angeles, 1935–1986" (doctoral dissertation, University of California, Irvine, 1987), 98.

38. Earl Caldwell, "City in California, 72% Black, Looks to Future Despite Woes," *New York Times*, January 19, 1972, 18.

39. Alejandro A. Alonso, "Territoriality among African-American Street Gangs in Los Angeles" (master's thesis, Department of Geography, University of Southern California, 1999), 90, 94, 104.

40. Malcolm W. Klein and Cheryl L. Maxson, "'Rock' Sales in South Los Angeles," *Sociology and Social Research* 69 (July 1985): 561–65.

41. Widaatalla, "Effect of Racial Change," 83.

42. Los Angeles County Grand Jury, *Public Hearing: City of Compton* (1975), 13–14.

43. These "disaster areas" were National City (CA), McKeesport (PA), Huntington Park (CA), Baldwin Park (CA), Bell Gardens (CA), Paramount (CA), Covington (KY), Hoboken (NJ), Highland Park (MI), Chester (PA), East St. Louis (IL), Camden (NJ), Alton (IL), and Compton. Judith Fernandez and John Pincus, *Troubled Suburbs: An Exploratory Study* (Santa Monica: Rand, 1982), 77–78.

44. Elman, *Ill at Ease in Compton*, 14–17.

45. Ibid., 23–24.

46. Ibid., 201.

47. Ibid., 173–75.

48. Harry Dolan, "Lily-White No More," *New York Times*, July 9, 1967, 199.

49. Davis, *Dead Cities*, 279; Roberts, "Compton, Calif., 65% Negro," 65; Earl Caldwell, "City in California, 72% Black, Looks to Future Despite Woes," *New York Times*, January 19, 1972, 18.

50. Jean Douglas Murphy, "Doris Davis Running Hard and Fast," *Los Angeles Times*, September 23, 1973, sec. 10, 1, 18.

51. Terry McDermott, "Parental Advisory: Explicit Lyrics," *Los Angeles Times*, April 14, 2002, 1.

52. Jerry Adler, "The Rap Attitude," *Newsweek* (March 19, 1990), 56–58.

53. McDermott, "Parental Advisory," 1.

54. Ibid.

55. See, Murray Forman, *The 'Hood Comes First: Race, Space, and Place in Rap and Hip-Hop* (Middletown, Conn.: Wesleyan University Press, 2002), 193–96; Brian Cross, *It's Not about Salary: Rap, Race, and Resistance in Los Angeles* (London: Verso, 1993), 37.

56. Compton Avenue, the north-south thoroughfare, runs primarily through the Willowbrook section of Los Angeles and should not be confused with Compton Boulevard, the major east-west thoroughfare that runs through Compton.

57. Tricia Rose, *Black Noise: Rap Music and Black Culture in Contemporary America* (Middletown, Conn.: Wesleyan University Press, 1994), 4.

58. Bill Yousman, "Blackophilia and Blackophobia: White Youth, the Consumption of Rap Music, and White Supremacy," *Communication Theory* 13 (November 2003): 367.

59. See Kathy J. Ogren, *The Jazz Revolution: Twenties America and the Meaning of Jazz* (New York: Oxford University Press, 1989), and Lewis A. Erenberg, *Steppin' Out: New York Night Life and the Transformation of American Culture, 1890–1930* (Chicago: University of Chicago Press, 1981).

60. Yousman, "Blackophilia and Blackophobia," 369.

61. For work on the politics of place naming in general, see Cohen and Kliot, "Place-names in Israel's Ideological Struggle Over the Administered Territories," *Annals of the Association of American Geographers* 82 (December 1992): 653–80; Azaryahu, "The Power of Commemorative Street Names," *Environment and Planning D: Society and Space* 14 (1992): 311–30; L. D. Berg and Kearns, "Naming as Norming: 'Race,' Gender, and the Identity Politics of Naming Places in Aotearoa, New Zealand," *Environment and Planning D: Society and Space* 14 (1996): 99–112. For work on African American place naming, see Derek H. Alderman, "Street Names and the Scaling of Memory: The Politics of Commemorating Martin Luther King, Jr. within the African American Community," *Area* 35 (2003): 163–73; "Creating a New Geography of Memory in the South: (Re) Naming of Streets in Honor of Martin Luther King, Jr.," *Southeastern Geographer* 36: 51–69; Jonathan Tilove, *Along Martin Luther King: Travels on Black America's Main Street* (New York: Random House, 2003).

62. Lee Harris, "Paramount Erases 'Compton Boulevard,' Draws Fire," *Los Angeles Times*, November 27, 1986, 1; Fernandez and Pincus, *Troubled Suburbs*, 77. Paramount's ability to transcend its "disaster" reputation while Compton languished in it, speaks volumes about race relations and racial attitudes in Southern California, where Mexicans are generally regarded by whites as preferable to blacks. The heavy concentration of Latinos in Paramount (who represented more than 72 percent in 2000), for example, did not discourage the establishment of the Paramount Manufacturing & Distribution Center, a 200,000-square-foot facility in 1999. James Flanigan, "Manufacturing, Distribution Facility Opening in Paramount," *Los Angeles Times*, May 5, 1999, 2.

63. Shawn Hubler, "Racism Seen in Street Name Change," *Los Angeles Times*, December 31, 1989, 6.

64. Ibid.

65. Michele Fuetsch, "East Compton's Name Change Riles Officials," *Los Angeles Times*, August 9, 1990, pg. 1.

66. For a brief overview of the recent ethnic succession of Latinos throughout South Central, see Dowell Myers, "Demographic and Housing Transitions in South Central Los Angeles, 1990 to 2000," Population Dynamics Research Group, School of Policy, Planning, and Development, University of Southern California, Los Angeles, April 22, 2002.

67. See, for example, Regina Freer, "Black Brown Cities"; Albert Camarillo, "Black and Brown in Compton"; Michele Fuetsch, "Latino Aspirations on Rise in Compton," *Los Angeles Times*, May 7, 1990, B1; "Latino Reaches Runoff in Compton Council Race," April 18, 1991, 2; Patrick McDonnell, "As Change Overtakes Compton, So Do Tensions," August 21, 1994, A1.

68. Freer, "Black Brown Cities," 23.

L.A. Race Woman:
Charlotta Bass and the Complexities of
Black Political Development in Los Angeles

Regina Freer

> The growth of Los Angeles and the development of the Negro people within its
> boundaries have been phenomenal. . . . I remember with fond devotion many of
> the old pioneers of Los Angeles with whom I have been associated through the
> years. . . . They shared in my hopes and ambitions to build a great city in which
> they had a stake for themselves and posterity.
>
> Charlotta A. Bass, Forty Years:
Memoirs from the Pages of a Newspaper (1960)

If she is remembered at all today, Charlotta Bass is typically recalled as a
black leftist journalist. Owner and editor of one of Los Angeles's first
black newspapers, the *California Eagle*, from 1912 to 1951, she is perhaps
best known for her lengthy battle against racially restrictive residential covenants. A journalist, activist, and candidate for several elected offices, including the vice presidency of the United States, Bass was a pioneer at the center of
the black community's fight for racial justice for much of the twentieth century. Yet, she is a relatively obscure figure even in her home base of Los Angeles. Her obscurity reflects the broader absence of attention to the pre–Watts
1965 history of Los Angeles's black community. The twentieth-century history of African Americans in Los Angeles is much less defined than the histories of other cities such as Chicago and New York (Harlem). The dominance
of scholarly inquiry into the time period surrounding the city's two cataclys-
mic civil disturbances in 1965 and 1992 has meant that subtle understanding
of the earlier historical development of black Los Angeles, and how it does or
does not compare to black communities elsewhere, is only just beginning to
emerge.[1] Because Charlotta Bass lived it and chronicled it in her paper, her life
offers a path to a richer understanding of the forces impacting the development of Los Angeles black life, in particular black political life prior to 1965.

While blacks were first elected to city government in Chicago and New
York in the 1920s and 1930s, Los Angeles did not see its first black city
councilperson until the 1960s.[2] Limited at first by its small size and later by

gerrymandering of local politicians, the L.A. black community was forced to pursue politics outside of the formal electoral arena.[3] Despite these obstacles, black residents were politically active, doggedly working against local racism in the public and private sectors. A consideration of Bass's life allows us to examine the limits and possibilities of the Los Angeles black community in the mid-twentieth century—how it was distant in many ways from other major centers of black life, with its particular struggles over home ownership, leisure space, and job prospects. With L.A.'s specific multiracial milieu, and its unique struggles between communists and anticommunists, the history of black politics in Los Angeles was the site of distinctive struggles around equality and justice.

Whether she was protesting discriminatory hiring at the Southern California Telephone Company or in the war industries, seeking to stop production of the racist film *Birth of a Nation*, or decrying residential segregation, Charlotta Bass put a premium on racial fairness and equity. Very much a "race woman," she set aside class privilege to militantly advocate on behalf of the entire black community, prioritizing and evaluating issues based upon their relationship to the advancement of the downtrodden of the race. But even in the universe of other race men and race women active in the first half of the twentieth century, Bass's positions offer a layer of complexity and nuance that distinguishes her. Indeed, it makes sense to view her not simply as a "race woman" but specifically as an L.A. race woman. Bass's politics were a direct engagement with the particular demography, geography, politics, and economics of Los Angeles and African Americans's expectations of what life should be like in the city. Her political life thus offers a lens for understanding that before the rise of black power movements in the 1960s, Los Angeles's black community actively confronted and resisted racial oppression, despite and in some ways because of the limited opportunities that existed for black advancement. Picking up on the work of Lonnie Bunche, Lawrence de Graaf, Douglas Flamming, Gerald Horne, Josh Sides, and others, this article seeks to resurrect Los Angeles as a site of significant black history-making even before Watts exploded.

Shaping the Destiny of a Community, a Race, and a Nation

Little is known about Bass's early life. Born Charlotta Amanda Spears in Sumter, South Carolina, in 1879 or 1880, she moved to Rhode Island after high school and began working in the newspaper business.[4] Like many of those who came to the region, Bass migrated to Los Angeles in 1910 on the advice of her physician, though her specific ailment is unknown. Soon after arriving in the city, she took a job selling subscriptions to the small African American newspaper, the *Advocate* (later renamed the *Eagle*). Just before he died in 1912, the paper's founder, John J. Neimore, asked Bass to take over the paper. Changing the name to the *California Eagle* in 1913, Bass hired Joseph Blackburn (J. B.) Bass, who eventually became the editor of the paper as well as Bass's husband.[5]

From the beginning of their association with the paper, this husband-wife team used the *California Eagle* as a vehicle for advancing a range of social justice causes. Like most black newspapers of that period, the *California Eagle* served as a source of both information and inspiration for the black community, which was largely ignored or negatively portrayed by the white press. After J. B. Bass's death in November 1934, Charlotta Bass expanded the paper's political advocacy, highlighting many of her issues and causes. Bass also used her weekly column "On the Sidewalk" and her editorial page contributions to draw attention to social and political conditions as well as to promote campaigns to reform what she considered to be a pattern of injustice. At its height in the 1940s, the paper had a circulation of 17,600, meaning that a quarter of the black population of Los Angeles read the *California Eagle*.[6] Bass wrote her last column for the *California Eagle* on April 26, 1951, and sold the paper soon after.

During this same period, Bass was also involved in local and national politics. She entered the electoral arena with a nonpartisan run in 1945 for a seat on the Los Angeles City Council representing the 7th district, which was at the time 45 percent African American.[7] She lost this race but went on to run on the Progressive Party ticket for Congress in 1950, challenging Sam Yorty (who won the race, served in Congress, and later went on to become the mayor of Los Angeles).[8]

In 1952, Bass's political horizons expanded beyond Los Angeles when she was selected by the Progressive Party as the first black woman to run for vice president. At the Progressive Party's national convention, Bass was nominated by Paul Robeson, with W. E. B. Du Bois seconding the nomination.[9] The Progressive Party's slogan in 1952—"win or lose, we win by raising the issues"—reflected Bass's own orientation toward electoral politics as a forum (sometimes successful, sometimes marginalized) for political education.[10] It also reflected the larger reality for blacks in Los Angeles, who experienced few electoral wins prior to the 1960s.

Bass continued her strong social justice advocacy even after selling the *California Eagle* and after her 1952 campaign for vice president. Suffering from health problems, she moved to Lake Elsinore, a small town east of Los Angeles, and purchased a home in the late 1950s or early 1960s. There, she turned the garage into a community reading room and a voter registration site for local African Americans. In addition to continuing her civil rights activism, Bass also joined protests against apartheid in South Africa and on behalf of prisoners' rights in the state of California until she suffered a stroke in 1966 and was placed in a Los Angeles nursing home, where she died in 1969.[11]

For more than forty years, Bass was at the center of black political life in Los Angeles. Indeed, her life and that of the *California Eagle* parallel the pre-1965 twentieth-century history of black L.A. But more than simply paralleling the history and chronicling it, she actually embodies the dominant paradox of this history—one shared by the city as a whole—namely the familiar trope of sunshine and noir. While L.A. offered unique opportunities for African Americans, these prospects bred high expectations that were met with stern white resistance. The fact that a woman could hold a leadership position within the black community so early in the twentieth century, and for so long, is an indication of the unique opportunities for political change offered by L.A. At the same time, the fact that this woman used this opportunity to confront resistance to black progress signals that advancement in the city was in fact limited.

At the time of Bass's arrival in L.A., the black community enjoyed a number of conditions that distinguished it from black communities in the South and the North. The population was relatively small. For example, in 1920, while New York City's black population was 152,465 and Chicago's was 109,458, Los Angeles's was only 15,579.[12] Though newly established, this community could remarkably point to the existence of antidiscrimination laws on the books, even if they weren't enforced.[13] Prior to the 1920s, blacks in Los Angeles enjoyed residential dispersion that distinguished them from most of their counterparts elsewhere in the country. Whereas blacks who migrated to northern cities in the 1910s generally moved into highly segregated, spatially isolated, and concentrated all-black residential neighborhoods, in Los Angeles during this time period, black migrants lived in a number of racially diverse geographic areas in the city, including downtown, along Central Avenue, in northwest portions of the city, east in Boyle Heights, in the southeastern corner of the city, and in the western section of the city proximate to Jefferson Boulevard.[14] Dispersion of the black community reflected the city's image as an anti-urban garden city that was built out instead of up.[15] The vastness of Los Angeles, its low population density, and the relatively small size of the black population minimized whites' animosity toward black residents.[16] Likewise, black Angelenos lived in a multiracial, rather than a biracial, environment, with Mexicans, Japanese, and others sharing white animus. Blacks were attracted to Los Angeles because the lifestyle encouraged by these demographic and spatial dimensions offered such a contrast to the overt racial violence of the South and the growing ghettos and slums of the northern cities. African American residents of Los Angeles and visitors from elsewhere spread the word that Los Angeles was "wonderful. Nowhere in the United States is the Negro so well and beautifully housed . . . Out here in this matchless Southern California there would seem to be no limit to your opportunities, your possibilities."[17]

In a place like Los Angeles in the early twentieth century, there was room for pioneering black female leadership, and the environment afforded some space for such a pioneer to challenge discrimination. The lure of the city with its open space and amenable climate shaped the direction of such challenges. Access to Los Angeles's version of the American Dream was a central goal for black Angelenos. Though conditions and priorities changed over time, African Americans in the city consistently measured their success more by their relative position to whites than by comparing their condition to blacks elsewhere. The political issues they pursued and the strategies they engaged in reflected this point of view, and Charlotta Bass adhered to it as much as anyone.

Developing Strategies for Resistance:
The UNIA, the NAACP, and Early Black Los Angeles

As the black community grew from 7,599 in 1910 to 15,579 in 1920, circumstances began to change, and the relative anonymity of the black population faded. Just prior to the decade of the 1920s, racial segregation began to harden in Los Angeles and in the nation as a whole, as evidenced by a rise in the use of racially restrictive housing covenants and the increasing activity of the Ku Klux Klan.[18] By 1920, most blacks lived in a concentrated area stretching thirty blocks south from downtown along Central Avenue. Nearly 75 percent of the black population lived in three of the city's twelve assembly districts.[19] While this concentration did not match that experienced by northern blacks, it did represent a palpable shift for those black Angelenos who witnessed it.

Disturbed by these changes, Bass and other activists in the black community sought out strategies for addressing the increasing gap between migrants' expectations and an ever-harsher racial reality.[20] The disjuncture between the idyllic image of Los Angeles as a haven for black progress and the reality of racism in the city represented a lasting challenge for activists such as Bass, namely how to call attention to the inequities experienced by L.A.'s blacks when they were perceived as doing well relative to blacks in other parts of the country. The search for appropriate uplift strategies led them to connect to national racial justice movements and experiment with a variety of techniques, including building black institutions and pursuing integration into white ones.

One approach pursued by Bass was her simultaneous membership and leadership in the National Association for the Advancement of Colored People (NAACP) and the Universal Negro Improvement Association (UNIA), two organizations engaged in a fierce battle in the 1920s over the best strategy for black uplift, integration or separation. The Los Angeles chapter of the NAACP, founded in 1914, was led by many of the city's most established black elites.[21] In line with the national NAACP's principles, the Los Angeles chapter sought to encourage advancement of the race by challenging Jim Crow practices, often relying upon the court system. The pursuit of civil rights and integration, especially in employment, were at the forefront of the organization's agenda.[22] Marcus Garvey's UNIA had a very different strategy for racial uplift. Permitting blacks to admit their lack of faith in a white-run judicial system, the organization's Los Angeles Division 156, established in 1921, was nationalist, appealed more to the working class, and focused on building black collective political and economic strength separate from the white community. Garvey himself accused the NAACP and its then-leader W. E. B. Du Bois of hating the black race and pursuing its destruction.[23] The well-known feud between Du Bois and Garvey characterized the rivalry between these two organizations.

While both organizations were home to race men and women, there were important strategic distinctions between them. Those who supported an integrationist strategy belonged to the NAACP, and those who supported a separatist strategy joined the UNIA. We might expect Charlotta Bass, as a race woman, to be a member of one of these organizations, but she was simultaneously a member and leader of both, and the *California Eagle* actively promoted both the NAACP and the UNIA, often on the same page of the paper. Why and how could she belong to both, and what does her simultaneous membership tell us about the impact of Los Angeles on black political development?

First, it is important to note that Bass's role as publisher of the city's most prominent black newspaper meant she was one of the most important conduits for information on community activity. Because the mainstream press largely ignored communities of color, black residents of all classes and ideological orientations looked to the *California Eagle* for news. Like the Forum, a civic organization established in L.A.'s black community in 1903 and dedicated to the promotion of debate and discussion, the *California Eagle* saw to it that the heterogeneity of black political thought had a "forum" for exchange. Bass affiliated with the group and carried their discursive format into the paper.[24] There was also likely a business imperative for Bass's attachment to both groups. Seeking to maintain the broadest readership possible amid such a small black community, she could ill afford to alienate potential subscribers.

Aside from Bass's own personal and professional interest in joining these groups, the larger significance of this occurrence lies in the fact that she could hold these simultaneous affiliations with any level of comfort. How could this be acceptable to black activists and considered a viable strategy for resistance? In his history of the UNIA in Los Angeles, Tolbert suggests a potential explanation for the possibility of Bass's dual membership—the distance between Los Angeles and the national home of both groups, New York City. As he explains, the local groups were mainly support groups for New York headquarters.[25] Removed from the heat of the fire between the two groups, blacks in Los Angeles could conceivably combine the messages of each without worrying about having their loyalty to either group questioned. Admittedly, few people aside from Bass and her husband had overlapping membership, but this argument about distance from the controversy is suggestive of the larger importance of Los Angeles's distance from other centers of black life in allowing for the development of innovative resistance strategies. In fact, according to Tolbert, West Coast members of the UNIA were most attracted to the organization's economic empowerment program and less moved by separatism and the potential of returning to Africa.[26] One of the leaders of the Los Angeles chapter, Noah Thompson, was even active in attempts to improve race relations in the city while he was active in the UNIA.[27] It is also telling that Bass and others in Division 156 broke away from the national UNIA less than a year after the chapter was established in a dispute over local control of finances. They formed a new organization, the Pacific Coast Negro Improvement Association (PCNIA) and continued to work on black economic empowerment.[28] Bass maintained her membership and activity in the NAACP until her death.

The small size of Los Angeles's black community is another important factor explaining the emergence of a resistance strategy that combined membership in the UNIA and the NAACP. Community leaders like Bass could ill afford a pitched battle over strategy or recruitment of group members when the numbers were so small. The community was becoming large enough to foment resistance, but was still small enough to encourage a degree of cohesiveness. As Bass sought to put Los Angeles on the map in national black activist circles, her sensitivity to the need for such unity was apparent. She implored: "We believe that it is possible for the Negro people of California to develop something better than New York's Harlem, and the message we broadcast to you . . . is to forget petty prejudices; religious, sectional and political differences and remember only that we have a common cause."[29] Clearly identifying Harlem's prior leadership in the fight for black advancement, Bass argues for new, West Coast–generated strategies that avoid sectarianism like that which divided the NAACP and the UNIA.

It is also interesting to note that the Basses, Thompson, and other UNIA members were solidly middle-class citizens. Elsewhere, the organization primarily attracted a working-class constituency. The distinct class appeal of the UNIA was apparently ignored in Los Angeles. The newness of the black community, the relatively large middle class and the uniqueness of its unprecedented levels of black home ownership may have minimized perceptions of class distinctions among black Angelenos, including Bass.[30]

Because the pre-1920s black community followed the dispersed pattern of residential development typical of Los Angeles and because their numbers were so small and they shared space with other minority groups, African Americans could establish organizational capacity in the political realm without posing much of a threat to white residents. This increased capacity to pursue black uplift connected black Angelenos to activists across the country, facilitating transmittance of the message that Los Angeles was a relatively hospitable locale for black migrants. As word spread and the population expanded in the 1920s, so did white awareness of black presence in the city. The black community's organizational capacity was increasingly required to respond to growing white hostility in housing, public space, and in the job market.

The Fight for Fair and Adequate Housing

Housing desegregation was not an issue unique to Los Angeles blacks. All over the country, blacks battled racial residential restrictions. There were, however, unique elements in the battle in Los Angeles that influenced political activism around the issue. The early and lengthy prioritization of housing desegregation by Bass and other African American activists in Los Angeles suggests the centrality of home ownership to the allure of the city. As much as anything, home ownership epitomized the American Dream for migrants to Los Angeles. The city was built on real estate speculation and growth of subdivisions.[31] Thus, it is not surprising that this element of the dream would be the site of white protection and black desire. The importance of this issue also signals the prominence of the middle class, who were more apt to be home owners, and their particular issues within the black community. The longevity of Bass's association with housing discrimination provides an opportunity to assess changes in the political priorities and strategies of the African American community over time. Likewise, her focus on housing demonstrates the importance of this issue to black politics in L.A.

Central to the emergence of housing desegregation as a key priority for black Angelenos was the widening disconnect between the relative accessibility of home ownership and the increase in racially based restrictions that grew along with the size of the black population in the 1920s. While blacks in the South and North did not necessarily expect to own homes or live in integrated neighborhoods just after the turn of the century, many blacks in Los Angeles realized such expectations. As an example, in 1910, 36.1 percent of African Americans owned their own homes as compared to 2.4 percent in New York City.[32] Not only did Los Angeles blacks experience high levels of home ownership, but relative to blacks elsewhere they were a geographically dispersed community and lived among a variety of racial groups. This housing situation led national black leaders and black real estate agents within the city itself to declare Los Angeles to be a paradise for blacks. Sidney Dones, owner of the Bookerite Investment Company, a prominent black real estate firm in the 1910s and 1920s was one of the biggest promoters of black home ownership possibilities. In the text of a September 1919 advertisement that appeared in the *California Eagle* under the glaring headline, "It Pays To Own Your Own Home If You Live in Los Angeles," Dones declared that Los Angeles was, "first and foremost a city of HOMES. The man who owns his own home, who has definitely and finally taken title to a piece of ground and the house thereon . . . He is considered a steady, stable, settled CITIZEN of Los Angeles. He has evinced his belief in the progress and stability of the city" (emphasis in original).[33] Home ownership was a quintessential component of the American Dream for all Los Angeles residents, and for blacks it was additionally a key element of citizenship.

In a relative sense, Los Angeles did offer unique opportunities for blacks. However, there was a harsh reality underneath this illusion of freedom. In order to address increasing injustice, black political leadership in the city had to move beyond comparisons to blacks elsewhere and approach racial inequity in local terms that recognized black Angelenos' limited opportunities relative to whites in the city. Home ownership was an obtainable goal for whites in the city, and blacks set their sites on this same goal.

Based on the centrality of the issue for local African Americans, Bass became an advocate for fair and adequate housing even before it became a key civil rights issue of the 1940s and 1950s. Through the pages of the *California Eagle*, through her work with a variety of community organizations, and in her electoral campaigns, she was deeply engaged in housing issues, fighting against racial restrictions and resulting overcrowding and slum conditions and eventually supporting public housing and rent control programs. On the housing issue, as with others, she used the *California Eagle* to educate and mobilize the black community.

Racially based restrictive covenants became more prevalent throughout the city in the late 1910s and had enormous impact in fostering residential segregation. Written into property deeds, these covenants restricted sale of property to whites only (often just white non-Jews). Yet, unlike in other cities, this practice had the ironic effect of fostering the development of diverse neighborhoods with a dividing line that separated whites from a host of other racial and ethnic groups, including blacks.[34] As a result of these restrictions, housing for blacks, Mexicans, and others was isolated and segregated from whites in a small number of forcibly created mixed-race neighborhoods within the city. For blacks, this meant increased concentration in an area of the city south of downtown, along Central Avenue. As populations expanded with increased migration, overcrowding and slum conditions grew as well. Landlords capitalized on these patterns of segregation by overcharging residents and creating what amounted to slum housing conditions.

The early campaigns to end discrimination in housing focused on gaining equal access to home ownership. Often when individuals and families purchased and occupied homes in violation of restrictive covenants, they were subject to harassment by neighbors. Some even faced eviction when brought to court by real estate agents eager to obtain their property. Indicative of the unique and early prioritization of housing issues for black Angelenos, as early as 1914, Bass actively involved herself in the defense of black home owners' rights in the city. When Mrs. Mary Johnson appealed to the *California Eagle* for help after literally being kicked out of her newly purchased home by white neighbors, Bass "discussed the situation with some club women, and that evening a brigade of a hundred women marched to the Johnson home."[35] The women were ultimately successful in getting the sheriff to help Mrs. Johnson back into her home.

Housing problems became acute in the 1940s as the war industries attracted unprecedented numbers of African Americans to the Central Avenue district of Los Angeles. For example, in 1943, at the peak of black migration to the city, more than six thousand African Americans came each month.[36] When conditions inevitably worsened in this confined area, mobilization against restrictive housing practices grew significantly among communities of color. New forms of individual resistance and political action took root, largely ignored by the white press and also largely absent in historical accounts of the housing issue in this period. African American residents, in particular, organized to push for changes in this more pernicious form of segregation and, as a kind of individually oriented civil disobedience, even intentionally violated the laws that allowed restrictive practices.

Racial restrictions in housing became a dominant theme in the pages of the *California Eagle*. In an August 5, 1943, editorial, for example, Bass wrote:

> While we emphatically support the demand for increased emergency housing in the Negro districts of Los Angeles it is certainly obvious that the *FUNDAMEN-TAL* housing necessity in Los Angeles is the total destruction of property restrictions. Today it is a fact that Negroes are confined to a ghetto area comprising only *FIVE PERCENT* of the residential area of the city.[37] (emphasis in original)

Bass's 1942 battle with the residents of Maywood, a restricted working-class suburb southeast of Los Angeles, typifies the valence of home ownership for whites and blacks in the city. Maywood's residents exemplified the California Dream of accessible home ownership and independence. They were working-class, lived close to growing industrial areas, and for them a home represented the good life.[38] They also saw their property values as being tied to the maintenance of barriers to nonwhite residents. When the city's property restrictions came up for renewal, Bass published an "Open Letter To The Citizens Of Maywood," calling for an end to the policy. In addition to appearing in the *California Eagle*, the letter was published by a local Maywood paper, the *Southeast Herald*. Bass and other activists also attempted to rally community opposition to restrictions by attending public meetings and passing out literature to city residents. Despite Bass's attempts to tie property restrictions to fascism and Hitler, Maywood's chamber of commerce voted to uphold racial property restrictions and "Keep Maywood White."[39]

Bass combined direct engagement in support of residents battling restrictions with use of the *California Eagle* to publicize such cases and mobilize community support. The *Laws* case of the 1940s was perhaps the most famous of these. This black family purchased a home in Watts in 1936, knowing that it was a restricted area, meaning blacks could purchase homes there but could not occupy them. When they decided to occupy their home in Watts, an area south of the Central Avenue district, the Laws pushed against the southern boundary of the city's increasingly rigid line of segregation. Throughout the duration of this black family's seven-year battle to occupy their home free of harassment, the Laws benefited not only from Bass's leadership in the activist Home Protective Association, formed to pursue such cases, but also from continuous coverage on the pages of the *California Eagle*.[40]

In writing about the *Laws* case, Bass made the point of connecting this struggle to America's effort in World War II, highlighting the fact that members of the family were jailed for occupying their home despite being employed in the defense industry and having a son-in-law overseas fighting with Allied forces.[41] Bass employed the strategy of many black activists and black journalists who participated in the "Double V" campaign during and after World War II—victory against fascism abroad and victory against racism at home.[42] While desegregation of the war industries and opposition to racial violence were common tenets of the Double V campaign in most cities, including Los Angeles, it is significant that Bass identified desegregated housing as a fundamental component of the local effort, again illustrating the valence of the issue for the city's residents. After the end of the war, Bass, the Home Protective Association, and the *California Eagle* also pushed for desegregated housing for veterans.

Unprecedented WWII population growth brought increased diversity to the black community, including class diversification. This diversity was represented in the housing issue whereby the more upper and middle class members of the community, represented by groups like the NAACP, continued to focus efforts on restrictive covenants and individual home owner's rights, while Bass and others supplemented this issue with attention to a fight for public housing and rent control—issues of greater concern to working-class residents.[43] These divisions proved to be important markers of change in the city's black politics.

While Bass used the *California Eagle* to highlight issues commonly pursued by race women in other cities, such as anti-lynching legislation, her prioritization of accessible housing reflects the unique expectations of black Angelenos compared to those elsewhere.[44] As these expectations went unmet, resistance fomented.

Race and Leisure Space

Consumption and leisure were common pursuits for black migrants in the early part of the twentieth century, and these elements of the American Dream were a part of what attracted them out of the South. Access to consumer goods like beauty products and automobiles and the ability to enjoy leisure time in music clubs and entertainment venues were heavily advertised by the black press as pleasures offered to those willing to migrate.[45] What made Los Angeles unique in this regard was how consumption and leisure were so tied to outdoor activity and recreation. A key feature of boosterism of the city of

Los Angeles has long been the climate and access to recreational space.[46] Black migrants were as prone to this attraction as whites. As the black population expanded in the 1910s and 1920s and residents increasingly sought access to such spaces, whites responded by raising the bars of restriction. Public beaches, a key locale for recreation and leisure in the city, became a defining site for civil rights struggles for black Angelenos.[47]

In 1911, a black couple, the Bruces, purchased beachfront property in Manhattan Beach, just south of Los Angeles. They developed a resort, "Bruces' Beach," that soon attracted large numbers of African Americans who recognized it as a hospitable location for recreation. This hospitality soon ran afoul of local white residents, and black visitors were increasingly harassed. The Ku Klux Klan attempted to intimidate the Bruces directly by threatening them and vandalizing their property. Official harassment of the Bruces came in the form of Manhattan Beach officials' attempts to condemn their property and turn it into a park. The Bruces sued the city, and they were given the right to buy elsewhere in Manhattan Beach and to receive compensation for their loss. However, they were not allowed to purchase beachfront property elsewhere, and no-trespassing signs soon appeared on their former property. In the late 1920s Bruce's Beach ceased to exist in a formal sense.[48]

Charlotta Bass and the *California Eagle* followed the Bruces' case much as they would the Laws's housing restrictive covenant case. In addition to publicizing the plight of the couple with articles under headlines like "What's The Matter With Bruce's Beach" and "Arrest Girl While Bathing At Manhattan Beach," the paper rallied black residents to support them.[49] Activists embarked on a public battle to pursue black access to Los Angeles's coastline. As Bass herself noted, "This is not the Bruce's [sic] fight. It is a fight for all the people. The NAACP and other organizations must see that the Bruce's [sic] are given a fair chance."[50] Residents were encouraged to attend public meetings in protest, and bathers were urged to "plunge in the ocean," daring local officials to confront them.[51]

As much as anything, "sunshine" in Los Angeles was experienced in leisure spaces like parks, pools, and beaches. Like blacks elsewhere, black Angelenos fought for equal access to public and private accommodations, including trolley cars, restaurants, theaters, and hotels, but it was their battle for outdoor leisure space that set them apart. This battle was initiated in the 1910s, during the earliest development of the black community, indicating its centrality to place-making in the city.

Employment Discrimination

The fact that black Angelenos pursued access to leisure space did not mean they or other city residents had an inordinate amount of leisure time. Like blacks elsewhere, they were focused on the need to secure employment and economic security. Employment discrimination, like housing discrimination, was not an issue unique to Los Angeles's black residents. However, it was uniquely manifested in the city in ways that structured their activism. The timing of industrial development, the multiracial character of the city, in particular the presence of a Mexican American population, changing labor union politics, and the expansion of WWII employment centered in the city all impacted black politics around this issue. Whereas housing opportunities contributed to the image of Los Angeles as a paradise for blacks, limited job opportunities and exclusion from unions worked in the opposite direction.

Prior to World War II, blacks who moved to Los Angeles found it more difficult to break into the industrial labor market than did their counterparts who migrated to the north. Because Los Angeles's manufacturing emerged during an era of surplus labor, and because even when conditions changed, employers preferred to hire Mexican labor, blacks were largely shut out of most industries.[52] Unions were complicit in this discrimination. This meant that when unions began pushing back against open shop restrictions in the city, blacks were not a part of the movement.[53] Likewise, in the 1930s, when the Congress of Industrial Organizations began to organize black workers elsewhere, blacks in Los Angeles saw little benefit because they weren't employed in organized sectors of the labor market.

In her autobiography, Charlotta Bass says she moved to Los Angeles to improve her health and only later gave thought to employment opportunities.[54] Like most African Americans who came to the city in the early part of the twentieth century, she was not motivated to migrate by the prospect of access to industrial jobs that lured some southern blacks to the North. The "garden city" that attracted her and other residents was built and sold as a foil to industrial cities of the North. While it offered sunshine, open space, and the possibility of home ownership, it did not initially offer much access to industrial jobs. The limited job opportunities partly explain why the black population remained relatively small until WWII. Nonetheless, Bass pushed for black access to the labor market even before the economic expansion brought on by the war industries. As mentioned in a 1927 *Eagle* description of Bass, she identified with workers' rights and thrived "in an atmosphere of the women-workers and the men-toilers, and never was framed into life to be an idler, a drone, a gossiper or a society-belle."[55] So long as blacks were denied job market access afforded to whites and others, desegregated employment would be a political issue for the community.

World War II was truly a watershed moment for the development of Los Angeles as a whole and black Los Angeles and black resistance in particular. As the West Coast center for wartime industries, the area attracted migrants from all over the country looking for work. African Americans flocked to the region following Roosevelt's June 21, 1941, signing of Executive Order 8802 in response to pressure from activists such as A. Phillip Randolph to integrate the war industries.[56] The fact that Los Angeles was a center for the war industry meant that jobs in that industry joined home ownership as a central component of the Los Angeles version of the American Dream. Thus, the campaign to desegregate the industry took on particular urgency for Bass and other black activists.

Locally, Bass joined with the Reverend Clayton Russell of the People's Independent Church, an activist black congregation in South Los Angeles, as co-leader of the Los Angeles Negro Victory Committee to insure that blacks fully participated in the region's defense industry.[57] She used the pages of the *California Eagle* to help organize members of the black community to demand their right to work. One of the Victory Committee's campaigns sought to insure the rights of African American women to obtain jobs in the shipbuilding enterprises. Acting on behalf of women who complained directly to Bass and the *California Eagle* about discrimination by the United States Employment Service (the agency responsible for wartime hiring), Bass and Russell organized a meeting in July of 1942 at the Independent Church of Christ. Bass herself describes "a spirited meeting." "For the first time in Los Angeles," Bass wrote, "Negro women, led by a Negro preacher, decided that they were going to fight untidily[sic] for food, clothing and the comforts of life which were due them."[58] The next morning, these women converged on the U.S. Employment Service headquarters in protest and successfully convinced officials to lift the ban against hiring black women in the war industries.[59]

By the mid-1940s, with blacks' unprecedented World War II–related entrance into the labor market, the black community in Los Angeles had new leverage to call for union desegregation. The CIO pragmatically responded to pressure and began to focus on organizing blacks in the war industries and promoted them to leadership positions within the organization.[60] As Bass asserted in writing about the CIO's Anti-discrimination Committee,

> The unprecedented industrialization of the Negro in our state must be followed
> by his full integration in the labor movement. It is heartening to find that the

labor movement is alive to the Negro's particular problems and is determined to find them, fight them . . . [61]

Prior to World War II, limited access to higher paying union jobs represented the version of noir that confronted blacks in L.A. to a greater degree than it did blacks elsewhere. WWII changed this, as the number of jobs expanded and the draft opened new opportunities. Yet and still, black Angelenos had to fight for access to the sunshine represented by wartime job growth in the city.

Multiethnic Coalitions and Competition

As the discussion of blacks and Mexicans in Los Angeles's labor market suggests, the city's multiracial character distinguishes it from other cities in the South and North, where blacks interacted solely with whites. Black politics were shaped by the unparalleled opportunities for interethnic and interracial contact in Los Angeles. The city's proximity to Mexico and Asia meant that black Angelenos were not the sole recipients of white racism, and it meant they were not alone in the quest for social, economic, and political equality. Just as political issues were uniquely shaped by the city, so too were options for allies and competitors.

Anti-Asian, particularly anti-Chinese, sentiment prevailed in California from the mid-1800s well into the twentieth century. Though black Angelenos could acknowledge that the presence of other people of color had the effect of refracting the effects of racism typically reserved for them, for blacks at the bottom of the class structure, competition in the labor market produced a context of heightened xenophobia.[62]

Early on, Bass and the *California Eagle* reflected such xenophobia. They were quite nationalist in their promotion of black interests and were not always consistent in appreciating the possible connectedness of oppression of blacks and other groups. For example, an August 1934 column in the *California Eagle* on race riots in Arizona between whites and Japanese asserts,

> White American landholders and business men should have foreseen the possibility of the country being overrun with aliens when the best of positions sublease and even the humble traditional job of private family domestic were given to the Japanese, Filipinos, Hindus and other non-citizen peoples while our young Afro-American citizens finish school to look in vain for work.[63]

In the same year, the *California Eagle* ran an article detailing the coordinated efforts of Bass herself and leaders from the Mexican community to call attention to discrimination against blacks and Mexican girls on a federally sponsored work project.[64] While these two articles may be interpreted as indicating inconsistency, in both cases the civil rights of blacks motivate the paper's concern.[65] Likewise, the two articles suggest a complex matrix of conflict and cooperation endemic to a diverse environment.

With the advent of World War II and increased integration of blacks into the work force, the white/other divide in Los Angeles became more salient, and African Americans began to see the advantages of building multiethnic coalitions.[66] For Bass, by 1943, the anti-Asian sentiment of the 1930s evolved into support for the rights of Japanese Americans. As an *Eagle* article notes, "Persecution of the Japanese-American minority has been one of the disgraceful aspects of the nation's conduct of this People's War."[67] In subsequent years, Bass would regularly include Asians in lists of groups who faced discrimination similar to that African Americans suffered.

In 1943, Bass and the *California Eagle* also played a visible role in supporting the Sleepy Lagoon defendants, a group of Mexican youths indiscriminately rounded up by Los Angeles police and charged with murder. In addition to serving on the defendants' Sponsors' Committee, Bass used the paper to inform black readers about the injustices suffered by the defendants. The *California Eagle* also reproduced a pamphlet detailing the story of the case and aided in the legal appeal. For Bass, "the case represented in all its horror the use of all the powers of local government to smear and terrorize an entire racial group."[68] In separating the *California Eagle* from the mainstream press, and the *Los Angeles Times* and Hearst papers in particular, she noted, "A sensation-mongering, circulation-mad metropolitan press was a prime factor in fanning the flames of race hate and suspicion before and during and after the long 'Sleepy Lagoon' trial."[69] Bass asserted that the proper role of the *California Eagle* was to advocate for marginalized communities that had suffered through the type of characterizations found in the mainstream press. This advocacy role extended beyond the black community to include Mexican Americans, situating Bass as one of the city's earliest advocates of a black-brown coalition, predating the coalitions of the 1970s such as that between the Black Panthers and the Brown Berets.

In addition to offering support to causes of other marginalized groups, black activists in Los Angeles in the 1940s and 1950s actively joined with them in pursuing racial justice. The participation of black Angelenos in multiracial (as opposed to biracial) civil rights organizations reflects strategic opportunity and innovation. While blacks and whites had a long history of organizing together in groups like the NAACP, multiracial civil rights organizing was much less common. One of Los Angeles's earliest incarnations of this type of organization was the city's chapter of the Civil Rights Congress (CRC), a national civil rights group affiliated with the Communist Party. In its most active East Coast chapters, the CRC focused primarily on the fight for the rights of working-class African Americans, but in Los Angeles it also advocated on behalf of Mexican Americans and other people of color.[70] The CRC's work was largely dedicated to fighting police brutality by publicizing complaints and providing legal support for victims. Charlotta Bass was a board member of the CRC, and many such brutality cases, including those involving nonblacks, found their way onto the pages of the *California Eagle*.

Just as the local Double V campaign reflected the particular significance of the housing issue in Los Angeles, so too did local blacks' extension of the campaign's moral argument to include Mexicans reflect a unique Los Angeles imprint. For instance, in a 1950 column, Bass highlighted the case of Jose Estrada, who had immigrated from Mexico to the United States in 1905 and, forty-five years later, faced deportation for "un-American activities." In her article Bass pointed out that Estrada deserved protections afforded all Americans. "He is married to a native Texan and has ten American-born children," Bass wrote. "Three sons served in the armed forces during World War II. . . . Each spent over three years fighting, one receiving the Purple Heart."[71] Her decision to focus on Estrada's "American-ness," as illustrated by his ties to this country and the patriotic actions of his children, was in keeping with her argument about the contradictory nature of American policy during the war, with discriminatory practices against blacks at home while the country was fighting a war for freedom and democracy abroad.

Bass's orientation toward an alliance with nonblack groups is most evident after World War II, but even prior to this there are indications of a willingness on her part to build coalitions in seeking racial justice, as in her advocacy for an alliance between blacks and Mexican Americans.[72] Her early xenophobia, which was reflective of the black community more broadly, was clearly tied to the concern that the advancement of other races would be a threat to black advancement, and her differentiation between Mexican Americans and Asian Americans demonstrated the complexity of the multiracial tensions and alliances of the time. Yet, the uniqueness of a multiracial and multiethnic city such as Los Angeles provided, if not demanded, an impetus for aligning the fight for black empowerment with that of other groups.

Seeing Red?

World War II profoundly impacted the terrain of black community politics in Los Angeles. As the population grew, class divisions became much more pronounced. Many members of the older, more established middle class sought to distance themselves from newer, more working-class migrants. Older black residents were resentful of newer residents who, they believed, were unrefined and undercut them in the job market, while newcomers felt the older residents were too timid and needed a more aggressive politics.[73] As the relative prioritization of restrictive covenants versus public housing suggests, the political priorities and strategies that appealed to each of these groups began to diverge. Despite such divergence, however, black activists were still unified in their desire to achieve parity with the city's white residents, and they constantly sought allies in this struggle. World War II Los Angeles offered a number of strategic options for pursuit of this goal. The increasing industrialization that accompanied the war build-up attracted union activists and communists seeking to build a proletarian movement. The city's strategic location on the pacific stage of the war, and the fact that it was home to the image-making factory, Hollywood, meant that anticommunist forces also focused on the city. L.A.'s black activists responded to these competing forces.

Up to the WWII era, Bass and her paper were adept at speaking to the needs and concerns of upper- and middle-class African Americans, and those of the working class as well. While she never abandoned the issues of more well-to-do community members, after the war she and other black middle-class leaders increasingly diverged on strategy. Their respective approaches to communism were a key example. Once again, Bass's life serves as a useful tool for understanding the contours of black political development in Los Angeles. The evolution of her own politics before and after the war, the alliances she formed, and the opposition she faced from within the black community all speak to the increasing diversity of black political positions in post–WWII Los Angeles.

There is some evidence that Bass was anticommunist early on in her career, but her position was one that was also sympathetic to communism in that she clearly understood why its ideological positions were attractive to those who experienced racial injustice. As she observed in an "On the Sidewalk" column in 1932,

> within the Negro group the masses are slowly but surely turning their faces and their political hope of independence toward the Communist party, and I fear that it will take a more drastic antitoxin than head beatings and breaking up meetings by brutal police officers to destroy the poison planted in the hearts and minds of those who have been so long misused and mistreated.[74]

Bass is critical of police harassment and brutality aimed at suspected communists, but her reference to communism as a "poison" clearly indicates her opposition to the ideology.

After World War II, Bass displayed a much more sympathetic point of view and worked closely with members of the Communist Party. This opened her up to a great deal of criticism from within the African American community. The widening of this fissure is reflective of the impact of anticommunism on black political development.

One possible reason that Bass and other black activists moved closer to communists in the late 1940s was the primary role of party members in the activities of the Civil Rights Congress. Los Angeles was a center for activism on the part of the Communist Party, and members there prioritized the fight against racism.[75] While local NAACP leadership weakened in the period, was increasingly reluctant to challenge racist practices on the part of city agencies, and moved away from direct action, the CRC stepped into the breach and became more active and more militant, especially around cases of racially motivated police brutality.[76] Throughout her career, Bass supported and even initiated militant protest and evaluated potential allies on the basis of their actions in defense or opposition to black rights. A *California Eagle* editorial criticized the local NAACP for being out of touch with community concerns and "more noted for its hesitancy than its militancy."[77] The hesitancy she detected was likely related to the desire of some NAACP leaders to work with white elected officials the CRC confronted.

Growing anticommunism also influenced the decline in militancy on the part of some black leaders in Los Angeles. Because the city was home to high levels of Communist Party activity, the influential film industry, and the growing military industrial complex, Los Angeles was also home to some of the most virulent anticommunism of the 1940s and 1950s.[78]

In the midst of the red scare and the McCarthy era many individuals and organizations sought to distance themselves from communism. Organizations such as the NAACP, the ACLU, and numerous labor unions purged themselves of suspected communists, and many former communists disavowed their previous ties. Those who continued to support communism and/or communists were increasingly isolated. As Jelani Cobb describes, many race leaders, including NAACP figures, pursued what he calls, "strategic anti-communism," in an effort to convince government officials of their loyalty and boost the likelihood of acceptance of their civil rights demands.[79] The late 1940s and early 1950s represented the height of such strategic thinking among black leaders, and as Gerald Horne notes, members of the Los Angeles NAACP strongly subscribed to it.[80] No longer distant from black politics elsewhere, Los Angeles became a key forcing ground for strategic anticommunism. Just as anticommunism was on the increase in the broader population of black activists, Bass was moving closer to Communist Party members and increasingly defended them, signaling a divide in black leadership.

In 1948 Bass explicitly denied that she was a member of the Communist Party and demanded retraction of this accusation made by another newspaper.[81] Despite her denial, the FBI considered Bass to be a communist and a subversive. Agents maintained surveillance of her activities, read each issue of the *California Eagle*, and made regular reports to FBI director J. Edgar Hoover.[82]

Bass was disturbed but unbowed by such attacks, and in her last column for the *California Eagle* in 1951 she directly addressed them,

> For many years the reactionary forces in this community have tried to crush me and *The California Eagle*. . . . Among them, I regret to say, are some of my own people, whom I have personally helped over the years to become successes in business, in the professions, and in political office. They have joined forces with the enemy of their own people and the enemy of democracy. Their fate is not difficult to foretell.[83]

While Bass maintained these commitments and refused to reverse her position regarding communist affiliation, the *California Eagle* began to lose readers in the mid- to late 1940s due to these attacks, resulting in financial losses. Bass eventually had to sell the *California Eagle* and thus lost her most powerful source of advocacy.[84]

Whereas Los Angeles's new, relatively small, and experimental black community of the 1920s advocated and allowed for a diversity of political strategies, by the late 1940s and 1950s, the battle over strategy for combating racial injustice was more pitched and less distant from national black politics. The community had grown, and divisions, especially those that were class based, mattered more. As the black population in Los Angeles grew and became more diverse in its political positions, it became, ironically, less distinguishable within the broader framework of black politics throughout the nation—in its increased importance, it became less easy to ignore but also less flexible because of the dictates of national racial politics.

Conclusion

To gain insight into Charlotta Bass's political life is to achieve some measure of understanding of how Los Angeles influenced and was influenced by black political development and how this community's struggle for empowerment coincided with and differed from those of blacks in other parts of the country. Like other migrants to the city, African Americans were attracted to Los Angeles's version of the American Dream. When white residents attempted to limit their access to home ownership, leisure space, and jobs, black Angelenos resisted and measured their progress relative to other residents of the multicultural city. While they confronted pitched job market competition and familiar white resistance to black advancement, blacks in L.A. did experience a form of refracted racism; they had unprecedented home ownership levels, racist violence was much less common than it was in the South, and the presence of other people of color meant white racism was not solely directed at the black community. But even while they recognized these relatively favorable circumstances, blacks in L.A. were not complacent; rather they used the circumstances to develop unique, aggressive forms of civil rights activism. They combined ideologies that elsewhere competed, chose multifaceted allies in their struggle, and demanded access to opportunities that blacks elsewhere did not expect to enjoy. Despite black Angelenos' recognition of their own unique struggles with injustice, however, Bass and her contemporaries faced a broader perception that the struggle they faced was negligible.

Developments that followed in the wake of Bass's most active years and after her death, including the Watts riots of 1965, which devastated South Los Angeles, and the 1992 Los Angeles riots after the trial of Rodney King, which were the most destructive this country has experienced, served to call attention to the unique conditions and struggles of Los Angeles's African American community. Unfortunately, these catastrophic incidents exemplify a radically different type of politics than that which Bass personified. It could be argued that her struggle to call attention to and eliminate racial injustice in Los Angeles long ago warned of the possibility for the explosions in 1965 and 1992. What is important is that Bass attempted to alert the city and the nation to the inequities that lay beneath the veneer of progress and opportunity. In the wake of Watts, one observer remarked that "other cities are old and have lived with this problem longer . . . Where the most hope is built up, the awakening to reality hurts the most." [85] Bass took advantage of the opportunities afforded by Los Angeles, she employed a hope-filled activism, and she attempted to awaken others to the realities of racism existing in this relatively young city.

Ironically, Bass's obscurity as a national civil rights figure speaks to the power of the image of Los Angeles as a relative paradise for blacks prior to 1965. Why examine a resistant figure in a place where folks have it so good—what's to resist? Using Bass to unearth a more than forty-year history of black response to the pattern of limits and opportunities offered by L.A. allows for a complicated view of the black community and the city as a whole. Just as assumptions about L.A. prior to 1965 are oversimplified, so too is scholarly and popular fascination with understanding L.A. as dystopia. Such a perspective truncates L.A.'s black history by locating its birth in Watts in 1965 and circumscribes black history-making to expressions of hopelessness. Political struggle like that practiced by Bass and other black Angelenos signals hope as much as it does frustration. Thus, resurrecting her legacy is more than an exercise in highlighting a history of disappointment for black Angelenos. The life of this L.A. race woman also shines light on the history of resistance and civil rights struggles in the city long before it was recognized on the national stage. This history of black struggle in Los Angeles signals sunshine as much as it does noir.

Notes

1. See Frederick E. Anderson, *The Development of Leadership and Organization Building in the Black Community of Los Angeles from 1900 Through World War II* (Saratoga, Calif.: Century Twenty-One Publishing, 1980); Susan Anderson "A City Called Heaven: Black Enchantment and Despair in Los Angeles," in *The City: Los Angeles and Urban Theory at the End of the Twentieth Century,* ed. Allen J. Scott and Edward W. Soja (Berkeley: University of California Press, 1996); Lonnie G. Bunche, "A Past Not Necessarily Prologue: The Afro-American in Los Angeles" in *20th Century Los Angeles: Power, Promotion, and Social Conflict,* ed. Norman M. Klein and Martin J. Schiesl (Claremont, Calif.: Regina Books, 1990); Lawrence De Graaf, "The City of Black Angels: Emergence of the Los Angeles Ghetto 1890–1930," *Pacific Historical Review* 5.39 (August 1970); Doug Flamming, "African-Americans and the Politics of Race in Progressive-Era Los Angeles," in William Deverell and Tom Sitton, eds. *California Progressivism Revisited* (Berkeley: University of California Press 1994); Gerald Horne *Fire This Time: The Watts Uprising and the 1960s* (Charlottesville: University of Virginia Press, 1995); Josh Sides, *L.A. City Limits: African American Los Angeles from the Great Depression to the Present* (Berkeley: University of California Press, 2003); Emory Tolbert, *The UNIA and Black Los Angeles* (Los Angeles: UCLA Center for Afro-American Studies, 1980); *Seeking El Dorado: African-Americans in California,* ed. Lawrence B. de Graaf, Kevin Mulroy, and Quintard Taylor (Los Angeles: Autry Museum of Western Heritage, 2001).

2. Sides, *L.A. City Limits,* 152–53.

3. James Grossman, *Land of Hope: Chicago, Black Southerners, and the Great Migration* (Chicago: University of Chicago Press, 1989), 4; Sides, *L.A. City Limits,* 15.

4. Biographical sources on Bass include Charlotta A. Bass, *Forty Years: Memoirs from the Pages of a Newspaper* (Los Angeles: self published, 1960); the Charlotta A. Bass Papers and Manuscript Collection at the Southern California Library for Social Studies and Research, Los Angeles; Jacqueline Leavitt, "Charlotta Bass, *The California Eagle,* and Black Settlement in Los Angeles," in *Urban Planning and the African American Community: In the Shadows,* ed. June Manning Thomas and Marsha Ritzdorf (Thousand Oaks, Calif.: Sage Publications, 1996); Gerda Lerner, ed., *Black Women in White America: A Documentary History* (New York: Vintage Books, 1972); Rodger Streitmatter, *Raising Her Voice: African-American Women Journalists Who Changed History* (Lexington: University Press of Kentucky, 1994); Gerald Gill, "From Progressive Republican to Independent Progressive: The Political Career of Charlotta A. Bass," in *African American Women and the Vote 1837–1965,* ed. Ann D. Gordon et al. (Amherst: University of Massachusetts Press, 1997); James Phillip Jeter, "Rough Flying: The California Eagle

(1879–1965)" (paper presented at the 12th Annual Conference of the American Journalism Historians Association, Salt Lake City, Utah, October 7, 1993); Marty Tippens, "Talking Back: How Publisher and Activist Charlotta Bass Challenged Inequality Through the California Eagle" (master's thesis, California State University, Northridge, 2001).

5. Bass, *Forty Years.*
6. Jeter, "Rough Flying."
7. *Los Angeles Times*, April 1, 1945, Part 2, 2.
8. Bass Collection, Box 1, folder titled "Bass Congressional Campaign 1950."
9. Leavitt, "Charlotta Bass."
10. Jeter, "Rough Flying," 13.
11. Bass, *Forty Years*, 179; Streitmatter, *Raising Her Voice*, 105–6.
12. Grossman, *Land of Hope: Chicago, Black Southerners, and the Great Migration*, 4.
13. See Anderson, "A City Called Heaven: Black Enchantment and Despair in Los Angeles," 336–64, for a discussion of path-breaking civil rights legislation in Los Angeles and California as a whole, ranging from the right to testify in court to equal public accommodation laws.
14. See De Graaf, "The City of Black Angels," 333.
15. William Fulton, *The Reluctant Metropolis: The Politics of Urban Growth in Los Angeles* (Point Arena, Calif.: Solano Press Books, 1997).
16. Sides, *L.A. City Limits*,16.
17. W. E. B. Du Bois, *The Crisis*, August 1913, 192.
18. On increasing segregation, see Bunche, "A Past Not Necessarily Prologue," 103–10. Bass and her husband fought a direct and personal battle with the Ku Klux Klan when the organization sued the couple for libel based on items published in the *California Eagle*. The Basses won the court fight. *California Eagle*, May 22, 1925.
19. De Graaf, "The City of Black Angels," 335–36.
20. In 1910, 83 percent of all black Angelenos had migrated to Los Angeles. Bunche, "A Past Not Necessarily Prologue," 103.
21. Tolbert, *The UNIA and Black Los Angeles*, 90.
22. Ibid., 93.
23. See "An Appeal to the Conscience of the Black Race to See Itself," originally published in Amy Jacques Garvey, ed., *Philosophy and Opinions of Marcus Garvey*, vol. 2 (New York: Universal Publishing House, 1925), 55–61.
24. For information on the Forum, see Tolbert, *The UNIA and Black Los Angeles.*
25. Tolbert, *The UNIA and Black Los Angeles*, 93.
26. Ibid., 66.
27. Ibid., 75.
28. Ibid., 67.
29. *California Eagle*, "In New York," January 14, 1927.
30. In 1910, almost 40 percent of blacks in Los Angeles County owned their own homes, compared to only 2.4 percent in New York and 8 percent in Chicago. Sides, *L.A. City Limits*, 16. On the small number of black professionals in L.A. prior to WWII, see Gill, "From Progressive Republican to Independent Progressive."
31. Carey McWilliams, *Southern California: An Island on the Land*, 10th ed. (Layton, Utah: Gibbs Smith, 1995).
32. Bunche, "A Past Not Necessarily Prologue," 103.
33. *California Eagle*, September 27, 1919.
34. Sides, *L.A. City Limits*, 18.
35. Bass, *40 Years*, 95.
36. Sides, *L.A. City Limits*, 43; Bunche "A Past Not Necessarily Prologue," 117.
37. *California Eagle*, August 5, 1943.
38. See Becky M. Nicolaides, "The Quest for Independence: Workers in the Suburbs," in Tom Sitton and William Deverell, eds., *Metropolis in the Making: Los Angeles in the 1920s* (Berkeley: University of California Press, 2001), for a discussion of early white suburban development in Los Angeles.
39. *California Eagle*, "On the Side Walk—An Open Letter To The Citizens Of Maywood" March 26, 1942; *California Eagle*, "Maywood-Bell Editor Hopes to Keep Out 'Undesirables,'" March 26, 1942.
40. The Home Protective Association was formed specifically to rally support for the Laws family. The group later offered help in other similar cases. See Bass, *Forty Years*, 197.

41. Ibid., 110.
42. The Double V campaign was initiated on February 7, 1942, in the pages of the *Pittsburgh Courier*—one of the widest-read black newspapers in the 1940s. The campaign involved articles, editorials, letters to the editor, and an official logo. Black newspapers across the country, including the *California Eagle*, picked up the cause, demanding that African Americans called to fight in the war receive full citizenship rights at home. See Patrick S. Washburn, "The Pittsburgh Courier's Double V Campaign in 1942," *American Journalism* 3.2 (1986): 73–86.
43. Horne, *Fire This Time*, 33.
44. For a discussion of issues pursued by race women more broadly, see Darlene Clark Hine and Kathleen Thompson, *A Shining Thread of Hope: The History of Black Women in America* (New York: Broadway Books, 1998).
45. Alan D. DeSantis, "Selling the American Dream Myth to Black Southerners: The Chicago *Defender* and the Great Migration of 1915–1919," *Western Journal of Communication* 62.4 (fall 1998): 494.
46. McWilliams, *Southern California: An Island on the Land*, 96–112.
47. For more information on the connection between race and leisure space in Los Angeles, see Lawrence Culver, "The Island, the Oasis, and the City: Santa Catalina, Palm Springs, Los Angeles, and Southern California's Shaping of American Life and Leisure" (doctoral dissertation, University of California, Los Angeles, 2004).
48. *Los Angeles Times*, July 21, 2002, "Resort Was an Oasis for Blacks Until Racism Drove Them Out."
49. *California Eagle*, July 1, 1927; July 8, 1927.
50. Bass, *Forty Years*, 56.
51. *California Eagle*, "What's The Matter With Bruce's Beach," July 8, 1927.
52. Sides, *L.A. City Limits*, 24–25.
53. For a discussion of the relationship between blacks and unions in Los Angeles, see Tolbert, *The UNIA and Black Los Angeles*, 37, and Flamming, "African-Americans and the Politics of Race in Progressive-Era Los Angeles."
54. Bass, *Forty Years*, 27.
55. Louis Michel, "Managing Editor C. A. Bass' Travelogue Lecture Has Teeth," *California Eagle*, May 5, 1927.
56. Josh A. Sides, *Working Away: African American Migration and Community in Los Angeles from the Great Depression to 1954* (doctoral dissertation, University of California, Los Angeles, 1999), 79–82.
57. Gill, "From Progressive Republican to Independent Progressive," 162.
58 Bass, *Forty Years*, 74.
59. Ibid., 74.
60. Sides, *L.A. City Limits*, 63–64.
61. *California Eagle*, "A Great Ally Comes to the Fore," August 27, 1942.
62. See Tomas Almaguer, *Racial Fault Lines: The Historical Origins of White Supremacy in California* (Berkeley: University of California Press, 1994), 153–59, for a discussion of the connection between blacks, anti-Asian hostility and the California labor market.
63. *California Eagle*, "Anti-Japanese Race Riots," August 31, 1934.
64. *California Eagle*, "Mexican, Negro Leaders Open Discrimination Fight Charge Against Officers at Projects," October 26, 1934.
65. See Almaguer, *Racial Fault Lines*, 204, for a discussion comparing attitudes toward Asians and Mexicans.
66. For more information on how World War II impacted Bass and other African American leaders and their perspective on interracial cooperation in particular, see Kevin Allen Leonard, "'In the Interest of All Races': African-Americans and Interracial Cooperation in Los Angeles During and After World War II," in *Seeking El Dorado*, ed. de Graaf, Mulroy, and Taylor.
67. *California Eagle*, "A Point Well Taken, We Think," November 11, 1943.
68. Bass, *Forty Years*, 124.
69. Ibid., 124.
70. See Civil Rights Congress Collection at the Southern California Library for Social Studies and Research.
71. "Father Of Vets To Be Deported," *California Eagle*, February 23, 1950.
72. Leonard, "'In the Interest of All Races.'"
73. Horne, *Fire This Time*, 34.
74. *California Eagle*, "On the Sidewalk," July 1, 1932.

75. Dorothy Ray Healey and Maurice Isserman, *California Red: A Life in the Communist Party* (Urbana: University of Illinois Press, 1993); and Sides, *L.A. City Limits,* 142.
76. Sides, *L.A. City Limits,* 140–45. For a fuller discussion of the Civil Rights Congress and Los Angeles's black community, see Josh Sides, "You Understand My Condition: The Civil Rights Congress in Los Angeles's African-American Community, 1946–1952," *Pacific Historical Review* 67.2 (May 1998): 233–58.
77. *California Eagle*, March 30, 1950.
78. Ibid.
79. Jelani Cobb, "Antidote to Revolution: African American Anticommunism and the Struggle for Civil Rights, 1931–1956" (doctoral dissertation, Rutgers University, 2003).
80. Horne, *Fire This Time,* 173.
81. Bass Collection, Box 1, folder titled "Letters to C. A. Bass 1940's," "Notice of Libelous statements Published and Demand for Retraction," dated August 31, 1948.
82. Streitmatter, *Raising Her Voice,* 102.
83. *California Eagle*, April 26, 1951.
84. According to Jeter, the *California Eagle's* circulation dropped from 17,600 in 1940 to 10,000 in 1950. Jeter, "Rough Flying," 11–12.
85. Reverend H. H. Brookins, *Los Angeles Times*, August 22, 1965.

"What's Good for Boyle Heights Is Good for the Jews": Creating Multiracialism on the Eastside during the 1950s

George J. Sánchez

Two magazine articles published in the mid-1950s pointed to the Boyle Heights neighborhood in East Los Angeles as an "example of democratic progress" to a national audience. The first, published in October 1954 in *Fortnight*, focused on the diverse group of Boyle Heights residents and organizations that gathered together to fight the proposed $32 million Golden State Freeway that would invade Hollenbeck Park and destroy some of the oldest mansions and social service agencies headquartered on Boyle Avenue. This article claimed that "few districts in America are as ethnically dynamic, religiously and politically tolerant, and community proud" as Boyle Heights. Its population was depicted as more civic-minded than the residents of any other neighborhood, with more than a hundred coordinating councils, fifty community centers and associations, and "probably more social workers per cubic feet of sorrow than anywhere else in the world."[1]

While this article and a similar one that followed in *Frontier* in 1955, "U.N. in Microcosm," both saw the Mexican-American dominated Community Services Organization (CSO) as the most vibrant organization in the Boyle Heights scene, they credited the Jewish community for first instilling a spirit of working together across ethnic lines. "It was the Jews who supplied the initial energy to create ethnic understanding and work-activities on the Heights," reported *Fortnight*, while *Frontier* proclaimed that "the Jews have worked hard for the advancement of the area as a whole."[2] Both articles referred to the support of the Jewish community for Mexican-American Edward Roybal for city council, even when he ran against "one of their own." Joe Kovner, publisher of the *Eastside Sun* and member of the Eastside Jewish Community Center Board, was highlighted as having campaigned vigorously for Roybal and quoted as saying, "Eddie was the best man. What's good for Boyle Heights is good for the Jews. We keep pounding away on the theme of sticking together. An injury to one is an injury to all."[3]

These articles were written at a time, however, when Boyle Heights was becoming less, not more, ethnically diverse. By 1955, Mexicans had grown to form almost half of the Boyle Heights residents, and it appeared that their numbers would only increase dramatically over the next few years. The Jewish population, by contrast, had plummeted by more than 72 percent in the past fifteen years, and now made up less than 17 percent of the area's population. The Boyle Heights community, once considered the centerpiece of Jewish life in Los Angeles, had collapsed in the postwar period due to out-migration. Other ethnic communities, most notably the Japanese American and African American populations, had held steady at less than 5 percent since 1945. Why then, in the wake of Mexican ascendancy and lessened demographic diversity, did Boyle Heights gain a reputation as the seat of "democratic progress" for Los Angeles of the mid-1950s?

The answer lies, in large part, on the actions of a select group of Jewish residents of Boyle Heights in the late 1940s and 1950s that either remained in Boyle Heights or moved into the area as most others were moving out. These residents came from both liberal and leftist political viewpoints and were committed to building a new multiracial community in Boyle Heights, while Southern California as a whole was becoming more suburban and conservative. Fighting the literal geographic movement of Jews into white America, they collaborated with leaders from the growing Mexican American population and from the smaller ethnic communities on the Eastside to leave a legacy of political interracialism, commitment to civil rights, and a radical multiculturalism in Boyle Heights, despite the growing conservative climate of the 1950s.

Los Angeles's Geography of Difference

Boyle Heights can still be found nestled at the eastern edge of the city, directly across the Los Angeles River from downtown. As the population of L.A. grew in the twentieth century and city limits expanded westward, northward, and southward, the area known in the 1781 charter as Paradon Blanco (or White Bluffs) remained the easternmost community within city limits. In the late nineteenth century, city officials placed Evergreen Cemetery in this remote, sparsely populated outpost, and renamed the area Boyle Heights, after a wealthy Irish immigrant to the city. Although just beyond walking distance to the downtown area, Boyle Heights remained largely rural until World War I, because public transportation to the Eastside and bridges over the unstable Los Angeles River were lacking. From the 1880s to the 1920s, the city solved both these problems by building and expanding several bridges to span the unruly river, and by extending an interurban railway network across the river to Boyle Heights.[4]

As Los Angeles's population boomed in the early twentieth century, local officials attempted to keep two discrete migrant streams—one of midwestern "folks" and another of distinctively working class and ethnic newcomers—carefully separated from one another in Los Angeles through an intricate residential segregation that placed American-born Anglo newcomers on the west side of the city, while foreign-born and nonwhite residents found themselves largely confined to the east side. While both sides of Los Angeles had stately Queen Anne homes at the turn of the century, city zoning ordinances in 1908 made Westside L.A. the first urban area in the United States exclusively reserved for residential land use.[5] This government action, coupled with racial segregation initiated by the real estate industry, which took the form of universal restrictive covenants on the west side of the city, meant that the area west of downtown Los Angeles was marked as middle class and a zone of whiteness.

Eastside and Southside Los Angeles, on the other hand, were allowed to develop industrial sites, and immigrants followed these to take up residence near work opportunities. Given their exclusion from the growing middle-class Protestant communities on the west side of the city, working-class migrants from Mexico, Asia, the American South, and the urban Northeast and Midwest all settled in large numbers in these industrial zones, including Boyle Heights. By 1940, the Jewish population of Boyle Heights totaled about 35,000, the Mexican population about 15,000, and the Japanese population approximately 5,000, with smaller numbers of Italians, Armenians, African Americans, and Russian Molokans. These groups had substantial interaction with each other in neighborhood institutions, businesses, schools, and playgrounds. Although Jews never made up a majority of the Boyle Heights population, that neighborhood came to be known as Los Angeles's "Lower East Side," or the principal community in Jewish Los Angeles. During the two decades before World War II, Boyle Heights developed as a uniquely working class Jewish community, full of Jewish-owned businesses along its major thoroughfare, Brooklyn Avenue. Many Jewish workers brought with them a tradition of radical politics and enthusiastic trade unionism. Their militancy made Boyle Heights home to local chapters of the Workmen's Circle and the hatters, carpenters, and garment workers unions.[6]

For Jews in Boyle Heights, this working-class community contrasted sharply with a more elite Jewish community that developed about the same time in

Westside L.A. A Hollywood collection of Jewish studio chiefs, actors, directors, producers, and writers created a new ethnic community, rooted in the movie industry, which one author has described as "an empire of their own."[7] Having broken through restrictive covenants early on to establish a stronghold in several Westside residential communities, this part of Jewish life in Los Angeles represented an intense desire for upward mobility and ethnic assimilation. As several film historians have made clear, Jews helped create white Americanness in the early twentieth century through movies that stressed ethnic assimilation, even while they battled local discrimination by the Protestant elite of Los Angeles.[8] Most important for our purposes, the two poles of Jewish ethnic identity—the separate world of working-class ethnicity and the middle-class ideal of assimilation—were mapped onto the very geography of the city of Los Angeles.

This geography of difference—which had been rooted in inequalities based on social class and an inclusive sense of ethnic "otherness"—was radically altered in the late 1930s and 1940s by a changing ideology of race and a growing lack of tolerance for social mixing. As historian Matthew Jacobson makes clear, the mid-twentieth century "saw a dramatic decline in the perceived differences among these white Others," where new racial ideologies were busy "creating Caucasians, where before had been so many Celts, Hebrews, Teutons, Mediterraneans, and Slavs."[9] The popular use of the term *Caucasian* grew dramatically during this period, and Jewish placement on one side or the other of the line between Caucasian and non-Caucasian was critical in defining the boundaries of this newly important division in American life.[10] Jacobson concentrates on the ideological and cultural transformation of this division in the 1940s, but clearly sees this new racial ideology also grounded in material and geographic considerations, when "the racial revision of Jewishness into Caucasian whiteness would become the invisible mask of *Jewish* privilege."[11]

Boyle Heights, by the World War II era, was not only an anomaly of this new racial ideology; it increasingly became a target for government social engineering designed to separate the races geographically. Through applied social science research, fiscal policy, and direct intervention, the federal government reshaped local communities through housing and transportation policies, and in doing so, was an active presence in redefining the terms of racialization. This did not bode well for multiracial Boyle Heights, which would now be consistently and negatively compared to other neighborhoods in Los Angeles in ways that made it a prime target for government-sponsored reform. In 1939, for example, the Federal Housing Authority gave its lowest possible rating to Boyle Heights specifically because its racial diversity supposedly made it a bad risk for housing assistance:

This is a "melting pot" area and is literally honeycombed with diverse and subversive racial elements. It is seriously doubted whether there is a single block in the area which does not contain detrimental racial elements and there are very few districts which are not hopelessly heterogeneous.[12]

This complex transformation of the terms of racialization was never anticipated by the local population as the United States entered World War II in December 1941. The disruption caused by the war led many individuals and families to leave Boyle Heights in the early 1940s, many for the first time in their lives, and while this disruption was seen as temporary by most, it quickly became clear that it would be difficult to resume life as normal immediately after the war. California, known for its booming population growth since the late nineteenth century, experienced a population explosion that was phenomenal during and immediately after the war. By 1946, the population of the state reached nine million, when it had been less than seven million in 1940.[13] In Boyle Heights, World War II veterans from all racial groups were joined by returning Japanese Americans released from internment camps in 1945, as well as Mexican immigrant *braceros* making their way to urban centers from the San Joaquin and Imperial valleys. It was not uncommon to see families doubling up temporarily in the immediate postwar period within the single-family residences that marked so much of Boyle Heights. This overcrowding occurred throughout Southern California but was particularly acute in working-class communities like Boyle Heights. And many who first looked to return to Boyle Heights could find little housing to match their family needs or pocketbooks, with vital mortgage assistance now funneled away from multiracial communities.

Other communities located in Westside Los Angeles or in the San Fernando Valley were ready to take their positions as leading centers for permanent Jewish settlement in Los Angeles. The Fairfax district—located in the midcity area west of downtown and close to the flourishing Miracle Mile shopping district—already housed four Jewish congregations in 1940, and its expansion of middle-income housing prompted Boyle Heights Jews to consider moving west for resettlement. The Walter N. Marks Company, owned by a young Jewish real estate developer, helped develop a hospitable business climate along Wilshire Boulevard, while the Metropolitan Life Insurance Company purchased exhausted oil fields from Fairfax to Cochran just north of this area and petitioned the city of Los Angeles to annex the region in 1941. Their housing project, which would later be called Park La Brea, would open up the neighborhood for widespread settlement, even though Jews seemed confined to only certain buildings within the enormous complex. Ten other annexations followed this large one, creating new urban settlements in the middle of the city of Los Angeles.[14]

In the San Fernando Valley, residential development was even newer than that over the hill in the Fairfax district. Next to new industrial plants placed there during the war and later converted to nonmilitary use, planned communities sprouted up in Panorama City, North Hollywood, and elsewhere to take advantage of a geographic area almost the size of Chicago. By 1950, only New York City could boast of having added more people to its population during the 1940s; the Valley had reached more than 400,000. In 1950, the *Valley Jewish Press* reported that there were about 22,000 Jewish families living in the Valley.[15] The San Fernando Valley, however, would contain fewer than 5,000 African Americans and other "nonwhites" in 1950, so its growth was highly regulated on racial grounds.

As agricultural land was turned into single-family tract housing, racially restrictive covenants continued to operate, but these new restrictions explicitly limited buyers to those of the "Caucasian race." The new color line placed Jews decidedly into the "white race," but continued to exclude Blacks, Asians, and probably most Mexicans. Added to this dynamic in the postwar period was the rise of specific Jewish builders who invested and sold real estate properties, particularly targeting Jewish newcomers by advertising in the local Jewish weekly newspaper. Chudacoff's Coronet Construction Company, for example, advertised a three-bedroom home that could be obtained by veterans for only a $350 down payment toward the $11,350 total cost. Estimated at 20 percent of the city's home builders and accounting for almost 40 percent of the market, Jewish builders grew to represent 19 percent of the total monies raised by the United Jewish Welfare Fund by 1954, replacing film magnates as the leading entrepreneurs in the Jewish community of Los Angeles.[16]

Even after May 3, 1948, when the United States Supreme Court ruled that racially restrictive covenants were discriminatory and could not be enforced, discriminatory practices continued against "non-Caucasians" by real estate agents, local property owners associations, and lending companies until the 1970s. For example, when Julius Blue, an African American World War II veteran, and his wife saw an August 1948 advertisement offering "wonderful terms" to GIs in Allied Gardens, a new development of 392 single-family homes in Van Nuys, they jumped at the chance to improve their housing circumstances. The promoters of the development, however, refused to show them floor plans and instead gave them a mimeographed sheet reporting the following:

No person whose blood is not entirely that of the Caucasian race (and for the purpose of this paragraph no Japanese, Chinese, Mexican, Hindu, or any person of the Ethiopian, Indian, or Mongolian races shall be deemed to be Caucasian) shall at any time live upon any of the lots in said tract 15010.[17]

An extensive December 1948 report from the Anti-Defamation League made clear that this was not an isolated incident in Southern California. In El Monte, the realty board expelled a member in August 1948, Maurice Curtis, who sold a house to a Mexican American in violation of the Realtor's Code of Ethics and the board's own constitution, which stated: "A realtor should never be instrumental in introducing into a neighborhood a character of property or occupancy, members of any race or nationality, or any individuals whose presence will clearly be detrimental to property values in that neighborhood."[18] Cross burnings, threatening phone calls, property damaging, and personal physical abuse were all parts of enforcing racial restrictions before and after the Supreme Court decision, but so was open and organized opposition to blacks, Latinos, or Asian Americans moving into specific neighborhoods. From Kiwanis Clubs in Eagle Rock to Security First National Bank of Huntington Park, various local institutions worked hard to keep areas strictly limited to Caucasians.[19] What is critical about the postwar legal and illegal restrictions, for our purposes, was that Jews and other European ethnics had, for the most part, moved across the line of exclusion into the world of Caucasians.

Of course, most Jews who purchased new homes in these areas did not migrate from Boyle Heights, but rather were complete newcomers to Southern California altogether. Deborah Dash Moore reports that during the peak year of 1946, 500 newly arrived Jews poured into Southern California each week, making up roughly 13 percent of all newcomers to Los Angeles during this period. The city's Jewish population, estimated at 130,000 before the war, grew to more than 300,000 by 1951. By 1950, only 8 percent of adult Jews in Los Angeles had been born in the city. By the end of the 1950s, only one Jewish head of household out of six had been a prewar resident, and more than half of all Jewish household heads had arrived since the end of World War II. With this accelerated migration to Los Angeles, even while those from other faiths were also pouring into the city, the overall Jewish population of the county grew from 4 to 7 percent of the total. In 1940, Los Angeles Jewry ranked seventh among the nation's cities; by 1955, Los Angeles ranked second only behind New York, and within a few years, only behind New York and Tel Aviv as the world's largest Jewish cities.[20]

This overwhelming of the local population by newcomers was nothing new in Los Angeles, of course, neither within specific ethnic groups nor for the population as a whole. But for Jews in Boyle Heights, it meant that the historic importance and respected place of Boyle Heights among Los Angeles Jewry was forgotten. New families quickly were establishing themselves elsewhere in Los Angeles, and communal institutions, from schools to synagogues, raced to serve this new population, often moving up economically by taking advantage of new industrial and entrepreneurial occupations as well as suburban living. Jewish institutions in Boyle Heights immediately had to consider their own future, given the falling Jewish population in the district, as well as the monumental growth of local Jewish populations elsewhere in Southern California.

"A Laboratory and Training Ground for Democracy"

While new suburban Jewish communities were sprouting up all over Southern California, Boyle Heights surprisingly experienced a renaissance of sorts in the post–World War II period. Jews who staunchly decided to remain in Boyle Heights were joined by newcomers attracted by the history of Jewish local radical tradition and multiracialism. Indeed, after World War II political radicalism increasingly became associated with promoting and defending multiculturalism throughout Southern California.[21] As the rest of the Los Angeles basin became increasingly stratified by race and class through growing residential restrictiveness and the growth of overwhelmingly white suburbs, it was neighborhoods like Boyle Heights that emerged as models for interracial harmony and cooperation. The combination of political radicalism and racial diversity in a relatively small neighborhood like Boyle Heights made the two seem uniquely intertwined in Southern California, and various leftist organizations utilized this combination to defend their politics in the McCarthy period of antiradicalism. Boyle Heights, therefore, became something of an ideological bunker, somewhat protected by its geographic isolation, defending its residents from outside attack, while nurturing a particular brand of radical ideology and multicultural sensibility.

The transformation of Boyle Heights from a nominally Jewish enclave to a predominantly Mexican community with a selective Jewish population committed to multiracialism meant that new individual and institutional efforts were required to achieve ethnic cooperation. The postwar demographic transformation of Boyle Heights created the conditions for a neighborhood that collectively saw its fate as intertwined across ethnic lines, and mobilized to protect the community against encroachments and attacks hoisted onto the area. Even while the Jewish community of Los Angeles as a whole was transformed by the demographic changes, clearly becoming "white" in the racial hierarchy of the region both geographically and politically, Jews in Boyle Heights chose a different path. Increasingly, those Jews who decided to remain in Boyle Heights battled to retain an ethnic community tied to its working-class origins, leftist sensibilities, and ethnic distinctiveness.

Growing up in the 1940s, Leo Frumkin remembered that unique mix of Jewish and multicultural sensibilities that shaped Boyle Heights in the postwar era. Living with an extended family whose politics ranged from social Democrats who voted for Roosevelt to communists, Frumkin helped organize a Socialist Youth Club at age sixteen, when he was in eleventh grade at Roosevelt High School. While leftist Jews had been attracted to the heterogeneous Boyle Heights neighborhood since the early 1930s, Frumkin's youth was spent in a Boyle Heights neighborhood in which secularists and leftists already dominated the Jewish landscape. He remembers the Jewish community of Boyle Heights of his youth in very specific religious and political terms:

> I would say, 85 percent of the population were secular Jews. I hear there were so many synagogues here, so many synagogues there. I remember three. That's all. Three is all I remember. You never saw anybody with yarmulkes . . . So it was a secular community. And of this 80 or 85 percent who were secular Jews, I would say 10 or 20 percent of them were apolitical. Liberal, but apolitical. The balance of them, let's say 60, 70 percent of the Jewish population, were pretty evenly divided between communist and socialist. So there were discussions going on all the time . . . But the community was extremely political, extremely political.[22]

In 1945, when the Los Angeles Board of Education allowed fascist Gerald L. K. Smith to speak at Polytechnic High School, Frumkin helped organize a protest composed in part of five hundred to six hundred students out of Roosevelt High School. The protest also included students from Hollenbeck Junior High School in Boyle Heights, as well as Jefferson High School in South Los Angeles. The unity between Boyle Heights and South Los Angeles, two racially mixed areas—albeit increasingly becoming dominated by Mexican and black populations—became a staple of leftist political organizing in the postwar era. By the time the protest march arrived at the L.A. Board of Education offices downtown, the group numbered close to one thousand students, having marched from both Eastside and Southside Los Angeles.[23]

Frumkin already saw the distinction between his community of Boyle Heights and the growing Jewish community on the Westside in 1945. There was "an unspoken solidarity among all the neighbors" on the Eastside, including the 60 percent of his neighbors who were Mexican. "We never had a lock on our door, never had a key. You just didn't do it. I don't know if it was unspoken, but as poor as we were, nobody stole from anybody else." In this working-class solidarity, a certain level of contempt was reserved for the more middle-class surroundings on the Westside.

> When we would smoke, for instance, we would keep the cigarettes in the car. We would never dump them out in East L.A. When we used to go to West L.A. to the Jewish Community Center to dances, we'd dump all our ashtrays out, because we knew the streets were going to be cleaned there. But we never did it here.[24]

Indeed, one Jewish institution that profoundly changed its orientation, melding new programs with a traditional spirit drawn from its origins in the social settlement house movement, was the Soto-Michigan Jewish Community Center in Boyle Heights. This uniquely American institution affected all Jews in the neighborhood, both religious and secular, and potentially could reach beyond the Jewish community to serve all peoples in a given neighborhood. The Boyle Heights area had been served by a Jewish community center since the 1920s, after a group of community leaders presented the need for such a center to the Federation for Jewish Charities in 1923. In 1934, a new center complex was established at the corner of Michigan and Soto Streets, renaming itself the Soto-Michigan Jewish Community Center, along with continuing its emphasis on serving youth in the community.[25]

In the post–World War II period, the Soto-Michigan Jewish Community Center began to distinguish itself through innovative programming aimed at addressing the changing nature of the Boyle Heights community and the need for increased intercultural work in the neighborhood. Led by Mel Janapol, board member in charge of "intercultural activities," this effort began by inviting non-Jewish youth from outside the community to a model seder at the Jewish Center. At the same time, youth director Mark Keats organized the first Friendship Festival in spring 1949 at the Fresno Playground, to "bring together Mexican, Japanese, Negro, and Jewish youth in a cooperative venture."[26] By the following year, the "Festival of Friendship" had grown to include a three-hour formal arts program, a parade, food sales, and an art exhibit. More than 12,000 people attended, with 1,500 participating in the parade alone. Later that year, a late autumn intercultural week included a Jewish-American cultural night next to evenings dedicated to the cultural contributions of Japanese Americans, Negro Americans, and Mexican Americans.[27]

The paid and volunteer staff members of the Soto-Michigan Jewish Community Center were critical to the expansion of this effort toward minority populations in Boyle Heights. Mark Keats, the co-coordinator of the "Festival of Friendship," quickly became acknowledged within the center as the general community relations person for his sustained work with the non-Jewish youth of Boyle Heights. In addition to the summer festival, Keats organized celebrations of Negro History Week and Mexican Independence Day at the center. He also worked directly with youth and parents groups at Pico Gardens public housing project in his role as youth project worker. This activity was fostered by the multicultural ideology of the Soto-Michigan Center, which Keats explained in this manner: "Our feeling is that each group has a culture which it should be proud of, should retain, and add to the American culture, so that our total culture can be richer than it is at the present time."[28] While Keats's activity expanded beyond the walls of the Soto-Michigan Center, Janapol and other Jewish leaders were committed to seeing the Soto-Michigan Center expand its activities to all the youth in the surrounding community. By 1952, a report on center activity showed that almost 15 percent of participants at Soto-Michigan were non-Jews.[29]

As Jewish adult membership and participation lagged in the late 1940s and early 1950s, Mel Janapol, as director of the Community Relations Committee, encouraged the board to take a wider look at the very meaning of community in Boyle Heights by actively engaging both Jewish and non-Jewish groups in the immediate neighborhood. In late 1949, Janapol and his committee contacted B'nai B'rith, the American Jewish Congress, the Japanese American Citizens League (JACL), the Community Services Organization (CSO), and other groups to meet on future programming at the center. Janapol reported that while "they recognized the essential Jewish purposes of the Center . . . [they] felt that there were many common platforms on which all groups could unite for discussion and debate." The group decided to pursue "programs which would be in line with all the philosophy of the Jewish Community Center, and at the same time could be of service to the various cultural groups of the area." In particular, they supported town meetings on controversial subjects. Their first forum, held April 12, 1950, focused on the hydrogen bomb, and the Community Relations Committee announced the event in both English and Spanish over loudspeakers in various areas of Boyle Heights, through literature in four different languages, and in several paragraphs publicizing the event in the *Daily News* and other metropolitan newspapers.[30]

This intercultural work on the part of the Soto-Michigan Jewish Center increasingly received praise from within and outside of the Jewish community of Los Angeles. The director of the Soto-Michigan Center, Joseph Esquith, told the board in April 1950 that "the intercultural activities of the Center . . . continue to grow with Soto-Michigan becoming the laboratory and training ground for democracy." After a particularly successful intercultural week in

November 1950, when more than four hundred people attended the Japanese-American night, the board of the Soto-Michigan Center unanimously commended Mel Janapol, chairman of the Community Relations Committee, for "the finest job in intercultural activity being done in the entire city." By 1951, Director Esquith spoke in front of the Los Angeles Community Chest Budget Committee regarding this intercultural work, which then became a model for a citywide intergroup committee sponsored by the Community Chest. Moreover, the Soto-Michigan Board received numerous commendations from various ethnic organizations following intercultural programming, such as one from Tats Kushida, regional director of the JACL, in November 1950, "expressing pleasure in having participated in the intercultural program and offering future cooperation wherever possible." In 1951, letters of commendation followed from the Parents Group of Pico Gardens, the Community Services Organization, the *Asociacion Nacional de Mexico-Americanos* (ANMA), and Mayor Fletcher Bowron, all extolling various activities involving intercultural programming.[31]

While board members of the Soto-Michigan Center rightly took great pride in opening up new avenues for intercultural activity, they also worried about the repercussions of a dwindling Jewish community in Boyle Heights. Nowhere was this more evident than in their collective concern over the turnover in their own board membership due to individuals leaving Boyle Heights for other parts of Southern California. As early as March 1950, Sidney Katz, member of the board's Budget Committee, expressed concern that young leadership at the center was absent from the Eastside, and "that the shift in population accounted in part for the lack of local leadership."[32] Throughout the early 1950s, various committees of the center experienced formal resignations due to active members moving out of the Boyle Heights region. This undoubtedly led to a certain openness toward who was a legitimate member of the community, and the board allowed, and possibly even encouraged, Jewish entrepreneurs who no longer lived in Boyle Heights to assume leadership positions. William Phillips, for example, owner of Phillips Music Store on Brooklyn Avenue, was elected second vice president of the board of directors in April 1950, almost one year after he had moved residentially to Beverly Hills.[33]

The personal history of William Phillips, and his famed Eastside music store, is a strong indication of the sort of adaptation to new realities that characterized the decision making of Jewish entrepreneurs in Boyle Heights. Originally founded during the Great Depression, Phillips Music Store decided to stay in the community after World War II and adapt its merchandise to the new populations of Boyle Heights. Committed to the ideals of diversity, William Phillips, the store's owner, even went so far as to encourage a returning Japanese American from the internment camps, Kenji Taniguchi, to open his sporting goods store inside of the music store in the 1950s until it took off on its own. During the 1950s, many budding Latino musicians coming out of Roosevelt High School credited Phillips with introducing them to a wider network of musicians from Central Avenue or the Hollywood Studios. Phillips was considered such an integral part of the changing community that he was selected to chair the Citizens Committee to Re-Elect Roybal for City Council in 1951.[34]

Like many other businessmen from the Jewish community, however, Phillips residentially moved out of the Eastside even while keeping his business located in Boyle Heights. He and his wife moved from the City Terrace neighborhood in 1949, concerned about its rising crime rate, to the "poor side" of Beverly Hills, south of Wilshire Boulevard. Phillips, however, kept his music store in Boyle Heights until the mid-1990s, and remained an active presence in both the institutional Jewish community of the Eastside, as a member of the board of directors of the Soto-Michigan Jewish Community Center, and in the interracial group that formed to support city councilman Edward Roybal, who represented the district from 1949 to 1963 before moving to the U.S. Congress.[35]

Part of the reason that some Jewish businessmen remained in Boyle Heights, despite the exodus of many Jewish customers, was that certain critical groups of Jewish residents also opted to stay in the Heights, regardless of a larger demographic transformation. While many young couples just establishing themselves decided not to start families in Boyle Heights in the postwar period, elderly Jews, particularly those whose children had already left the family, stayed behind in the community in which they felt comfortable and that had met their needs in the past. Politically, Jews who were traditionally Democratic in their political orientation took advantage of newfound economic and social benefits in suburban communities. On the other hand, Jews who were committed leftists—be they socialist, communist, or embedded in secular Yiddish culture—received less cultural benefit from leaving the Eastside and chose to remain in Boyle Heights or City Terrace, where established unions and leftist organizations remained centered. In short, specific groups of Jews resolutely stayed in Boyle Heights long after most others had abandoned the Eastside. This steadfastness altered the nature of the Jewish community of Boyle Heights that worked with the wider multiracial population of the neighborhood during the 1950s.

Radical Innovations and Multicultural Perspectives

Boyle Heights was increasingly associated with political radicalism in the late 1940s and 1950s, as political ideologies in greater Southern California moved decidedly to the right. Although Boyle Heights had a long tradition of working-class politics and was home to various labor unions before World War II, after the war institutions in the area were specifically attacked for harboring communists, socialists, and sympathizers. In and out of the Jewish community, Boyle Heights grew to be seen as an anomaly in Southern California by the early 1950s, and for being sympathetic to liberal and leftist causes. This growing reputation led many leftists, including those in the Jewish community, to remain in Boyle Heights while political moderates left, and it encouraged leftists from other parts of Southern California to move into Boyle Heights just as it was becoming known as a Mexican American "ghetto" neighborhood. To study radicalism in Southern California during the 1950s, therefore, requires a spatial investigation of Boyle Heights and its continued reputation for political tolerance and radical ideologies.

Many radicals from various backgrounds had been drawn to Boyle Heights years before the 1950s, with some of the most well known leftists in Los Angeles migrating there to establish ties to other activists within this tolerant working-class community. Dorothy Healey, who would later become the most important Communist Party organizer in California, moved to Soto Street in 1931 on assignment for the Young Communist League.[36] Saul Alinsky spent summers as a child with his father in Boyle Heights, an experience that would influence him in the late 1940s to fund the work of the Community Services Organization through his Chicago-based Industrial Areas Foundation.[37]

Another leftist family that had settled in Boyle Heights during the 1930s displays the multigenerational aspects of a radical tradition in the neighborhood. Russian-born Rose Chernin, who would later become executive secretary of the Los Angeles Committee for Protection of the Foreign Born, moved to Boyle Heights in the mid-1930s, after joining the Communist Party in New York City in the late 1920s. What pulled Rose Chernin to Boyle Heights was family; her parents and aunt's family had already moved there from New York. Rose described Boyle Heights of the 1930s as a community of "working people; it had trade unionists, cultural groups, a synagogue, kosher stores, a place where you could buy a Yiddish newspaper and books."[38]

Unlike other Jews in the postwar period, some deliberately chose Boyle Heights in which to raise families, even after exploring other options in Southern California. Ida Fiering had been born in Boyle Heights in 1926, into a Jewish family with a strong socialist background, committed to the preservation of Yiddishkeit culture. Her parents, both born in Kiev, Russia, came to the United States in 1910 and into the City Terrace section of Boyle Heights in 1922. Her father had been among the charter members of the Painter's Union, Local 1348. After attending Malabar Elementary, Belvedere Junior High, and Roosevelt High School (class of 1945), Ida herself attended Berkeley and UCLA before marrying in 1949. After the newlywed couple lived in East Hollywood for one year, they decided to move back to Boyle Heights to start a family and raise their children in what remained of Yiddish culture in the area in 1950. Like many on the left in Boyle Heights during the 1950s, Ida would be involved in secular Jewish organizations such as the Jewish People's Fraternal Order (JPFO) and the City Terrace Cultural Center, but she also majored in Spanish at UCLA, participated in the campaign of Ida Alvarez for state assembly, and claimed a Latina neighbor as her best friend.[39]

This stark political geography of Southern California increasingly made Jewish individuals and institutions in Boyle Heights targets for the growing anticommunist movement in California in the postwar period. On September 7, 1948, Joseph Esquith, the director of the Soto-Michigan Jewish Center, was summoned to testify in front of California's Un-American Activities Committee, chaired by state senator Jack Tenney, a right-wing Republican from Los Angeles. The California committee, which lasted from 1941 to 1949 under Tenney's command, shared information with the federal House Un-American Committee (HUAC), utilizing many of the same tactics of public confrontation, humiliation, and red-baiting pressure in front of media and public officials. Tenney, well known for his anti-Semitism by 1948, often equated communism with Judaism in confronting Jewish witnesses.[40]

Early in the hearings, Tenney accused the Soto-Michigan Center of allowing communist front organizations to use the center, charging that the center's staff, member organizations, and programming all contained communists. His evidence was based in the fact that movies prepared by the Peoples Educational Center had been shown, the Actors Laboratory Theatre had presented several plays, and the International Workers Order had been allowed to rent the facilities. Committee counsel R. E. Combs read into the record references from the *People's Daily World* in which activities at the Soto-Michigan Center had been listed. The most damning evidence to the committee was that the center received substantial funding from the Community Chest, which Tenney alleged was used to fund "communist propaganda."[41]

Esquith, for his part, responded eloquently, reminding the committee that the center "was a laboratory of democracy where free speech, free association, and free assemblage flourished."[42] The Soto-Michigan Center welcomed all groups, in a tradition of an open forum that hearkened back to the social settlement period at the beginning of the twentieth century, its only explicit exception being overt political parties.[43] When the center's board met one week later on September 14, they rushed to support Mr. Esquith and the reputation of the Soto-Michigan Jewish Community Center, unanimously passing a resolution protesting Tenney's attack, condemning the committee's action, and demanding an immediate public response on the part of the Jewish Centers Association governing board. Al Waxman, member of the Soto-Michigan Center board and editor of the *Belvedere Citizen*, felt that "the entire Jewish community was on trial in not having made an immediate answer to the Tenney attack."[44]

However, an immediate and supportive response was not forthcoming from the Jewish Centers Association (JCA), the newly formed umbrella organization (1943) responsible for coordinating activities, controlling finances, and setting policy for all the Jewish community centers in Los Angeles.[45] Instead, the association and the individual centers held a tension-filled joint meeting that, while reaffirming established policies toward openness, also made it clear that the JCA was concerned about getting smeared and labeled by the broad stroke of communism or communist sympathizer.[46] On September 23, the president of the Welfare Federation of Los Angeles wrote to Sam Bates, president of the executive board of the Soto-Michigan Jewish Community Center, asking for "a statement from your Board as to what steps have been taken to investigate and determine whether or not there are grounds for such allegations" as put forward by the Tenney Committee.[47] As the Boyle Heights group received letters of support from various labor unions for their position, a special committee was formed to investigate the situation at JCA urging.[48]

Their report, which showed that less than 3 percent of the total attendance at the center came from accused "communist" organizations, did not satisfy the Welfare Federation of Los Angeles, who continued to worry about being branded as a potential communist front organization. By the end of 1948, the Welfare Federation issued a directive to all its agencies, including the Soto-Michigan Center, to deny its facilities to any organization on the attorney general's subversive list, which had been created by the Tenney Committee. The Soto-Michigan board rejected this directive, claiming that it infringed on its right to set its own policy and that it contradicted the open forum philosophy of the Jewish Centers movement. While this tension led to a standstill between the two organizations, others in the wider Jewish community had already begun to purge perceived communists from their midst. The Jewish

People's Fraternal Order (JPFO), which met regularly at the Soto-Michigan Center and was considered "an integral part of the Jewish Community of Boyle Heights," was challenged as a member within the Los Angeles Jewish Community Council in 1949 and 1950. By early 1951, as the Cold War heated up in Korea, the JFPO had been purged from local ties to the organized Jewish community for being subordinate to the International Workers Order and, therefore, to Moscow.[49]

Most historians of the McCarthy period in Los Angeles have focused on attacks on University of California professors and leftists in Hollywood as defining the era.[50] In working-class districts of Southern California, however, the anticommunist crusade hit labor union and ethnic community leadership with a vengeance that was only hinted at on the west side of town. A series of legislative acts in the late 1940s and early 1950s targeted suspected and former communists, particularly those who had been born abroad, with deportation, denaturalization, and unlimited detention without benefit of trial. The 1947 Taft-Harley Act made it illegal for communists and those "calling for the overthrow of the U.S. government" to participate in American labor unions. The Internal Security Act of 1950 allowed the federal government to deport aliens who admitted or were suspected of ever having joined the Communist Party or any affiliated group. But the law that solidified and expanded the reach of the anticommunist crusade was the McCarren-Walter Act of 1952, which included the provision that naturalized aliens could be "denaturalized" if found to have been communist sympathizers at the time of their citizenship statement of allegiance. Not surprisingly, the U.S. Justice Department almost immediately began to focus on former union leaders in this growing anticommunist campaign, including many who had participated in the growing labor movement of the late 1930s centered in Boyle Heights.

As the implications of these acts for the working-class communities of Southern California became clear, one organization, formed in 1950, took as its sole focus the protection, legal and otherwise, of those held under threat of deportation: the Los Angeles Committee for the Protection of the Foreign Born (LACPFB). The LACPFB was ostensibly a branch organization of the American Committee for the Protection of the Foreign Born, identified as a communist-front organization based in New York City.[51] While the American Committee had branches across the country, the Los Angeles–based group was by far its largest. Yet the very different histories of the two organizations point to a history of difference between East Coast and West Coast versions of radicalism, immigration, and multiracialism. The American Committee was formed in New York in the early 1930s, working overwhelmingly with European immigrant groups that dominated East Coast unions, and was an important Popular Front organization of the late 1930s and early 1940s. By 1959, the American Committee was moribund.[52] The Los Angeles Committee was formed at the height of the anticommunist campaign of the 1950s, dominated by a multiracial group of activists who were often those targeted by the McCarren-Walter Act itself, and lasted well into the late 1960s, when the organization changed its name and became part of the radical milieu of the New Left period.

Most important for our purposes, the LACPFB emerged out of the multiracial communities of Los Angeles's Eastside and Southside, most notably from Boyle Heights. Rose Chernin, from a strong Jewish radical tradition in Boyle Heights, became the organization's executive director in 1951, promptly leading to her arrest later that year under the antiradical Smith Act. However, the largest national group the L.A. Committee sought to protect in Southern California was Mexican, with fourteen Mexican nationals targeted for deportation as early as 1953 out of a total group of eighty. Russia, with thirteen, and Poland, with six, were next in line, and most of these were undoubtedly Jewish. The truly international character of the work was indicated by the diversity of the numbers that followed.[53] By the time the committee looked back on its work from 1965, it had processed 225 cases of threatened deportation and/or denaturalization.[54]

Boyle Heights, and the Eastside in general, probably led the count of those targeted for deportation, and therefore attracted a large amount of the attention of the L.A. Committee. While the LACPFB maintained its major office in downtown Los Angeles, it established an Eastside branch at 3656 East 3rd Street within three years of its founding, with activities directed at the Mexican community by Josefina Yanez. The Eastside Committee for the Protection of the Foreign Born, however, included active members from both the Jewish and the Mexican communities of Boyle Heights. This defense committee was initially formed around fourteen deportees who lived in East Los Angeles in 1953. When "Operation Wetback" was launched in 1954 by the Immigration and Naturalization Service to apprehend "undocumented aliens" in the American Southwest, the LACPFB was uniquely positioned to place this heightened assault on Mexican aliens in a wider historical framework.[55]

In Los Angeles, the unique diversity of the membership of the LACPFB made its protest against the racial profiling of Mexicans by the INS a distinctively multiracial appeal. In May 1954, the LACPFB issued a call to "all democratic-spirited, fair-minded Americans" to protest the actions of the U.S. Immigration and Naturalization Service in raids conducted throughout Los

Angeles. Utilizing the recently approved provisions of the McCarren-Walter Act, the INS had launched mass detentions of Mexican nationals in open-air pens in Elysian Park in downtown Los Angeles under a campaign called "Operation Round-Up." The LACPFB called this campaign a "concentration camp order" by Attorney General Brownell, using rhetoric that could be identified as harassment "by the 350,000 members of the L.A. Jewish Community who are reminded of other pogroms and other concentration camps when they saw or heard of the noon-hour sweep-down on Wilshire Blvd.'s Miracle Mile, wherein 212 young Mexican workers were carried off summarily."[56]

In this manner, the LACPFB flyer went on to link oppressive detention in World War II by the U.S. government of Japanese Americans, with that of Germany under Hitler, pogroms in Eastern Europe, and the actions of the U.S. Immigration Service in the 1950s. It sought to remind "all other Americans who recoil to think that—in our America—people are sought out by the color of their skin; are followed, fingered and picked up on the streets, in their homes and their factories as 'alien,' as 'illegals,' and who can say how many citizens among them." In short, the shared racial histories of various groups that had made up Boyle Heights and other working-class communities in Los Angeles were now marshaled, by the LACPFB, to come together to support the latest victims of mass arrests and unfair jailings: the "thousands of defenseless Mexican nationals" being targeted by the INS.[57]

The Los Angeles Committee replicated this multiethnic appeal in almost all their publications and public pronouncements. The programs from their yearly conferences almost always contained specific appeals to the "Japanese American community" or the "Jewish community" or the "Mexican American community." Rather than collapse all the disparate histories together into one large melting pot approach, the LACPFB consistently kept separate appeals distinct, while placing them all in the same program, brochure, or flyer. The consequence of this sort of political approach, if not its intention, was to both utilize and foment a multiracial sensibility that could be used no matter what specific group was targeted in anti-immigrant measures. Most of these appeals relied on a shared history from neighborhoods like Boyle Heights, as well as an attempt to link histories across the current geographic and social divides in a city like Los Angeles.

Even their major fund-raising annual event had this same sort of focus. The "Festival of Nationalities" seemed patterned after the Soto-Michigan Center's "Festival of Friendship," although this one-day event was intended to raise operating expenses for the LACPFB. Held every year from 1950 until well into the 1960s at the Croatian-American Hall and Picnic Grounds just outside Boyle Heights at 330 South Ford Avenue, this Sunday event saw "garden and meeting turned into booths and squares offering the good, rare foods of many countries." The festival was billed as an "all-day tribute to the Armenians, Mexicans, Africans, Poles, Greeks, Koreans, Jews, Hungarians, Italians, Czechoslovaks, Yugoslavs, Russians, English"—in other words "those who built Los Angeles" and "those who made our country."[58] In the organization's own internal get-togethers, the same spirit of multiculturalism prevailed. When the seven-year deportation case against Edo Mita, the Japanese-born editor of the LACPFB's newsletter, the *Torchlight*, was won in 1958, the LACPFB celebrated by sponsoring an "International Smorgasbord Dinner." Held at the Hungarian Hall just west of downtown, the celebration included "turkey, ham, chicken-flavored Japanese sushi, Mexican guacamole, delicious Hungarian cakes, West Indian punch, Jewish delicacies, Italian antipasto . . . and more."[59]

What the LACPFB could not prevent, however, was the growing tension within various ethnic communities over radicalism in the 1950s, particularly the ideological attack that consistently linked communist infiltration with multicultural sensibilities. A significant segment of American patriotism of the 1950s linked Americanism to staunch anticommunism and support for McCarthyite tactics of exposure and humiliation.[60] Not only did this ideology expand within the growing suburban communities of the United States, but also in ethnic communities trying to reposition themselves around a growing civil rights agenda that could be successful in conservative times. No community better exemplified this growing split, on both ideological and geographic lines, than Los Angeles's Jewish community.

One 1958 incident best exemplifies how far away Jewish members of the LACPFB had moved from establishment Judaism in Los Angeles. Mainstream Judaism was now firmly situated out of Boyle Heights and on the west side of the city, where a middle-class liberal, antiradical sensibility prevailed. On February 7, 1958, the *B'nai B'rith Messenger* reported that Marion and Paul Miller had been honored by the Los Angeles City Council for "their distinguished service to their country," the latest of a long line of commendations for the couple who lived in Rancho Park on the Westside, which also included the honor of naming Marion Miller "outstanding Jewish woman of the year." These accolades came to them because they had been paid informers to the FBI and various anticommunist government committees about the inner workings of the Los Angeles Committee for the Protection of the Foreign Born from 1950 to 1955. Marion Miller, at the urging of the FBI, rose to become the recording secretary for the LACPFB, earning $80 a month for her efforts. Herman Gluck, author of the article, felt that "the whole Jewish community has reason to be proud of these intrepid spirits" due to "their patriotic and self-sacrificing service performed in imminent peril of discovery." The article ended with an emphatic ethnic ring: "The Millers are Jews—good Jews—and I, as a Jew, am as proud of them as I am of Einstein." [61]

Even more revealing was the fact that the citation was presented to the Millers by Rosalind Wyman, the first Jew elected to the Los Angeles City Council in the twentieth century. Often discussed as the second liberal on the council in the 1950s—joining Edward Roybal from Boyle Heights—Wyman critically shaped her political ideology from the postwar suburban sensibilities of Los Angeles's Westside liberalism. While this liberalism included moderate support for civil rights efforts in the city, it also was staunchly anticommunist. Wyman joined the vast majority of her colleagues after 1952 in viewing public housing, for example, as a suspicious socialist experiment, and she led efforts within the city council from 1956 to 1958 in handing over Chavez Ravine to Walter O'Malley to facilitate the move of the Brooklyn Dodgers to Los Angeles. [62]

Not surprisingly, this honor incensed the Los Angeles Committee for the Protection of the Foreign Born, especially its executive director, Rose Chernin, who clearly saw the work of the committee as exemplifying the better half of Jewish tradition during the 1950s. She orchestrated a letter-writing campaign to the city council, particularly directed at Wyman, protesting the honor. One of the committee's biggest supporters, Charlotta A. Bass, editor of the *California Eagle*, Los Angeles's main African American newspaper, wrote Councilwoman Wyman directly to protest an honor for someone "who would spy for a fee." [63] But no one wrote to the city council with more wrath than Rose Chernin:

> We of the Committee, are shocked at this action on the part of the City Council. It is our considered judgment that the Council acted very unwisely in choosing a paid informer to honor as an example for Young Americans . . . It is our considered judgment that this can be construed as a slur on the Jewish Community . . . We believe that an aroused citizenry should protest the action of the L.A. City Council in wasting time to glorify an informer, who like Marion Miller, for $80.00 a month, which she was receiving according to her own statement under oath in Washington, would sell her birthright as an American of Jewish parentage. [64]

This incident clearly showed that the bifurcation of the Jewish community in 1950s Los Angeles had been firmly implanted. While the LACPFB would continue to work on behalf of the undocumented in the 1960s, and Rose Chernin increasingly found sympathetic speaking audiences on college campuses, the local activity of the committee binding various communities together would decline precipitously after 1958. [65]

By 1958, even the liberal Jewish tradition in Boyle Heights began to dwindle considerably due to the aging of the population and the mounting pressures on individuals and institutions that remained in Eastside L.A. to move out. In that year on September 4, the Eastside Jewish Community Center's board met for the last time, formally dissolving after selling the property on Michigan and Soto Streets to the All Nations Foundation. In the six previous years, the Jewish Centers Association had merged the two Eastside centers, cut the resulting organization's budget dramatically, reduced staffing, and finally decided to completely close their Eastside work and completely shift operations to the west side of the city.[66]

For the diminishing numbers of individual Jews who remained in Boyle Heights, it became more and more difficult to retain the quality of Jewish life that had drawn them to Boyle Heights in the first place. Leo Frumkin, who lived in the house in which he had been born in 1928, finally moved out to Monterey Park in 1958 "because the house literally began to fall apart" and he was able to buy a tract home further east for $18,000. By this time, most of his friends, both Jewish and Mexican, had already moved out of the neighborhood to Lakewood and other lower-middle-class neighborhoods farther east near expanding employment opportunities.[67] Another Jewish family, who found themselves to be the last remaining Jews on their block in Boyle Heights, were concerned about their child remaining at his middle school, as it gained a reputation for growing violence and tension. So the father picked the largest Mexican boy in his neighborhood and paid him to protect their son through junior high school in the late 1950s.[68]

Jewish families were faced with difficult choices, and most of them would eventually move out of the neighborhood, no matter how committed they were to Boyle Heights. Committed socialist Ida Fiering, who had been born in Boyle Heights and returned there to raise her own family in 1950, faced a painful dilemma for herself and her family in the fall of 1961. As she surveyed the roster of her child's fifth-grade class, Ida came to the startling conclusion that her son was the only Jewish child left in his class at Malabar Elementary School. Indeed, by 1960 only 4 percent of all Jews in Los Angeles now lived in Boyle Heights.[69] With her strong commitment to raising children in a Jewish environment steeped in radical tradition, Ida and her husband now decided to leave Boyle Heights. This move was made with utter reluctance and ambivalence, given the family's deep roots to the cultural and political history of working-class Jewish life in East L.A.[70]

Only two significant groups of Jews remained in Boyle Heights after the late 1950s, and each remained significantly separated from the rest of L.A.

Jewry. The Jewish elderly of Boyle Heights tended to maintain their residences if their families could not convince them to move out and if their health remained good. As one elderly Jewish woman who had spent thirty years in the garment industry put it, "I'll spend my last days here. And why not? My husband is dead, my children are all grown up. Why should I bother my children, they have their own families. I visit them, once in a while, they come here to take me for a drive, that's all."[71] Harry and Hilda Hoffman, for example, remained in their City Terrace home until 1965, when their grown children "were getting tired of ferrying them to the West Side where all their social activities seemed to be taking place."[72] For those who needed additional care, a move into the Jewish Home for the Aged on Boyle Avenue remained an option until the site was sold in the 1970s and became the Japanese Home for the Aged.

But the longest lasting remnants of Jewish Boyle Heights were the Jewish-owned businesses along Brooklyn Avenue that catered to a multicultural clientele. The owners of Canter's Delicatessen had kept open the original shop on Brooklyn Avenue even after opening a new Fairfax branch in 1948. By the early 1970s, however, even Canter's on Brooklyn shut its doors. Only Phillips Music Store and Zellman Clothiers would remain in Boyle Heights until the 1990s, even though their owners now lived outside the neighborhood, as they adapted to meet the buying needs of the growing Mexican immigrant community.[73] And Jews transplanted to other parts of Los Angeles continued to venture back to the "old neighborhood," and specifically to these businesses, if they wanted to connect to a part of their youth and a time in which Jews lived in a multiracial working-class enclave in Los Angeles.

Forgetting and Remembering Multiracialism

In December of 1998, First Lady Hillary Rodham Clinton kicked off the West Coast version of a White House initiative dedicated to preserving historic American sites by visiting a run-down, largely abandoned synagogue located in Boyle Heights. The selection of the Breed Street Synagogue for preservation was intended to evoke a particular kind of historical remembrance, one intended to connect generations of immigrants and immigrant children from different backgrounds together—while ignoring the complex history of racial interaction in Boyle Heights. While Clinton addressed a crowd of about five hundred made up of local politicians, academic conservators and historians, and representatives of Los Angeles's dispersed Jewish community, local Mexican American residents stood on the sidelines, curious and somewhat bemused. "This shul and the work we are doing together to preserve it for future generations is an important statement," the First Lady told the crowd. "We believe that there must be continuity between generations . . . Boyle Heights immigrants today can think back to those immigrants 60 to 70 years ago who did not speak English—they spoke Yiddish. In honoring this particular building, we honor the past."[74]

Mrs. Clinton's comments reflect an assumption by most Americans that the racial diversity we now see in urban America is a recent phenomenon, and that the changing demographics of American cities are simply a continuing saga of ethnic succession, with one immigrant group gradually and naturally replacing another group of former newcomers as they move up the economic ladder. The complicated racial history of Boyle Heights points instead to a story in which few population movements are "natural," much discontinuity between generations and groups is evident, and the geography of urban America has been decidedly shaped by racialized policy and political turmoil. Moreover, these comments speak to the way in which we have collectively forgotten the history of racial interaction in the past, and the particular way in which the legacies of racial conflict in Los Angeles are erased from the urban landscape.[75]

This particular "forgetting," however, was initiated by the very anticommunist forces that sought to silence progressive politics in the 1950s. From the deportation of ethnic labor leaders to the outright banning of certain forms of speech, the McCarthy and Tenney Committees, and the government bureaucrats who carried out radical purges, began the process of making sure that the history of leftist multiracial organizing in Boyle Heights would be erased. Moreover, ethnic organizations of all groups with an interest in the neighborhood, from the Jewish Centers Association to the Community Services Organization, had to be careful to hide, if not outwardly attack, any connections to leftist organizers who might threaten their own funding or standing in the wider public of Southern California. Yet, it was the ethnic nationalisms of the 1960s, with their focus on empowerment from the grass roots that would be drawn from single ethnicities, that insured the "forgetting" of this multiracial movement.

The multiracialism that had begun as a homegrown neighborhood movement in Boyle Heights would be difficult to sustain once significant numbers of individuals left the confines of the neighborhood for personal, political, or professional reasons. Yet many of the central players continued to be involved in efforts at racial justice in the wider context of Southern California as the civil rights movement gained steam nationally. In 1952, Mel Janapol, who had led the Eastside Center's efforts at multicultural programming, stepped down as board president, and his wife, Esther Janapol, left the board to concentrate her efforts on working directly with Edward Roybal on juvenile delinquency programs. Indeed, many members of the Eastside Center remained loyal supporters, as well as staffers, for Roybal on the city council, leading his efforts at reelection into the 1960s.[76]

The politically committed Jews who moved out of Boyle Heights in the late 1950s and 1960s did not generally leave their politics and multiracial sensibilities behind them. But unlike earlier generations of Jews who moved westward into the suburban communities within the city of Los Angeles, many moved east into the growing multiracial cities increasingly reshaping eastern Los Angeles County, along with former Mexican American and Japanese American residents of Boyle Heights. While this geographic mobility moved them outside of the electoral politics of the city of Los Angeles, they often entered the new racial politics of the county's modest suburbs, such as Monterey Park.[77] Membership in the Monterey Park Democratic Club, for example, included a large number of Jewish Americans, prompting Matthew Martinez, a former Monterey Park City Council member, to note, "All of these people were part of the Democratic Club who were fighting from a strong, heartfelt view of what the Constitution stood for—everybody's equality, everybody's rights."[78]

In the late twentieth century, Jewish Boyle Heights would increasingly become part of the historical memory of a few, rather than a continued part of the present of the neighborhood, yet in time the nature of even this historical memory would be recast by a new Los Angeles desperate for stories of multiculturalism in the city's past. Mrs. Clinton's commemoration of the Breed Street Synagogue was one attempt to recast this history as a story of ethnic succession, but what was missed was the radical politics and multiracial collaborations that had often marked Boyle Heights as a particular site of ethnic cooperation in the midst of racial segregation and political conservatism in Southern California of the 1950s. It is this story that better situates our own search for neighborhoods of diversity that truly worked together in the past and our hope for a multiracial Los Angeles that can work together in the future.

Notes

1. "Boyle Heights: A Sociological Fishbowl," *Fortnight*, October 20, 1954, 20–23.
2. Ibid., 21; Ralph Friedman, "U.N. in Microcosm; Boyle Heights: An Example of Democratic Progress," *Frontier: The Voice of the New West*, March 1955, 12.
3. *Frontier* article, 12; quote is from *Fortnight* article, 21.
4. Robert Fogelson, *The Fragmented Metropolis: Los Angeles, 1850–1930* (Berkeley: University of California Press, 1967), 88, 93, 173; Scott L. Bottles, *Los Angeles and the Automobile: The Making of the Modern City* (Berkeley: University of California Press, 1987), 14–15; Ricardo Romo, *East Los Angeles: History of a Barrio* (Austin: University of Texas Press, 1983), 68, 78–79, 81.
5. Dana Cuff, *The Provisional City: Los Angeles Stories of Architecture and Urbanism* (Cambridge, Mass.: MIT Press, 2000), 100, 116.
6. Max Vorspan and Lloyd P. Gartner, *History of the Jews of Los Angeles* (San Marino: Huntington Library, 1970), 117–19; David Weissman, "Boyle Heights: A Study in Ghettos," *The Reflex* 6.2 (July 1935): 30–31; David Philip Suldiner, "Of Moses and Marx: Folk Ideology Within the Jewish Labor Movement in the United States" (doctoral dissertation, University of California, Los Angeles, 1984), 222–32; Wendy Elliot-Scheinberg, "Boyle Heights: Jewish Ambiance in a Multicultural Neighborhood" (doctoral dissertation, Claremont Graduate University, 2001), 98–142, 234–48.
7. Neil Gabler, *An Empire of Their Own: How the Jews Invented Hollywood* (New York: Crown Publishers, 1988).
8. See Gabler, *An Empire of Their Own*, and Michael Rogin, *Blackface, White Noise: Jewish Immigrants in the Hollywood Melting Pot* (Berkeley: University of California Press, 1996).
9. Matthew Frye Jacobson, *Whiteness of a Different Color: European Immigrants and the Alchemy of Race* (Cambridge, Mass.: Harvard University Press, 1998), 14.
10. See Jacobson, *Whiteness of a Different Color*, 91–135, 171–99, and particularly 92. See also Karen Brodkin, *How Jews Became White Folks and What That Says about Race in America* (New Brunswick, N.J.: Rutgers University Press, 1998).
11. Jacobson, *Whiteness of a Different Color*, 197.
12. Home Owners Loan Corporation City Survey Files, Area D-53, Los Angeles, 1939. National Archives, Washington, D.C., 7. Also quoted in George Lipsitz, *Time Passages: Collective Memory and American Popular Culture* (Minneapolis: University of Minnesota Press, 1990), 137.
13. Kevin Starr, *Embattled Dreams: California in War and Peace, 1940–1950* (New York: Oxford University Press, 2002), 193.
14. Lynn C. Kronzek, "Fairfax . . . A Home, A Community, A Way of Life," in *Legacy: Journal of the Jewish Historical Society of Southern California* 1.4 (Spring 1990): 15, 23–36; Eshref Shevky and Marilyn Williams, *The Social Areas of Los Angeles: Analysis and Typology* (Berkeley: University of California Press, 1949), 157–59.
15. Letter from Morris J. Kay, publisher, *Valley Jewish News*, to John Anson Ford, February 9, 1950, John Anson Ford papers, Box 75, Folder B IV 5i cc(15), Huntington Library.
16. Deborah Dash Moore, *To the Golden Cities: Pursuing the American Jewish Dream in Miami and L.A.* (New York: Free Press, 1994), 42–44; Jackson Mayers, *The San Fernando Valley* (Walnut, Calif.: John D. McIntyre, 1976), 172; James Thomas Keane, *Fritz B. Burns and the Development of Los Angeles: The Biography of a Community Developer and Philanthropist* (Los Angeles: Thomas and Dorothy Leavey Center for the Study of Los Angeles, 2001), 70–71; Greg Hise, *Magnetic Los Angeles: Planning the Twentieth-Century Metropolis* (Baltimore: Johns Hopkins University Press, 1997), 186–215.
17. Memorandum from Milton A. Senn, director, Anti-Defamation League of B'nai B'rith, December 31, 1948, "Report on Efforts in the Los Angeles Area to Circumvent the United States Supreme Court Decisions on Restrictive Covenants," 8. John Anson Ford papers, Box 75, Folder B IV 5i cc(13), Huntington Library.
18. Ibid., 3.
19. Ibid. Tellingly, the only mention of restriction targeted specifically against Jews in this 1948 ADL report was in Lake Elsinore, located in the mountainous region of Riverside County, quite a distance from the major urban or suburban neighborhoods of metropolitan Los Angeles; 5.
20. Moore, *To the Golden Cities*, 23.
21. On the local level, see Mario T. Garcia, *Mexican Americans: Leadership, Ideology, and Identity, 1930–1960* (New Haven: Yale University Press, 1989), 221–22; and Lisa McGirr, *Suburban Warriors: The Origins of the New American Right* (Princeton, N.J.: Princeton University Press, 2001), 182–85. On the national level, see Mary L. Dudziak, *Cold War Civil Rights: Race and the Image of American Democracy*

(Princeton, N.J.: Princeton University Press, 2000), 26–29.

22. Transcript of interview with Leo Frumkin, conducted by Ken Burt and Sojin Kim, Tarzana, California, December 19, 2001, Japanese American National Museum, 7–8.

23. Ibid., 4–7. For an earlier example of Jewish student radicalism in Boyle Heights, see Abraham Hoffman, "Jewish Student Militancy in the Great Depression: The Roosevelt High School Blowouts of 1931," *Branding Iron: Los Angeles Corral*, no. 121 (March 1976), 6–10.

24. Ibid., 9.

25. Herbert Morris Biskar, "A History of the Jewish Centers Association of Los Angeles with Special Reference to Jewish Identity" (doctoral dissertation, University of Southern California, School of Social Work, 1972), 42–45.

26. Minutes of the Board Meeting of the Soto-Michigan Jewish Community Center, May 18, 1949, Box 9, Jewish Centers Association (JCA), Histories file, Archives, Jewish Community Library, Jewish Federation Council of Los Angeles.

27. Minutes of the Board Meeting of the Soto-Michigan Jewish Community Center, June 13, 1950, and October 10, 1950, Box 9, JCA.

28. "Boyle Heights, California: A Sociological Fishbowl," *Fortnight*, October 20, 1954, 23. Keats also set up an intercultural teenage chorus, met regularly with a Mexican American boys group that met at the center, and was a principal organizer of the Hollenbeck Coordinating Youth Council, an activist group set up in the wake of the city's Zoot Suit Riots of 1943.

29. Minutes of the Board Meeting of the Soto-Michigan Jewish Community Center, June 13, 1950, and January 8, 1952, Box 9, JCA. Indeed, Keats would go on to photograph many of the most progressive and intercultural activities of the 1960s, as evidenced by his photographic collection now available at the Southern California Library for Social Studies and Research, Los Angeles, California.

30. Minutes of the Board Meeting of the Soto-Michigan Jewish Community Center, November 10, 1949, February 14, 1950, March 14, 1950, and April 12, 1950, Box 9, JCA; Biskar, "A History of the Jewish Centers Association," 67–69.

31. Minutes of the Board Meeting of the Soto-Michigan Jewish Community Center, November 14, 1950, January 9, 1951, and October 30, 1951, Box 9, JCA.

32. Minutes of the Board Meeting of the Soto-Michigan Jewish Community Center, March 14, 1950, Box 9, JCA.

33. Interview with William Phillips, conducted by Tamara Zwick, February 22, 1990; Minutes of the Board Meeting of the Soto-Michigan Jewish Community Center, April 12, 1950, January 9, 1951, and February 12, 1952, Box 9, JCA.

34. Text in museum exhibition, "Boyle Heights: The Power of Place," Japanese American National Museum, Los Angeles, California, September 2002–February 2003; "Bill Phillips Elected to Head Citizens Committee to Re-Elect Roybal," *Eastside Sun*, February 1, 1951; Anthony F. Macias, "From Pachuco Boogie to Latin Jazz: Mexican Americans, Popular Music, and Urban Culture in Los Angeles, 1940–1965 (doctoral dissertation, University of Michigan, 2001), 127.

35. Interview with William Phillips; JANM exhibition.

36. Dorothy Healey and Maurice Isserman, *Dorothy Healey Remembers: A Life in the American Communist Party* (New York: Oxford University Press, 1990), 39.

37. Rozina Lozano, "The Struggle for Inclusion: A Study of the Community Services Organization in East Los Angeles, 1947–1951" (senior thesis, Stanford University, 2000), 19.

38. Kim Chernin, *In My Mother's House* (New York: Ticknor & Fields, 1983), 161–62, 177–78; Healey and Isserman, *Dorothy Healey Remembers*, 135.

39. Interview with Ida B. Fiering, conducted by Leslye Sneider, February 23, 1990.

40. Edward L. Barrett Jr., *The Tenney Committee: Legislative Investigation of Subversive Activities in California* (Ithaca, N.Y.: Cornell University Press, 1951), 37–39; Moore, *To the Golden Cities*, 201–2.

41. Transcript, vol. 48, 55, quoted in Barrett, *The Tenney Committee*, 38.

42. Moore, *To the Golden Cities*, 201.

43. See Biskar, "A History of the Jewish Centers Association," 67–68.

44. Minutes of Board Meeting of Soto-Michigan Jewish Community Center, September 14, 1948, Box 9, JCA.

45. Biskar, "A History of the Jewish Centers Association," 46–51.

46. Moore, *To the Golden Cities*, 201.

47. Barrett, *The Tenney Committee*, 38.

48. Moore, *To the Golden Cities*, 201–2; Barrett, *The Tenney Committee*, 39; Minutes of the Board Meeting of Soto-Michigan Jewish Community Center, December 14, 1948, Box 9, JCA.

49. Minutes of the Board Meeting of the Soto-Michigan Jewish Community Center, December 14, 1948, Box 9, JCA; Biskar, "A History of the Jewish Centers Association," 68-69; Moore, *To the Golden Cities*, 202–5.

50. See Kevin Starr, *Embattled Dreams: California in War and Peace, 1940–1950* (New York: Oxford University Press, 2002), particularly chapters 10 and 11, for one of the best accounts emphasizing the cultural tension between Southern California "folks" like Tenney and Sam Yorty, who led the anticommunist crusade, and elite liberals and leftists in Hollywood and on campuses.

51. The one book dedicated to the AFCPFB, which directly calls the organization "a tool of American communism" (1) is John W. Sherman, *A Communist Front at Mid-Century: The American Committee for Protection of the Foreign Born, 1933–1959* (New York: Praeger Publishers, 2001).

52. See Sherman, *Communist Front*.

53. Following Mexico, Russia, and Poland, the national origins of targeted deportees of 1953 were (in diminishing order): Armenia, England, Greece, Japan, Austria, Italy, Korea, Romania, and Sweden. Eight other countries had one member each represented in the 80 total targeted deportees of 1953. By 1954, the group of deportees had grown to 110. *The Torch*, May 1953, 7, "Correspondence and Publicity: 1953" Folder, Box 14, American Committee for the Protection of the Foreign Born, Labadie Collection, Department of Special Collections, University of Michigan Library, Ann Arbor, Michigan.

54. 1965 program for Fifteenth Annual Conference, Folder 20, Box 1, Los Angeles Committee for the Protection of the Foreign Born (LACPFB) papers, Southern California Library for Social Studies and Research, Los Angeles, California.

55. For a fuller account of the relationship between the LACPFB and the Mexican American left, see Jeffrey M. Garcilazo, "McCarthyism, Mexican Americans, and the Los Angeles Committee for Protection of the Foreign-Born, 1950–1954," *Western Historical Quarterly* (autumn 2001): 273–95.

56. "A Call to the People of Los Angeles!!" LACPFB: Correspondence and Publicity, 1954 folder, Box 14, ACPFB, Labadie Collection, Department of Special Collections, University of Michigan Library, Ann Arbor, Michigan.

57. Ibid.

58. *Torchlight*, May 1954, LACPFB: Correspondence and Publicity 1954 folder; and program for "Festival of Nationalities," June 7, 1953, LACPFB: Correspondence and Publicity 1953 folder, Box 14, ACPFB, Labadie Collection, Department of Special Collections, University of Michigan Library, Ann Arbor, Michigan; Festival of Nationalities poster, June 14, 1964, folder 21; and press release for the Third Annual Festival of Nationalities Conference, 1954, Folder 22, Box 1, LACPFB papers, Southern California Library for Social Studies and Research, Los Angeles, California. See also Chernin, *My Mother's House*, 243–44; and Garcilazo, "McCarthyism," 283–84.

59. Flyer for Edo Mita Victory Celebration, Folder 22, Box 1, LACPFB papers, Southern California Library.

60. One of the best studies of this kind for Southern California is Lisa McGirr, *Suburban Warriors*, 29–53, which focuses on Orange County, California.

61. Hershel Gluck, "City Council Honors Marion and Paul Miller: Jewish Couple 'Led 6 Lives' for Their Country," *B'nai B'rith Messenger*, February 7, 1958, 4.

62. See Neil J. Sullivan, *The Dodgers Move West* (New York: Oxford University Press, 1987), 103–5, 145–46, 154–55; and Eric Avila, *Popular Culture in the Age of White Flight: Fear and Fantasy in Suburban Los Angeles* (Berkeley: University of California Press, 2004), Chapter 5.

63. Charlotta A. Bass to the Honorable City Council, Att. Mrs. Rosalind Wyman, undated, Folder 25, Box 1, LACPFB papers, Southern California Library.

64. Rose Chernin to Los Angeles City Council, February 11, 1958, Folder 25, Box 1, LACPFB papers, Southern California Library.

65. Garcilazo, "McCarthyism," 294.

66. Facts about the Eastside Jewish Community Center of the Jewish Centers Association, prepared for Budget Subcommittee #10, Community Chest–Welfare Federation of Los Angeles, February 1954, Jewish Centers Association files; Minutes of the Eastside Jewish Community Center, 1954 to 1958, Jewish Centers Association, Box 9.

67. Interview with Leo Frumkin, 35–36.

68. Interview with Richard Duran, conducted by Stephanie Duran, February 18, 1990.

69. Vorspan and Gartner, *History of the Jews of Los Angeles*, 297; Moore, *To the Golden Cities*, 58; Elliot-Schienberg, "Boyle Heights," 11.

70. Interview with Ida B. Fiering, conducted by Leslye Sneider, February 23, 1990.

71. Quote is from *Fortnight* article, 21.

72. Abraham Hoffman, "My Boyle Heights Childhood, Los Angeles, 1940–50s," *Western States Jewish History* 35.1 (fall 2002): 81.

73. Kronzek, "Fairfax," 36–37; interview with William Phillips, conducted by Tamara Zwick, March 5, 1990; Leilah Bernstein, "The Changing Flavors of Jewish Cooking in Southern California," *Los Angeles Times*, March 24, 1999, Metro, B1; Matea Gold, "Era Ends as 78-Year-Old Men's Store Calls It Quits," *Los Angeles Times*, October 4, 1999, Metro, B1.

74. Joseph Trevino and Caitlin Liu, "First Lady Visits Historic Synagogue, Movie House," *Los Angeles Times*, December 11, 1998, Metro, B1.

75. See Norman M. Klein, *The History of Forgetting: Los Angeles and the Erasure of Memory* (London: Verso, 1997) for a longer exploration of this subject.

76. When Roybal decided to give up his council seat in 1962 to run for the U.S. Congress, the shift in Jewish geography in Los Angeles led the city's Democratic Party establishment to pick African American Gilbert Lindsey to replace him, leaving Latinos and the Eastside in general left out and forgotten in the new multiracial coalition. See Raphael J. Sonenshein, *Politics in Black and White: Race and Power in Los Angeles* (Princeton, N.J.: Princeton University Press, 1993), 31, 43–51, 61–66.

77. Leland T. Saito, *Race and Politics: Asian Americans, Latinos, and Whites in a Los Angeles Suburb* (Urbana: University of Illinois Press, 1998), 133–35.

78. Saito, *Race and Politics*, 64.

The Art of the City:
Modernism, Censorship,
and the Emergence of
Los Angeles's Postwar Art Scene

Sarah Schrank

I n the 1960s, the *New York Times*, *Art News*, *Art in America*, *Vogue*, and *Time* magazine covered the Los Angeles art scene and, for the first time, brought its young artists to the forefront of national media attention.[1] *Vogue's* November 1967 issue featured a six-page article by critic John Coplans on the most prominent of Los Angeles's artists, including Edward Kienholz, Ken Price, Craig Kauffman, Billy Al Bengston, Larry Bell, and Robert Irwin. Los Angeles, a city notorious for a lack of civic culture and a hostility toward modernism, suddenly hosted the most exciting trends in contemporary American art, including "junk," "assemblage," "finish-fetish," and the city's own "L.A. Look." Coplans wrote that:

> As few as ten years ago southern California was an intellectual desert. No institution in Los Angeles had enough insight, determination or vitality to bring to bear the kind of pressure needed to create an environment in which art could flourish as a living and vital entity. Given this background, the blossoming of the Los Angeles area as a center of modern art during the past decade seems nothing short of miraculous.[2]

According to Coplans, Los Angeles had spent the past decades in a creative vacuum only to produce a new generation of brash male artists whose hipness was overshadowed only by their genius. He argued that L.A.'s artists "were driven by a compulsive search for quality in their own work" and "by an insistent demand to see first hand the important art of their time."[3]

Despite the city government's internal battles over public art, including a 1951 ban on abstract painting and sculpture and the attempted closure of Edward Kienholz's 1966 exhibit at the Los Angeles County Museum of Art, these artists, known as members of the Ferus Gallery group or, less generously, the Venice Beach "mafia," had indeed emerged as significant Los Angeles–based artists. Today examples of Kienholz's politically and sexually explicit assemblages can be found in most major American modern art museums; Robert Irwin designed the gardens of the new Getty Museum; along with Ed Ruscha, Craig Kauffman, Ken Price, Larry Bell, and Billy Al Bengston, they form the mainstay of the postwar Southern California modernist canon.

Both the Ferus Gallery and Venice Beach have become mythic spaces in Los Angeles cultural lore as sites where a handful of ragtag bohemians produced their artwork on the margins of the city. Even as municipal and county authorities clamped down on artistic expression, these artists overcame local provincialism to emerge stars of the post–abstract expressionism, pop art world. Reiterating Coplans's themes, and going so far as to claim the new art scene as emblematic of the city, in an article enticingly titled "California's Cool Comers," *Time* magazine pointed out that

> in the Southern California landscape, there have sprung up like desert flowers a new variety of artists. [The artists] vary widely but are united by a common dedication to "cool" materials far divorced from the conventions of oil paint and bronze—plastics, neon, acrylics, Plexiglas, aluminum. They also share a preoccupation with a visual illusionism that plays with space and color to make the eye see beyond the surface of the work, perhaps inspired by the clear, bright light of Southern California (on its non-smoggy days).[4]

Not only were the artists themselves cool, but their "cool" materials suggested an inherent connection with the contemporary regional economy. By drawing attention to the artists' use of postwar urban industrial materials, evidence of Los Angeles's economic affluence, *Time* reaffirmed the youthful freshness of the scene, implying a disconnect from any previous historical context.

Yet it was neither inevitable that Los Angeles would host this innovative and commercially successful modern art scene, nor did it spring from nowhere, as implied in the mainstream magazines. Rather, Los Angeles's 1960s art world, and its current prominence as an international art center, benefited from decades of struggle between diverse creative communities and Los Angeles's conservative authorities, including the city council, the Los Angeles Police Department, and the county board of supervisors. Instead of emerging from an "intellectual desert," artists, art spaces, and artworks were products of complex negotiations between civic elites, government officials, and the residents of the city. The question ought not be from what did this art scene emerge, but how did *Los Angeles* end up hosting it when the city had been riddled for decades with the contradiction of desperately wanting highbrow art status without nurturing an art community, indeed, crushing any signs of an avant-garde? This article suggests that the answer lies in the relationship between various arts communities, Los Angeles's historical booster investment in the arts, and the tenacity of specific artists in the face of political repression and spatial isolation.

Artwork and civic imagery formed an integral part of Los Angeles's civic identity from early in the city's Anglo history. From the turn of the century through the 1920s, newspaper, oil, real estate, and tourist interests promoted Los Angeles as a fertile, sunny, open shop paradise with the economic promise of a big city but the feel of a midwestern town. For civic boosters like Harrison Gray Otis, Harry Chandler, and Charles Lummis, fine art was the means by which Los Angeles could attain what they felt were the finer qualities of a major city without the undesirable ones like mass immigration and union disruptions. A citizens' committee received a city charter and established the Municipal Art Commission in 1911, making Los Angeles one of the first American cities to establish a civic body overseeing art and urban aesthetics. The commission saw itself as a control mechanism over the entire infrastructure of the city from the height of public buildings to the design of every lamppost. In a 1924 annual report, the commission stated that it was responsible for approving the design and construction of every "public building, bridge, approach, fence, retaining wall, lamp, lamp post or other similar structure proposed to be erected by or under the authority of the city." Design and construction also included the commissioning and mounting of any civic art, including "all paintings, murals, decorations, inscriptions, stained glass, statues, bas reliefs and other sculptures, monuments, fountains, arches, gates and other structures of a permanent character intended for ornament or commemoration."[5] Such design concerns, from large monuments to the minutiae of ornamentation on public buildings, underscored the extent to which Los Angeles's civic leaders were concerned with urban aesthetics.

Meanwhile, elite art clubs, like the California Art Club and Artland, served as the cultural deacons of Los Angeles, organizing fund-raising drives and helping the Municipal Art Commission articulate an identifiable aesthetic for the city. In 1926 Artland announced in its monthly newsletter that Los Angeles must build a civic cultural center worthy of the Greeks, a veritable "Temple of Art," if the city were to grow and prosper as its wealthy Anglo boosters hoped.[6] The publicized design plan featured a complex built to early modern English specifications including turrets, stone walls, and a drawbridge. While never built, this extraordinary image of civic grandeur carried through much of the 1920s when urban boosters were hard at work selling their city to white, middle-class Americans. Thus, in 1929, the *Los Angeles Examiner* could unblushingly write, "the glory that was Greece was the glory of its unparalleled achievement in the arts. Our artists are earnestly endeavoring to make a similar achievement known the world over as the glory that is Los Angeles."[7] The city was unsuccessful in building any major art institutions or achieving international cultural status during the 1920s, in part because the city council rejected Aline Barnsdall's offer of thirty-six acres of prime Hollywood real estate to build an art center. The oil heiress's eccentric modernist art tastes, her single motherhood, and her socialist politics rendered her a local embarrassment, and the city council and the art clubs spent years mired in legal wrangling over what to do with Barnsdall's Olive Hill property.[8] Eventually the city begrudgingly took the land but only because Barnsdall threatened to turn her property over to the leftist supporters of Tom Mooney if the city did not oblige her, a threat Barnsdall backed up by erecting huge signs on Olive Hill demanding that the California courts immediately release the beleaguered labor activist.[9]

The economic and social conditions of the 1930s proved the civic aspirations of the 1920s too exclusively Anglo-Saxon and bourgeois to fully withstand the challenge of multiethnic modernism, though whitewashing ensured a relative degree of political conservatism in public art. Nevertheless, the Depression marked a creative time for Mexican, Jewish, and African American painters in Los Angeles, many of whom produced murals and appeared in local exhibits. For example, in 1932, renowned Mexican painter David Siqueiros created a mural on Olvera Street, in the newly renovated downtown plaza. What was requested was a festive work for the Mexican-themed tourist district, an exotic but playful piece that inspired and soothed. Instead, Siqueiros produced *Tropical America*, a mural with images of severe native statuary and an angry eagle Mike Davis describes as "evok[ing] the imperial savagery at the origin of the Anglo occupation [of Mexico]."[10] Rather than re-create the Spanish fantasy past or reinforce the local booster mythology of virgin land and orange groves, Siqueiros was inspired by the recent repatriation of Mexican Americans and the plight of migrant farmworkers.[11] Investors in Olvera Street didn't care for the artist's reinterpretation of Los Angeles history and the mural was whitewashed and Siqueiros deported.[12]

Throughout 1936 and 1937, David Siqueiros's twenty-three-year-old protégé, Myer Schaffer, painted hospital murals depicting interracial relationships and critiquing the social-economic causes of disease among the poor and people of color. Like Siqueiros's *Tropical America*, however, Schaffer's work also met the municipal whitewash brush; the majority of his murals were destroyed or altered by the end of the decade. After the Los Angeles Tuberculosis Sanitarium whitewashed a clenched fist from one of his panels, Schaffer credited the federal arts project with encouraging public art in Los Angeles but kept track in the *Jewish Community Press* of the increasing number of social content murals whited out by local authorities.[13]

African American artists too found their 1930s reception to be a mixed one. In 1935, sculptor Beulah Woodard became the first African American to exhibit at the Los Angeles County Museum, showing Afro-centric masks, which were reviewed in the press as "bizarre" artifacts rather than serious artwork. Likewise, in 1937, the Los Angeles Negro Art Association was invited to exhibit at the prestigious Stendahl Gallery but on the back patio rather than in the main gallery.[14] The 1930s marked a complicated moment when the civic hyperbole of the 1920s seemed outdated as progressive public art challenged the old booster images and promoted art as a tool of social revolt, yet the new modernist work was evidently too political and too ethnic to receive more than trite recognition from the city at best, and censorship or destruction at worst.

Disrupted by the war effort, artists took up the 1930s challenge to Los Angeles's restrictive art codes after World War II, but the climate of the cold war made art a particularly volatile site in municipal politics. For a brief period from 1948 to 1951, Los Angeles hosted a remarkable art program of festivals, community centers, galleries, and children's classes, all sponsored by the publicly funded Municipal Art Department, created in 1925. Kenneth Ross, the department's dynamic new director, shifted away from the art clubs' early-twentieth-century goal of creating one central highbrow civic institution, such as an art museum, toward a broader emphasis on community art projects and local cultural centers.[15] In the spring of 1951, the *Los Angeles Times* announced the Art Department's introduction of a "new approach to art with a program intended to bring the enjoyment of art into reach of every person in the city." Instead of supporting one art center, founded on the principles and ideologies of elite Angelenos, the new program promised "to give art exhibits, lectures, films, forums, painting demonstrations, and instructions in arts and crafts in community buildings . . . in every community area."[16]

In October 1951, the Municipal Art Department opened its Annual All City Outdoor Art Show, a two-week festival of art exhibitions held in ten public parks scattered throughout the city, with the largest exhibit held at the Greek Theater in Griffith Park. Started in 1950, the Outdoor Art Show was the foundation of Ross's community-based approach to civic culture, an approach that "encourage[d] public participation in the arts and reached as many people as possible through the media of television, festivals, expositions, and decentralized exhibits."[17] In effect, Ross's art shows turned Los Angeles's public parks into a decentralized civic arena where Angelenos from different neighborhoods could participate in their own community or take a free bus shuttle to any of the other parks. The festivals were popular, attracting upwards of fifty thousand people each year. And, starting with the first festival in 1950, Ross included black and Latino neighborhoods. South Park, located in southern Los Angeles, diagonally between the Crenshaw district and Watts, was chosen by the Municipal Arts Department as one of the ten public parks to host the festival. Ross appointed Beulah Woodard, the same artist who exhibited African masks at the Los Angeles County Museum in 1935, as the director of the South Park festival.[18] Underscoring the explosive potential of racial diversity, Ross did not publicize his support of the black festival. The tenth park was advertised only in the black newspaper, the *California Eagle*, not the *Los Angeles Times*.

Despite the festival's widespread popularity, it soon became clear that it wasn't going to simply close at the end of its run. The *Los Angeles Times* published dozens of letters describing the festival as a "chamber of horrors" and "an insult to the people of Los Angeles."[19] Letters from the San Fernando Valley Professional Artists' Guild and the Coordinating Committee for Traditional Art were also sent to the mayor's office voicing the complaint that modern art was overrepresented and contained communist content.[20] In response, city councilman Harold Harby, chairman of the Building and Safety Committee, opened a public investigation of the art show in Griffith Park. He asked that Kenneth Ross and a select group of exhibiting artists appear in council chambers on October 24 to answer to accusations that there had been a "heavy communist infiltration" of the exhibit. Among the artists in question were Bernard Rosenthal, whose sculpture *Crucifixion* was deemed sacrilegious; Rex Brandt, whose painting of a boat was said to have incorporated a hammer and sickle on the sail (fig. 1); and Gerald Campbell, whose landscape painting was considered nonrealistic (fig. 2).

The hearing, with all of its Tenney committee and HUAC resonance, proceeded in a theatrical manner. Artists displayed their work and fielded questions. Campbell was baited by Harby, who called his painting "screwball art" because the moon depicted in it "wasn't even round." After the end of the long day of testimony, the only conclusion drawn by the Building and Safety Committee was that another public hearing should take place a week later.[21] At the second hearing, Ross defended the exhibit and asked the council to rescind its accusations in the interest of "a constructive program of art for the City of Los Angeles." Ross stated that the council's behavior was ruining Los Angeles's reputation as an art center: "Many thoughtless and unnecessary things have been said . . . , some spokesmen not realizing that the words with which they

Figure 1.
Rex Brandt, *Surge of the Sea*, 1951.
Municipal Art Department All City
Art Show Exhibition Catalog.

Figure 2.
Gerald Campbell, *Landscape*, 1951.
Municipal Art Department All City
Art Show Exhibition Catalog.

describe a work reveal at once their own lack of knowledge. These statements . . . are going to be repeated nationally and unfortunately will not only make those who utter them seem ridiculous, but will make the city itself the laughing stock of rival cities."[22]

A week later the Building and Safety Committee issued the statement that while they "did not believe that any individual artist at this exhibition was a Communist; . . . [they] were equally firm in the belief that [modernists] were being unconsciously used as tools of the Kremlin."[23] As far-fetched as this may appear, in equating modern art with communism at the height of the cold war, Harby subjected to scrutiny all art under municipal auspices. That which was not censored through innuendo was effectively censored through the passage of two committee recommendations. The first forced Kenneth Ross to submit his annual budget to the council for consideration if he wished to continue the All City Art Show, limiting his control over public exhibits. The second divided all city-sponsored exhibits into two, one modern and one traditional, with the Municipal Art Department funding both equally.[24] This meant that the same allocation of funds used for one exhibit would now be used for two. Additional funding had to come from private sources. Jurisdiction over the All City Art Shows thus shifted from the public realm of the Municipal Arts Department to the state-incorporated private organization, the Municipal Art Patrons. The two resolutions passed with a council vote of twelve to one.[25]

Public reaction was so overwhelmingly negative that three months later, the city council rescinded its official statement that the artists involved were unwittingly communist infiltrators. The Building and Safety Committee, however, stepped up its campaign to undermine Kenneth Ross. Despite Ross's compliance with the council's motion that he submit all plans to the council for consideration, Harby remained unsatisfied that his committee had enough of a grip on the city's public art program.[26] Following the 1952 municipal elections, when mayor Fletcher Bowron was ousted in favor of Norris Poulson, candidate of Harby and the anti–public housing factions, the Building and Safety Committee ordered an audit of receipts from recent city sponsored art exhibits. With headlines like "Housing Row Echo Heard in Art Talk" on the front pages of the local papers, the political connections between the recently crushed public housing campaigns and the censorship of public art was not lost on Los Angeles residents.[27] Though the audit proved nothing if not Ross's absolutely scrupulous use of funds, the Municipal Art Patrons withdrew all future funding and bankrupted the Municipal Arts Department. As the city had undermined public housing, public art too would fall victim to red-baiting and bankruptcy. Ross spared few words in responding to Harby:

The artistic policy of the Arts [Department] can be stated in very simple terms: Los Angeles is a city of heterogeneous population and taste. This heterogeneity is part of its richness and is the fertile soil in which, through understanding, tolerance, and objectivity, a mature and significant art can flourish. [S]o long as there is a broad base of expression in the City's artistic program . . . a bigoted insistence on uniformity should not be made by . . . anyone else in the community.[28]

Buttressed by the publicity surrounding the abandonment of "socialistic" public housing, Harby led a crusade against another of Bernard Rosenthal's pieces, this one entitled *The Family* (fig. 3). During the summer of 1954, the city council proclaimed outrage that the new $6 million Police Department Building in downtown Los Angeles was to feature a piece of bronze at a cost of $10,000, an amount included in the total cost of the building.[29] According to Rosenthal, the fourteen-foot sculpture "depicted a mother, father, adolescent child, and infant" and symbolized "the American family protected by the police."[30] Though the Municipal Arts Department and the Board of Public Works had approved the sculpture almost two years earlier, upon viewing a model of the sculpture, Harby called a hearing to discuss revoking Rosenthal's contract.[31] With the exception of councilman Ed Roybal, who several times during the hearing pleaded that the proceedings not turn into another "art hassle," the city council unanimously attacked Rosenthal and Kenneth Ross for purportedly moving ahead with secret plans to install a modernist sculpture on a public building. Harby went so far as to say "this art has been shoved down the throats of the people by a subversive clique."[32] The strongest condemnation of the

Figure 3.
Bernard Rosenthal, *The Family*, 1955. *Los Angeles Examiner* Collection, courtesy of University of Southern California, on behalf of the USC Specialized Libraries and Archival Collections.

sculpture came from councilman Debs who stated that it shows "the artist's low opinion of the American family—without eyes, ears, noses, or brains."[33] Despite the council's efforts, lawyers for the Municipal Art Department found that there was no legal basis upon which to cancel Rosenthal's contract.[34]

With plans moving ahead to install the statue in the interim, the city council received letters from both supporters and detractors of Rosenthal's work. The California Watercolor Society and art teachers across the city wrote the council asking them to give up their efforts to block the statue's installation. Author Irving Stone asked the city council to "hold steadfast in support of [the] excellent Rosenthal sculpture and not allow Harby and the crackpot fringe to disgrace us once again in the eyes of the cultivated world."[35] Art instructor Richard Cassady simply asked, "Why does it always have to be the Los Angeles city council [who] make asses out of themselves?"[36] These supporters reiterated a complaint similar to the one they had expressed during the 1951 Greek Theater hearings: the council's reactions embarrassed the city by attracting negative national attention to Los Angeles's art scene. Rosenthal's detractors, however, had a new complaint. Rather than red-baiting *The Family*, and accusing the artist of promoting communist-influenced art, this time conservative art clubs, as well as private citizens, objected to the vagueness of the statue's ethnic and racial identity. In their letters, detractors revealed what it was about *The Family* that so disturbed them: E. Nealund wrote that "we resent this hideous, abominable thing named faceless, sexless art, costing [us] the sum of $10,380. It is a brazen insult to our intelligence and to our American way of life." The Highland Park Art Guild wrote that "the public is tolerant of private preferences in the arts but regards public representations of itself with a jealous eye." The board of directors of the Women's Club of Hollywood wished to go on record "as being unanimously opposed to this statue. [We] believe it to be an ugly representation of American life." Lastly, F. A. Lydy wrote:

> The Los Angeles press has quoted the sculptor as stating that his faceless and distorted creation is "designed to be seen in its 14-foot size at a distance, with faces kept in simple outline so they cannot be construed as belonging to any definite race or creed in preference to any other." It should not be forgotten that this nation was founded by members of a distinct race whose descendents represent 90% of our present citizenry. Since when, and upon whose authority, is it prohibited to place statuary bearing a likeness of average citizens composing a 90% majority in or upon our public buildings?[37]

These letters deride Rosenthal's *The Family* for appearing un-American, unbeautiful, unwhite, and unrepresentative of Los Angeles's public. In fact, many complaints focused on the "faceless" nature of the artwork, offended that it did not have the characteristics of a "distinct race" but, instead, stood in for anyone the viewer wanted. Harold Harby told the *Los Angeles Examiner* that "[*The Family*] is a shameless, soulless, faceless, raceless, gutless monstrosity that will live in infamy!"[38] Despite the protests, on January 20, 1955, under the watchful gaze of security guards, Los Angeles's Board of Public Works installed Bernard Rosenthal's sculpture on the front of the new downtown Police Department building. Fears that anti–modern art and patriotic protest groups such as the Highland Park Art Guild, the Native Daughters of the Golden West, and the Keep America Committee would steal or vandalize the publicly funded artwork prompted the irony of hiring private guards to oversee municipal police property. Reporters were admitted to the construction grounds only with special permits. And, once the piece was installed, the National Sculpture Society and the Christian Nationalists joined others in picketing the sculpture, proclaiming that "the statue is not representative of our culture."[39] Despite threats of imminent destruction and fears that it would "surely prove deleterious to morality," the sculpture stands today outside the same building.[40]

It was in this context of artistic struggle and repression that the major art scenes of the 1960s would develop, but on the margins of Los Angeles's civic art world, as artists and proponents of public art programs were wracked by ugly cultural politics, red-baiting, and racism. Not surprisingly, the city's 1950s campaign of humiliating public hearings and a calculated lack of municipal funding either forced its avant-garde to retreat underground or pushed promising talent out of the city. The two scenes that emerged most prominently were Venice and the Ferus Gallery. The evidence suggests that clues to their survival lay in the artists' efforts to overcome urban sprawl and disparate art communities to form concentrated scenes. At the same time, the appropriation of a bohemian, beat identity by cultural entrepreneurs harnessed popular support and publicity for the artists. The city council's efforts to eradicate modern art backfired by pushing young artists out of mainstream art forums and into alternative and underground scenes at precisely the moment that a local and national audience was prepared to receive both the scene and the hype. It was in the coffeehouses of Venice that the beats took hold in the early 1950s, and it was in commercial coffeehouses in other parts of Los Angeles that entrepreneurs took hold of the beats, creating a hugely popular and profitable alternative fashion for teenagers and tourists. The more Los Angeles pushed to close down the coffeehouses, the more popular coffeehouses became. And it was Ferus, conveniently located on the gallery strip in West Hollywood, that generated a market of avant-garde collectors and a loyal audience for Los Angeles's pop art and 3-D installations of found materials. This art market helped solidify a scene that strengthened the artists' community and helped overcome the sprawl that left artists isolated and vulnerable to the city's assaults. In 1956, local gallery owner Herman Cherry pessimistically pointed out that

> Los Angeles is a community where artists live under the strangest conditions of any of our major cities. To visit an artist or a gallery one has to brave the nerve-wracking traffic. . . . It makes it exceedingly difficult for artists to get together. There is nothing like . . . a Greenwich Village, or the Left Bank. Efforts in the past to find a meeting place have always failed and were doomed to fail from the nature of the place.[41]

Both Venice Beach and the Ferus Gallery served as spaces to counteract the effect of sprawl and isolation, as well as functioning as centers of "cool" where creative folk and clever entrepreneurs devised artistic personae for the city by playing off Los Angeles's own repressive cultural policies.

Considered by critics to be the runt sibling of the better-known bohemian art circles of the beat generation, New York City's Greenwich Village and San Francisco's North Beach, mid-1950s Venice nevertheless had a vibrant scene of poets, novelists, painters, and other colorful characters. Venice, the early-twentieth-century urban-bourgeois fantasy of developer Abbot Kinney, who had hoped to bring genteel culture to Los Angeles, was by the postwar period a decaying wreck of peeling paint, ostentatious stucco and stinking sewers. Its proximity to the beach, however, and its cheap rents, made it attractive to every type of alternative lifestyle follower, including artists, writers, musicians, student drop-outs, dope smokers, Zen masters, vegetarians, gay men, and lesbians. The Gas House coffeehouse and the Venice West Café functioned as town hall, watering hole, and crash pad for the authors and painters who lived in or visited the beach. Both coffeehouses exhibited and sold artwork produced in the community and hosted live music and poetry readings, creating a civic art center for Venice residents.

The most famous resident of "Venice West" was writer and beat guru Lawrence Lipton. Lipton surrounded himself with lesser known painters and writers of the era like Arthur Richter, Stuart Perkoff, and Charles Newman, but also occasionally hosted famous guests like Allen Ginsberg, Jack Kerouac, Lawrence Ferlinghetti, and Kenneth Rexroth. Frustrated by his lack of writing success, and feeling put out by the lack of attention to the Venice scene, Lipton set out to show the world that Los Angeles did have a beat art culture as good as anything one could find in other cities. The result was his 1959 tome, *The*

Holy Barbarians. Meant as a sociological history of Southern California beat culture, it was interpreted by reviewers and Americans across the country as a guidebook to coolness, a veritable how-to guide to becoming a beatnik.[42] It was both tourist guide and a call to arms:

> Our barbarians come bearded and sandaled, and they speak and write in a language that is not the language of conventional usage. This is not, as it was at the turn of the century, the expatriates in flight from New England gentility and bluenose censorship. It is not the anti-Babbitt caper of the twenties. Nor the politically oriented alienation of the thirties. The present generation has taken note of all these and passed on beyond them to a total rejection of the whole society, and that, in present-day America, means the business civilization. The alienation of the hipsters from the squares is now complete.[43]

Whatever Lipton's personal motives in writing the book, the result was a remarkably successful advertisement for the neighborhood. Complete with photographs of "real" beats and a glossary of beat jargon, *The Holy Barbarians* attracted thousands of tourists and reporters to Venice Beach throughout the summers of 1959 and 1960 (figs. 4 and 5). The influx of cultural voyeurs in shorts and suntan lotion ended what local "old-timers" felt was the genuine Venice experience of bohemian community and anonymity. Lipton's clever encapsulation of the beat experience also attracted unwanted attention from the Los Angeles Police Department, who hoped to track down the narcotics users described in *The Holy Barbarians* in the hopes of a headline-grabbing bust. Even more damaging, however, the media attention armed "square" home owners with sensationalist ammunition about the freaks in their midst. Organized into groups like the Venice Civic Union and the Women's Civic Club of Venice, home owners took the opportunity created by the publication of *The Holy Barbarians* to rid themselves of their neighborhood's bohemian element. In the *Los Angeles Times,* Alfred S. Roberts, president of the Venice Civic Union, complained that since the publication of Lipton's best seller, "beatniks have been pouring into Venice from everywhere. We've got to get on our feet and scream and get these people out of here."[44]

While home owners flipped their collective wigs and wrote angry letters to the papers and the city government, cultural entrepreneurs capitalized on the public interest in hanging out with the beats. In 1959 alone, more than fifty coffeehouses (eateries that didn't serve alcohol) opened in the broader Los Angeles area, from Malibu to the Sunset Strip and Pasadena to as far south as Laguna Beach. With cover charges and seventy-five-cent cups of coffee, these cafes were serious business enterprises with an eye for fashion. Herb Cohen, who opened Cosmo Alley and The Unicorn, required his waitstaff to dress in

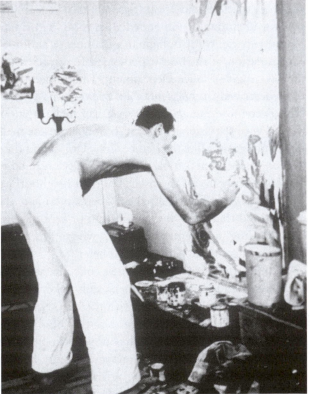

Figure 4.
The Venice West Café, 1959. Photograph by Austin Anton from Lawrence Lipton's *The Holy Barbarians*.

Figure 5.
Poet-painter Charles Newman, 1959. Photograph by Austin Anton from Lawrence Lipton's *The Holy Barbarians*.

"beatnik style to provide atmosphere for the 'square' eager to glimpse the beat world."[45] The *Los Angeles Mirror News* published a series of tourist guides to the beat generation that listed the new cafes along with descriptions of the artwork and the art scene found inside. For example,

> Café Frankenstein, Laguna Beach. Covered inside and out with murals by Burt Schoenburg. Dark atmosphere, several folk singers, a biographer who will write one's life story for 30 cents. Mostly college types; Cat's Pajamas, Arcadia. Walls adorned with ceramics, oils, watercolors, ink drawings by Bill Garner. Mostly San Gabriel customers in teens and early 20s; Club Renaissance, Sunset Boulevard. Has a membership gimmick. Very commercial. Sells records, sandals, books, pottery, ceramics. [Features] experimental films, low budget operas and dramas, pantomime, poetry, small jazz groups. Mostly Hollywood crowd; Dragonwyck, Pasadena. Entire place painted black. Paintings on the walls but one can't see them. Predominantly Negro.[46]

Stories of the economic threat to bar and nightclub owners and tales of thousands of teenagers flocking to late night and possibly racially integrated dens of iniquity made the newspapers frequently enough to pressure both city and county authorities to look into the "coffeehouse problem."[47] Soon the Los Angeles County Board of Supervisors required all coffeehouses to have entertainment licenses.[48]

The ordinance did not simply create an inconvenience and an expense for their owners; it gave the Los Angeles County Sheriff's Department the power to grant the permits at its own discretion. As a result, the police had the power to control sites of cultural activity, usually by making arrests, orchestrating drug searches, and planting spies, as well as through general surveillance. Like San Francisco's North Beach and New York's Greenwich Village, Venice's emergent beat scene was targeted as a center of cool and the police worked hard to infiltrate it. An undercover officer from San Francisco reported that for five months he "faked marijuana dreams, played the harmonica, and even wrote beatnik poetry nobody liked."[49]

In Los Angeles, though, artwork itself contributed to the suspicious nature of the bohemian community. Coffeehouses displaying paintings and sculptures attracted the most attention from the Los Angeles Police Department and the county sheriff's office. An anonymous coffeehouse owner reported in the *Los Angeles Times* that "the average cop thinks there is something subversive about any place with paintings on its wall. He thinks an artist is a suspicious character partly because of the way he may dress and partly because the officer holds art itself suspect."[50] With artwork already historically proving politically problematic in Los Angeles, the concentration of an art scene in

Venice focused municipal authorities' attention on the subversive nature of artists themselves. Another series of public hearings began in August 1959 when Eric "Big Daddy" Nord, owner of the Gas House, requested an entertainment license from the city government. (The Gas House was named for the impending execution of Caryl Chessman.) Venice civic groups stalled the possibility of Nord receiving his license by demanding an investigative public hearing into the subversive goings on at his popular coffeehouse. The Gas House hearings were held at the Los Angeles Police Department Building in the new civic center, where in 1955, conservative art groups and councilman Harold Harby had attempted to stop the installation of Bernard Rosenthal's sculpture *The Family*. According to the papers, Big Daddy Nord took a look at the infamous Rosenthal sculpture and said: "Man, I thought the fuzz were strictly squaresville but dig that chopwork. We're home!"[51]

The first opponent of an entertainment license was A. S. Roberts, representing the five-hundred-member Venice Civic Union. His objections to the Venice beats were that "they drink, make a lot of noise, and act in ways unbecoming normal citizens. I went to the Gas House and saw a bathtub in the middle of it with a man just sitting in it. Just sitting in it!" Roberts's testimony was followed by that of Miss Edgar Hersford, president of the Women's Civic Club of Venice. Upon visiting the Gas House on the fourth of July, Hersford was horrified to find that the beats were "standing around smoking, drinking coffee, and acting nonchalant." Lawrence Lipton responded, "The lady is quite right, of course. It's sinful to be nonchalant. We shall endeavor to be more *chalant* in the future."[52]

Yet it was the idea of an art community, indeed, an artistic civic body, that formed the basis of the Gas House proprietors' arguments in favor of an entertainment license. When the hearings continued on September 2, Al Matthews, attorney and co-owner of the Gas House, told Police Commissioner Thomas Mulherin that "he intend[ed] the Gas House to be an artistic workshop where artists of all kinds [could] strive for freedom of expression—and fail if they wish." Lipton, Nord, singer Julie Meredith, and other representatives of the Venice art community supported Matthews by displaying paintings and sculptures at the hearing as evidence that they were indeed artists invested in their community and not the drug-addled troublemakers the police made them out to be. As further evidence of their dedication to civic spirit, they brought along brightly painted garbage cans to place along the beach.[53]

After months of hearings testimony, Police Commissioner Mulherin refused Big Daddy Nord the entertainment license on the grounds "that some of the so-called beatniks are of bad moral character . . . and that issuance of an entertainment license would increase the problems of the Police Department."[54]

Nord kept the coffeehouse open anyway and was arrested, charged, and convicted of operating without the license. Shortly thereafter, in 1960, the city council's Building and Safety Committee condemned and destroyed the building.[55] Six years later, the Venice West Café closed in the wake of city council hearings to ban bongo drumming at the beach.[56]

The coffeehouse closures only added to the publicity generated by Lipton's *The Holy Barbarians,* turning Venice into a national phenomenon. *Life* magazine picked up the story of the Gas House and ran a piece called "Squaresville, U.S.A. vs. Beatsville" comparing the life of a "square" family living in Kansas to the Venice beats.[57] By encouraging the arrival of more young people, which, in turn, provoked greater crackdowns on the coffeehouses, the national media attention did little to benefit the Venice art scene, which was losing all of its cultural institutions.

Meanwhile, in the midst of a campaign of police repression and censorship, an increase in the number of commercial art galleries in the West Hollywood area, including La Cienega Boulevard, Melrose Avenue, and Sunset Boulevard, exposed the influx of private money into the city's art culture, the growing concentration of an art scene, and a new entrepreneurial savvy on the part of a young generation of artists and collectors. Whereas the first decades of the century saw few commercial galleries established in the city, the late 1950s and early 1960s witnessed the opening of more than one hundred in a few short years and within a couple of square miles. The major La Cienega galleries included Ferus, Primus, Massa, the Ceeje Gallery, and the Galleria Gianni. Galleries off of La Cienega on Melrose Avenue and Beverly Boulevard included the Comara and the Galerie de Ville. Going west on Sunset one found the Everett Elin and the Dwan.[58] The majority, however, opened on La Cienega, creating Los Angeles's first concentrated gallery scene. Dubbed the "New Left Bank" by both the popular media and the national art press, La Cienega Boulevard became a tourist destination. As with the coverage of the beat coffeehouses, newspapers listed weekly tours and special events taking place in the galleries.[59] These tours helped collectors find new talent and the collectors could learn what to look for by attending art appreciation courses at UCLA geared especially toward teaching them how to evaluate the avant-garde in their midst.[60]

At the forefront of the gallery boom, Edward Kienholz and Walter Hopps opened Ferus at 736A La Cienega Boulevard on March 13, 1957. Through a system of barter and trade, Kienholz had already established himself in the middle of La Cienega in 1956 at the Now Gallery. Shortly after Now's opening, Kenneth Ross approached Kienholz and asked if he would set up the

1956 All-City Outdoor Art Show in Barnsdall Park. The censorship, hearings, and audits had ruined Ross's annual public art festival, and by 1956, the All-City Art Show's budget was only $5,400, reduced from the $40,000 allotted in previous years.[61] Left with a tiny budget, the Municipal Art Department needed a contractor who would work for next to nothing, and it appears Kienholz fit the bill. Backed by an army of laborers (many of whom were artists from the Now Gallery), and paid only $1000.00, Kienholz put together the show, including promotion, booth construction, and selection of almost 1,800 artworks.[62] Despite the tiny budget and the enormous amount of labor required, the All-City Art Show was a success, lauded by the mayor's office as "the largest of its kind in the country" (fig. 6). In two and a half days, the festival attracted more than 18,000 people who viewed the work of more than a thousand local artists, both amateur and professional.[63] Working for the city allowed Kienholz to invite other young artists to take part in a mainstream exhibition. Having learned that Kienholz was the city's art festival contractor, Walter Hopps asked if he could have a booth in which to display work from his own avant-garde gallery, the Syndell Studio, in exchange for helping Kienholz set up the festival. Kienholz agreed and the ensuing partnership resulted in the cofounding of the Ferus Gallery.[64]

As fortunate as Kienholz was to get the job with the city, introducing Los Angeles to its own avant-garde was not so simple. Municipal authorities (probably representatives from the Art Department hoping to prevent another embarrassing public art controversy) perused the exhibits and prevented Walter Hopps from displaying one of his own pieces because of its resemblance to pubic hair.[65] One censored piece amid one thousand would certainly seem to indicate that the city was loosening its grip on modernist exhibitions in public spaces, but the experience of the Ferus Gallery,

Figure 6.
All City Art Festival in Barnsdall Park, 1956. Photograph by Edward Kienholz, © Nancy Reddin Kienholz.

not to mention that of the Venice Beach scene, would imply otherwise.

Between March 1957 and November 1958, the Ferus Gallery featured more than thirty-five artists who lived, worked, or hung out in Venice Beach, West Hollywood, and other west-side neighborhoods. Together, Kienholz and Hopps created an irreverent space that eventually hosted many of Los Angeles's most famous artists of the late 1950s and 1960s. The original gallery artists included Kienholz himself, Wallace Berman, Billy Al Bengston, John Altoon, Craig Kauffman, George Herms, and Ed Moses. Run as part artists' cooperative, part studio, and part gallery, Ferus offered a means for young, experimental, and predominantly male artists to exhibit new and potentially controversial work in a city with a history of cultural censure. The artwork exhibited at the Ferus Gallery demonstrated the complicated relationship between art, images of Los Angeles, and postwar prosperity. Postwar prosperity, with its suburban expectations and colorful consumer durables, contributed to a new materialism that could be attained by more Americans than ever before and, through television, could be coveted by nearly everyone else. Some artists, influenced by the film industry, television, and Southern Californian popular culture, embraced the elements of postwar materialism. Billy Al Bengston's neon-colored paintings of motorcycle parts and Ed Ruscha's famous pop images of landscaped wordplay helped define an image of Los Angeles as a newly developed frontier, optimistic, and prosperous (though often tinged with dark surrealism). Others, such as Wallace Berman, George Herms, and Ed Kienholz, critiqued material prosperity with often elaborate installations made of garbage and found objects, creating a style art critics described as "junk art," often freestanding objects and sometimes entire rooms created from materials gathered from the trash, the beach, or the street. The work of many of these Los Angeles junk artists eventually sold in La Cienega Boulevard galleries, appeared in the Los Angeles County Museum of Art and the Museum of Modern Art in New York, and were part of traveling art exhibits.[66] Ironically, as Thomas Crow points out, the art forms that made Los Angeles famous developed out of the artists' marginality. As a result of the city government's censure and Los Angeles's isolation from the national art market, Crow argues, local artists did not expect to sell anything anyway, so works made out of cheap and disposable materials were particularly attractive: "largely excluded from participation in any real art economy, [these artists] were regularly drawn to the cheap disposability of collage and assemblage (much work in the period was never meant to be permanent). On a cognitive level, they exploited these means in order to make sense of their own marginality, recycling the discards of postwar affluence into defiantly deviant reconfigurations."[67]

Ferus became most notorious for the arrest of Wallace Berman shortly after it opened. A private person, Wallace Berman spent ten years experimenting with painting, drawing, and assemblage before holding a public exhibit.[68] While he restricted his own artwork to private parties, Berman promoted his friends' work throughout Los Angeles's bohemian arts community. Berman collected the writings, poetry, photographs, and drawings of the Los Angeles underground art scene and printed them in a periodical called *Semina*.[69] *Semina* served as a textual means of holding together a scattered artists' community and a creative response to the repressive political environment. At the height of Los Angeles's cultural censorship, *Semina* represented an art scene that, until the opening of Ferus and the appearance of the Venice beats, had little geographical space to inhabit—just a textual one. However shy and unassuming Berman might have been, Kienholz and Hopps managed to convince him to exhibit publicly in their new gallery.

On June 7, 1957, Berman set up a display of collages and assemblages, the centerpiece of which was a sequence of four large wooden pieces, *Homage to Herman Hesse*, *Vertitas Panel*, *Cross*, and *Temple*. Each piece resembled heavy, old-fashioned furniture and represented religious, sexual, and domestic themes familiar to those who knew Berman and his family. Outside the intimate group of Venice and Ferus artists, however, Berman's work was open to harsher scrutiny and criticism. An unidentified visitor took offense at a tiny photograph of two people engaged in sexual intercourse suspended from *Cross* and reported to the Los Angeles Police Department that Berman exhibited "lewd and lascivious pornographic art."[70] The police phoned the gallery to give advance notice of their inspection and advised Berman that he could remove objectionable material before they arrived. Berman left the artworks intact. When the Hollywood vice squad arrived, dressed as tourists in Hawaiian shirts, they asked, "Where's the art?"[71] The police walked past the offending photograph and arrested Berman for an ink drawing, created by another artist, which was lying on the floor. Berman was found guilty and sentenced to either thirty days in jail or a $150 fine. Actor Dean Stockwell paid the fine, and shortly thereafter Berman and his family left for San Francisco, damning Los Angeles as the "city of degenerate angels."[72]

Curiously, this incident received no press coverage yet has been documented in every source discussing the Ferus Gallery at length. Peter Plagens includes the arrest in a litany of oppressive acts committed by the City of Los Angeles during the 1950s. In her retrospective catalog of the Ferus exhibitions, Betty Turnbull depicts the event as an unwelcome intrusion into the gallery's sanctity. Rebecca Solnit, in her 1990 survey of the cold war–era California arts scene, describes the arrest as a "disaster."[73] Photographs taken at the time of the arrest by Ferus associate Charles Brittin depict Berman as a martyr, "in dim, streaming light a bearded artist shrinking from the officers who loom over him."[74] Richard Cándida Smith argues that the arrest reveals the innocence of this generation, artists and police alike. Kienholz describes Berman's arrest quite differently. In a 1976 interview, Kienholz referred to the incident as a "big farce." Berman and the other artists hoped that there would be some "hue and cry over the intrusion of police in the arts, which [they] expected. It didn't work."[75] In a recent public discussion at the Getty Research Institute, Brittin remembered that Kienholz had, in fact, waved the drawing at the police and asked, "Is *this* what you're looking for?"[76] A historiographical perspective offers two interpretations: one, of an overly oppressive police intrusion on a peaceful creative haven, and two, a purposefully provocative encounter on the part of the artists meant to draw public attention to themselves.

Placed within the context of Los Angeles's outrageous restrictions on the arts, Ferus serves as a valuable analytical site, because it highlighted the connections between the two main streams of postwar Los Angeles art: the politically irreverent and socially critical art culture of the Venice Beach community and the commercial gallery row on La Cienega. As *Vogue* celebrated Los Angeles's masculine modernism in 1967, *Art News* and the *New York Times* referenced the La Cienega gallery strip as "Los Angeles' Left Bank," or the "West Coast Madison Avenue."[77] These two qualities, bohemian aesthetic and commercial advertising enterprise, characterized a dialectic in which Los Angeles artists found themselves allied with the antimaterialist ideologies of the beats at the same time that they self-consciously commodified their "bohemian" identity. Bought out by suave New York art entrepreneur Irving Blum in 1958, Ferus soon lost much of its ramshackle cooperative feel and became a successful commercial enterprise. Under Blum's guidance, the gallery was moved across the street and given a swank new exterior, and the thirty-five original artists were scaled to six or seven artists, including Kauffman, Bengston, Bell, Price, and Ruscha, artists who had become the forefront of the L.A. Look with its neon colors, hard lines, plastic, and industrial paint. Blum also exhibited major New York names like Andy Warhol, in his first California exhibition, and Roy Lichtenstein. The most interesting aspect of Blum's ownership of the gallery, however, was his capitalization on the bohemian "authenticity" and masculinity of the early Ferus and the Venice Beach community. Blum advertised his artists in major art magazines and journals in the United States and Europe. These advertisements were posters of the featured artist, usually in characteristically macho poses on a surfboard or motorcycle, or roughhousing with

Figure 7.
Ken Price, Ferus Gallery Announcement, 1961. Courtesy of Ken Price Studios.

other men (fig. 7). These images commodified the artists themselves, in part by playing off the bohemian hype of Venice Beach. With its masculine bohemian edge, capitalization on Venice, and Blum's masterful salesmanship, Ferus helped lay the groundwork for the commercial success of Los Angeles's contemporary art.

The paring down of the gallery created bitterness for artists throughout Los Angeles. Matsumi Kanemitsu, a local Japanese American painter would call the Ferus the "Venice Mafia" for its insularity, whiteness, and capitalizing on the beats.[78] And, in fact, under Blum's leadership, the Ferus was reshaped from a dark, hidden artists' studio located off an alley into a bright, highly visible commercial gallery with easy street access off of La Cienega, while the artwork exhibited within it changed from deeply personal junk sculpture and assemblage to pop, a commercially successful art movement that both celebrated and critiqued the very consumer culture that the original Ferus artists tried to circumvent.

Edward Kienholz, who always remained bitter about Blum's involvement in the gallery, nevertheless kept his ties to Ferus and had a one-man show there in 1962. His exhibit, "A Tableau at the Ferus," included the freestanding installation of a brothel named "Roxy's." Despite its overtly sexual nature (one of the prostitutes would gyrate when a spectator pressed a foot pedal) the exhibit survived scrutiny by city authorities. In an interview, Blum explained why the exhibit could remain open: "There were several attorney friends of the [Ferus] gallery by that time, and anytime that possibility [of censorship] surfaced, I think they were able to use their good offices and their influence to persuade people of the legitimacy of what the gallery was up to."[79] Clearly, the gallery had experienced significant change when one considers the response to

Wallace Berman's more innocuous exhibit five years earlier. With broadening commercial appeal, the Ferus Gallery could, by 1962, attract powerful friends whose influence served as a buffer against Los Angeles's provincial attitudes.

Yet, when Kienholz's work appeared in the newly opened Los Angeles County Museum of Art in 1966, the city council and the county board of supervisors reacted violently against the exhibit. Los Angeles municipal and county authorities did not appreciate Kienholz's vision of a brothel (*Roxy's*) nor his tableau of an adolescent sex romp in the backseat of a used car (*Backseat Dodge '38*) in a publicly funded civic space. In a letter to Edward Carter, the president of the Los Angeles County Museum Board of Governors, county supervisor Warren M. Dorn wrote that it was "tragic to me that with so much talent available we should have this kind of depressing, nauseating and revolting expression displayed in our magnificent new public facility."[80]

In response, the county board of supervisors voted to close down the show. This decision was partially supported by the city council, which split down the middle over a resolution to support the board of supervisors "in their efforts to uphold high moral standards by publicly objecting to the Kienholz exhibit. . . . which is partly supported by public funds."[81] While the county and city officials argued over the exhibit, record numbers of visitors lined up to visit the exhibit in the new museum. Henry Hopkins, chief of the museum's educational services, told the *Los Angeles Times* that he expected more than 300,000 visitors. The museum's director, Kenneth Donahue, refused to close the exhibit without a direct order from the museum's board of governors, which the board did not issue.[82] The exhibit remained open.

The Kienholz show at the Los Angeles County Museum of Art signified the arrival of Ferus artists into the mainstream of the Los Angeles, indeed the American, art world. The controversy over the content of the show illustrated that public space was still vulnerable to censure in Los Angeles but that there was enough money and influence supporting the avant-garde from the private sector to prevent the type of censorship that occurred in the early 1950s.

By creating communities, challenging municipal and county authorities, and playing off Los Angeles's complex and contradictory cultural politics, local artists built the city into the country's second art center, and their scene held a place in the international art world of the 1960s. Even the *New York Times* was forced to admit that Los Angeles "has come to deserve its title of the Second Scene," pointing out that "the sensuous colors and 'object' quality of Los Angeles art mirrors perfectly the affluence of California life."[83] While the city basked in cultural acclaim in the national press, the acrid smoke of the 1965

Watts Riot was still singed on buildings in South Central Los Angeles. Watts Towers Art Center directors, Noah Purifoy and Judson Powell, addressed the impact of social inequity and troubled race relations on the city in sculptures also created from urban industrial materials, but in a different context from that of the Venice and Ferus artists. Purifoy and Powell gathered the melted neon, broken glass, and twisted plastic debris from burned stores, homes, and cars and built stark yet beautiful objects. Their exhibit, "66 Signs of Neon," traveled across the country to Washington, D.C., and was presented in Europe as well. Unlike the pieces that Los Angeles junk and pop artists built from the detritus of affluence or the by-products of a growing high-tech industry, Purifoy and Powell's work emerged from the debris of want and frustration (fig. 8). And, unlike cultural promoters who had once claimed Los Angeles "the Athens of America," with artwork the key to international cosmopolitan status, "66 Signs" pointed toward the ill effects of urban growth, affluence, and a civic culture that benefited the wealthy at the expense of poor and minority neighborhoods. With Los Angeles's heralded arrival on the national art scene in the late 1960s, a perceptible tension developed between the pop art that seemed to bolster Los Angeles's image and the artful criticism that commented on the city's enduring social crises (fig. 9). Though the artwork produced by Venice and Ferus artists had originally proven a counterpoint to Los Angeles's early booster images, the impact of cultural commodification, media attention, and a new art market rendered it without a historical context or an obviously critical perspective.

Mike Davis articulated this recurring tension in the well-known "Sunshine or *Noir*" chapter of *City of Quartz: Excavating the Future in Los Angeles*, the brilliant critique that started many Los Angeles scholars on their investigative urban journeys. Davis argued that as both utopia and dystopia, booster excess and failed promise, Los Angeles had become a "stand-in for capitalism," a convenient metaphor for the appropriation of cultural forms by corporate entities.[84] Yet a historical examination of art's centrality in multiple communities allows us to see that Los Angeles, with its self-conscious mythologies and strange paradoxes, reveals complex relationships between visual culture, urban space, and civic life that belie the hegemony of cultural representation. Standing above the 405 freeway, the privately funded Getty Museum, a bastion of modernist high culture easily viewed from miles away, has become a civic symbol of power and cultural status. At the same time, in underfunded enclaves throughout the city, public art programs, restoration projects, festivals, and murals are continuously planned and launched by local artists and community groups. Currently the Los Angeles Cultural Affairs Department

Figure 8.
Noah Purifoy and Judson Powell, *66 Signs of Neon*, 1966, Germany. Courtesy of Noah Purifoy Foundation.

Figure 9.
Billy Al Bengston, *Skinny's 21*, 1961. Courtesy of Wendy Al and Billy Al Bengston.

sponsors twenty-five community art centers citywide and protects more than 1,500 murals. Despite budgetary cutbacks for the arts (which have worsened precipitously in recent months), the demise of public space, and its history of censorship, Los Angeles still hosts an active art culture in the shadow of the city's corporate cultural institutions. Art remains a significant component of the city's cultural life, and the communities of artists continue to grow. Our ability to experience and support them, however, depends on our willingness to seek them out. As Phil Ethington argues in his examination of the haunted spaces left by freeway overpasses, Los Angeles's constructed commuter aesthetic of expansive space and familiar sameness "can only temporarily abolish the spontaneous profusion of the unique and particular."[85] The same is true for Los Angeles's art scenes. The trick is to get off the freeway to find them.

Notes

1. *Art in America*, April 1963, 127; *Art News*, March 1965, 29–61; *Vogue*, November 1, 1967, 184–233; *Time*, August 30, 1968, 38; *New York Times*, May 29, 1969.
2. John Coplans, "Art Blooms," *Vogue*, November 1, 1967, 184–233.
3. Ibid., 186.
4. "A Place in the Sun," *Time*, August 30, 1968, 38.
5. The Municipal Art Commission, *Los Angeles Annual Report 1921–1929*, Section 165, California File #128811, Huntington Library, San Marino, California.
6. *Artland* 1.2 (May 1926): 7; California File #259694, Huntington Library, San Marino, California.
7. *Los Angeles Examiner*, May 21, 1929.
8. Kathryn Smith, "Frank Lloyd Wright, Hollyhock House, and Olive Hill, 1914–1924," *Journal of the Society of Architectural Historians*, March 1979, 18–19; Edmund Teske, interviewed by Susan Larsen, California Oral History Project, Archives of American Art / Smithsonian Institution, Washington D.C., 1980, 45–46; letter from Aline Barnsdall to John Anson Ford, January 17, 1944, John Anson Ford Papers, Box 42, Folder BIII, 10d bb (1), Huntington Library, San Marino, California; Francis William Vreeland, "City Should Acquire All of Olive Hill," *California Graphic*, March 31, 1928, 5; California Art Club Scrapbook, Jan. 1928–July 31, 1928, Box 1/5, Archives of American Art / Smithsonian Institution, Washington, D.C.; "Battle Over Barnsdall Gift: Owner Erects Huge Signs on Olive Hill Land," *Los Angeles Express*, September 8, 1931; "Council's Plan for Park Vote Brings Protest," *Los Angeles Express*, April 3, 1931.
9. "Battle Over Barnsdall Gift."
10. Mike Davis, *City of Quartz: Excavating the Future in Los Angeles* (London: Verso, 1990), 33–34.
11. Shifra Goldman, "Siqueiros and Three Early Murals in Los Angeles," *Art Journal* 33.4 (summer 1974): 322–24.
12. E. F. P. Coughlin, "Deportation Looms for Noted Mexican Artist on Eve of Greatest Triumph," miscellaneous newspaper clipping, October 8, 1932; Myer Schaffer, "Murals in Southern California," *Jewish Community Press*, September 3, 1937, 153–54, Myer Schaffer Papers, Archives of American Art/ Smithsonian Institution, West Coast Regional Center, San Marino, California.
13. Schaffer, "Murals in Southern California," 154.
14. Alma May Cook, "Beulah Woodard Masks Gain Attention," *Los Angeles Herald Express*, September 9, 1935; Jack Austin, "Dark Laughter in American Art: A Brief Appreciation of the Negro Artists of Southern California," *Critic of Critics*, May 1931, Museum of Natural History, Los Angeles County Scrapbook #17; Los Angeles Negro Art Association, *First Annual Exhibition-Painting and Sculpture*,

Los Angeles, November 15 to 27, 1937, Anton Blazek Papers, Microfilm LA 8, #565, Archives of American Art/Smithsonian Institution, West Coast Regional Center, Huntington Library, San Marino, California.

15. Public Relations Office, Cultural Affairs Department, City of Los Angeles, interview with Sandra Rivken by the author, February 20, 2001.

16. "City Takes New Approach to Art," *Los Angeles Times*, April 23, 1951.

17. Kenneth Ross, "Large Art Center City's Greatest Lack: Cultural Facilities Drop Behind Needs of Growing Population," *Los Angeles Times*, August 23, 1953.

18. "Outdoor Art Shows Chairmen Appointed," *California Eagle*, September 14, 1950; "South Park Art Festival Success," *California Eagle*, October 19, 1950, Microfilm Reel No. 37, Southern California Library for Social Research, Los Angeles, California.

19. "Reactions of Viewers at Art Show," *Los Angeles Times*, October 22, 1951.

20. Building and Safety Committee Report, dated November 5, 1951, submitted to the city council on November 6, 1951, Council File No. 50460, Los Angeles City Archives.

21. Public Hearings Proceedings, October 24, 1951, City Council File No. 50460, Los Angeles City Archives.

22. "Art Exhibit at Griffith Park" hearings transcript, October 31, 1951, Council File No. 50460, Los Angeles City Archives.

23. Building and Safety Committee Report.

24. Ibid.

25. Transcript of council proceedings, November 6, 1951, Council File No. 50460, Los Angeles City Archives.

26. Art Commission Proposal for 1952–53 Fiscal Year, submitted by Kenneth Ross to the Building and Safety Committee, April 15, 1952, Council File No. 50460, Los Angeles City Archives.

27. "Housing Row Echo Heard in Art Talk: City Councilmen's Ill Humor Bounces Back in Near Revival of Fracas over Paintings," *Los Angeles Times*, January 15, 1952.

28. Letter to the city council from Kenneth Ross, Municipal Arts Department, December 30, 1953, Council File No. 61479, Los Angeles City Archives.

29. "Art Row of '51 Recalled," *Los Angeles Examiner*, July 25, 1954.

30. "City Art Chief Denies Board OK'd Statue," *Los Angeles Examiner*, July 26, 1954.

31. "Statue Issue Stirs Council," *Los Angeles Examiner*, July 27, 1954; "Ex-Commissioner Contradicted," *Los Angeles Examiner*, July 29, 1954.

32. "Ex-Commissioner Contradicted."

33. "City Art Chief Denies Board OK'd Statue."

34. "Disputed Statue OK: Council Lacks Power to Cancel Pact," *Los Angeles Examiner*, August 27, 1954.

35. Telegram to the city council from Irving Stone, Beverly Hills, n.d., Council File No. 64746, Los Angeles City Archives.

36. Letter to the city council from Richard F. Cassady, filed July 30, 1954, Council File No. 64746, Los Angeles City Archives.

37. Letters to the city council from E. Nealund, the Highland Park Art Guild, the Women's Club of Hollywood, and F. A. Lydy, n.d., Council File 64746, Los Angeles City Archives.

38. *Los Angeles Examiner*, January 21, 1955.

39. *New York Times*, March 21, 1955.

40. Ibid.

41. Herman Cherry, "Los Angeles Revisited," *Arts Magazine*, March 1956, 18.

42. John Arthur Maynard, *Venice West: The Beat Generation in Southern California* (New Brunswick: Rutgers University Press, 1991).

43. Lawrence Lipton, *The Holy Barbarians* (New York: Julian Messner, 1959), preface.

44. Patrick McNulty, "Beatniks and Venice Square Off in Fight," *Los Angeles Times*, August 3, 1959.

45. Frank Laro, "Tourists Make Beatniks Flee Coffeehouses," *Los Angeles Times*, June 2, 1959.

46. *Los Angeles Mirror News*, June 2, 1959.

47. Nightclub owners' concern about the popularity of the coffeehouses encroaching on their business went so far as a $100,000 damage suit lodged against Herb Cohen for purposefully turning a nightclub into a "beatnik hang-out." "Judge Hears Beat Café Suit," *Los Angeles Examiner*, December 17, 1959.

48. "All-Night Coffeehouses to Pay Entertainment Tax," *Los Angeles Examiner*, January 28, 1959; McNulty, "Beatniks and Venice"; "Police Oppose Permit: Beatnik Hearing Becomes Fuzzy," *Los Angeles Examiner*, September 2, 1959; "Gas House Defended," *Los Angeles Examiner*, September 3, 1959; "Beatniks

'Cut Out' of Hearings: Police Examiner Biased, They Say," *Los Angeles Examiner*, September 9, 1959; "Squareville Heatnik Scorches Beatniks," *Los Angeles Examiner*, October 28, 1959; "Judge Hears 'Beat' Café Suit."

49. "Spy Can't Wash," *Los Angeles Examiner*, January 25, 1960; "Beatnik Dicks," *Los Angeles Examiner*, November 18, 1959; "Beatnik Police Nab 85 in New York Dope Raids," *New York Times*, November 9, 1959.

50. Laro, "Tourists Make Beatniks Flee."

51. "Beats Want to Be Pals, Dig It?" *Los Angeles Examiner*, August 29, 1959.

52. Ted Thackery Jr., "Gas House Hearing a 'Drag, Man,'" *Los Angeles Examiner*, August 28, 1959.

53. "Gas House Hearing: Beatniks Described as New Religion," *Los Angeles Herald*, September 3, 1959; "Gas House Defended," *Los Angeles Examiner*, September 3, 1959; Thackery Jr., "Gas House Hearing a 'Drag, Man.'"

54. "Beatniks Lose New Round on Gas House," *Los Angeles Examiner*, December 22, 1959.

55. "Gas House Real Gone in Venice," *Los Angeles Examiner*, April 1, 1960; "Gas House Operator Guilty— No License," *Los Angeles Examiner*, February 16, 1961. Serge Guilbaut, "The Bingo-Bongo Art Scene," *Journal of the Los Angeles Institute of Contemporary Art* 5 (April–May 1975).

56. Maynard, *Venice West*, 166–68.

57. "Squaresville, U.S.A. vs. Beatsville," *Life Magazine*, September 1959.

58. Arthur Millier, "Three Views of La Cienega," *Los Angeles Magazine*, July 1966, 31–33; Janice Lovoos, "Galleries in Los Angeles," *Studio International*, December 1963, 260–62; Gerald Nordland, "City's Amazing Art Expansion Evident in Tour of Galleries," *Los Angeles Mirror*, December 5, 1960; Henry J. Seldis, "L.A. Becomes Hub for Art: City West's Most Active Market; La Cienega Is 'Gallery Row,'" *Los Angeles Times*, February 8, 1959, part v, 12.

59. Peter Selz, "Los Angeles," *Arts Magazine*, February 1958, 20–21; Seldis, "L.A. Becomes Hub for Art"; Nordland, "City's Amazing Art Expansion"; Alfred Frankfurter, "Los Angeles: The New Museum," *Art News*, March 1965, 30–63; John Coplans, "Los Angeles: The Scene," *Art News*, March 1965, 29–61; Grace Glueck, "Los Angeles Regains Vigor as an Art Center," *New York Times*, May 29, 1969.

60. Edward Kienholz, interviewed by Lawrence Weschler, Los Angeles Art Community Oral History Project, University of California, Los Angeles, 1977, 287.

61. Letter to the Municipal Finance Committee from the Mayor's Office, June 24, 1957, Council File No. 79872, Los Angeles City Archives.

62. Letter to the Municipal Art Department from Sherman Sternberg, financial analyst for the City Council, 17 June 1957, Council File No. 79872, Los Angeles City Archives.

63. Letter to the Municipal Art Department from Sherman Sternberg.

64. Kienholz, Los Angeles Art Community Oral History Project, 93–94.

65. Ibid.

66. See Harvey Molotch, "L.A. as Design Product: How Art Works in a Regional Economy," in *The City: Los Angeles and Urban Theory at the End of the Twentieth Century*, ed. Allen J. Scott and Edward W. Soja (Berkeley: University of California Press, 1996), 225–75.

67. Thomas Crow, *The Rise of the Sixties: American and European Art in the Era of Dissent* (New York: Harry N. Abrams, 1996).

68. Assemblage can mean paper collage, paintings containing non-art materials like string, broken glass, or ashes, or freestanding sculptures incorporating various mundane materials and objects of everyday life.

69. Betty Turnbull, *The Last Time I Saw Ferus* (Newport Beach: Newport Harbor Art Museum, 1976), 7.

70. Rebecca Solnit, *Secret Exhibition: Six California Artists of the Cold War Era* (San Francisco: City Lights Books, 1990), 22.

71. Richard Cándida Smith, *Utopia and Dissent: Art, Poetry, and Politics in California* (Berkeley: University of California Press, 1995), 226.

72. Smith, *Utopia and Dissent*, 227; Solnit, *Secret Exhibition*, 23; Turnbull, *The Last Time I Saw Ferus*, 7.

73. Solnit, *Secret Exhibition*, 22.

74. Ibid., 23.

75. Kienholz, Los Angeles Art Community Oral History Project, 148–50.

76. Charles Brittin, discussion panel at the Getty Research Institute, November 18, 2003, author's notes.

77. Jules Langsner, "Local Avant-Garde," *Art News*, November 1956; Langsner, "America's Second Art City," *Art in America*, April 1963, 127; Janice Lovoos, "Galleries in Los Angeles," *Studio International*, December 1963, 260; Glueck, "Los Angeles Retains Vigor as an Art Center."

78. Marjorie Rogers, interview with Matsumi Kanemitsu, Oral History Transcript, Oral History Program, University of California, Los Angeles, 1977.

79. Lawrence Weschler and Joann Phillips, "At the Ferus Gallery, Irving Blum," Oral History Transcript, Oral History Program, University of California, Los Angeles, 1984, 93.

80. Letter from Warren M. Dorn, Supervisor, Fifth District to Edward W. Carter, President, Boards of the County Arts, County of Los Angeles, March 17, 1966, Jan Butterfield Scrapbook, Archives of American Art/Smithsonian Institution, West Coast Regional Center, Huntington Library, San Marino, California.

81. City Council Resolution presented by Councilmen John S. Gibson and Louis R. Nowell, March 29, 1966, City Council File No. 129016, Los Angeles City Archives.

82. Harry Timborn, "Art Show to Open with Heavy Guard," *Los Angeles Times*, March 30, 1966.

83. Glueck, "Los Angeles Retains Vigor as an Art Center."

84. Davis, *City of Quartz*, 18.

85. Philip J. Ethington, "Ghost Neighborhoods: Space, Time and Alienation in Los Angeles," in *Looking for Los Angeles: Architecture, Film, Photography, and the Urban Landscape*, ed. George G. Salas and Michael S. Roth (Los Angeles: Getty Publications, 2001), 29.

Bringing Music to the People: Race, Urban Culture, and Municipal Politics in Postwar Los Angeles

Anthony Macías

I n April of 1940, swing big-band leader Jimmie Lunceford held a concert at the Shrine Auditorium in central Los Angeles, just southwest of downtown.* According to one contemporary account, "their angers flamed by free liquor, 6,000 assorted white, Negro, Mexican, and Filipino jitter-bugs . . . suddenly went wild, smashing windows, flashing razors, and swing-ing fists" in a disturbance that called for twenty-five police officers and left seven people injured. This sensationalistic story described a "riot" provoked by a rival promoter's saboteurs, but trumpeter Gerald Wilson, who performed that night in the Lunceford Orchestra, simply recalled that "they had so many people they had to stop the dance."[1]

One month after this incident, the Los Angeles Police Department refused to issue a Mexican American social organization called La Fiesta Club a per-mit to host a concert featuring the Benny Goodman Orchestra at the Shrine Auditorium. According to the *California Eagle,* the city's oldest African Ameri-can newspaper, the L.A.P.D. officers, along with conservative Los Angeles City Council members, were afraid that whites, blacks, Mexicans, and Filipinos might be allowed to dance together.[2] Also in May of 1940, Mayor Fletcher Bowron prohibited public entertainment establishments from serving alcohol after two in the morning, in an attempt to curtail what a *California Eagle* reporter called the "swarms of white visitors making the rounds" on Central Avenue, the heart of the city's African American jazz district.[3]

As these instances illustrate, popular music and dance performances pro-voked reactionary regulation by the established authorities. This antagonistic relationship suggested a broader social dynamic in which two contrasting models of civil society—one of multiracial musicians, dancers, and entrepre-neurs, the other of white urban elites and law enforcement—played out in multiple music venues, with the public freedom and cultural values of Los Angeles at stake. Reacting to the cross-cultural swing scene, local politicians and municipal arts administrators created a Bureau of Music in order to encourage patriotic citizenship, prevent juvenile delinquency, and bring proper music to the people of the city. After World War II, this dialectic took a new turn, as disc jockeys, dance promoters, and independent record store and record label owners began attracting white youths to rhythm and blues (R&B). In response, the city music bureaucrats tried to replace the popular musical participation of R&B with a more wholesome, state-sanctioned version. When even larger numbers of whites became involved in what would become rock and roll, the forces of law and order intensified the antagonism as they continued to suppress, rather than supplant, the race mixing in their midst. Ultimately, the educational infrastructure, cultural production, and grassroots initiatives of musicians, promoters, and fans brought music to more people, and brought more people from different neighborhoods together, than the official middle-class music programs of the city government did.

Indeed, beginning in the 1930s, when Mexican deportation drives, restrictive housing covenants, and anti-miscegenation laws were the order of the day, successive generations of Angelenos defied the city's rule of racial separation and white domination, creating a multicultural urban civility as they intermingled in dance halls, ballrooms, and auditoriums.[4] This civility was far from utopian, given the existence of sporadic racial prejudice within and between different groups. Nevertheless, dance music facilitated intercultural affinities that went beyond mere politeness or courtesy to include respect and tolerance. In diverse but distinct music scenes, people sustained egalitarian social relations in the face of blatant attacks on their civil liberties. As part of a cultural corollary to ongoing political struggles for dignity and equality, jitterbugs, zoot-suiters, and R&B lowriders exercised their right to freedom of assembly in public spaces.

During the early 1940s, with the rise of the bold, baggy zoot suit, African American hep cats and "slick chicks," along with Mexican American *pachucos* and *pachucas*, became the catalysts for a heated showdown over the public face of the modern metropolis. Not every Mexican American sported the "draped" zoot style, but many of them traversed Los Angeles, dancing the jitterbug to swing music with mixed-race audiences near MacArthur Park at the Royal Palms Hotel, and downtown at the Avadon and Zenda Ballrooms, as well as the Million Dollar and Orpheum theaters. Relying heavily on public streetcars, Mexican Americans also mixed with African Americans at the Club Alabam, Jack's Basket Room, and the Elks Hall on Central Avenue, as well as the Plantation Club in Watts, where they would see bandleaders like Count Basie and Jimmy Lunceford. For example, as a teenager, Soledad "Chole" Camarena, who was disdainfully called a *pachuca* by many of her elders for wearing a powder blue zoot suit, would often go dancing in South Central with the *pachucos* from her Lincoln Heights neighborhood, but they never experienced any interracial violence. As Camarena recalls, "the blacks were friendly as long as the Mexicans talked to them."[5]

On the east side, Boyle Heights trumpeter Paul Lopez explains that formal "black-and-white" balls would be held at "Mexican social clubs," while some "Mexicans would go" dancing "among the Americans" at big band ballrooms throughout the entire Los Angeles area.[6] Significantly, Mexican Americans even patronized several establishments that typically refused to admit African Americans, such as the Palladium Ballroom in Hollywood, the Trianon Ballroom in South Gate, and the Aragon Ballroom in Venice. By participating in the swing music scene, male and female Mexican American youths, often still in high school, contributed to the city's urban culture as dancers, musicians, and singers. Carey McWilliams has observed that during the war years many young Mexican Americans were lured beyond their neighborhoods "into the downtown shopping districts, to the beaches, and above all, to the 'glamor' of Hollywood."[7] In a 1942 study surveying 213 "Mexican boys" aged thirteen to eighteen, the majority of respondents "indicated no serious handicap in their search for amusement, except . . . at certain public beaches, because of their Mexican appearance," while 76 percent "felt that there were enough good places to which they could take a girl to dance."[8]

Yet the other 24 percent encountered racist resistance, and in this same study, 63 percent of the respondents "felt that the police treated Mexican boys more unfairly," while 51 percent claimed to have "been taken to the station for questioning when they had done nothing wrong."[9] In East Los Angeles, police officers "routinely raided parties," "broke up outdoor games and gatherings," "chased young people out" of public parks after sundown, or arrested them for loitering, then beat them "while in custody until they confessed their guilt."[10] Even though Mexican Americans were relatively freer to move about a wider range of the city in their search for public amusements than African Americans were, doing so exposed them to further police discrimination. For instance, in 1943 Alfred Barela and a group of his friends were unjustly detained and harassed by police officers in the beach community of Venice. In a letter to the Los Angeles municipal court judge who had dismissed the charges of disturbing the peace, Barela proclaimed, "We're tired of being told we can't go to this show or that dance hall because we're Mexican or that we better not be seen on the beach front, or that we can't wear draped pants or have our hair cut the way we want to."[11]

In the spring of 1943 several incidents occurred at the Lick Pier amusement park in Venice, where brazen Mexican American zoot-suiters would walk the boardwalk arm-in-arm, four abreast, forcing the locals to disburse before them.[12] In May of 1943 a mob of five hundred white sailors and civilians assaulted a smaller group of Mexican American teenagers exiting Venice's Aragon Ballroom after an evening of dancing.[13] In front of two thousand spectators, the police arrested the victims, many of them from the Alpine Street barrio near Chinatown, but the charges of disturbing the peace were eventually dismissed due to insufficient evidence.[14] Three weeks later, the Alpine, Chavez Ravine, downtown, Boyle Heights, East Los Angeles, and Watts districts erupted into a domestic battle zone as white servicemen and civilian vigilantes, with the cooperation of white Los Angeles Police Department officers, physically put Mexican Americans and African Americans back in their place during the so-called zoot-suit riots.

The African American campaign for a "Double Victory" over racial intolerance abroad and at home had already forced the creation of the Fair Employment Practices Commission, which, despite its halfhearted enforcement, enabled young working-class Angelenos of color, especially Mexican Americans, to cash in on the regional defense-industry economic boom.[15] Decked out in their finest attire, they asserted themselves about town with greater self-confidence. The national press demeaned black and brown zoot-suiters as draft-dodging "dandies," while the local newspapers not only reported the racial comeuppance of supposedly bloodthirsty Mexican "hoodlums," but slanderously denigrated the virtue and respectability of supposedly hypersexual Mexican American "zoot girls" in the public sphere.[16] With the War Production Board rationing fabric, the federal government even filed an injunction against one of the main Los Angeles stores selling zoot suits on the grounds that it used too much cloth. On June 9, 1943, after the worst of the rioting, the Los Angeles City Council got into the act, passing a resolution that officially prohibited wearing zoot suits within the city limits, declaring such action not only "a public nuisance," but also a misdemeanor punishable by thirty days in jail.[17]

Perceiving zoot-suiters as disturbers of the peace and public nuisances, Los Angeles officials responded to the multiracial music culture by creating their own contrasting version. In August of 1944, the city council established the Los Angeles Bureau of Music as part of the Municipal Art Department.[18] Emphasizing the need to recognize "the personal and social power of music," proponents such as Arthur Leslie Jacobs, a musician and member of the Church Federation of Los Angeles, argued that "the Bureau of Music has an important function in city government as it brings people together to make music, and in so doing makes them better neighbors and citizens."[19] To win the support of the Los Angeles City Council and Mayor Bowron, the Music Bureau's founding fathers employed the rhetoric of civic responsibility, claiming that music should receive the same support given schools, libraries, and museums. Artie Mason Carter, founder of the Hollywood Bowl, articulated the bureau's raison d'être, insisting that music, like education, is one of the "community necessities of daily life and should be brought easily within the reach of all."[20]

With its official slogan of "More Music for More People," in 1947 the bureau began a program of youth choruses, adult choruses, and community sings that soon became its signature feature. The program, which presented community singing, followed by talent show-style local entertainment, garnered high praise.[21] *Los Angeles Times* reporter Lee Shipey stated that "in one district a Mexican group and an Anglo-Saxon group combined with such perfect teamwork that all their friends and relatives grew friendlier when they gathered to applaud them. In (another) chorus there are Negroes, Nisei, Chinese, Russian, Spanish and Anglo-Saxon singers creating harmony, both musical and social."[22] Writing about the bureau's efforts in the Chavez Ravine area for the magazine *Music of the West*, Isabel Morse Jones claimed that "this Palo Verde district has been a center of city tensions between the Mexicans and the surrounding neighborhoods. The chorus is helping to relieve those tensions and bring harmony."[23] A journalist from the *California Eagle* attested that in the East 14th Street neighborhood, just south of Pico Boulevard, people no longer worried about juvenile delinquency because from 400 to 600 children, and their parents, turned out for the events sponsored by the Bureau of Music. Despite initial reservations, "the community sings caught on and now neighborhood youths are staging their own acts to supplement the Monday night programs."[24]

Mayor Bowron also lauded the bureau's ameliorative effects, and reaffirmed its overall mission, declaring that because

> the people of this city should have music in their lives, the Music Bureau has endeavored to carry music to all the people. Through the remarkable organization of youth choruses . . . thousands of our growing boys and girls in all sections of this vast community . . . will be better citizens and ours will be a better city in which to live.[25]

The portrayal of the Music Bureau as a deterrent to juvenile delinquency reveals a faith in both cultural determinism and progressive reformism. That it was also depicted as a means toward racial harmony reflects a belief in liberal integrationism. As David Theo Goldberg notes, however, the integration model purported to improve race relations and minority social conditions, "yet the central values continued to be defined monoculturally."[26] Accordingly, the bureau's attempts at exposing all young people to the character-building glories of Western musical masterpieces were flawed by its own cultural biases.

For example, as the *Music Journal* reported in 1952, the Music Bureau presumed that "in an impoverished area where little familiarity with great musical traditions is found among the youngsters," people did not really want such exposure to the arts anyway.[27] By this logic, the various community sings are deemed successful precisely because they are tailored

> to the wishes of the participants. Thus there is no attempt to force a group of Mexican children of little musical experience into the preparation of a Bach cantata for a youth chorus festival program. (Talented members of any chorus naturally have the opportunity to audition for any of the Bureau's several concert-type choruses.) On an occasion when folk songs were a feature of such a festival they had a starring part, however.[28]

Apparently, the music bureaucrats felt that low-income Mexican residents were fit to perform only their quaint folk songs and that they possessed neither the aptitude nor the desire for classical music. In reality, unbeknownst to most Anglo Angelenos, not only were there minority musicians with classical training, but a Mexican American teenage violinist from Roosevelt High School, Edmundo "Don Tosti" Tostado, had held the concert chair as concertmaster of the Los Angeles All-City High School Symphony Orchestra from 1939 to 1941.[29] Moreover, two Mexican American Angelenos, drummer/timpanist Chico Guerrero and bassist Tony Reyes, as well as Mexican trumpeter Rafael Mendez, played for Hollywood studio orchestras during the 1940s, although ethnic Mexicans were excluded from the Los Angeles Philharmonic Orchestra, the city's premier cultural institution.[30] Nevertheless, in the Music Bureau's hierarchical cultural scheme, which made clear distinctions between "the 'highbrow' music-lover" and "the person of little musical knowledge who enjoys community singing," there were no trained Mexican musicians, since Mexican folk songs did not impart any true musical knowledge or experience.[31]

The Music Bureau relegated the city's rich tradition of ethnic Mexican community singing to the periphery, devaluing a poetic oral culture in which traditional lyrics are sung in unison, across generations, at baptisms, *quinceañeras*, weddings, anniversaries, and other social gatherings. For instance, pianist Eddie Cano, who received formal classical training as a youth in Chavez Ravine and Lincoln Heights, vividly recalled "his uncles and family friends performing traditional Mexican music on the porch of his grandfather's house on Sundays."[32] In South Central Los Angeles, Jaime Corral's immigrant mother would sing mariachi and *ranchera* songs with Mexican neighbors on her front porch or at house parties, with somebody invariably accompanying her on acoustic guitar. In 1944, at the age of six, Jaime started singing the popular *rancheras* of Jorge Negrete and Pedro Infante before this audience of neighbors, one of whom taught him the basic chords on the guitar.[33] In addition to these unofficial Mexican choral programs and community sings, Chico Sesma describes hearing Mexican music wafting out of homes and stores while walking down the streets of Boyle Heights, while even some jazz-loving, jitterbugging *pachucos* played acoustic guitar and composed *corridos*.[34]

The Los Angeles Music Bureau never fully incorporated the diverse cultural practices of Mexican Americans, but it did offer more than a hundred summer concerts a year on a rotating basis in the city's public parks, including Lincoln Park and Hollenbeck Park, both in neighborhoods fast becoming majority ethnic Mexican. The bureau tried to consider the varied tastes of its constituents, contracting the Los Angeles Symphony and Civic Center Orchestras, but also the Mexican Tipica Orchestra, which was, with its singers, dancers, and conductor Jose Cordova Cantu, "extremely popular in East Los Angeles."[35] However, apparently these free concerts never came to any predominantly black neighborhoods, nor were existing South Central Los Angeles orchestras or musicians from the Jim Crow black Local 767 of the American Federation of Musicians' Union invited to perform. In this case, the Music Bureau acknowledged Mexicans but ignored blacks, thus casting doubt on its assertion that the city's "music program reaches *all* of its citizens," from the San Fernando Valley to the San Pedro Bay, from Westwood to Lincoln Heights.[36]

If Mayor Bowron, the city council, and the music bureaucrats wanted a working model for successful public music programs, supplemented with private support, that stimulated interest in the arts while bringing together the diverse citizenry of Los Angeles, they needed to look no further than the mixed-race urban cultures of Boyle Heights and South Central Los Angeles. In Boyle Heights, Roosevelt High School provided concert and swing orchestras, as well as excellent courses in music theory, composition, and arranging, while the nonprofit Neighborhood Music School, originally modeled after Progressive settlement schools, gave personal lessons in instrumentation, music theory, and classical music technique, at little or no cost.[37] In Watts, Jordan High School offered music classes and a swing band, while private instructor Lloyd Reese ran a one-man conservatory out of his home, teaching musical mechanics, harmonics, and philosophy. Reese also organized a weeknight swing band rehearsal at a South Central recreation center playground, where young Mexican American and African American musicians from throughout the city would come to practice, and a Sunday rehearsal at the black musicians' local, where his students and other musicians would work out their experimental ideas.[38] Private music teachers like Bill Green also flourished in South Central Los Angeles, as did private institutions like the Gray Conservatory of Music and the Western School of Music.

At Jefferson High School, visionary music teacher Samuel Browne taught classes in reading, arranging, composing, theory, harmony, counterpoint, classical, and opera, encouraging his African American and Mexican American students to find private teachers for intensive study of their respective instruments. In addition to conducting the school orchestra and organizing student jam sessions, Browne scheduled concerts for his school swing band at predominantly white schools like Fairfax High on the west side and Taft High in the San Fernando Valley. Browne also conducted field trips to the Hollywood rehearsals of jazz stars, while professional musicians, Jefferson High alumni, and visiting artists alike would not only play school assemblies, but would talk to, sit in with, and try out new arrangements on, his young music students. Browne created the best music program in the city, and one of the best in the nation, on a par with those at public high schools like Cass Technical and Miller in Detroit, Wendell Phillips in Chicago, and Douglas, Manassa, and Booker T. Washington in Memphis. These high school music programs treated jazz music as a serious discipline, emphasizing its theory and its practice, and were thus at least thirty years ahead of the rest of the country, including most college-level courses.[39]

Jefferson, Jordan, and Roosevelt High Schools not only provided vocational training and professional advice for musicians who were already working night jobs throughout the city, but their programs also turned at-risk youths toward a life of continuing education and study. However, when proponents of the Los Angeles Music Bureau spoke of bringing music to the people, they were not talking about jazz music, nor even all the people. The Music Bureau touted its claim that "Los Angeles is the *first and only* major city in this country to have an organized music program for all its citizens which emphasizes participation," and that "Los Angeles is actively using music as a moving force in drawing together the scattered communities which comprise this metropolitan area of more than 2,000,000 people."[40] Yet these statements ignored a musically mature listening, dancing, and performing public that was already participating in musical expression, and was already connected through both organized and informal networks.

As the summer concert park series illustrated, the Music Bureau neglected certain areas. In fact, rather than bind together the area's "scattered communities," the bureau merely attempted to oversee and administer them. In the bureau's model of municipal integrationism, the twelve different community sings under its auspices were "each of a markedly different character, reflecting the working, economic, racial, and general cultural backgrounds of the participating community."[41] Paradoxically, the community sings were described as tying Southern California's decentralized municipalities "into the metropolis as a whole," but they were "virtually autonomous community enterprises operated under the supervision of the city's Music Bureau."[42] While the local dance music scenes had already successfully achieved a functional integration, the bureau, depicting itself as an equal-opportunity vehicle for uniting Los Angeles, pursued a policy of scientific management that included the appointment of a "city music coordinator."[43] Furthermore, the bureau enjoyed a city budget that expanded from $4,000 in 1944 to $100,000 in 1952, and several of the community sings even had their own bank accounts.[44]

The youth choruses and community sings, along with the civic symphony and public park performances, were evidently popular, boasting impressive attendance figures that expanded from almost 6,000 in 1945 to almost 419,000 in 1952.[45] Although it is difficult to determine the exact attendance figures for the countless swing, R&B, and rock-and-roll concerts, not to mention the various Latin music performances, in and around Los Angeles since the middle 1930s, the city's multicultural urban civility arguably drew together more people from more neighborhoods than municipal and county music programs. Still, when Los Angeles County board supervisor John Anson Ford wrote in 1948 about providing young people "with a priceless opportunity to grow in their . . . understanding of a great and noble art," he was referring to the Los Angeles Philharmonic Orchestra's series of Symphony Concerts for Youth, not the city's public school music programs and orchestras or its neighborhood music schools and instructors, and certainly not its nightclubs, dance halls, and ballrooms.[46] Tellingly, the majority of the Los Angeles County Music Commission's funds supported the Hollywood Bowl, the Los Angeles and Long Beach Philharmonic Orchestras, the Civic Light Opera, the Guild Opera, and other highbrow cultural activities, consciously avoiding "a destructive competition with commercial entertainment in the area."[47] Municipal and metropolitan music programs were indeed competing with an urban popular culture that increasingly blurred the lines between high and low, but local politicians and arts patrons, in their efforts to imbue their fellow Angelenos with moral uplift, cultural refinement, and virtuous citizenship, could not see past their own ideological preconceptions.

In this postwar battle over the hearts and minds of the people, the city's elite did not form a monolithic bloc but included both conservative and liberal factions. The conservative faction was represented by politicians, urban planners, and corporate leaders interested in economic development and the removal of urban "blight," and by the Los Angeles City Council, which continued its wartime jumble of politics and morality.[48] For example, the city council voted against a proposed 1949 ordinance that would have made it illegal for the white musicians' union local "to refuse membership to Negroes." Contentious councilmen rushed through and defeated the measure "to avoid trouble" with the black community, and to avoid "dissension," which they claimed "is exactly what the Communists want."[49] In support of conservative politicians and businessmen, and representing a propertied silent majority, Los Angeles law enforcement agencies provided the muscle to regulate the dancing bodies of residents in a vain attempt to control the widespread race mixing that accompanied the city's "musical miscegenation."[50]

The liberal faction was represented by John Anson Ford, who championed racial integration and subsidized music, and by the Music Bureau, which countered "attacks made by various taxpayers' groups . . . opposed to municipal support of the arts."[51] Music continued to be presented as the perfect tool to produce enlightened citizens, but by 1948, a contingent within the liberal faction also promoted a broad concept of "recreation" that excluded many public amusements, but included athletics and dancing. Hence Mayor Bowron, John Anson Ford, and the other county board supervisors consistently advocated parks and recreation monies, in tandem with officially sanctioned social activities, as a means to defeat juvenile delinquency. Jaime González Monroy, program director of the East Los Angeles Young Men's Christian Association, argued that recreation was not only the "means of bringing youth of all groups together," but the medium through which "many of the evils of racial misunderstanding and conflicts would certainly be lessened."[52] However, even though recreational programs were offered as panaceas against prejudice, and as positive alternatives to the temptations of street life, some observers, such as University of Southern California student Kiyo Umeda, noted that many Los Angeles social agencies discriminated against people who were *pachucos* or suspected gang members.[53]

While the municipal music proponents stressed highbrow cultural enrichment, some of the recreation advocates emphasized physical and emotional release, including social dancing. Thus, in 1952, the Los Angeles Metropolitan Recreation and Youth Services Council extolled the benefits of "wholesome" recreation for young people, listing "dancing and other social events," as well as "music and rhythmic activities" as two of its official categories. Recreation, the council explained, releases the tension of "mental and emotional strain," providing "opportunities to use abilities, muscles, impulses, tendencies, not permitted use during work," while "discharging aggression" and "satisfying social hunger." In addition, recreation "maintains emotional balance," granting "temporary escape from intolerable realities."[54]

Yet African Americans already possessed a long tradition of refreshing the body and relaxing the mind after a hard week's labor. As Robin Kelley claims, in darkened dance halls, blues clubs, and jook joints, black workers, in spite of occasional fights, reinforced a sense of community and expressed an often socially circumscribed sexuality. By reclaiming their overworked bodies for pleasure, they undermined capitalist labor discipline and the Protestant work ethic, and by "dressing up," they constructed "a collective identity based on something other than wage work."[55] As Rosa Linda Fregoso argues, dance, with its "ritual properties," is also "central to the everyday life of Chicano and Chicana working-class culture," not just as "an end in itself," but as a pleasurable and meaningful "means to express one's relation to the world through stylized movement."[56] In Los Angeles, the communal, emotionally engaging vernacular traditions of Mexican Americans and African Americans almost certainly reached more people, and better reflected the multiracial character of the city, than the official ersatz version of expressive culture.

Rather than wait for the city's Music Bureau to bring music appreciation to a public park near them, or for the county board of supervisors to fund their social activities, many Mexican American and African American communities drew upon their own resources. By July of 1946, the Catholic Youth Organization had enrolled more than five thousand Mexican American boys and girls in athletics, orchestral music, dramatics, art, and dancing programs, with ninety-one gangs represented.[57] In Mexican districts like La Colonia, in the heart of Watts, the Catholic Church would host *jamaicas*. These bazaars, or charity sales, were more like block parties, since residents would come out and dance to *rancheras*, polkas, and swing tunes.[58] Weekly dances were sponsored by Mexican American neighborhood associations, while informal "home parties" enticed adults and youths and often included African Americans, Italian Americans, and Irish Americans, thereby "maintaining social cohesion and developing community ties."[59]

In 1950 a cross-cultural "Twilight 'Til Dawn" benefit dance to raise money for the Boy Scouts of Los Angeles was held at El Sombrero, a downtown Latin nightclub owned by a wealthy Mexican couple. With members of the Alta Qualidad Club assisting the local black hostesses, this philanthropic event boasted Joe Adams, the first African American disc jockey in Los Angeles, as the master of ceremonies. Revealing the breadth of popular styles missing from the municipal music programs, the evening's entertainment included a jazz contest for local musicians, "nimble swing . . . square dancing," solo performances by soprano and jazz vocalists, a rhythm-and-blues vocal harmony group, and a Latin band.[60] During the postwar years, the Armenta Brothers band would play at Our Lady of Lourdes Catholic Church in East Los Angeles, while all around the city enterprising young people hired bands to play at neighborhood playgrounds, and car clubs organized dances and "battle of the bands" concerts in which Mexican American groups "played R&B and Latin music."[61]

These grassroots initiatives complemented a bustling, multiethnic commercial dance scene during the late 1940s, a transitional postswing period in which black musical styles like jump blues, gospel, urban blues, and boogie-woogie blended into a new genre called rhythm and blues. In fact, from 1945 through the early 1950s, Los Angeles was home to the largest number of independent R&B labels in the country, including Modern, 4 Star, Exclusive, Excelsior, Aladdin, Specialty, and Imperial.[62] For several years in the mid-1940s, at least half of the nation's best-selling R&B recordings came out of Southern California.[63] Nevertheless, the county board of supervisors and Los Angeles Bureau of Music concept of music participation did not encompass the exciting "race music" that circulated throughout the urban soundscape via record retailers, jukebox operators, nightclub promoters, and, especially, white disc jockeys. Al Jarvis became the first disc jockey in Los Angeles to play jazz on his 1930s radio program, "Your Make-Believe Ballroom." Hunter Hancock followed in 1943 with his one-hour show, "Holiday in Harlem," and its opening refrain: "From blues to ballads, from bebop to boogie, featuring the very best in Negro entertainment." In 1948, Hancock became the first disc jockey to play an all-rhythm-and-blues format with his daily three-hour program, "Harlem Matinee," which was quite popular among Mexican Americans and African Americans.[64]

In 1948, Johnny Otis, the veteran Central Avenue swing drummer, singer, bandleader, and composer, brought the gutbucket grooves of his Barrelhouse Club in Watts to a largely Mexican American audience at the Angeles Hall on First Street in Boyle Heights.[65] By 1950 Otis began promoting and starring in Sunday shows at the Angeles Hall, where Boyle Heights resident Ed Frias remembers Mexican Americans and African Americans from "different segments of the city" gathering to see local black "honking" tenor saxophonists Cecil "Big Jay" McNeely, Joe Houston, and Chuck Higgins.[66] In this exuberant, swaggering style, the "honkers" would make their horns squeal, bleat, and growl, hitting one low note repeatedly in extended solos that worked the crowd into a frenzy. Regular Angeles Hall acts Big Jay McNeely, Johnny Otis, and the Armenta Brothers continued to draw enthusiastic fans through 1955.[67] The Mexican Americans and African Americans who met there were the primary rhythm-and-blues fans in Los Angeles, but despite many cultural affinities, their social interaction had its limits.

For example, Ed Frias remembers seeing "black guys with Anglo girls, but you did not see black guys with Chicana girls. That was a no no . . . among the Mexicans."[68] In 1951 and 1952, Chole Camarena, who had gone dancing on Central Avenue in the war years, would see Joe Liggins and the Honeydrippers at the Angeles Hall, where she and her Lincoln Heights friends would chat with Mexican Americans from other neighborhoods over pitchers of beer. Among the regular patrons, there were two young African American men who would ask Chole and her Mexican American friend Mable to dance. The two young women always said yes, but the exchange was limited to the dance floor, for as Chole says, "We did not socialize with them or bring them home with us." Nonetheless, their willingness to dance with black partners earned them "bad reputations" as "nigger lovers."[69] In essence, the antiblack bigotry of Camarena's Mexican American companions was stronger than, but compatible with, their love of African American music.

In fact, Mexican American fans, particularly car club members, played a key role in the success of local African American artists, as R&B records became the cruising anthems of neighborhood lowriders.[70] For instance, one night in 1950, Big Jay McNeely, the "king of the honking tenor saxophonists," drew so many cars to neighboring drive-in theaters at Whittier and Atlantic Boulevards in East Los Angeles that traffic was blocked "in every direction." According to then-novice Anglo American disc jockey Dick "Huggy Boy" Hugg, "the place went so crazy the sheriffs had to come out to control things."[71] In their McNeely mania, Mexican Americans showed the way to other Angelenos, and their taste for rhythm and blues "was greatly responsible for the music's early exposure to and acceptance by young whites around Los Angeles."[72] In fact, Huggy Boy himself was introduced to African American music by Mexican Americans while working and living in East Los Angeles in the late 1940s.[73]

By the summer of 1950, white Angelenos were getting hip to the raucous R&B of Big Jay McNeely, whose band typically included his brother, Bob, on baritone saxophone; drummer Jimmy Wright, a white hipster who cruised his customized convertible with Huntington Park car clubs; white guitarist "Porky" Harris, an ex-sailor who usually played in hillbilly bands; and, on occasion, Mexican American saxophonist Jess Rubio, from Anaheim, Orange County.

McNeely became very popular in white, working-class towns in southeast Los Angeles such as Huntington Park, Lakewood, and South Gate. McNeely was also big in Bell, which Britt Woodman, an African American trombonist from Watts, described as "prejudiced," and in Bell Gardens, which had been derisively labeled "Billy Goat Acres" because of the many "Okies" who settled there in the 1930s.[74] These communities "became bastions of rhythm and blues fever very early, thanks in part to the car clubs and the kids' growing love of honking saxophonists."[75] Apparently, any anti-Negro sentiment these white youths may have harbored was also compatible with their love of black music.

Once African American R&B caught on among working-class Mexican Americans and European Americans in east and southeast Los Angeles, it was not long before the music reached a broader, citywide audience. This process advanced apace in the early 1950s, when jazz promoter and "pop" radio disc jockey Gene Norman would throw R&B "Jubilees" featuring Wynonie Harris and Big Jay McNeely at the Shrine Auditorium. In downtown Los Angeles, Huggy Boy promoted Big Jay at the Orpheum Theater, while Hunter Hancock hosted McNeely at the Olympic Auditorium, both to mixed Anglo and Mexican American audiences. As McNeely claims, "the authorities were trying to shut me out of Los Angeles. They didn't like me playing at the high schools or the theaters, 'cause I was bringing whites and Spanish and black kids together and rilin' 'em up." During this time McNeely also played in the Orange County town of Fullerton, and in the recently developed San Fernando Valley, where "the audience would be all white."[76]

Emotionally expressive African American rhythm and blues called out to white youths within a context of increasing suburbanization. After World War II, housing shortages, postwar prosperity, population growth, and white flight from the central city, among many factors, led to a suburban home-owning boom that complemented the national baby boom. Yet in the subdivisions of identical tract houses along the Los Angeles periphery, many youths were raised in a monotonous cultural environment characterized not only by racial homogeneity and social conformity, but by a profound estrangement between neighbors, and between parents and children.[77] In contrast, black music and dance, which emphasize "personal stylization" and "individual improvisation . . . within a communal tradition and collective setting," appeared very appealing, as did the "back-and-forth interaction" between spectators and performers typical of African American celebration.[78] The subliminal tonality and ecstatic crescendo of wildly hypnotic honking tenor saxophone solos in general, and Big Jay McNeely's bottom-heavy sound and full vibrato technique in particular, induced a heightened emotional state.[79] As a new generation of white Angelenos discovered how "black social dancing circulates social energy," rhythm and blues opened a new front in the culture war over virtuous citizenship and proper civil society.[80]

For example, in the early 1950s, Johnny Otis hosted weekly half-hour television programs on three local stations, but in response to whites socializing with African, Mexican, and Asian Americans, police officers would "hassle the kids standing in line to get into the television show."[81] Despite rumors of impending racial strife or gang violence, as Otis remembers, "We never had any trouble, the people got along great."[82] Of course, there were still occasional inter- and intra-ethnic tensions, but Southern California's popular music and dance culture continued to bring young people together in a creative manner. For instance, by 1950, when the large record stores downtown and in Hollywood would not even stock records by black artists, a local African American entrepreneur, John Dolphin, purchased late-night airtime on a local radio station and hired a disc jockey to broadcast from his twenty-four-hour record store, Dolphin's of Hollywood. The store was actually located at East Vernon and Central avenues in South Central Los Angeles, but Dolphin reportedly reasoned, "If Negroes can't go to Hollywood, then I'll bring Hollywood to Negroes." Dolphin even built a small, Hollywood-quality recording studio in the back of his store, so that he could record new songs from local artists, press the records on his own label, then sell them right on the premises.

In late 1953, Huggy Boy began hosting a live rhythm-and-blues program from the large front window of Dolphin's establishment. Yelling "Keep alive and listen in!" over the show's blaring tenor saxophone theme song, "All Night Long," Huggy Boy would invite all of his listeners to turn their cars around and drive to "Vernon and Central, Central and Vernon."[83] As a result, R&B stars, actors, Mexican Americans from the east side, and whites from throughout the city and suburbs gravitated to John Dolphin's record store after hours, making it "the most happening place in Los Angeles." On weekend nights Vernon Avenue traffic would be bumper to bumper, while Huggy Boy addressed the people cruising outside the store, his voice echoing from their automobile radios. Restless white youths, some of whom traveled more than thirty miles from the suburban San Fernando Valley, ignored their parents' advice and drove to the commercial heart of black Los Angeles to buy hard-to-find R&B records.[84] Needless to say, the cultural tourism of curious Anglos was taken quite seriously by Los Angeles law enforcement.

Compared to the 1940s swing scene, R&B had crossed over to a young white audience on an unprecedented scale. This new problem required a new solution. In 1950, Chief of Police William H. Parker had begun to transform the Los Angeles Police Department into a professional, mobile, aggressive force.[85] More than any of his predecessors, Chief Parker crusaded against race mixing and inner-city vice, to the point of using inflated crime statistics and dubious racial theories to scare up funding resources and amass political power.[86] In the name of fighting juvenile delinquency, drugs, and gangs, police officers zealously reinforced the racial status quo by patrolling the physical boundaries between areas. For instance, Newton Street Division policemen would enter John Dolphin's store, turning whites away or escorting them from the premises with the warning that "Central Avenue was too dangerous for white people." According to the Los Angeles *Sentinel*, an African American publication, one night a dozen officers formed a human chain at the front door, "terrifying Caucasian customers . . . and rousting them from the neighborhood." Huggy Boy recalls that after two o'clock in the morning when the bars closed, Dolphin's and the neighboring barbecue restaurants would be packed, but uniformed police officers "would chase away the white kids," while undercover agents would search blacks on "suspicion of" selling drugs. In late 1954, Dolphin gathered a petition of 150 black business people from the neighborhood protesting these tactics. Sergeant George Restovich countered that the gatherings violated a ten o'clock curfew, and that other businessmen complained about teenagers assembling on sidewalks while Dolphin's outside loudspeaker blared music onto the street.[87]

In short, when whites joined Negroes and Mexicans in greater numbers, the rhythm-and-blues scene was deemed subversive. As the leading independent label distributors reported to *Billboard* magazine in 1952, "a major portion of the R&B sides now being sold are bought by Spanish and mixed-nationality buyers," due largely to promotion by Los Angeles disc jockeys.[88] In 1954, so many white teenagers were buying rhythm-and-blues records that it caused a national moral furor over allegedly "obscene" lyrics. In Long Beach, after a local radio station banned R&B records, the sheriff's department went even further, banning "offending" records from all area jukeboxes. In 1955, twenty-five leading Los Angeles disc jockeys bowed to censors at the Junior National Audience Board by agreeing to "avoid public airing of records which [were] believed objectionable."[89]

Among the local disc jockeys, Huggy Boy played more risqué songs than his rivals, much to the delight of his young listeners, who soon began to engage in an entirely new kind of music participation. In particular, Mexican Americans, who made up a considerable part of his audience, requested songs on Huggy Boy's dedication shows, declaring their love and broken hearts, while representing their neighborhoods, during the night's broadcast.[90] Another white disc jockey, Art Laboe, became the first to play rock and roll in Los Angeles when he debuted in 1955. Laboe was also one of the first, along with Huggy Boy, to openly welcome Mexican Americans onto his program, playing their dedications on the air. Beginning in 1956, Laboe's live remote transmissions from local drive-in restaurants in Hollywood and midcity attracted such a legion of lowriders that a two-hundred-car capacity restaurant was built in southwestern Los Angeles to accommodate his following. Teenage Mexican American car customizers from all across the city finally found a place in which they could congregate, and a medium through which their voices could be heard, as Laboe aired thousands of dedications.[91]

While young people found new outlets for their self-expression, the powers that be cracked down on allegedly obscene cultural influences. For example, by 1955 Johnny Otis operated his own studio and record label, and he also had a daily radio program through which he showcased and disseminated R&B styles. Consequently, he encountered stiff opposition from "major record companies, publishing firms, radio and TV stations, ballrooms, and police departments," as well as "church and parent groups" alarmed about the negative effect of rhythm and blues on white youth.[92] Undaunted by the arbiters of morality, Otis continued to promote the southern California dance parties he staged with business partner Hal Zeiger. According to Otis, "as the music grew in popularity, more and more white kids came to our dances, sometimes . . . even dancing with African American and Mexican American teenagers." Glaring officers who "hated to see white kids attending the dances with Black and Chicano youngsters . . . would stand around . . . harassing [the teenagers] with bullshit questions, checking their ID's." As this campaign of intimidation intensified into one of sabotage, the policemen even invoked obscure Progressive-era laws designed to restrict underage youth dancing.[93]

In a parallel development, in 1956 the Los Angeles County Board of Supervisors, voting on an existing law that all public dance areas must be walled, rejected a new licensing code amendment that would have allowed parks to sponsor dancing in the open. Even John Anson Ford, the longtime liberal politico, objected to liberalizing the rule, claiming that it "would lead to a lot of dancing in the darkness," and thus "might contribute to 'increased juvenile delinquency.'" Whether Ford's reservations reflected a fear of actual criminal acts by minors, or merely of youth sexuality, the board effectively outlawed dancing by young people in public parks, even as civic resources in poorer neighborhoods dwindled.[94]

In Los Angeles County, laws regarding public park dances may have been strict, but laws regarding general underage dances were relatively lax. In Los

Angeles, on the other hand, all public dances within city limits needed board of education permit approval, effectively restricting them to school grounds. By 1956, this limitation on all-ages dances, along with disruptive police harassment, spurred promoters like Johnny Otis to move their events outside of Los Angeles.[95] Art Laboe, who had begun to emcee live music shows in 1957 at the Shrine Auditorium and the Orpheum, United Artists, and Paramount Theaters downtown, also looked to neighboring independent cities.[96] Nineteen miles to the south in Long Beach, three thousand to four thousand teenagers at a time would pack the Civic Municipal Auditorium to enjoy the steady backbeat and ribald lyrics of African American artists, while Otis and his partner Zeiger "often paid off the firemen and police" to avoid trouble.[97] The multicultural urban civility of the swing and R&B eras thus changed over time, adapting to new tactics in an intensifying culture clash with municipal authorities.

Art Laboe had also been renting the Long Beach Municipal Auditorium, but both he and Otis began staging the majority of their dances at the American Legion Stadium in El Monte, a blue-collar city twelve miles east of Los Angeles in the San Gabriel Valley.[98] Friday and Saturday night rhythm-and-blues dances at the El Monte Legion Stadium drew up to two thousand black, white, Asian American, and Mexican American teenagers from all over Los Angeles city and county, becoming an alternative cultural institution from the mid-1950s through the mid-1960s. Linked by radio stations and freeways, young people converged in El Monte, where, as Laboe remembers, "white kids from Beverly Hills, black kids from Compton, and local Chicano kids used to come . . . every weekend."[99] Marta Maestas recalls that, at a time when interracial dating "was unacceptable," at El Monte in the mid-1950s, "it was Latina women with a black man. It was black girls with Latino boys. But, it was kind of an easy mix."[100]

Richard Rodriguez, who grew up in nearby Duarte, claims that by the late 1950s you would see "more blacks dating white girls and Chicana girls" at the El Monte Legion Stadium dances, and "every now and then you might see a white man with a black girl or a white man with a Mexican girl, or vice versa." Rodriguez recalls, "when I went to El Monte, I felt that I could date anybody I wanted to; I could dance with anybody I wanted to"; nevertheless, "if you dated a black girl, your parents would probably move out of the area."[101] While racial interaction still had limits, a new generation increasingly participated in cross-cultural socializing, as well as occasional drinking and fighting in the parking lot, where young people also engaged in necking, and more, in the backseats of cars, confirming John Anson Ford's worst fears of dirty dancing and delinquent behavior after dark.[102]

In 1956, the El Monte City Council revoked the dance permit they had issued to Hal Zeiger on the grounds that "rock and roll creates an unwholesome, unhealthy situation," but Otis fought back against what he called "racism, under the guise of all-American morality." Arguing that the decision was designed to prevent youth race mixing, Otis, joined by Al Jarvis and Hunter Hancock, representatives of the American Civil Liberties Union, the National Association for the Advancement of Colored People, and the recently integrated musicians' union Local 47, successfully pressured the council into rescinding their ban.[103] In Los Angeles, the Bureau of Music continued to promote "good citizenship through music" as late as September 1957, but the youth choruses and community sings must have been a harder sell compared to the El Monte Legion Stadium's "raw sexual energy" and lively musical participation, which included multiracial dance contests that produced popular Mexican American dance steps like the Pachuco Hop and the Corrido Rock.[104] In this charged atmosphere, audiences were thrilled by regular performers like The Penguins, Jesse Belvin, Don & Dewey, the Carlos Brothers, Rosie & the Originals, Sal Chico's Masked Phantom Band, the Salas Brothers, Cannibal and the Headhunters, and Thee Midnighters.

The Jaguars, an R&B vocal harmony quartet composed of two African Americans, a Mexican American, and an Italian American from Fremont High School in South Central Los Angeles, were also popular at the El Monte dances. After appearing on Hunter Hancock's R&B television program, "Rhythm and Bluesville," the Jaguars became an instant local success in 1955. Carrying popular music to all corners of the area, they played not only the El Monte Legion Stadium and the Long Beach Municipal Auditorium, but also Santa Monica's Pacific Ocean Park, and, crossing into Music Bureau territory, the Hollywood Bowl.[105] Another El Monte regular, Ritchie Valens, was a product of racially diverse San Fernando High School, as reflected in his first band, the Silhouettes, a rhythm-and-blues unit composed of African Americans, Mexican Americans, Italian Americans, and a Japanese American. Valens bridged cultures with his music, which incorporated black R&B, white country and western, and traditional Mexican styles, at public schools and private parties throughout the San Fernando–Pacoima area.

For instance, Valens played many house parties for the local Mexican American car club, the Lobos, and for white car clubs like the Igniters, the Drifters, and the Lost Angels, whose members, despite some initial racist reservations, were soon won over. According to Silhouettes' saxophonist Walter Takaki, "Ritchie actually got the two gangs, the Lobos and the Angels, a little bit closer together. Whenever he was playing, they would get along just fine."[106]

Even the Silhouettes' rehearsals would often become spontaneous dances as neighborhood teens gathered outside the garage of Valens's African American neighbors, Conrad and Bill Jones.[107] In late 1958, as a solo artist achieving national popularity, Valens performed from Hawai'i to New York, then combined Los Angeles radio station appearances with recurring performances at Pacific Ocean Park, El Monte Legion Stadium, Long Beach Municipal Auditorium, and even Disneyland in Anaheim. With each performance, Valens sparked moments of creative connection, bringing together people from different ethnicities and backgrounds. Moreover, Valens, along with many of the era's local musicians, inspired an entire generation of Angelenos to pick up an instrument and start a rock-and-roll garage band.

The cultural practices and entrepreneurial infrastructure associated with an irrepressible R&B scene complicate pessimistic assessments of postwar Southern California that overemphasize the domination of politicians and the police. Like its swing predecessor, R&B resisted social segregation and highbrow reification by fostering contact and comprehension, as well as musical and physical expression, in public spaces. Yet the interracial tensions, and uneven rates of economic, social, and spatial mobility, between Mexican, African, Anglo, and Asian Americans complicate optimistic assessments that overemphasize the resistance of postwar subcultures and youth cultures. The simultaneity of cooperation and conflict, of fellowship and friction, qualifies both pessimistic and optimistic historical interpretations. A pragmatic reading, on the other hand, suggests that urban dance scenes brought people together without completely erasing personal prejudice or the institutional racism that privileged whites and some Mexican Americans over African Americans. Such an interpretation acknowledges internal dissension, but still recognizes that people could be bound together by music, dance, car culture, and clothing styles more than they were separated by race or class.

A pragmatic approach illuminates the full story, warts and all, but still recognizes the power of music to provide not only the soundtrack to a shared expressive culture, but an impetus to question the patronizing moral values and divisive ethnic notions of the status quo. Without romanticizing interethnic and interclass cultural sharing, scholars can gauge the transgressive potential of musical dialogues within and across community boundaries. Without overestimating the control of the elites or the opposition of the people, we can better understand the practical possibilities and limitations of popular music and dance, as well as "the ways in which audiences, through their own agency, both challenge and reproduce the dominant ideology."[108]

For a time, postwar liberals retained the Progressive reformers' faith in the ability of social engineering to transform society, as city leaders tried to engage with, and invest in, the life experiences of young Angelenos. Unfortunately, musical uplift went hand in hand with municipal regulation and punitive policing. In response to the legal challenges; the social, economic, and political gains; and the cultural incursions made by racial groups, local authorities attempted to maintain a sense of order by monitoring and disciplining the musicians, dancers, and listeners who navigated the topography of metropolitan Los Angeles. In contrast, from social dancing to music education, grassroots activity, and entrepreneurial production, the city's multicultural urban civility more successfully brought music participation to more people, connecting an often fragmented populace in its leisure. In other words, music teachers, record store owners, disc jockeys, concert promoters, nightclub impresarios, and professional performers more fully realized the original goal of the Los Angeles Music Bureau's programs. Ultimately, the diverse, street-oriented urban culture represented a more populist public sphere than the one envisioned by the city councilmen, county supervisors, and cultural institution apparatchiks who privileged classical symphonies and choral sings when increasing numbers of Angelenos wanted raunchy rockers, romantic ballads, and mellow instrumentals.

These competing visions of Los Angeles, from above and below, both hinged on the cultural influence of the region's two largest racial minorities. Yet due to the logical imperatives and racialized rewards of a systemic "possessive investment in whiteness," the dialectic between these two models of civil society developed without reconciliation, without a synthesis between antithetical worldviews.[109] And so this unresolved relationship continues, from the culture wars of the 1960s to those of the present. By studying the power struggles over public space and common values in the past, perhaps we can learn from the lessons of Los Angeles to ensure a truly democratic American culture for the future.

Notes

* For critical feedback on earlier drafts, thanks to Danny Widener, Eric Avila, the members of the Los Angeles History Research Group at the Huntington Library, and the readers and editors at the *American Quarterly*. For funding support, thanks to the University of California, Los Angeles, where I was an Institute of American Cultures/Los Tigres Del Norte postdoctoral fellow at the Chicano Studies Research Center. Throughout this essay, "Mexican American" is used rather than "Chicano/a," although many Mexican Americans of the period simply referred to themselves as "Mexican." "Ethnic Mexican" is used to denote both Mexicans born in Mexico and Mexican Americans together. "Anglo" or "white" is used to generally describe Southern California European Americans, a population group that included white ethnics such as Italian or Jewish Americans, as well as poor white migrants from

Oklahoma, Arkansas, and Texas, and their postwar suburban children. "African American" and the later term "black" are used, although the period term "Negro" is occasionally used in context.

1. Jack Hirshberg, "6,000 Jitterbugs Riot at Lunceford Date," *Metronome* 56 (April 1940), 10, as quoted in David W. Stowe, *Swing Changes: Big-Band Jazz in New Deal America* (Cambridge, Mass.: Harvard University Press, 1994), 31. For Gerald Wilson's assessment, see Clora Bryant et al., eds., *Central Avenue Sounds: Jazz in Los Angeles* (Berkeley: University of California Press, 1998), 325–26.

2. "Leaders Protest Dance Hall Ban," *California Eagle* (May 30, 1940), 1. Yet in 1940 the L.A.P.D. allowed twenty Ku Klux Klansmen to march uninterrupted through the streets of downtown to city hall. See Ralph Eastman, "'Pitchin' up a Boogie': African-American Musicians, Nightlife, and Music Venues in Los Angeles, 1930–1945," in *California Soul: Music of African Americans in the West*, ed. Jacqueline Cogdell DjeDje and Eddie S. Meadows (Berkeley: University of California Press, 1998), 80.

3. Bryant et al., *Central Avenue Sounds*, 199; *California Eagle* (May 16, 1940), B 2.

4. My use of the term *civility* is inspired by Roger Keil, who writes about the "contradictory civility" of Los Angeles, where workers of color began "to claim spaces of alternative civility" after the 1992 uprising, building "a civil society from below" through "a network of democratic self-organization." See Roger Keil, *Los Angeles: Globalization, Urbanization and Social Struggles* (Chichester, England: John Wiley & Sons, 1998), 34–35.

5. Soledad "Chole" Camarena Ray, interviewed by the author, Colton, California, August 19, 1999.

6. Paul Lopez, interviewed by the author, Los Angeles, Californa, September 2, 1998.

7. Carey McWilliams, *North from Mexico: The Spanish-Speaking People of the United States* (New York: Praeger Publishers, 1990; originally 1948), 218.

8. Charles Dinnijes Withers, "Problems of Mexican Boys" (master's thesis, University of Southern California, 1942), 83.

9. Ibid.

10. Eduardo Obregón Pagán, *Murder at the Sleepy Lagoon: Zoot Suits, Race, and Riot in Wartime L.A.* (Chapel Hill: University of North Carolina, 2003), 49.

11. Alfred Barela, letter to the Honorable Arthur S. Guerin, May 21, 1943, as quoted in George J. Sánchez, *Becoming Mexican American: Ethnicity, Culture and Identity in Chicano Los Angeles, 1900–1945* (New York: Oxford University Press, 1993), 253.

12. Beatrice Griffith, *American Me* (Westport, Conn.: Greenwood Press, 1948), 18.

13. Ibid.; Pagán, *Murder at the Sleepy Lagoon*, 163.

14. See Rodolfo F. Acuña, *Occupied America: A History of Chicanos*, 5th ed. (Pearson Longman, 2003), 251.

15. Despite widespread discrimination in the war industries, Mexican Americans were often hired at places that did not hire African Americans. See Kevin Allen Leonard, "'Brothers Under the Skin'? African Americans, Mexican Americans, and World War II California," in *The Way We Really Were: The Golden State in the Second Great War*, ed. Roger W. Lotchin (Chicago: University of Illinois Press, 2000), 191.

16. Robin D. G. Kelley, *Race Rebels: Culture, Politics, and the Black Working Class* (New York: Free Press, 1996), 172; McWilliams, *North from Mexico*, 231; Griffith, *American Me*, 322, n 6.

17. William Overend, "The '43 Zoot Suit Riots Reexamined," *Los Angeles Times,* May 9, 1978, sec. 4, 5; Mauricio Mazón, *The Zoot Suit Riots: The Psychology of Symbolic Annihilation* (Austin: University of Texas Press, 1984), 75; McWilliams, *North from Mexico*, 225; "Zoot Suit Riots," VHS, directed by Joseph Tovares (PBS, *The American Experience*, 2002).

18. C. Sharpless Hickman, "Civic Music Administration in Los Angeles," *Music Journal* 10.4 (April 1952): 21.

19. City of Los Angeles brochure, undated, John Anson Ford Collection, Box 41, Folder 9, Huntington Library, San Marino, California.

20. City of Los Angeles brochure.

21. Hickman, "Civic Music Administration," 34; C. Sharpless Hickman, "Community Sings in Los Angeles," *Music Journal* 10.28–29 (January 1952): 28–29.

22. City of Los Angeles brochure. Nisei refers to the American-born, second-generation children of Japanese immigrants.

23. Ibid.

24. Ibid.

25. Ibid.

26. David Theo Goldberg, *Multiculturalism: A Critical Reader* (Oxford: Blackwell Publishers, 1994), 6.

27. Hickman, "Civic Music Administration," 34.
28. Ibid., 33.
29. Don Tosti, interviewed by the author, Palm Springs, California, August 20, 1998; Chico Sesma, interviewed by the author, Boyle Heights, California, September 4, 1998.
30. A handful of African American Angelenos worked in Hollywood studio orchestras in the 1940s and 1950s; Paul Lopez interview. Mexican American pianist Eddie Cano, whose uncle and grandfather were professional classical musicians, recalls that the Los Angeles Philharmonic Orchestra was "locked up" to Mexicans, and that by the 1950s there were "one or two blacks," but they "had a hell of a time getting in there." See Steven Loza, *Barrio Rhythm: Mexican American Music in Los Angeles* (Urbana: University of Illinois Press, 1993), 262, 156–57. By the early 1950s there was a Mexican American clarinetist in the Los Angeles Philharmonic. See David Reyes and Tom Waldman, *Land of a Thousand Dances: Chicano Rock 'n' Roll from Southern California* (Albuquerque: University of New Mexico Press, 1998), 23.
31. City of Los Angeles brochure.
32. Loza, *Barrio Rhythm*, 262.
33. Jaime Corral, interviewed by the author, Alhambra, California, July 19, 1999.
34. Chico Sesma interview. On *pachucos* writing *corridos* and other topical songs, see Griffith, *American Me*, 51; George Barker, "Pachuco: An American-Spanish Argot and Its Social Functions in Tucson, Arizona," *University of Arizona Social Science Bulletin* 18.1 (January 1950): 27–29.
35. Hickman, "Civic Music Administration," 32; City of Los Angeles brochure; "Outline of Tentative Program for the Belvedere Park Lake Dedication," John Anson Ford Collection, Box 41, Folder 7, Huntington Library. The Spanish word *tipica* translates as characteristic or traditional, with rural, "roots," or folkloric connotations.
36. City of Los Angeles brochure.
37. Chico Sesma interview; Paul Lopez interview; Don Tosti interview; "Los Angeles Neighborhood Music School Fills Need in Community," *The Southwestern Musician* 15.7 (June 1949).
38. Eric Porter, *What Is This Thing Called Jazz? African American Musicians as Artists, Critics, and Activists* (Berkeley: University of California, 2002), 62–63; Anthony Ortega, interviewed by Steven Isoardi, 1994, #300/498, Oral History Program, U.C.L.A., Department of Special Collections.
39. Bryant et al., *Central Avenue Sounds*, 325, 327.
40. City of Los Angeles brochure.
41. Hickman, "Community Sings," 46.
42. Ibid., 28.
43. Hickman, "Civic Music Administration," 21.
44. C. Sharpless Hickman, "Municipal Music and Money," *Music Journal* 10.5 (May 1952): 32; Hickman, "Community Sings," 29.
45. Hickman, "Money," 23.
46. Letter dated February 14, 1948, John Anson Ford Collection, Box 41, Folder 10, Huntington Library.
47. "1951–52 Statement of Program," John Anson Ford Collection, Box 40, Folder 5, Huntington Library.
48. On "blight," see Raúl H. Villa, *Barrio Logos: Space and Place in Urban Chicano Literature and Culture* (Austin: University of Texas Press, 2000), 71.
49. Charles Emge, "L.A. Council Votes Down Anti-Discrimination Law," *Down Beat* 16.3 (November 4, 1949).
50. On "musical miscegenation," see Michael Rogin, "Black Face, White Noise: The Jewish Jazz Singer Finds His Voice," *Critical Inquiry* 18 (spring 1992), 440; and Nelson George, *The Death of Rhythm and Blues* (New York: E. P. Dutton, 1989), 86.
51. Hickman, "Community Sings," 21.
52. "Peace and Brotherhood and Citizenship" pamphlet, John Anson Ford Collection, Box 60, Folder 14, Huntington Library.
53. Ibid.
54. "Over-All Outline Plan of Recreational Services Which Should Be Offered in the Los Angeles Area," May 20, 1952, John Anson Ford Collection, Box 61, Folder 2, Huntington Library.
55. Kelley, *Race Rebels*, 46–50.
56. Rosa Linda Fregoso, *The Bronze Screen: Chicana and Chicano Film Culture* (Minneapolis: University of Minnesota Press, 1993), 26.
57. Joseph P. Hill, "The Church and the Zoot-Suiter," Conference Report: Catholic Council for the Spanish Speaking, 1946, 16.

58. Anthony Ortega, interviewed by Steven Isoardi. Pomona disc jockey and club promoter Candelario Mendoza also mentions *jamaicas*; Candelario Mendoza, interviewed by the author, Pomona, California, December 10, 2003. Eduardo Pagán describes wartime Pacoima church bazaars as often flirtatious social functions. See Pagán, *Sleepy Lagoon*, 49.

59. Pagán, *Sleepy Lagoon*, 49.

60. "Twilight 'Til Dawn Dance to Benefit Boy Scout Jamboree," *California Eagle* (May 18, 1950).

61. Ed Frias and Lucie Brac Frias, interviewed by the author, Pasadena, California, August 17, 1998; Reyes and Waldman, *Land*, 20, 30.

62. George, *Death of Rhythm and Blues*, 26–28.

63. Jim Dawson, "Boogie Down on Central: Los Angeles' Rhythm and Blues Revolution," in liner notes to compact disc, *Central Avenue Sounds: Jazz in Los Angeles (1921–1956)* (Rhino, 1999), 65.

64. Dawson, "Boogie Down," 64–65; Molina, *Barrio Guide*, 5; Ruben Guevara, "The View from the Sixth Street Bridge: The History of Chicano Rock," in *The First Rock & Roll Confidential Report: Inside the Real World of Rock & Roll*, ed. Dave Marsh et al. (New York: Pantheon Books, 1985), 116.

65. Guevara, "View," 115.

66. George Lipsitz, "Land of a Thousand Dances: Youth, Minorities, and the Rise of Rock and Roll," in *Recasting America: Culture and Politics in the Age of Cold War*, ed. Lary May (Chicago: University of Chicago Press, 1989), 274; Ed Frias interview.

67. Reyes and Waldman, *Land*, 20–21.

68. Ed Frias interview.

69. Chole Camarena Ray interview.

70. Jim Dawson, *Nervous Man Nervous: Big Jay McNeely and the Rise of the Honking Tenor Sax* (Milford, New Hampshire: Big Nickel Publications, 1994), 96–97.

71. Ibid., 70.

72. Ibid., 76.

73. Reyes and Waldman, *Land*, 49.

74. Dawson, *Nervous*, 71–72; Bryant et al., *Central Avenue Sounds*, 115. On "Billy Goat Acres," see Leonard Pitt and Dale Pitt, *Los Angeles A to Z: An Encyclopedia of the City and County* (Berkeley: University of California Press, 1997), 44–45.

75. Dawson, *Nervous*, 71.

76. Reyes and Waldman, *Land*, 49; Dawson, "Boogie," 83; Dawson, *Nervous*, 60–61, 79, 68.

77. See D. J. Waldie, *Holy Land: A Suburban Memoir* (New York: St. Martin's Press, 1997), which is about growing up during the 1950s in the Los Angeles suburb of Lakewood, California.

78. William D. Piersen, "African American Festive Style," in *Signifyin(g), Sanctifyin', & Slam Dunking: A Reader in African American Expressive Culture*, ed. Gena Dagel Caponi (Amherst: University of Massachusetts Press, 1999), 429, 418.

79. On the ways that Big Jay McNeely used his formal music training, and the primal tension and religious fervency produced and released by the best honkers, see Dawson, *Nervous*, 73, 75, 41.

80. Guthrie P. Ramsey Jr., *Race Music: Black Cultures from Bebop to Hip-Hop* (Berkeley: University of California Press, 2003), 177.

81. George Lipsitz, "Cruising Around the Historical Bloc: Postmodernism and Popular Music in East Los Angeles," in *Time Passages: Collective Memory and American Popular Culture* (Minneapolis: University of Minnesota Press, 1990), 141–42.

82. Ibid., 142.

83. Dawson, *Nervous*, 88–89; Art Fein, *The L.A. Musical History Tour: A Guide to the Rock and Roll Landmarks of Los Angeles* (Winchester, Mass.: Faber and Faber, 1990), 43–44.

84. Molina, *Barrio Guide*, 6; Dawson, *Nervous*, 98, 92; Reyes and Waldman, *Land*, 49.

85. Terry McDermott, "Behind the Bunker Mentality," *Los Angeles Times*, June 11, 2000, A 28.

86. Mike Davis, *City of Quartz: Excavating the Future in Los Angeles* (New York: Vintage Books, 1992), 294.

87. Dawson, *Nervous*, 92, 93, 98.

88. Ibid., 75–76.

89. Michael T. Bertrand, *Race, Rock, and Elvis* (Urbana: University of Illinois Press, 2000), 70.

90. Molina, *Barrio Guide*, 6.

91. Reyes and Waldman, *Land*, 45–46; Molina, *Barrio Guide*, 5.

92. Johnny Otis, *Upside Your Head! Rhythm and Blues on Central Avenue* (Hanover, N.H.: Wesleyan University Press, 1993), 60–61.

93. Otis, *Upside Your Head!* 60–61. Chief Parker also used similar methods when he invoked a long-dormant statute, the Criminal Syndicalist Law, to arrest John Harris, a black Angeleno labor and civil rights activist, in 1966. Thanks to Ralph Shaffer for this information.

94. Program Study Report, May 17, 1956, John Anson Ford Collection, Box 61, Folder 5, Huntington Library.

95. Reyes and Waldman, *Land,* 45; Molina, *Barrio Guide,* 5; Otis, *Upside Your Head!* xxvi, 61.

96. Molina, *Barrio Guide,* 5.

97. Otis, *Upside Your Head!* 61–62.

98. Ibid., 60–61.

99. Matt Garcia, "'Memories of El Monte': Intercultural Dance Halls in Post–World War II Greater Los Angeles," in *Generations of Youth: Youth Cultures and History in Twentieth-Century America,* ed. Joe Austin and Michael N. Willard (New York: New York University Press, 1998), 161.

100. Matt Garcia, *A World of Its Own: Race, Labor, and Citrus in the Making of Greater Los Angeles, 1900–1970* (Chapel Hill: The University of North Carolina Press, 2001), 208.

101. Ibid., 207–8.

102. Ibid., 206.

103. Otis, *Upside Your Head!* xxvii, 61.

104. R. Freese, "Good Citizenship through Music," *Choral Guide* 10.22–23 (September 1957); Garcia, *World,* 206; Guevara, "View," 118; Pagán, *Sleepy Lagoon,* 53.

105. Tom Reed, *The Black Music History of Los Angeles—Its Roots: A Classical Pictorial History of Black Music in Los Angeles from 1920–1970* (Los Angeles: Black Accent on L.A. Press, 1992), 382–83; Molina, *Barrio Guide,* 63.

106. Beverly Mendheim, *Ritchie Valens: The First Latino Rocker* (Tempe, Ariz.: Bilingual Press, 1987), 34, 36.

107. Larry Lehmer, *The Day the Music Died: The Last Tour of Buddy Holly, the "Big Bopper," and Ritchie Valens* (New York: Schirmer Books, 1997), 50.

108. Robin D. G. Kelley, "Notes on Deconstructing 'the Folk,'" *American Historical Review* 97.5 (December 1992): 1408.

109. See George Lipsitz, *The Possessive Investment in Whiteness: How White People Profit from Identity Politics* (Philadelphia: Temple University Press, 1998).

The Battle of Los Angeles: The Cultural Politics of Chicana/o Music in the Greater Eastside

Victor Hugo Viesca

Chicanos are, when you call yourself that, you know your history, you know where you came from, you know where you need to go.
—Yoatl, Aztlán Underground[1]

I try to find my own Chicana sensibility in the dance.
—Martha Gonzales, Quetzal[2]

East Los Angeles is the center of a flourishing musical cultural scene with a renewed "Chicana/o" sensibility.[3] This scene is being led by a collective of socially conscious and politically active Latin-fusion bands that emerged in the 1990s, including Aztlán Underground, Blues Experiment, Lysa Flores, Ozomatli, Ollin, Quetzal, Quinto Sol, Slowrider, and Yeska. These groups compose original songs that weave together the sounds of the Americas, from soul, samba, and the *son jarocho* to reggae, rumba, and rap. Multilingual lyrics in Spanish, English, *Caló,* or Nahuatl that speak to themes of urban exile, indigenous identity, and multiracial unity are layered over the music to produce a sonic Chicana/o imaginary of the global city in the twenty-first century.[4] Several of the bands within the scene have released full-length albums on their own independent record labels such as Xicano Records and Film (Aztlán Underground and Quinto Sol), De Volada Records (Slowrider and Blues Experiment), and Lysa Flores's Bring Your Love Records (see discography). The bands often collaborate with one another, producing or playing on each other's records and touring on the same bill. While their music is sold primarily in California, where they perform most often, the Eastside scene is building an enthusiastic and global following through the growing popularity of Quetzal and Ozomatli. Since releasing their self-titled debut in 1998, Quetzal has released two successful and critically acclaimed albums on the premier folk label Vanguard Records. Ozomatli has sold more than half a million records of their first two CDs, their eponymous debut and the Grammy award–winning *Embrace the Chaos* (2001).

The popularity of the Eastside scene in California reflects a consumer market inhabited by millions of Latina/os with a bilingual and bicultural sensibility.[5] Latina/os make up a third of California's population and a near majority of Los Angeles County residents. Notably, more than 70 percent of Latina/os in Los Angeles are of Mexican origin.[6] The musicians and the audience of the Eastside scene are predominantly bilingual ethnic Mexican and Latina/o youth of the one-and-a-half, second, and third generations.[7] The cultural formations of the East L.A. scene emerge from this Latina/o population, as subjects of their lyrical voices, as potential consumers, and, most important, as cultural producers.

Along with visual artists, activists, and audiences, the musicians of the Eastside scene form an emergent cultural movement that speaks powerfully to present conditions. This community represents a form of political possibility that inheres in postindustrial culture, one that is grounded in the new spatial and social relations generated in Los Angeles in the transnational era.[8] Thus, it is critical that we consider how these cultural activities reveal an understanding and negotiation of these forces. The very conditions of oppression and disenfranchisement that characterize the new economy have enabled (and required) a particular counterresponse, a response that is necessarily different from older forms of struggle. The Eastside scene is both a product of and a means for countering the impact of globalization on low-wage workers and aggrieved racialized populations. The Eastside scene serves as a floating site of resistance, a mechanism for calling an oppositional community into being through performance. Groups within the scene link together diverse parts of a spatially dispersed community through the activities of live performance, listening to recordings and radio, and following the bands to marches, demonstrations, and direct action protests.

The term *East L.A.*, or *the Eastside*, is commonly used in Los Angeles and within the scene as a reference to the many predominantly ethnic Mexican enclaves of the city. In the 1960s and early 1970s, East Los Angeles became the core site of musical production for a wave of Chicano bands and individual musicians. Although hundreds of groups performed in the Eastside, only a few reached national recognition, including Thee Midnighters, the Village Callers, Cannibal and the Headhunters, El Chicano, and Tierra.[9] In 1980, the poet Luis Rodriguez recalled this 1960s–1970s musical movement in spatial terms: "They were rock artists based in East Los Angeles. They were part of a phenomenon known on the West Coast as the 'Eastside sound.'"[10] The contemporary Eastside, however, has expanded well beyond its traditional urban boundaries since the 1960s. Victor Valle and Rodolfo Torres have used the term *Greater Eastside* to describe the majority Latina/o districts of East Los Angeles County (see fig. 1).[11]

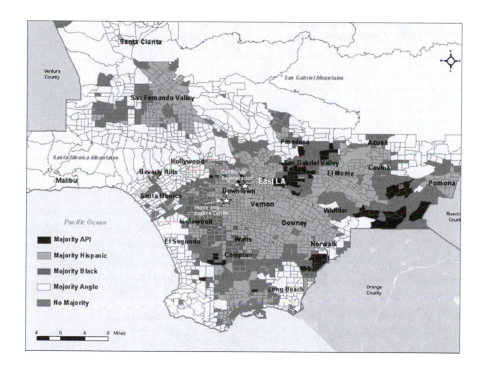

Figure 1.
Los Angeles County: Racial and Ethnic Diversity, 2000. Courtesy of Michelle Zonta and Paul Ong of the UCLA Lewis Center for Regional Policy Studies, with additional imaging by Melany de la Cruz.

The Eastside continues to represent a resource of identification and prestige for contemporary Chicana/o musicians. Javier Villalobos, the drummer for the Latin-reggae band Quinto Sol, notes the cultural meaning of the neighborhoods, industrial zones, cultural institutions, and commercial districts that make up the Greater Eastside: "It starts here. Home, East L.A. . . . planting the seed to let you know where you come from and where you are headed—to not forget your roots and culture."[12] Quetzal opened its album *Worksongs* (2003) with "This Is My Home," a ballad about their lifelong love of East Los Angeles. The Eastside scene fashioned by these artists and their audiences is a social institution embedded in a network of other institutions concentrated in the Greater Eastside. Crucial nodes in the network include local businesses such as Candelas Guitars in Boyle Heights, whose traditional Mexican guitars have been popular with Eastside musicians since the 1950s, and small cafés like the Troy in Little Tokyo, Luna Sol in Pico Union, and the mobile Eastside Café, whose tiny stages gave space to young musicians. Established community and cultural arts centers such as the city-managed Plaza de la Raza in Lincoln Heights and the privately endowed Self-Help Graphics in East Los Angeles proper, as well as experimental community cultural centers such as the seminal Peace and Justice Center in Downtown, Centro de Regeneracion in Highland Park, and the Aztlán Cultural Arts Foundation in Lincoln Heights, have probably played the most critical role in the development of the scene. These community centers offer not only a place to perform but additional services such as studio space, temporary jobs, and even temporary housing. While several of these venues were short-lived, usually lasting a year or two in the mid to late 1990s, their legacy lives on in the music and growing success of the bands they helped nurture.

The emergence of the current Eastside scene paralleled the rise of a postindustrial economy in Los Angeles. When local auto, tire, and steel plants shut down or moved elsewhere in the 1970s, the working-class suburbs of Southeast and Greater Eastside Los Angeles were repopulated in large numbers by ethnic Mexicans taking advantage of the cheap rent available in areas abandoned by white flight.[13] In the 1980s, as the city began to reindustrialize into a new economy based on high-skill, high-tech industries on one end and industries that relied on low-wage, often immigrant, labor at the other, Mexican and Central American immigrants swelled the Latina/o population in the Greater Eastside, where much of Los Angeles's manufacturing sector remained. Often fleeing the civil wars taking place in their homelands, Salvadorans, Guatemalans, Hondurans, and Nicaraguans joined Mexican immigrants in providing the bulk of the labor force for the low-wage sectors of the new economy. Their settlement revived once-abandoned communities in the South-east and South Central sections of the county.[14] While ethnic Mexicans and Central Americans make up a clear majority of the population in the Greater Eastside, several areas include significant numbers of Asian-Pacific Americans and African Americans. The rise of multiracial communities in the postindustrial era is reflected in the predominantly Asian American and Latina/o suburb of Monterey Park in the San Gabriel Valley and the transformation of the eastern half of South Central Los Angeles from predominantly black into majority Latina/o neighborhoods. The traveling cultures of the Asian, Latin American, and African diasporas have influenced the formation of a multiracial urban culture in Los Angeles. The shifting dynamics of Chicana/o culture as represented in the Eastside scene are shaped by and yet are a part of the multiracial and multinational reality of the Los Angeles polity.

Economic restructuring altered not only the demographic landscape of the Eastside but also the life chances of a new generation of youth. The deindustrialization of the local economy displaced thousands of African American and Mexican American workers and restricted their mobility. African Americans presently constitute the bulk of the jobless poor in Los Angeles, with Latinas/os making up the majority of the working poor. Latinas/os are overwhelmingly concentrated in the low-wage sectors of the reindustrialized economy and currently make up 57 percent of the poor in Los Angeles County and only 27 percent of those with incomes in the "middle or above."[15] The massive unemployment that economic restructuring has brought forth and the increasing profitability of the drug trade have made criminals out of many African American and Latina/o youth looking for a way to get paid. Los Angeles "gangsta rap" and the "narco-corridos" of the Mexican *banda* music scene attest to these consequences. Anti-gang initiatives and increased surveillance in the inner city by the Los Angeles Police and Sheriff Departments has led to massive arrests and the establishment of criminal records for thousands of African American and Latina/o youth, making it even more difficult for them to find employment.[16]

Furthermore, the coming of age of the Chicana/o youth culture from which the Eastside scene stems took place in an era of political repression against the state's burgeoning population of color. Since 1994, California voters have been presented with and passed Proposition 187, which sought to restrict rights to education and health care for undocumented immigrants; the anti–affirmative action Proposition 209; and the anti–bilingual education Proposition 227. In 2000 California voters overwhelmingly passed Proposition 21, the "Gang Violence and Juvenile Crime Prevention Act," meant to stiffen penalties for juvenile offenders while allowing more juveniles to be tried as adults.[17] These measures sought to blame California's most vulnerable populations for the destructive consequences of urban austerity and economic restructuring on the state economy in the 1990s. Undergirded by "the possessive investment in whiteness," these California public policies, as well as private prejudice, are a form of white identity politics that have worked to maintain, and increase, white privilege.[18] Governor Pete Wilson, in his support of Proposition 187, for example, relied more on his whiteness than on his political record to secure his reelection in 1994 despite his low approval rating. The majority-white electorate who passed the proposition chose to ignore the essential role of immigration and immigrant labor in maintaining both a prosperous state economy and middle-class comfort. As Lisa Cacho has argued, "Proposition 187 was not an attempt to close national borders, but an attempt to create borders within the nation."[19]

Along with the Zapatista rebellion in Chiapas, discussed below, Proposition 187 served as a catalyst for the Eastside scene's commitment to activism on behalf of immigrants and people of color. According to Robert Lopez, former guitarist for the band Ollin and co-owner of the now-defunct Luna Sol Café, "We were all playing political benefits during the uprising in Chiapas, and when Proposition 187 passed, we decided to put a compilation out to record a period of our history."[20] *Sociedad=Suiciedad*, a compilation album that includes songs by Ozomatli, Aztlán Underground, Ollin, Blues Experiment, and Quinto Sol, was released on the independent punk label BYO Records in 1997 (see fig. 2).

The Eastside scene's history of formation, the multiplicity of its sounds, and its commitment to political activism and coalition building all illuminate the relations between culture and politics at the present moment. The musical practices of the East L.A. scene echo the dislocations and displacements endemic to global cities in the transnational era, but they also reflect the emergence of new forms of resistance that find counterhegemonic possibilities within contradictions. In culture and in politics, groups in the Eastside scene proceed through immanent critiques and creative reworkings of already existing social relations rather than through transcendant teleologies aimed at the establishment of utopian sites and subjects. Rather than a politics of "either/or" that asks people to choose between culture and politics, between class and race, or between distinct national identities, this cultural movement embraces a politics of "both/and" that encourages dynamic, fluid, and flexible stances and identity categories.

The Chicana/o Cultural Politics of the Eastside Music Scene

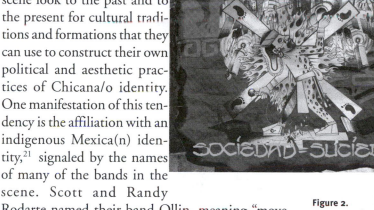

Figure 2.
Courtesy of NUKE from the Under The Influence Crew.

Musicians in the Eastside scene look to the past and to the present for cultural traditions and formations that they can use to construct their own political and aesthetic practices of Chicana/o identity. One manifestation of this tendency is the affiliation with an indigenous Mexica(n) identity,[21] signaled by the names of many of the bands in the scene. Scott and Randy Rodarte named their band Ollin, meaning "movement" in the indigenous language of Nahuatl.[22] Quetzal retains the Nahuatl name for a native bird of southern Mexico that is considered sacred by the Aztecs and the Mayans. Ozomatli is named after the Aztec god of dance who is represented as a monkey figure in the famous Aztec Sun Stone. Quinto Sol refers to the historical period of the fifth sun, the present era according to Aztec philosophy. Aztlán Underground uses the name of the original homeland of the Aztecs, Aztlán, to signify their indigenous identity and origin in the Southwest. This understanding of Aztlán was popularized by Chicana/o artists and activists of the Chicano movement in the 1960s, who reclaimed much of the United States Southwest as the homeland of the Chicano/Mexicano nation. The band names that do not explicitly suggest an indigenous Mexican identity implicitly signal their affiliation with other recognizable ethnic Mexican cultural formations. Slowrider, for example, alludes to the popular barrio art of car customizing, or lowrider culture, while Yeska is slang for marijuana, evoking the 1940s' Pachuco argot of *Cálo*.

The connection to Mexican culture is further expressed in the use of traditional Mexican music styles and instruments. The *son jarocho*, an Afro-Mexican song and dance form originating in Vera Cruz, Mexico, is an important element in the music of Quetzal. Quetzal Flores, its founder and lead guitarist, composes much of the band's music around the rhythms of his *jarana*, the small, four- to eight-stringed guitar that is the main instrument of the *son jarocho*.[23] When performing and recording songs in the *jarocho* style, band member Martha Gonzales stomps on the *tarima*, a wooden box with sound holes that is an essential percussive element of the Veracruzan *son*. Raul Pacheco, guitarist and vocalist for Ozomatli, makes use of the *bajo sexto*, a twelve-stringed Mexican bass guitar that is the rhythm instrument for *conjunto* groups that play music from the northern states of Mexico as well as the Texas-Mexican variation, *Tejano*. The hardcore/hip-hop sound of Aztlán Underground is layered with the percussion, flutes, and rattles of indigenous Mexico.

These expressions of indigenous and ethnic Mexican identity are not anchored in claims for a separate nation-state of Chicana/os based in the Southwest. Rather, these stylistic markers are used to reaffirm an ethnic origin and identity that precedes the nation-state. As Aztlán Underground explained,

> We wanted to bring back the understanding of Aztlán and place of our origin. The connection to the land that was torn from us. To dissect the way in which they have colonized us and made us believe in the white ways and not our own from the Spanish to the English. We wanted and want to resurrect our true identity is how we started. So we united the ancient with the present by fusing our native instruments with hip-hop and our message to create a bridge to our identity.[24]

This turn toward traditional musical practices is similar to the experience of East L.A. band Los Lobos, who first used the *son jarocho* and other traditional Mexican music styles in their own Latin-rock fusions in the late 1970s. Their adaptation of traditional Mexican elements highlighted the impact of the Chicano movement in East Los Angeles just prior to their emergence. As Steven Loza noted, "A large part of the group's desire to appropriate folkloric jarocho genres into their repertoire was based on an urge not only to preserve such music, but to promote it as a viable art form in an urban and, in many respects, a culturally hostile environment."[25] The musicians of Los Lobos are mentors to the East L.A. scene. David Hidalgo played the *requinto doble* and accordion on Ozomatli's song "Aqui No Sera" on their debut album, and saxophonist Steve Berlin produced Quetzal's third album, *Worksongs* (2003).

In the context of the contemporary economic and political marginalization of ethnic Mexicans in Los Angeles, the musical practices that emerge from the Greater Eastside continue to serve as a strategic site for the production and negotiation of emergent national, racial, class and gendered identities. Although Chicano/a culture speaks to the shared experiences, institutions, and practices of Mexican Americans as a distinct ethnic community, other expressions of cultural affiliation are also at play. Interethnic identification and unity through culture rather than nationality or color are integral components of a new Chicana/o sensibility being forged in the current East L.A. scene. Neither assimilationist nor separatist, this complex of Chicana/o cultural production affirms its cultural heritage and history of place in Los Angeles while creatively engaging in and adapting to the diversity of communities and cultural forms that make up the city.

One of the most vital influences of the Eastside scene has come from Mexican immigrant culture. The *banda* music scene that dominates much of the Mexican immigrant cultural, social, and radio space of Los Angeles has captured the imagination of thousands of Mexican American youths in the Greater Eastside. *Banda* originated in Sinaloa, Mexico, and was transformed into "techno-*banda*" in the 1980s when musicians in northwestern Mexico adapted elements of rock and roll and replaced traditional brass instruments and bass drums with the electric bass, modern drums, timbales, and synthesizers. *Banda's* popularity exploded in Los Angeles in the early 1990s as local Spanish-language radio stations began programming the music in response to the musical preferences of recent immigrants. Nightclubs, radio stations, and swap meets that catered to the emerging ethnic Mexican majority in Los Angeles produced a thriving dance and music scene based on the sound of the *tambora* (bass drum) and the dance of the *quebradita* (little break). Many of the immigrants in the initial market audience had come from rural areas that had not previously sent many migrants to Los Angeles. This audience responded enthusiastically to *banda's* rural immigrant identity. *Banda* artists presented themselves in the *vaquero* (cowboy) style of dress, wearing hats, boots, and jeans, and sang of life on the ranch and the experiences of crossing the border in the *ranchera* voice of the region.[26] In the nativist era of Pete Wilson and Proposition 187, *banda* was a potent source of community prestige for ethnic Mexicans who turned to the musical culture as an active affirmation of their own Mexican background. Mexican American youths and adults now compose a major base of consumers and producers of this transnational musical culture, and the music's impact has transcended the *banda* scene itself.[27] Ozomatli, Ollin, and Quetzal all incorporate elements of *banda* and *ranchera* music into their repertoire.

The Eastside hardcore (punk) scene was another formative musical culture influencing the East L.A. scene. Members of Aztlán Underground, Blues Experiment, Ollin, Quinto Sol, and Slowrider actively engaged in this precursory scene. Punk produced by ethnic Mexican and Latina/o youth in East and Southeast Los Angeles has had a popular following since the late 1970s, despite little radio airplay, minimal recorded work and record labels, and only a few short-lived clubs.[28] Punk is often performed in backyard gatherings, one of the more common ways to celebrate the weekend in the working-class suburbs of the Greater Eastside. The Rodarte twins of Ollin and Robert Tovar of Blues Experiment, as well as members of Aztlán Underground and Quinto Sol, paid their dues in hard-core bands such as Bloodcum, Peace Pill, Subsist, and Golpe de Estado.

The popular music that dominates the audible spaces of contemporary urban radio and local nightclubs has been a fundamental element of the new musical practices of the Eastside scene as well. The increasing popularity of Jamaican reggae in the urban United States is reflected in the music of both Quinto Sol, which blends roots-reggae with Latin rhythms like cumbia, rumba, and son, and Yeska, whose take on Jamaican ska is fused with the sounds of Latin jazz. The electronica sounds of dance music can be heard in the work of Quetzal and the remixes of Slowrider. Yet it is hip-hop that has had the most generative influence on the Eastside scene. Ozomatli and Slowrider incorporate a DJ and an MC into their albums and live performances. One of the pioneers of West Coast *and* Chicano rap, Aztlán Underground is considered one of the innovators of the rap-rock genre.[29] Rap groups that are affiliated with the Eastside scene, such as 2Mex, the Black Eyed Peas, and La Paz, record more traditional versions of hip-hop by rhyming over break beats produced electronically.

The cultural hybridity of the Eastside scene is not new to urban Chicana/o musical practice. The rise of Eastside jump blues bands like the Pachuco Boogie Boys in the 1940s and the growth of the Eastside sound in the 1960s and 1970s showed particular affinities between ethnic Mexicans and African Americans in music, audiences, and band membership.[30] What is different about the contemporary Eastside scene is the politicization of these hybrid practices into new forms of political expression. The evolving social movements and cultural practices of Chicana/os are producing an emergent form of oppositional identity that not only draws on their history and collective memory but speaks to new ways of thinking and practicing community across national and ethnic lines. The use of the *son jarocho* by Quetzal, for example, is not only an expression of Mexican identity, but it is a link to the cultural struggles waged by African slaves. As Quetzal Flores explains, "We performed at an academic conference in Kentucky about the influence black culture had on the Americas earlier this year. One of the professors made the point that, as maniacal and genocidal as slavery was, black culture survived and thrived. That's son. The slaves had drums; the Spaniards took them away. The slaves said, 'All right, fuck you. I'll stomp on wood then,' and created this wondrous music. It shows how rich humans are. Human resilience will always prevail. And that's what we try to convey—the problems and beauty of Los Angeles."[31] Quinto Sol bassist Martin Perez characterized his band's movement away from punk to the Latin fusion style and community-oriented lyrics that distinguishes the East L.A. scene as a desire to raise the political consciousness of his community. According to Perez, "We used to play in punk rock bands that maybe were politically aware but not too conscious. That was why we started playing roots. We saw what Bob Marley was doing for his people and we thought, 'Hey, our people need a message too.'"[32] Aztlán Underground echoed this sentiment when asked about the formation of the group: "By 1988, when we first were turned on to black nationalist groups such as Public Enemy and BDP (Boogie Down Productions) in hip-hop, we were moved by their message and realized that there was nothing for our people to look to and we were confined to embracing the dominant culture. Ways of the Iztac.[33] So we wanted to break the notions that we were illegal by affirming to our people our native identity and roots, which are lost in these western schools that teach us George Washington is our father, huh!!" [34]

The political ideology of Chicana/o identity manifested in the current Eastside scene is distinct from previous generations of Chicano nationalism and expression. Several activists and later critics have pointed to the exclusive and masculinist aspects of the "Chicano" subject of the political and cultural movement of the 1960s and 1970s.[35] Richard T. Rodriguez has noted how the representations of Chicano nationalism in contemporary "Chicano rap" echo the dominant masculinism of the past. The masculinist element of Chicano rap, such as (Kid) Frost's representation of "La Raza," makes it susceptible to sexism while its concern with traditional notions of Mexican culture such as *la familia* or *carnalismo* (brotherhood) may reproduce within in it notions of the Chicana/o community as exclusively or predominantly masculine.[36]

In contrast, the East L.A. scene acknowledges and attempts to sustain a vision of gender equity and respect for different sexual orientations. As Quetzal Flores has noted, "[T]he whole East L.A. scene is into the mode of making a conscious effort to acknowledge the struggle of women and for us as men to act on that as well."[37] The participation of woman is critical to the male-dominated Eastside scene. Martha Gonzales and violinist Rocio Maron are central members of Quetzal and their cultural community. The music they produce stakes a claim for a particular female perspective. As Martha notes, "I learned the traditional *tarima* but then took it out of its element into rock 'n' roll. It's not just about the footwork, but there's an upper body movement that affects the sound as well. I try to find my own Chicana sensibility in the dance."[38] The folk-rock of Lysa Flores eloquently expresses a Chicana standpoint as well. Flores composes songs that deal with her quotidian struggle as a proud and independent woman of color, reflected in her representation as "Queen of the Boulevard" in her self-produced album *Tree of Hope* (1998). Indeed, Chicana feminists are at the forefront of this scene, including spoken word artists such as the all-female crew Cihuatl Tonalli (Woman Force), and the women of color performance art collective Mujeres de Maiz (Women of the Corn).

Another aspect of the new political ideology is being shaped by the struggle to build a politicized cultural community. Quetzal Flores, a child of organizers for the United Farm Workers, argues that Chicana/o identity has to be reformulated in terms of community: "I think that being Chicano now is still valid and still very important in terms of identity and self-determination, but I think more and more people are starting to take this position: how to create an identity as a way to build a foundation so that you can communicate and collaborate with other communities."[39] This idea of community building extends through all of the groups of the Eastside scene. These artists have not only shared the stage at concerts throughout Los Angeles, but have also come together to record and/or produce one another's albums. Yet this collaborative work is not limited to musicians. In addition to the women's collectives mentioned above, visual artists, dramatists, and filmmakers have been an important element in the constitution of the East L.A. scene. Chicano visual artists Chaz Bojorquez and Joseph "NUKE" Montalvo designed the cover art for two independent compilation albums: *Sociedad=Suiciedad* (1996) and the 2000 release *Mex-America*.[40] The Chicana/o comedy troupe ChUSMA, Spanish slang for "Outcasts," have collaborated with the East L.A. music scene since their founding in 1997. The Latina/o theater troupe Culture Clash's critical and popular play *Chavez Ravine* (2003), about the displacement of an ethnic Mexican community in 1950s Los Angeles, was supported by Ollin's musical production. Additionally, the media-arts collective Smokin' Mirrors has produced videos for Quetzal ("Grito de Alegria" and "Elegua Jarocho") and Aztlán Underground ("Blood on Your Hands").

The practices of community building through cultural expression within the East L.A. scene are largely inspired by the rebellion in Chiapas, Mexico. The rebel army of the Ejercito Nacional de Liberacion Nacional (EZLN) has been waging a decade-long struggle for the dignity, voice, and autonomy of Indian and peasant communities of the southern region of Mexico and against the policies of neoliberalism, such as NAFTA, that have devastated their way of life. As they noted in an interview, Aztlán Underground is "[v]ery influenced by the EZLN."[41] This influence is reflected on the cover of their album *Sub-Verses* (2003), adorned with a colorful and defiant image of a Zapatista woman soldier. Quetzal is also deeply influenced by the Zapatista struggle. The song "Grito Alegria," on Quetzal's self-titled debut album, is a tribute to the Zapatista vision of community and collective struggle. The chorus of the song is drawn from the Zapatista slogan "El pueblo unido jamas sera vencido (The people united will never be defeated)." These groups, along with Ozomatli, who originally called themselves "Todos Somos Marcos (We are all Marcos)" in honor of the *subcommandante* and spokesman of the EZLN, have played at several concerts to raise funds for the movement in Chiapas. Quetzal, Quinto Sol, Aztlán Underground, and several local Chicana/o visual artists and activists, have traveled to Chiapas to meet with the rebels and to act as human rights observers.[42] The significance of the Zapatista struggle for an alternative imaginary of democratic politics has not been lost on the artists and activists of the East L.A. scene. The Zapatista politics of consensus that has opened up grassroots networks of solidarity and produced respect for different political traditions has provided the East L.A. scene with a model for a more inclusive democratic politics in a multiracial city such as Los Angeles.[43]

Yet, more than just an attempt at affecting a politicized Chicana/o identity, the East L.A. scene emerged in the battle over a space to practice, perform, and produce a creative community. In the mid-1990s the struggle over the Peace and Justice Center was an important vehicle for the development of this cultural movement and its expression of a renewed Chicana/o consciousness. In March 1995, Wil-Dog Abers (future bassist of Ozomatli) and Alfredo Ortiz (drummer for Yeska), along with several other, mostly African American and Latina/o workers, took over the Emergency Resources Building in downtown Los Angeles in an attempt to organize a union among the youth who worked for the Los Angeles Conservation Corps (LACC), a federally funded jobs program.[44] Local youth working for the corps were trained and employed at minimum wages with no benefits and offered few long-term job prospects. Up to two thousand youth a year—from thirteen- to twenty-three-year-olds—work for the LACC, making it one of the largest youth employers in Los Angeles. The jobs performed by these youth include gardening, landscaping, and janitorial work at schools and other government buildings. Much of their trash pickup is now done in industrial zones—a free government service to corporations. These maintenance jobs used to be done by unionized employees. In California, thousands of such workers have been laid off—their places taken by minimum-wage earners, such as the LACC youth, or others. One of the main organizers of the strike, Lilia Ramirez, noted how much the uniforms the youth were given reminded her of the bright orange jumpsuits prisoners in the L.A. County jail wore: "Is that what they see us as?"[45] If not seen as criminals, these youths were certainly looked upon with disdain. "McDonald's is the best job these kids will get," a manager told Ramirez at an LACC meeting called to address the strike.[46] In the meantime, upper-level management, many of whom were from out of state, received high wages and lavish benefits from the $6.5 million annual budget.

Conflict began when Carmelo Alvarez, a longtime activist from the Pico Union area and the corps' only Latino site director, began protesting the discrepancy between management and the youth workers.[47] Soon after, a meeting of the Conservation Corps management was called to question the tactics of Alvarez, who wanted to find more creative and productive ways to train youth. As Carmelo argued at the time, "They only see us as a cheap labor force. The corps has potential to do great things in the community, but how can they be involved in the kids' futures if they have them pushing brooms and picking up trash?"[48] Despite the protests of the youth workers, Alvarez was fired in a subsequent meeting that included the board of directors of the LACC. Corps workers at the Emergency Resources Building, where Alvarez was program director, also protested the firing and refused to leave the site. In response, agency managers shut down the building and threatened to call in the police. Carmelo, Lilia, Wil-Dog, and Alfredo Ortiz were joined by more than thirty co-workers in staging a takeover of the building. Together, they mounted a two-month sit-in.[49]

The protesters demanded union representation, better wages, benefits, and the opportunity for advancement for corps youth. The LACC responded by giving the organizers of the sit-in "voluntary resignation" slips. Negotiations, prompted by bad publicity for the corps, did not bring about a union but did manage to secure access to the locked-out downtown building for a period of twelve months. The activists transformed the building into a nonprofit community arts center.[50] While music concerts took place on weekends, the week was dedicated to workshops in studio mixing, theater production, poetry writing, silk-screening, and community organizing. The programs and workshop activities were organized by the youth themselves. As Lilia Ramirez put it, "Carmelo helped us to get consciousness, but he doesn't tell us what to think and do. The kids, we run this center. [It is] the kids who are hired to make the program, not the administrators. That's why we created this center, so we could raise the kids to another level of consciousness."[51] The type of organizing practiced at the Peace and Justice Center relied on the interests of youth to get them politically active and interested in acquiring the skills in creative production, which can lead to real jobs in a postindustrial economy staked on the fields of communications and informational technologies.[52]

This local struggle for a community center that promoted political consciousness and training for the new economy also produced Latin bands. The soul band Blues Experiment was born at the center and fund-raising parties brought together the members of Ozomatli for the first time. As Wil-Dog notes,

> After the strike, we were given access to this new community center dedicated to youth and art. We had to raise money for the building, so I called all these musicians I knew. Ozomatli got together during the first five gigs. It was a jam thing where everyone's musical past came out. We never set out to play this style. It's just what everybody knew.[53]

Several fledgling bands took advantage of this experiment in urban cultural politics in downtown Los Angeles. Predominantly Chicana/o groups Rice and Beans, Ollin, and Quetzal, as well as multiracial groups like the Black Eyed Peas, became the official "House Bands" of the center. The bands were given studio space to practice their art. A few individual musicians, such as Randy Rodarte of Ollin and Blues Experiment guitarist Robert Tovar, actually lived at the center free of charge. Many of these bands performed before large, multiracial audiences at the monthly "Unity Fests." These popular events brought together artists, activists, and members of the diverse communities of Los Angeles through a celebration of local urban creativity, including DJ-ing, graffiti demonstrations, skateboarding, and spoken word (see fig. 3).

The Peace and Justice Center was shut down by the City of Los Angeles in 1996, a year after it was taken over by the youth of the Conservation Corps. While it no longer exists, its impact persists. The Peace and Justice Center contributed a great deal to the development of local bands, and its legacy is readily seen in the activism of several of the music groups and activists with ties to center. Groups in the Eastside scene who performed, practiced, or stayed at the center continue to organize spaces for creative expression and political education. These bands have performed at music festivals raising awareness about immigrant, indigenous, and youth rights, often for little or no compensation. They often provide the sound at local demonstrations against police abuse and the death penalty and, since the fall of 2001, in protests against the "War on Terror" being waged by the United States in Afghanistan and Iraq.

The Peace and Justice Center was a vital space for collective political mobilization, a repository of social memory about past struggles for social change,

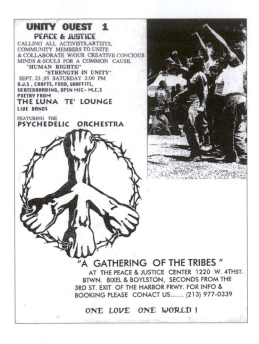

UNITY QUEST 1
PEACE & JUSTICE
CALLING ALL ACTIVISTS,ARTISTS,
COMMUNITY MEMBERS TO UNITE
& COLLABORATE W/OUR CREATIVE CONCIOUS
MINDS & SOULS FOR A COMMON CAUSE.
"HUMAN RIGHTS!"
"STRENGTH IN UNITY"
SEPT. 23 ,95 SATURDAY 2:00 PM
D.J.S , CRAFTS, FOOD, GRAFFITI,
SKATEBOARDING, OPEN MIC- M.C.S
POETRY FROM
THE LUNA TE' LOUNGE
LIVE BANDS

FEATURING THE
PSYCHEDELIC ORCHESTRA

"A GATHERING OF THE TRIBES "
AT THE PEACE & JUSTICE CENTER 1220 W. 4THST.
BTWN. BIXEL & BOYLSTON, SECONDS FROM THE
3RD ST. EXIT OF THE HARBOR FRWY. FOR INFO &
BOOKING PLEASE CONACT US....... (213) 977-0339

ONE LOVE ONE WORLD !

Figure 3.
Courtesy of Lilia Ramirez.

and a site for imagining and enacting new social relations in the era of globalization. The multiracial politics of the center emerged from young people's shared experience of racialization and class and spatial location in Los Angeles since the 1970s. Chicana/o activists and artists did not deny their ethnicity in creating a space that would foster interethnic coalitions, but rather drew on their cultural identities to reposition their struggle as connected to other marginalized groups. Collectively and in their own ways, the Chicana/o bands from East Los Angeles have taken the lessons learned from social movements, past and present, to generate their own notions of Chicana/o identity through their encounter with contemporary social dynamics and affiliations with other communities' struggles for self-determination.

Conclusion

In August of 2000 the internationally popular rock-rap group Rage Against the Machine performed for the thousands gathered in the "designated protest area" of the Democratic National Convention (DNC) held at the Staples Center in downtown Los Angeles. In solidarity with the demonstrators, lead singer Zach de la Rocha stormed through Rage's tribute to Mayan and Mexica resistance, "People of the Sun," and songs from their 2000 release *The Battle of Los Angeles*, including "Maria," about the struggle of Latina immigrants, and "Guerilla Radio."[54] The latter song remarks on de la Rocha's work with Centro de Regeneracion in Highland Park, a Chicana/o cultural center he cofounded in 1996, where, among other activities, he subsidized the micro-radio station Radio Clandestina.

Although Rage Against the Machine emerged out of the hard-core scene in Orange County, the group was affiliated with the East L.A. scene through the activism of de la Rocha, who was a resident of East Los Angeles and the son of Roberto "Beto" de la Rocha, a well-known artist, activist, and founding member of the seminal Chicano art group Los Four. Zach's Chicano identity informed his band's commitment to the struggles of immigrants, people of color, and the Zapatistas. Rage provided access to progressive organizations and media by setting up tables for such groups in their concert performances and by offering links to their organizations on Rage's official Web site. In 1999 Rage invited Aztlán Underground to open its concerts in Mexico City, while Ozomatli opened what turned out to be Rage's final show at Los Angeles' Grand Olympic Auditorium in 2000.

The possibilities of collective organization that had been practiced at the Peace and Justice Center inspired Zach de la Rocha's formation of another significant but also short-lived experiment in community building through cultural practice. He renamed the People's Resource Center in Highland Park the Centro de Regeneracion.[55] There, many of the same artists and activists who had participated in the struggle over the Peace and Justice Center maintained their commitment to providing youth a space for cultural expression and training. Along with music workshops and the development of Radio Clandestina, Centro members also organized graffiti workshops and youth film festivals.[56] Although the Centro lasted only two years, it was an important space in the ongoing institutionalization of the community politics, cultural practices, and social networks of the Eastside scene in the nineties.

The cultural politics waged by the contemporary Chicana/o music scene in Los Angeles registers in precise and detailed fashion the injuries done to low-wage workers and racial others by globalization and transnationalism. But new social forces create new social subjects, who in turn create new social imaginaries. At the very moment when political and economic leaders scapegoated multilingual "mongrel" communities and cultures, music groups associated with the East L.A. scene challenged the cultural and political pretensions of white/Anglo culture. In the process, they exploited the contradiction between the nation's political reliance on fictions of cultural homogeneity and the nation's economic dependence on securing low-wage labor, markets, and raw materials from Latin America, Asia, and Africa. Speaking from the interstices between commercial culture and the new social movements, Chicana/o musical culture and its political work offers us invaluable bottom-up perspectives on the terrain of counterpolitics and cultural creation at the beginning of the twenty-first century.

Selected Discography

Aztlán Underground
Decolonize, D3 Entertainment, 1995
Sub-Verses, Xicano Records and Film, 1998

The Blues Experiment
....*Que Pasa?*, The Blues Experiment, 2000

Lysa Flores
Tree of Hope, Bring Your Love, 1998

Ollin
Sons of the Shaking Earth, Ollin, 2001

Ozomatli
Ozomatli, Almo Sounds, 1998
Embrace the Chaos, Interscope, 2001
Street Signs, Concord Records, 2004

Quetzal
Quetzal, Son del Barrio, 1998
Sing the Real, Vanguard, 2002
Worksongs, Vanguard, 2003

Quinto Sol
Kwikakali, Xicano Records and Film, 1999
Barrio Roots, Xicano Records and Film, 2003

Rage Against the Machine
Battle of Los Angeles, Epic/Sony, 1999

Slowrider
Mas Alla, !De Volada Records!, 2000
Nacimiento, !De Volada Records!, 2002
Historias en Revisión, Nomadic Soundsystem, 2003

Yeska
Skafrocubanjazz, Aztlán Records, 1998

Various
Mexamerica, Angelino Records, 2000
Sociedad=Suciedad, Better Youth Organization, 1997

Notes

1. Quoted in Brian Cross, *It's Not About a Salary . . . Rap, Race and Resistance in Los Angeles* (London: Verso, 1993), 264.
2. Quoted in Nancy Redwine, "Quetzal Flashes Its Brillance, in Two Shows," *Santa Cruz Sentinel*, December 11, 2003.
3. An earlier draft of this essay was prepared for the Mexican American Studies History Workshop, sponsored by the Center for Mexican American Studies and the Department of History at the University of Houston. I would like to thank the organizers of the workshop, Luis Alvarez and Raul Ramos, and all of the participants for their valuable suggestions and comments. I am also indebted to George Sánchez, Barry Shank, and Raúl Villa, readers for *American Quarterly*, for their helpful comments and prudent guidance on this article. This essay is dedicated to the work and vision of all of the organizers and artists of the Eastside scene.
4. See Janet L. Abu-Lughod, *New York, Chicago, Los Angeles: America's Global Cities* (Minneapolis: University of Minnesota Press, 1999). See also Saskia Sassen, *The Global City: New York, London, and Tokyo*, 2d ed. (Princeton, N.J.: Princeton University Press, 2001).
5. Lisa Catanzarite, *California's Growing Latino Population: Census 2000 Dismantles Stereotypes* (Los Angeles: UCLA Chicano Studies Research Center, March 2003). According to Catanzarite, 71 percent of Latinas/o adults and 80 percent of Latina/o youth, ages five to seventeen, in Los Angeles are bilingual.
6. U.S. Census Bureau, "*State and County Quick Facts*," HtmlResAnchor http://quickfacts.census.gov/qfd/states/06/06037.html (accessed on April 28, 2004).
7. I use "ethnic Mexican" to refer to people of Mexican descent residing in the United States, including native-born or U.S.–raised Mexican Americans and Mexican immigrants. I use "Latina/o" to describe U.S. residents of Latin American descent across race and national origin. The 1.5 generation refers to immigrants who were raised in the United States.
8. George Lipsitz, *American Studies in a Moment of Danger* (Minneapolis: University of Minnesota Press, 2001), 3–30.
9. Steven Loza, *Barrio Rhythm: Mexican American Music in Los Angeles* (Urbana: University of Illinois Press, 1993), 95–107.
10. Ibid., 95.
11. Victor Valle and Rodolfo Torres, *Latino Metropolis* (Minneapolis: University of Minnesota Press, 2000), 21.
12. *Quintosolmusic.com* (accessed on May 3, 2004).
13. Mike Davis, "L.A. Inferno," *Socialist Review* 22. 1 (January–March 1992): 57–81.
14. Nora Hamilton and Norma Stoltz Chinchilla, *Seeking Community in a Global City: Guatemalans and Salvadorans in Los Angeles* (Philadelphia: Temple University Press, 2001).
15. Manuel Pastor, "Economics and Ethnicity: Poverty, Race, and Immigration in Los Angeles County," in *Asian and Latino Immigrants in a Restructured Economy*, ed. Marta López-Garza and David R. Diaz (Stanford, Calif.: Stanford University Press, 2001), 106–7.
16. Mike Davis, *City of Quartz: Excavating the Future in Los Angeles* (New York: Vintage, 1992), 267–322. For a historical study of the criminalization of ethnic Mexicans in Los Angeles, see Edward J. Escobar, *Race, Police, and the Making of a Political Identity: Mexican Americans and the Los Angeles Police Department, 1900–1945* (Berkeley: University of California, 1999).
17. This latter proposition severely affects youth in Los Angeles County, the source for nearly one-third of the state's juvenile offenders, most of whom are African American or Latina/o. See Vince Beiser and Karla Solhei, "Juvenile Injustice: Proposition 21 Aims to Send Thousands of California Teenagers to Adult Prisons," *L.A. Weekly*, February 11–17, 2000.

18. George Lipsitz, *The Possessive Investment in Whiteness: How White People Profit from Identity Politics* (Philadelphia: Temple University Press, 1998).

19. Lisa Cacho, "'The People of California Are Suffering': The Ideology of White Injury," *Cultural Values* 4.4 (fall 2000): 390. Although the measures prescribed by Proposition 187 were ruled unconstitutional by the state, several aspects of the initiative survived as part of the Illegal Immigration Reform and Immigrant Responsibility Act and the Personal Responsibility and Work Opportunity Act that were signed into law by a democratic president in 1996.

20. Yvette C. Doss, "Choosing Chicano in the 1990s," in *Urban Latino Cultures*, ed. Gustavo Leclerc, Raul Villa, and Michael Dear (Thousand Oaks, Calif.: Sage Publications), 151.

21. Mexica is the proper name for the cultural group who migrated from Aztlán in the north to the central valley of Mexico, where they constructed the great city of Tenochitlan, now Mexico City, in the twelfth century.

22. Randy Rodarte, interview with author, October 21, 2003.

23. Quetzal Flores biography located at *quetzalmusic.org* (accessed April 28, 2004).

24. Quoted in Kurly Tlapoyawa and Ilwixochitl, "Q&A with AZTLÁN UNDERGROUND," in *Kuauhtlahtoa: Journal of Native Resistance*, n.d., http://www.mexika.org/CoverStory.html (accessed April 27, 2004).

25. Steven Loza, "From Veracruz to Los Angeles: The Reinterpretation of the Son Jarocho," *Latin American Music Review* 2.2 (1992): 188.

26. Helen Simonett, *Banda: Mexican Musical Life Across Borders* (Middletown, Conn.: Wesleyan University Press, 2001).

27. See Josh Kun's essay in this issue.

28. Duane Leyva, "Teenage Alcoholics: Punk Rock in East Los Angeles," HtmlResAnchor http://muisctap.net/DuanesPunkPitNotes/elapunk.pdf (accessed on June 29, 2004). One of the more popular groups to emerge out of the current scene is the hard-core bilingual group Union 13.

29. See the Aztlán Underground interview in Cross 1993.

30. Loza, *Barrio Rhythm*, 54–128. See also Anthony Macías, "Raza con Raza, Raza con Jazz: Latinos/as and Post World War II Popular American Music," in *Musical Migrations: Transnationalism and Cultural Hybridity in Latin/o America*, ed. Frances Aparicio and Candida Jaquez (New York: Palgrave MacMillan, 2003), 183–98; and David Reyes and Tom Waldman, *Land of a Thousand Dances: Chicano Rock 'n' Roll from Southern California* (Albuquerque: University of New Mexico Press, 1998).

31. Gustavo Arellano, "Have Jarana, Will Travel: Quetzal Find Success Making Money for Others," *OC Weekly*, November 28–December 4, 2003.

32. Quoted in "Quinto Sol," *Reggae Nucleus*, n.d., HtmlResAnchor http://www.quintosolmusic.com/news.htm (accessed April 27, 2004).

33. In Nauhuatl the term *iztac* refers to the color white.

34. Tlapoyawa and Ilwixochitl, "Q&A with AZTLÁN UNDERGROUND."

35. Angie Chabram-Dernersesian, "I Throw Punches for My Race, but I Don't Want to Be a Man: Writing Us—Chica-nos (Girl, Us)/Chicanas—into the Movement Script," in *Cultural Studies*, ed. Lawrence Grossberg, Cary Nelson, and Paula Treichler (New York: Routledge, 1992), 81–95; Ramón A. Gutiérrez, "Community, Patriarchy, and Individualism: The Politics of Chicano History and the Dream of Equality," *American Quarterly* 45.1 (March 1993): 44–72.

36. Richard T. Rodriguez, "The Verse of the Godfather: Unwrapping Masculinity, Familia, and Nationalism in Chicano Rap Discourse," in *Velvet Barrios: Popular Culture & Chicana/o Sexualities*, ed. Alicia Gaspar de Alba (New York: Palgrave Macmillan, 2003), 107–22.

37. Quoted in Chris Gonzales Clarke, "Forging the Sound of the New Millenium," in *Motion Magazine*, 1998, HtmlResAnchor http://www.inmotionmagazine.com/quetz.html (accessed April 27, 2004).

38. Quoted in Redwine, "Quetzal Flashes Its Billiance."

39. Quetzal Flores, interview with author, April 21, 2003.

40. *Sociedad=Suiciedad* (BYO Records, 1997). In the compilation *Mexamerica* (Angelino Records, 2001), East L.A. bands collaborate with musicians from Tijuana and Mexico City.

41. Tlapoyawa & Ilwixochitl, "Q&A with AZTLÁN UNDERGROUND."

42. Quetzal Flores, interview with author, April 21, 2003. In 1997 Quetzal and Martha co-organized the Chicano-Indigena Encuentro in Chiapas.

43. See Neil Harvey, *The Chiapas Rebellion: The Struggle for Land and Democracy* (Durham: Duke University Press, 1998). See also the essays collected in John Holloway and Eloína Peláez, *Zapatista! Reinventing Revolution in Mexico* (London: Pluto Press, 1998).

44. *Revolutionary Worker,* March 26, 1995, 1.

45. Lilia Ramirez, interview with author, November 5, 2002.

46. Ibid.

47. Ibid. Alvarez's critique was provoked when the money from a $250,000 grant provided by the Federal Emergency Management Agency to be used for transportation and day care for the young workers went missing.

48. Tina Barseghian, *Hollywood Independent,* April 12, 1995.

49. Lilia Ramirez, interview with author, November 5, 2002.

50. Marilyn Martinez, "Strike at Jobs Program; L.A. Conservation Corps Workers Stage Sit-In, Demand Benefits and Better Pay," *Los Angeles Times,* March 22, 1995; Fred Shuster, "Taste the New Salsa," *Los Angeles Daily News,* July 22, 1998; Josh Kun, "Around the World with Ozomatli," *Color Lines,* fall 1998; Alisa Valdes-Rodriguez, "Ozo Rising," *The Los Angeles Times,* July 25, 1999.

51. Quoted in Dianne Flowers, "Fight for Youth Center Continues in Los Angeles," *Peoples Tribune,* April 24, 1995.

52. Villa and Torres, 167–94. For the ways youth turn play into pay, see Robin D. G. Kelley, *Yo Mama's Dysfunktional! Fighting the Culture Wars in Urban America* (Boston: Beacon Press, 1997), 43–77.

53. Shuster, "Taste the New Salsa."

54. *The Battle of Los Angeles* (Epic 2000).

55. Kieran Grant, "Multiculturalism Thrives in L.A.'s Ozomatli," *Toronto Sun,* July 9, 1999.

56. Quetzal Flores interview, April 21, 2003.

What Is an MC If He Can't Rap to Banda? Making Music in Nuevo L.A.

Josh Kun

I Love Mexicans

In the weeks before the California recall election wrapped production on a hot new political farce starring Arnold Schwarzenegger, the governor-to-be hit the campaign trail. He wanted to make it clear that even though he opposes his gardeners and nannies having driver's licenses, and even though he supported Proposition 187 (California's notorious 1994 anti-immigration legislation), he actually likes Mexicans. Or at least that's what he told a crowd at the Inner City Games softball tournament in Santa Fe Springs, where he was forced to appear after he was disinvited from a Mexican Independence Day parade in East L.A.

"I love Mexico," he said. "I've done four movies down there."

For Schwarzenegger, Mexicans in California do not exist. There is only "Mexico," not actual Mexico, but virtual Hollywood Mexico: a distant "down there," a Mexico that is used, but never actually seen. This is not just an Arnold problem of course: Mexicans in California have long existed at the surreal junction between cinematic imagination and brutal political reality. By going "down there" to understand Mexicans in California, Schwarzenegger was eliding their very presence, ignoring the multiple ways in which Mexican immigration continues to transform the state he now governs, and reducing Mexicans "here" to a country "down there."

This rhetorical deportation of California Mexicans was, to say the least, a bold move, considering just how obvious a cover-up it was in a state that in 2000 became the first to have a "majority minority," with whites occupying a minority position for the first time since the nineteenth century. And, as Mike Davis and many other critics have argued, the prime impetus for this demographic shift has been the "Mexicanization" of Governor Schwarzenegger's very own backyard, Southern California.[1] In the 1990 census, Los Angeles County was 37.8 percent Latino, with Mexicans comprising almost 30 percent of the total (during the 1980s, the Latino population of L.A. and Orange counties grew by 1.5 million). In the city of Los Angeles alone, one out of every three residents was Mexican.[2]

Mexican Radio

While Schwarzenegger was busy pretending that the Mexicanization of "up here" hadn't happened, Mexican Los Angeles was doing its own publicity. The governor could have simply turned on the radio to hear it: the biggest urban hit of summer 2003, Akwid's "No Hay Manera (There's No Way)." Alongside MTV favorites like Lumidee, Wayne Wonder, Beyonce, and Sean Paul, Akwid provided the summer's most radical song—radical because of the cultural realities it fused and performed, radical because of where you could hear it and what that told you about the changing profile of Mexican Los Angeles. "No Hay Manera" got airtime on both KPWR 105.9, one of L.A.'s leading hip-hop and R&B stations ("urban," in industry parlance), and on La Que Buena (KBUE), one of the city's top regional Mexican music stations (home to traditional styles such as the accordion-driven trio and quartet sounds of norteño and grupero from northern Mexico, and the larger-scale brass marches of banda music from the northwest).

Where KPWR's target audience is generally thought to be primarily black and Latino (when in fact the station notes that its prime marketing target is L.A. Latinos), Que Buena's is predominantly immigrant Mexican. Never before had a song been on rotation cycles on both stations and in both markets—U.S. "urban" and Mexican "regional" at once—but there it was, a song that immediately shot to number seven on Billboard's specialty market Latin chart while also reaching the Top 20 on Billboard's overall, cross-market Heatseekers' charts. In its first three months on the shelves, Akwid's debut album, *Proyecto Akwid*, went platinum, a significant sales achievement in both the Latino hip-hop and Mexican regional markets.

"No Hay Manera," a song rapped in Spanish over samples of Mexican banda music mixed with West Coast hip-hop beats, was played first on La Que Buena, where the song's update of traditional banda styles found an immediate home with the station's listeners.[3] Hearing banda—albeit cloaked in hip-hop—on KPWR was the bigger coup, but one that still makes sense as the Mexicanization of Southern California has led to a dramatic transformation in the demographics of the region's radio markets. Whereas in the 1980s, Mexican and Latino radio audiences were considered specialty or niche markets better left to Mexican stations, Latinos in Southern California are now a primary and coveted segment of the city's overall market share. This is especially true for stations like KPWR, where "urban" increasingly signifies "Latino" as much it does "black." According to KPWR's senior vice president Val Maki, "We target Latinos, young Latinos. In Southern California, they are the new mainstream. Hip-hop is the global youth culture and the most popular music among young Latinos."[4]

Hip-hop may indeed be "the global youth culture," but its singular globality depends upon multiple localities—its creation, production, and reception within local and translocal sites such as Los Angeles. Hip-hop is not just popular *among* Latinos; hip-hop is a music *of* and *by* young Latinos, music they make as well as consume, music they customize and reinvent according to their own rules and styles. Akwid's "No Hay Manera," with its West Coast (U.S.) rhymes and its northwest coast (Mexico) tubas and trumpets, represents the relocalization of global hip-hop culture and its recontextualization in twenty-first-century Mexican Los Angeles. The popularity of *Proyecto Akwid* spawned an instant market-driven movement: the urban regional movement, a catch-all term for artists who blend regional Mexican music with hip-hop sensibilities. In the year after Akwid's debut, Los Angeles was flooded with "urban regional" releases from artists such as Jae-P, David Rolas, Mexiclan, and Flakiss (all signed to the Univision Music Group), and numerous Mexican regional artists—Adan Sanchez, Yolanda "La Potranquita" Perez—began incorporating hip-hop elements into their more traditional banda and norteño repertoires.[5] "We all grew up listening to Mexican music at home and listening to hip-hop with our friends," Akwid's Sergio Gomez has explained. "Our music is the inevitable outcome of this fusion between these two different cultures."[6]

As the pioneering anthem of urban regional music in Mexican Los Angeles, "No Hay Manera" is the perfect place to unpack the abstractions of "fusion" by focusing instead on what Theodor Adorno called the "congealed history" of the song—its historical layers, its union of disparate elements and epochs into a singular musical space.[7] What congeals in "No Hay Manera" are three issues I wish to highlight in the following pages: the ongoing Mexicanization of Southeast and South Central Los Angeles in the context of economic globalization and deindustrialization, and the subsequent centrality of Mexican migrant identity to the social structures and economic circuits of contemporary Los Angeles; the ongoing transformation of Mexican migrant cultural expressions from banda and norteño forms to new urban hybrids based in genre mixing, bilingualism, and generational reinvention; and the extent to which the creation of local musical forms in Los Angeles is both the *product* of the global flows of commercial popular culture and the *producer* of them. That is, Akwid's music responds to circuits of global culture, but as a local form it also changes what that global culture looks and sounds like.

Akwid's music and the urban regional movement that has sprung up around it offer a new version of the flexible ethnic identities that, as George Sanchez

has argued, have long characterized Mexican American identity in Los Angeles. In his study of Chicano identity between 1900 and 1945, Sanchez argues
that ethnicity "was not a fixed set of customs growing from life in Mexico, but
rather a collective identity that emerged from daily experience in the U.S."[8]
Akwid's music at the other end of the twentieth century supports this notion,
but also expands on it. As a music born of migration and globalization, it
performs an ethnic identity that is indeed based on a daily experience in the
United States, but one that remains influenced by and informed by a new set
of customs produced within U.S.–Mexico migration—customs based not only
on life in Mexico, but on life between Mexico and the United States. Instead
of being heard solely within the critical context of Chicano identity formation, then, Akwid's music forces us to listen as well for migrant identity formation—a kind of "becoming Mexican *in* America"—and how ethnicity is
further transformed by the experience of urban migration.

The new migrant L.A. ethnicity that Akwid performs requires a surrender-
ing of older models of nationalism and national identity as static entities per-
manently tied to fixed places on maps. In her recent critique of postcolonialism
within the diasporic circuits of economic globalization, Gayatri Chakravorty
Spivak urges us to think of nationalism as "a moving base . . . of differences, as
dangerous as it is powerful, always ahead or deferred by definitions, pro or
contra, upon which it relies."[9] The Mexicanization of South Los Angeles is
one local effect of what Spivak calls "the financialization of the globe, or globalization." Though Spivak's critique deals with labor—specifically that of
migrant women workers—and not culture, her analysis of nationalism's transformation within economic globalization is equally valuable when looking at
cultural workers like Akwid. She sees women workers as "victims below but
. . . agents above, resisting the consequences of globalization as well as redress-
ing the cultural vicissitudes of migrancy." One result is a new relationship
with the country of origin, so that "home" is no longer simply "a repository of
cultural nostalgia" but a part of "the geopolitical present."[10]

What I am suggesting here is that "No Hay Manera" in particular, and
Akwid's music and that of the urban regional movement more generally, enact
this very shift—from passive repository to active producer—even as it participates, via the recording industry, in the "financialization of the globe." Mexico
is not a repository of nostalgia here, but a generative, living source of knowledge and history—which is not, in any way, to write off the importance of
nostalgia as a potential mode of progressive thinking. Akwid's treatment of
the Mexican past through music is more akin to what Svetlana Boym has
called "reflective nostalgia," individually based nostalgia that *reflects on* na-

tional or collective pasts instead of attempting to restore and monumentalize them in the present. Reflective musical nostalgia, then, is not about memorializing a collective past, but is an individual musician's way of using the past, through performance, to structure the present as it "cherishes shattered fragments of memory and temporalizes space" without pretending to rebuild a mythical home.[11]

Where previous models of nation and home might see the migrant experience as simply adding new ingredients to the American cultural mix via paradigms such as the melting pot, Akwid's music points us elsewhere. The music may be located and produced within the geopolitical boundaries of the United States, but the transnational movements through space and time that it contains and performs beg a reevaluation of cultural production in Los Angeles. Akwid's music should not be heard solely as producing a "new" U.S. multicultural or postethnic national identity, and therefore enabling the typically reactionary state and federal "investments" in cultural diversity that so often result.[12] Indeed, instead of adding "No Hay Manera" to discussions of U.S. national identity, the song might be better heard through the ear of the new transnational cartography that Michael Dear and Gustavo LeClerc have recently dubbed "Bajalta California," the transfrontier "global metropolis" that joins Southern California to northern Mexico, "a single, integrated system of global significance." Following Dear and LeClerc, the Mexicanization of South L.A. that Akwid is a part of is a prime factor in the emergence of this region of transnational culture, economics, and identity.[13] By placing Akwid's South Los Angeles on the map of Bajalta California, the region's cultural products begin to be heard within new geopolitical contexts, with "No Hay Manera" as the soundtrack not to the formation of new national identities, but to the formation of new transnational, mobile ones.

I also want to offer Akwid's music as a way of understanding the transformation of Los Angeles's racial communities that does not necessarily replicate the apocalyptic tendencies of some recent L.A. urban theory that has developed in the noirish wake of Mike Davis's *City of Quartz: Excavating the Future of Los Angeles*.[14] Deepak Narang Sawhney's recent anthology, for example, *Unmasking L.A.: Third World and the City*, portrays Los Angeles as "an epic tale of racial disharmony, territorial conquest, and the attempted extermination of original peoples."[15] Sawhney rightly calls our attention to histories of economic apartheid, racial segregation, spatial incarceration, militaristic neighborhood policing, and reckless environmental destruction. But Akwid's "No Hay Manera"—a song produced at the juncture of Mexican immigrant and African American life in South Central L.A.—asks us to think about what cultural practices emerge within these systems of exploitation and abuse, within these histories of disharmony.

As Roger Keil points out, accepting Los Angeles as one big metaphor for global urban distress turns the lived city into "a place without people." He asks, "Where is the Los Angeles filled with human interaction, a place where incredibly complex social relationships . . . are reproduced daily?"[16] Indeed, what relationships are heard and performed in popular music? "No Hay Manera" is a reminder that for all of L.A.'s "global urban distress," the city is not simply a metaphor. It is a place where people respond to this distress using global and local languages, where people make culture happen by reinventing their identities in response to urban transformation and to the limits (and opportunities) of economic change within globalization. Indeed, while Akwid's music points to cross-racial dialogue and migrant cultural production, the social reality of urban racialization and discrimination never goes away. Just weeks after the release of *Proyecto Akwid*, the Gomez brothers were denied entrance to the Saddle Ranch restaurant on Los Angeles's Universal City Walk and roughed up by the club's bouncers because of "how they looked." The civil suit against the restaurant got under way just as their single began climbing the charts.

Akwid's music also urges us to reconsider another key theme in recent Los Angeles studies: the city as a site of collective amnesia, where ethnic and racial pasts are continually buried and erased in the drive to construct new urban presents. Norman Klein has rightly argued that L.A. is a city that has historically based its presence on its desire to erase itself. For Klein, L.A. history can be read as a "history of forgetting," in which urban development and demographic displacement create "social imaginaries" of erasure and absence, "built environments" that "contain an evacuation."[17] Yet I think it would be a mistake to accept these erasures and evacuations—for all of their urgent political and social import—as decidedly final. Indeed, popular culture and popular media within Los Angeles have historically counteracted urban amnesia. In the case of Mexican migrants, the preservation of memory in the face of erasure is a central facet of their cultural production. As I will argue below, "No Hay Manera" excavates buried memories and puts them into play within the present. The deindustrialized zone of South Central in which the song is produced may contain evacuation, but "No Hay Manera" is a good example of how expressive culture can fill those voids back up, reinserting memories of the past and even the immediate present into a social and economic landscape determined to forget them. The song demonstrates Iain Chambers's point about the role of popular music—what he calls a "journey in sound"—in maintaining memory and culture within the geopolitical and economic dispersals of globalization. The languages of popular music, he argues, "speak of the powers and potential of a specific cultural place where the inscription of memory and the prescriptions of the past come to be recited and resited."[18]

Straight Outta Michoacan

The place of Akwid is a double place, a translocal site sustained in the movement between Mexico and the United States. Akwid's Sergio and Francisco Gomez were born in the southern Mexican state of Michoacan and migrated in the 1980s to South Central Los Angeles, where they were raised. On the cover of *Proyecto Akwid,* they sport shaved heads and football jerseys and sit on the hood of a convertible Porsche between the two worlds they straddle: the tubas, beer, cacti, and Mexican flags of Michoacan, and the palm trees and office buildings of downtown Los Angeles. "We identify with this mix," Sergio Gomez has said. "We were brought from Mexico at a very young age and raised in L.A. and we spoke Spanish at home. But at school it was all English. [This mix] was something that always existed in the communities."[19] The Gomez brothers left Michoacan when they were nine, and their music carries this transnational migrant route with it—L.A. hip-hop done Mexican migrant style, or what one song proclaims, "tipo Hollywooood." They pile clapping g-funk beats and Spanish-language rhymes on top of the brassy horns of traditional Mexican regional music, especially the marching oom-pah of *banda sinaloense.* The album's opening skit dramatizes both the transnational migrant circuitry at work and their avowed merger of traditional (a Mexican *banda de viento*) and contemporary (hip-hop MCs) musical modes. Before we even hear any music, we hear the Gomezes preparing a banda de viento for their new style of banda hip-hop. The tubas, trumpets, and snare drums get in tune as the Gomezes warn the musicians that what they are about to play is like nothing they have ever played before.

The Gomez brothers have not always been this committed to translating traditional Mexican regional music into new hip-hop vocabularies. Before they were Akwid, they were Juvenile Style, rapping in English over stock nineties' West Coast beats and samples. In numerous press interviews, the duo have spoken openly about previously not wanting to, or knowing how to, mix their Mexican regional affiliations with the DJ Quik and NWA they grew up hearing in South Central. They had listened to the rough narco-corridos of Chalino Sanchez at home, but on the street, they belonged to the South Central L.A. hip-hop scene of the 1990s and were cautious about overidentifying themselves with their Mexican migrant roots. In the band's press release, Sergio Gomez explains it this way: "When you're young and you're growing up in an environment that is totally different than your culture, you find yourself being forced to adapt and assimilate, only to later evolve and reunite with your own roots."[20]

"No Hay Manera" tracks that evolution and that return. I focus on this one song not only because of its cross-market popularity in 2003 and its profound impact on the birth of other "urban regional" musical projects, but because of what the song itself contains. It is built on three separate musical layers, each of which tells its own story about Mexican migration to Los Angeles and the formation of identities in Mexican Los Angeles. The first layer consists of the lyrics themselves, a series of fairly typical hip-hop boasts in which Akwid brags about the inventiveness of its style, bridging the traditional with the new. "Como un corrido," they rap, "Akwid ha regresado con un nuevo sonido (Like a corrido, Akwid's back with a new sound)." Their rapping owes as much to the vocal styles of veteran L.A. African American MCs like Snoop Dogg, DJ Quik, and Ice Cube, as it does to the Spanish and Spanglish wordplay of the nineties' Chicano hip-hop scene (groups like Delinquent Habits, Proper Dos, Frost).

The song's second layer is the sample of Banda El Recodo's "Te Lo Pido Por Favor," which structures the melodies and rhythms of Akwid's verses and the lyrics and melodies of the chorus itself (Akwid's chorus comes directly from Recodo's). Banda El Recodo is perhaps commercial banda music's most recognizable, familiar, and endurable group. Named for El Recodo, a small Sinaloan village near Mazatlan, Banda El Recodo was founded in 1954 by Don Cruz Lizarraga and is currently still run by his son German. Although Recodo was originally a typical banda de viento, Lizarraga soon transformed the group into what would become the blueprint for a commercial *banda orquesta*, complete with music stands, suits and ties, and musicians organized into rows—a hybrid of U.S. big bands and Mexican orchestras. From 1954 to the present, Recodo has evolved along with the banda genre: from viento to orquesta to the more current "technobanda" style developed in Guadalajara that incorporates synthesizers, electric guitars, electric bass, and drum sets.[21]

Banda El Recodo was a perfect choice for Akwid to sample—a banda that signifies the transformation of banda music from a music of small-town Mexico to a transnational, commercial music fused with pop and rock elements that has become the soundtrack of Mexican migration to California. Recodo remains one of the most popular banda ensembles among Mexican immigrants in Los Angeles, which became, in the 1990s, banda's capital outside of Mexico.

Fueled by radio stations like KLAX (the top-rated station in L.A. in 1992), banda music spoke directly to the rising number of Mexican migrants who began arriving in South Los Angeles in the 1980s as a result of the Mexican economic crisis. This economic push only intensified in the 1990s when the passing of the North American Free Trade Agreement provided even more of an impetus for people to leave Mexico for higher-paying jobs in the United States. George Lipsitz has rightly called banda a register of "the dislocation of low-wage labor" and a signal of "a new cultural moment, one that challenges traditional categories of citizenship and culture on both sides of the border."[22] But he is careful not to lose the singularity of banda in Mexican Los Angeles by calling it a new form of Mexican American or even American music. As it grew in the 1990s, banda became more and more the music of Mexicans *in* the U.S., a music that refused to choose between assimilation and ethnic isolation and instead celebrated what Lipsitz calls "a re-combinant Mexican identity inside the U.S."[23]

The third layer of Akwid's "No Hay Manera" makes this point even more clear. The musicians do indeed choose a Banda El Recodo song to sample and rap over, but the song they choose has a history of its own—"Te Lo Pido Por Favor (I Ask You Please)" was originally written and recorded by veteran Mexican pop and mariachi star Juan Gabriel in 1986. Gabriel, a revered Mexican national icon, was like Akwid, born in Michoacan, and was also a product of the musical flows of the U.S.–Mexico border, having begun his career as a singer in the nightclubs of Ciudad Juarez (across the line from El Paso, Texas).[24] Yet Gabriel's enormous popularity (and his ability to traverse the worlds of radio pop balladry and traditional mariachi) has led him to become synonymous with Mexican national music, which makes Recodo's cover of him and Akwid's indirect sampling of him all the more relevant for Mexican migrants in Los Angeles—a "transborder population" in Ruben Martinez's words—who want to sustain a transnational balance between the United States and Mexico, blending patrimonies and preserving allegiances while creating new ones.[25]

When Gabriel recorded the song in the 1980s, the South Central neighborhood where the Gomez brothers were raised was a key hub in the emergence of postindustrial L.A. It was in the midst of a demographic transformation that had begun during the early stages of deindustrialization of South Los Angeles in the 1960s and 1970s. The accompanying white flight and displacement of manufacturing jobs opened up "rustbelt" communities like Southgate, Bell, Maywood, and Compton to new waves of Mexican immigrants taking advantage of the more relaxed immigration restrictions of the 1965 Hart Cellar Immigration Act.[26] As a result, through the 1970s and 1980s, the notion of

East L.A. as the exclusive capital of Mexican life in Los Angeles had been displaced by a constellation of southeastern and south central communities that Victor Valle and Rodolfo Torres have dubbed "the Greater Eastside." The suburban, deindustrialized Greater Eastside that the Gomez brothers migrated to and grew up in would also become known, especially in music circles, as "Nuevo L.A.," the part of the L.A. map (comprising more than a million people) most familiar to promoters and performers of Mexican regional music where Latinos make up roughly 90 percent of the population.[27]

The migrant audiences and migrant experiences that Akwid's music grows out of can be traced back to the key role that Southeast and South Central Los Angeles played in attracting more Mexican and Latino immigrants in the 1960s and 1970s, the very period when changes in national immigration policy helped secure the United States' dominance in the global economic system. As Saskia Sassen has argued of this period, "The central military, political, and economic role the U.S. played in the emergence of a global economic order contributed . . . both to the creation of conditions that mobilized people into migration, whether local or international, and to the formation of links between the U.S. and other countries that subsequently were to serve as bridges for international migration."[28] The rise of Mexican immigration that began in the late 1960s has led to what Mike Davis has called "the browning of L.A.'s industrial working-class" in several communities once populated by blue-collar whites and African Americans. Davis uses South Central and Southeast L.A., "Latino L.A.," as lead examples of how Latino immigration is transforming U.S. cities in terms of economics, culture, and politics. In a dramatic and highly symbolic example, Central Avenue, the former main street of black Los Angeles, is now 75 percent Latino.[29]

Akwid's arrival in Los Angeles in the 1980s was part of a larger wave of general Mexican immigration dominated specifically by migrants from their home state of Michoacan, a prolific "sender" state matched in the 1970s and early 1980s only by Jalisco.[30] Akwid's music, then, can also be heard as a product of the specific Michoacan sector of Mexican migration that has led to there being more than three million Michoacanos living and working in the United States who send home more than five billion dollars a year. In his study of migrants from Michoacan—specifically Purepeceha Indians from the pueblo of Cheran—Ruben Martinez characterizes the Mexican migrant trail not as a one-way route of departure and arrival, typical of classic twentieth-century models of European immigration, but as a mobile loop in both space and time. "The movement is circular," Martinez has argued. "You meet the future by moving out, render tribute to the past by coming back home to visit, and spend your hard-earned American dollars."[31] Roger Rouse, in his study of migration between Alguililla, Michoacan, and Redwood City, California, has called this Michoacan-California loop a "transnational migrant circuit" that leads to an "alternative cartography of social space."[32]

This migration back and forth from Michoacan produces new formations of community, identity, and culture within a "network of settlements" organized according to movements across transnational U.S.–Mexican spaces. The result is that now to be Michoacano, to be Purepecha, is to be part of this loop of traveling ideas and circulating culture. Martinez, for example, meets Chaco, who boasts of being 100 percent Purepecha while listening to house and banda and identifying with East L.A. To be Purepecha in the age of economic globalization and transnational immigration, Martinez argues, is to be a Tupac fan, wear an NBA jersey, and watch satellite TV in your village home.

Akwid members are neither Purepecha Indians nor direct participants in the transnational migrant loops that either Rouse or Martinez examines. But their experience in South Central Los Angeles as Michoacan immigrants, the way their music is born from these circulations of ideas and culture and these negotiations between past and future, is part of a new paradigm of Mexican migrant identity in which the local and global, the regional and the urban, the traditional and the modern, are not strictly opposed. Instead, they are mutually enabling, nearly complementary, nodes within a migrant, cross-border continuum both forced and enabled by the hand of economic globalization. What Martinez writes of the migrants he meets also applies to Akwid on the northern side of the borderline: "They can participate in—indeed, be protagonists of—transnational or 'global' culture even as they nurture the vestiges of their roots. In this context, the regional is global and vice-versa."[33] In songs like "No Hay Manera," the new loop of social space produced by this regional-global nexus is not just audible, but retheorized and reimagined at the level of music within the song's three layers of migrant sound.

The historical layers that congeal in "No Hay Manera" do not, however, tell us only about the resiting of identity in transnational movement. The song's sampled and covered layers—its congealing of Gabriel, Recodo, and Akwid—also involve passages in time, from recent pasts to immediate presents. The song participates in what Andreas Huyssen has explored as "the current transformation of the temporal imaginary" within "the globalization of memory."[34] The sample of Recodo covering Gabriel contains two of Huyssen's "present pasts" at once, two pasts kept alive within the present time of South Central. Akwid uses musical sampling, then, as a technology of migrant memory, a digital aide-memoire that does not just preserve memory within cultures of migration, displacement, and exile, but reanimates it by putting it into living dialogues with newly generated forms, generating "the memories needed to construct differential local futures in a global world."[35]

Ni De Aqui, Ni De Alla

The spatial and temporal movements of Akwid's music are typical of most of the artists who align themselves with the urban regional banner. In different ways, they all perform themselves as moving between spatial sites and, in a temporal move of counterassimilation, between Mexican pasts in Mexico and Mexican futures in the United States. The first artist to follow Akwid in this genre, the South Central rapper Jae-P, began his *Ni De Aqui, Ni De Alla* (*Not from Here, Not from There*) album with another "present past," as Pancho Huerta sings what at first sounds like a traditional acoustic Mexican corrido but then becomes a warning to listeners not to pirate what they are about to hear. The song is followed by the album's title track, which details an illegal border crossing into the United States from Mexico and highlights Jae-P's dual spatial belonging. That Jae-P chooses to rap from the point of view of an undocumented migrant when he himself was actually born in South Central only further highlights the centrality of migrant experience to the formation of identity in Nuevo L.A.

Jae-P dedicates his norteño-tinged hip-hop—"corridos just like rappin'"—to portraying a Mexican American urban experience that vacillates between the hood and the campo. On the CD's cover, his own image is superimposed onto a collage of a Mexican flag on a hillside and a strip of downtown L.A. Inside, there is a shot of him squatting in an underground tunnel that runs from the Tijuana border checkpoint directly to L.A.'s city hall. He boasts that he listens to La Que Buena and to KPWR (where "they freak the beat") and warns, "no desprecies mi sonido cuz it's born in LA (don't insult my sound . . .)." Where Akwid concentrates on the regional Mexican music it samples, language is the material Jae-P uses to build his one-tunnel, two-countries identity. He may make it in the United States, but he'll do it with two accents on his tongue, "dos accentos en la lengua." He tells us that while he learned to speak English (he also used to rap in it), he has no interest in assimilating. "I'm from Califas," he boasts, "pura sangre azteca (pure Aztec blood)." When he throws a "West Coast party," he does it Mexican style, "al estilo Mexicano."

Switching between Spanish and English is Jae-P's way of performing his temporal and spatial doubleness. His Spanglish fluency is not a mark of being lost between languages, but precisely the opposite, of being a master of both, knowing the right moment when to choose one or the other. Echoing the regional-global loop of Martinez's migrants, Jae-P wants to be able to embrace hip-hop without sacrificing corridos, without assimilating into whitewashed, English-only Americanism, without having to stop being a Mexicano in Los Angeles. "You want me to change my culture," he says. "Fuck that."

Other urban regional artists follow similar formulas, combining elements of hip-hop (sampled beats, rapping) with elements of Mexican regional music. David Rolas's *Nuestra Vida* starts with Cecilia Brizuela hyping Rolas in a traditional ranchera grito style that ends with her breaking into English and issuing a common hip-hop warning: "Don't hate the playa, hate the game." Yolanda Perez's debut album of otherwise straightforward Mexican regional songs also begins with a nod to hip-hop: a bilingual argument with her father (played by La Que Buena DJ Don Cheto) about her independence carried out over hip-hop beats and done in the style of a rap duet. Cheto raps in a heavily accented Spanish; Perez switches between Spanish and English: "Y voy a tener novio [I'm going to have a boyfriend] and I don't care if you get mad!" Later in the album, Perez delivers a romantic banda song in English, singing "You'll Lose a Good Thing" as if it were an R&B ballad performed by a Mexican banda.

All of these mergers of regional Mexico and regional Mexican L.A., of hip-hop with bandas and corridos, of two accents on one tongue and two flags in one heart, could only have come out of Nuevo L.A. at the turn of the twenty-first century, a time when both hip-hop and Mexican regional music are the dueling dominant forces in urban L.A. popular culture. In 2002, Mexican regional star Pepe Aguilar became the first artist in any genre to play a series of sold-out concerts at the prestigious Kodak Theater in Hollywood. The year 2001 saw the debut of Mex2TheMax, a Mexican regional music video show on KJLA-LATV that reaches more than three million homes throughout Southern California. Concerts by leading regional acts like Los Tigres del Norte and Lupillo Rivera regularly sell out multiple nights, and groups like Oxnard's Los Razos sell twenty thousand copies of an album in one week with virtually no mainstream publicity from their label.

What began in Los Angeles as largely the music of swap meets, homegrown indie labels, and car trunks is now central to the growing corporatization of Mexican media in the United States. The label that markets Akwid's music is part of the Univision empire that includes USA network, TelefuturaTV network, Univision Music group, Venevision, Galavision, and most recently, the Hispanic Broadcasting Company, the largest Spanish-language radio broadcasting company in the United States.

This is all happening, of course while hip-hop remains the dominant commercial force of American popular music and a major soundtrack to life in Los Angeles. From the high school cheerleaders who appear in Akwid's videos and stage shows to their football jerseys, from the live banda ensemble they often perform with to their samples and their beats, Akwid give us a fully integrated merger of hip-hop Mexican regional identities, a new hybrid that does not ask the musicians to choose one world over the other but allows them to flow between both. Where Jae-P declares that he is "ni de aqui, ni de alla," neither from here nor there, Akwid says that it is *de aqui;* it's just that *aqui* carries *alla* with it. In "No Hay Manera," there is no *aqui* without *alla*, no corridos without hip-hop, no hip-hop without banda, no L.A. without Michoacan.

The merger of Mexican regional music and L.A. hip-hop in urban regional music does not, of course, emerge from a historical vacuum. It speaks directly to two related histories of migrant cultural production in Mexican and African American neighborhoods in Los Angeles. First, as journalist Sam Quiñones has pointed out, with the success of Mexican corrido singer Chalino Sanchez in Los Angeles in the late 1980s, the early 1990s saw a sudden rise in young L.A. Mexicanos who, otherwise immersed in the popular styles of urban culture, now wanted to play Mexican regional music. What they once considered the corny and uncool music of their parents was now cool and rebellious, thanks to the underground popularity of Sanchez's raw tales of cross-border narco life. When Sanchez was killed in 1992, his popularity escalated even further. As one L.A. Mexicano noted, "When we were small, we always wanted to fit in, so we'd listen to rap. The other kids were all listening to rap, so I guess we felt that if we listened to Spanish music we'd be beaners or something. But after Chalino died, everybody started listening to corridos. People wanted to feel more Mexican."[36]

So kids who were hip-hop fans now also wanted to play corridos and banda, leading to the rise of the "chalinazo"—young L.A. Mexicans who fused their love for Sanchez's immigrant outlaw stance as a narco bad boy with the gangsta poses of NWA into "narcotraficante chic." What Quinones dubs the post-Chalino "Sinaloaization of L.A." led to the rise of gangsta regional/gangsta Mexicano hybridizations by Lupillo and Jenni Rivera, son and daughter of corrido singer and label owner Pedro Rivera—Long Beach twenty-somethings who started putting Stetson hats on the gangsta lean of Ice-T and fusing the iconography and attitudes of "the hood" with the iconography and attitudes of a rancho that they never lived on. But the Riveras never actually made hip-hop records. They stuck to corridos, rancheras, and banda, albeit with Lexuses on their album covers. The shift marked by Akwid and the rest of the regional urbanites is that they actually do both—they bring corridos and banda into the hip-hop form.

It Wouldn't Be L.A. Without Mexicans

There is a final "congealed history" in Akwid's "No Hay Manera," that of Mexican and African American musical dialogue in Los Angeles. More specifically, Akwid's regionalization of hip-hop reminds us that South Central and Southeast Los Angeles have long been vital spaces of exchange and coalition between black and Mexican communities. These populations often engaged in common struggles against legislative power, white supremacy, and urban renewal—even as these very forces conspire to keep them separated, divided, and more important, at war with each other. The South Central neighborhoods where Akwid grew up, which are now predominantly Latino, were once overwhelmingly African American, and the world they grew up in was based on the styles and sensibilities of African American hip-hop culture.

"It wouldn't be L.A. without Mexicans," Tupac Shakur rapped in 1996. "Black love, brown pride, . . . Pete Wilson tryin' to see us all broke, . . . out for everything they owed." The line is from Shakur's "To Live and Die in L.A.," a song that seems to be simply a rendering of black Los Angeles, specifically South Central Los Angeles, as "the city of angels in constant danger." Tupac's L.A. is a city divided by its neighborhoods, policed by "ghetto bird helicopters," and torn apart by the crack economy's war for drugs that turned into Darryl Gates and Nancy Reagan's war on drugs.

His L.A. may be the home of "niggas getting' three strikes tossed in jail," but it's also Nuevo L.A., Latino L.A., the L.A. of the Greater Eastside. South Central L.A. may be cemented in the public imagination as a black community by the media coverage of the 1992 uprisings (as the black home of a black riot), but it is well over half Latino. Tupac reminds us that African American cultural activism and struggle must be in chorus with Chicano resistance to nativist legislation like Proposition 187, precisely because Pete Wilson is trying to "see them *all* broke." Blacks and Mexicans in South Central L.A. may use some different instruments, may occasionally sing in different languages, but they hear the same song.

Just to prove Tupac right, Delinquent Habits—a hip-hop trio of a "guero loco," a Chicano, and a "Blaxican" best known for their use of Herb Alpert, mariachi, and tango records as samples—returned the favor by recognizing Tupac's recognition of Mexican L.A. The group built its song "This Is L.A." on a sampled loop of Tupac's verse. The exchange that these two songs represent—in George Lipsitz's formulation "the families of resemblance" they speak to—are of course also part of a "bloc of opposition," a pop musical conversation that rehearses and enacts a political coalition built on shared resistance to shared systems of oppression within Los Angeles.[37] "We might fight each other," Tupac sings, "but we'll burn this bitch down if you get us pissed." Part Los Ilegals "El Lay" (where the LAPD hunts undocumented Mexicans) and part NWA "Fuck Tha Police" (where the LAPD hunts blacks in Compton), Tupac's burning city is still fresh from the uprisings and intimate with the national guard, a Los Angeles ready to go up in flames, be torn down and built anew, always at war.

This black and Mexican back-and-forth is perhaps best summed up by Ozomatli, a band of multiracial urban fusionists, self-professed anarchists and red diaper babies who hail from across the Greater Eastside of Nuevo L.A. In 1998, in the middle of a beat-juiced Mexican ranchera hoedown they call "La Misma Cancion," the same old song, they asked: "What is a DJ if he can't scratch to a ranchera?" When you are a band of Chicanos and Salvadorans and Basques and Jews and Japanese and Filipinos and blacks and whites and browns, a band synonymous with post-urban uprising Los Angeles, the answer to that question is simple. The DJ who's been schooled on funk breakbeats or jazz bridges or Roland 808 kick patterns who can scratch to the Watts funk of Charles Wright or the South Central electro of World Class Wreckin Crew but who can't scratch to the accordions and rural romance of a Mexican ranchera is a DJ who will become obsolete. The DJ of Nuevo L.A. is no DJ if a ranchera can't be turned out under a stylus scratch so you can still get your groove on at a quinceñera. The same goes for any musician who can't reshape banda around a rhyme or any hip-hop crew who can't cut tubas from Banda El Recodo into a looped beat.

After all, the question they pose isn't even theirs. They're sampling too. It was first asked in the early 1980s by pioneering African American rap and electro artist Egyptian Lover. But when he asked it, it was just "What is a DJ if he can't scratch?"—one of L.A. hip-hop's first DJ dares. Ozomatli's addition to it ups the ante on the DJ's skill: it's no longer purely just about technical ability (can you scratch?); it's about creative selection (what can you scratch to?). For Ozomatli, the DJ can't just know hip-hop, can't just scratch over a James Brown "Funky Drummer" break, but must know what to do with the acoustic guitars, accordions, and simple snare steps of a ranchera or the tubas and snare rolls of a Banda El Recodo cover of Juan Gabriel. The ability of the DJ working in an African American art form to scratch over Mexican music is the ability to be a cultural cross-fader, a DJ who can cut between the cultures he or she lives in, a DJ who understands cultural exchange and cultural collision well enough to make music out of it. After all, part of the point of the scratch is to transform (there is even a specific kind of scratch that has been labeled "the transformer scratch"), to take one musical unit, change its shape, blur its message, reduce it to skeletal percussive noise, then allow it to gather itself and reform and rediscover its code, changed and different, a new sound with new tones.

So when Akwid sample Banda El Recodo covering Juan Gabriel, they up Ozomatli's ante and ask, "What is an MC if he can't rap to banda?" The question is actually a challenge, a challenge to contemporary Los Angeles to listen to itself, to turn on the radio and hear through the static of disharmony and urban unrest and hear—in beats, in tubas, in rhymes, and in samples—the sound of its communities, the sound of its dialogues, the new sound of Nuevo L.A.

Notes

1. Mike Davis, *Magical Urbanism: Latinos Reinvent the U.S. City* (London: Verso, 2000), 2.
2. Rodolfo F. Acuna, *Anything But Mexican: Chicanos in Contemporary Los Angeles* (London: Verso, 1996), 3.
3. Brass bands in northwestern Mexico have been performing "banda" music—literally "band music"—for more than a century. Born and developed in the state of Sinaloa under the influence of military marching bands, banda was initially an instrumental music limited to village brass bands playing trumpets, tubas, trombones, and drums, with no guitars and no vocalists. Over the last century, traditional banda ensembles like bandas de viento (wind bands) and bandas de orquesta (orchestra bands) gave way in the 1990s to the birth of "technobanda," a modernized banda style that added electric guitars, bass, and synthesizer to the traditional mix. The development of banda is chronicled in detail by Helena Simonett in *Banda: Mexican Musical Life Across Borders* (Middletown, Conn.: Wesleyan University Press, 2001).
4. Nicole Taylor, "Top Radio Stations: Ranked by Audience Share, Summer 2002," *Los Angeles Business Journal*, November 25, 2002, 1–2.
5. Yolanda Perez, *Dejenme Llorar* (Fonovisa); David Rolas, *Nuestra Vida* (Fonovisa); Jae-P, *Ni De Aqui, Ni De Alla* (Univision Music Group); Mexiclan, *Mexiclan* (Univision Music Group).
6. Mar Yvette, "Urban Legends: The Rise of Urban Regional," *Urban Latino Magazine*, November/December 2003. http://www.marpop.com/urbanregional.html.
7. Robert Witkin, *Adorno on Music* (New York: Routledge, 1998).
8. George Sanchez, *Becoming Mexican-American: Ethnicity, Culture and Identity in Chicano Los Angeles, 1900–1945* (New York: Oxford University Press, 1993), 11.
9. Gayatri Chakravorty Spivak, *A Critique of Postcolonial Reason: Toward a History of The Vanishing Present* (Cambridge: Harvard University Press, 1999), 363.
10. Ibid., 360.
11. Svetlana Boym, *The Future of Nostalgia* (New York: Basic Books, 2001), 49–50.
12. I realize that Spivak would no doubt disapprove of my insertion of popular culture into her analysis of agency and nationalism within globalization. She critiques the cultural studies tendency to culturalize transnationalism, arguing, "To recode a change in the determination of capital as a cultural change is a scary symptom of cultural studies, especially feminist cultural studies. Everything is being made 'cul-

tural'" (Spivak, *A Critique of Postcolonial Reasoning*, 412). My aim here is not use Akwid to culturalize economic globalization as a means of diluting the political and financial urgencies of labor inequities and social injustices within processes of immigration and diaspora. Yet I do want to make a case for the enduring importance of understanding culture's role in the forging of new identities and the performance of new communities, especially as modes of translocal articulation and social survival within globalization. Likewise, I think discussions and critiques of globalization must continue to consider culture's relationship to economic structures of displacement and labor migration.

13. Michael Dear and Gustavo LeClerc, "The Postborder Condition: Art and Urbanism in Bajalta California," in *Postborder City: Cultural Spaces of Bajalta California*, ed. Michael Dear and Gustavo LeClerc (New York: Routledge, 2003), 2.

14. Mike Davis, *City of Quartz: Excavating the Future of Los Angeles* (New York: Vintage, 1992), and *The Ecology of Fear: Los Angeles and the Imagination of Disaster* (New York: Vintage, 1999).

15. Deepak Narang Sawhney, "Journey Beyond the Stars: Los Angeles and Third Worlds," in *Unmasking LA: Third World and the City*, ed. Deepak Narang Sawhney (New York: Palgrave, 2002), 2.

16. Roger Keil, "Los Angeles As Metaphor," in *Unmasking LA*, 202.

17. Norman M. Klein, *The History of Forgetting: Los Angeles and the Erasure of Memory* (London: Verso, 1997), 10.

18. Iain Chambers, "Citizenship, Language, and Modernity," in *PMLA: Mobile Citizens, Media States* 117.1 (January 2002), 29.

19. Ramiro Burr, "New, Traditional Music Enjoying Broad Appeal," *Houston Chronicle*, January 14, 2004. http://www.chron.com/cs/CDA/ssistory.mpl/features/burr/2343330.

20. Official press release, *Akwid: Proyecto Akwid*, Unision Music Group, 2003.

21. Simonett, *Banda*, 169.

22. George Lipsitz, "Home Is Where the Hatred Is: Work, Music, and the Transnational Economy," in *Home, Exile, Homeland: Film, Media, and the Politics of Place*, ed. Hamid Naficy (New York: Routledge, 1999), 195.

23. Ibid., 210.

24. Banda El Recodo, "Te Lo Pido Por Favor," included on the compilation *Pa' Que Te Enamores* (ProTel, Universal, 2000); Juan Gabriel, "Te Lo Pido Por Favor," *Pensamientos* (RCA 1986).

25. Simonett, *Banda*, 85.

26. Victor Viesca, "Straight Out of the Barrio: Ozomatli and the Importance of Place in the Formation of Chicano/a Popular Culture in Los Angeles," *Cultural Values* 4.4 (October 2000).

27. Victor Valle and Rodolfo Torres, *Latino Metropolis* (Minneapolis: University of Minnesota Press, 2000); Valle and Torres, "Latinos in a Post-Industrial Order," *Socialist Review* 93.4; and for "Nuevo L.A.," see Simonett, *Banda*.

28. Saskia Sassen, "U.S. Immigration Policy Toward Mexico in a Global Economy," in *Between Two Worlds: Mexican Immigrants in the United States*, ed. David G. Guiterrez (Wilmington: Scholarly Resources, 1996), 214.

29. Davis, *Magical Urbanism*, 39.

30. Dolores Acevedo and Thomas J. Espenshade, "Implications of the North American Free Trade Agreement for Mexican Migration into the United States," in *Between Two Worlds*, 233.

31. Ruben Martinez, *Crossing Over: A Mexican Family on the Migrant Trail* (New York: Picador, 2002), 25.

32. Roger Rouse, "Mexican Migration and the Social Space of Postmodernism," in *Between Two Worlds*, 257.

33. Martinez, *Crossing Over*, 132.

34. Andreas Huyssen, "Present Pasts: Media, Politics, Amnesia," in *Globalization*, ed. Arjun Appadurai (Durham: Duke University Press, 2001), 74–76.

35. Ibid.

36. Sam Quinones, *True Tales from Another Mexico: The Lynch Mob, the Popsicle Kings, Chalino, and the Bronx* (Albuquerque: University of New Mexico Press, 2001), 24.

37. George Lipsitz, *Time Passages: Collective Memory and American Popular Culture* (Minneapolis: University of Minnesota Press, 1990), 158.

Fools Banished from the Kingdom: Remapping Geographies of Gang Violence between the Americas (Los Angeles and San Salvador)

Elana Zilberg

The topographical reform of the civic body by the unceremonious exportation and dumping of libido in the countryside and in the far away colonies . . . is the perfect representation of the production of identity through negation.

—Peter Stallybrass and Allon White[1]

This essay explores how the policing, incarceration and, most dramatically, the deportation of Salvadoran immigrant youth are reshaping the parameters of urban experience between Los Angeles and El Salvador. These disciplinary governmental practices have transformed the geographies of belonging, exclusion, and citizenship between the once putatively separate cultural and political spheres of the United States and Central America. Drawing on ethnographic fieldwork conducted with deported youth, the essay focuses on the crucial place of the city in the production of their transnational subjectivities. Following the work of James Holston and Arjun Appadurai, I argue that at this juncture in globalization and with the attendant unsettling of national citizenship, cities such as Los Angeles and San Salvador emerge as crucial spaces for the appearance of radically unfamiliar and new identities. They are key sites for the mediation between the national and the global and for the localization of global forces.[2] The role played by the city in mediating between the local, national, and global is most evident in the production of the deportation narratives under consideration here. In the case of deported Salvadoran immigrant youth, it is on the streets of the urban *barrio* that the United States is most effectively policing the boundaries of its nation-state.[3] Moreover, the emergent transnational identities of these youth are, in fact, created by the very forces of nationalism directed at them through the collusion between local law and federal immigration enforcement bodies.

The local police beat has thus become both a staging ground for managing the pressures of globalization and for the globalization of youth violence. Take, for instance, the corruption scandal surrounding CRASH (Community Resources against Street Hoodlums), the zero tolerance gang abatement unit in the Los Angeles Police Department (LAPD)'s Rampart division. That scandal, which erupted in 1999 in the heart of a Latino immigrant neighborhood just west of downtown Los Angeles, was in many ways a sequel to the 1991 Rodney King beating. Indeed, the Rampart police scandal brought back the ghost of King's bruised body in another form: the paralyzed, framed, and wrongfully imprisoned body of undocumented Central American immigrant and member of the 18th Street Gang, Javier Ovando. Under pressure of the corruption charges leveled against him, officer Rafael Perez agreed to cooperate with an investigation into the illegal activities of his unit. Perez's testimony described how he and his fellow CRASH officers engaged in bank robberies, drug deals, and organized prostitution rings. The officers were also accused of wounding and killing unarmed gang members and planting guns and drugs on their victims.

If not for the eruption of the scandal and the subsequent revisiting of his case, Javier Ovando would more than likely have been turned over to the Immigration and Naturalization Service (INS) and deported at the end of his prison term. Indeed, at the time of the scandal, the LAPD had targeted ten thousand purported gang members for deportation, and the INS and Border Patrol agents maintained a regular presence in LAPD's booking-and-charging out facilities. As a result of this collaboration, even when criminal charges against gang and purported gang members were overturned, the INS still maintained a deportation hold on them. According to the Federal Public Defender's office in Los Angeles, this tactic had been employed by the LAPD to push many a key hostile witness into and through the deportation pipeline, thereby hindering efforts of defense attorneys in pending cases against immigrant youth and of those seeking to prosecute rogue officers in the Rampart case itself.

As journalist Peter Boyer explained, "The [Rampart] investigation was a messy process, because it had no precedent. [Rampart CRASH officer] Perez [the key defendant and informant in the case] would tell the task force about a bad case, and the detectives would fan out to . . . village[s] in Central America" in search of wrongfully deported immigrants.[4] Rampart was an unprecedented scandal for the Los Angeles Police Department only because of its transnational dimensions. While Rampart police officers patrol a very limited and highly localized beat, their actions on the streets of L.A.'s urban neighborhoods have transnational reach. Well beyond the scope of the Rampart scandal, deportation, following incarceration, of immigrant gang youth has become a key management strategy for the United States. Zero-tolerance gang-abatement strategies combined with changes in immigration law as a result of the Illegal Immigration Reform and Individual Responsibility Act of 1996 have resulted in the deportation to El Salvador of thousands of Salvadoran immigrant gang youth—including permanent residents and some for nonviolent offenses.

Speaking from San Salvador, then twenty-seven-year-old deportee from Los Angeles Weasel explains his situation this way:

> I've got this document right here. It says my full name and it has a little box right here that's checked and it says deportable under section blah blah blah. Removed from the *States*. Anyways the bottom line is that I've been banished from the U.S., you know, like they used to do in the medieval days, they used to banish "fools" from the kingdom . . . people who did something that was considered a threat to the crown (in my case society). Anyway, that's how I felt. They kicked me out of society [the United States] and sent me into the jungle [El Salvador] to live alone in my own solitude.[5]

But Weasel is far from alone. He is surrounded by "fools," "homeboys" from "Elay" . . . "banished from the kingdom." Indeed, El Salvador is now host to a new social formation built on this puzzling relationship between space and identity. Deported Salvadoran immigrant gang youth—banished from the United States after spending the better part of their young lives in this country—are returned "home" to a place where, in their memory, they have never been. As Bulldog exclaimed five days after his rude return to El Salvador: "Shit, homes, I've never been here. I mean, I know I'm from here, homes, but I've never been here." And then with disbelief, "You from here too?"

Weasel, who left El Salvador for Los Angeles when he was five years old, continues thus:

> Ey, you know (a little laugh) . . . I went to kindergarten in Elay, elementary school, junior high school, high school. Man, I grew up singing—you know—my country 'tis of thee (he laughs again) . . . the song "America the Beautiful" . . . and—you know—pledging allegiance to the flag. Well, I grew up with all of that . . . and here they are, you know, twenty-something years later, kicking me out.[6]

When these Salvadoran immigrant gang youth, deported from the United States, run into each other in the busy, congested streets of El Salvador's capital, San Salvador, or in those cobbled streets of its dusty *pueblos* (towns), the first thing they ask one another is, "Where you from, homes?" This is a multiply determined question about origin, geography, affiliation, and identity, which takes this much in common—the territory of the Latino *barrio* in the United States.

Much of my research is set in Los Angeles and focuses on the contentious social production of the Pico Union district as a Central American immigrant *barrio*, where many of these deported youth are "from." Pico Union, which falls under the jurisdiction of the Rampart police division, is Salvadoran Los Angeles's symbolic, if not demographic, center. While still predominantly Mexican and Mexican American, it is also home to nearly every Central American community organization and has served as the central stage for their political protests and cultural production. My research there tracks the spatial logic of the cultural politics behind the expulsion of "fools" like Weasel "from the kingdom."[7] Yet as the emergent subjectivities of these transnational protagonists suggest, any such study must be agile enough to traverse local, national, and global scales and to track flows—material, discursive, and affective—between the immigrant *barrios* of Los Angeles and *barrios populares* (working-class neighborhoods) of San Salvador. Certainly, the inner-city *barrio* in Los Angeles is a complex articulation of local forces. It is a space acted on by the contradictory pressures of urban redevelopment and law enforcement agencies and social justice organizations, as well as the enabling and disabling everyday practices of residents themselves.[8] But there is still more at stake. There is the cultural politics of forced repatriation on the other side—in Central America. Indeed, the Central American *barrio* in Los Angeles is haunted with voices from and banished to El Salvador.

Youth deported from Los Angeles walking the streets of San Salvador calling themselves "homies" are the shock effects of globalization as it clashes with nationalism. They are the embodiment of a forced transnationality. While the literal mobility of these deported youth may have been arrested, contained, and reversed by the forces of nationalism, their narratives—which leak beyond the bounds of the nation-state—tell us volumes about the complex relationship between space and identity. They reveal a painful rupture between culture and nation, where cultural identity does not correspond to, but is, rather, excluded from national citizenship. It is to those narratives that I now turn and through them, to an interrogation of the ways in which the geographies of violence, of belonging and exclusion, of Los Angeles's immigrant *barrios* have been relocated and reinscribed within the post-civil war landscape of San Salvador's *barrios populares*.

Gato's Story

I met Gato in Modelo, a *barrio popular* in San Salvador, and territory to a *clika* (clique) of the gang La Mara Salvatrucha (MS). In Los Angeles, Gato was a veteran of the MS archrival, the 18th Street Gang. We began our conversation in English sitting outside his home, a modest concrete apartment, attached to a small liquor and convenience store run by his mother. Gato is fully conversant in both Spanish and English. However, as is clear from the transcription below, he is not a native U.S. English speaker. His speech—a mixture of street English, the Spanglish of Chicano gangs, and the *caliche* of Salvadoran colloquial Spanish—still marks him as Salvadoran, and as immigrant to the United States.[9]

Gato is originally from Modelo. I am confused and curious. How does he navigate this terrain living inside enemy territory and with the enemy? He begins to explain:

> G: First they told me, "Don't write on the walls." You know, write 18th Street . . . And I told them, "I won't do that."
>
> Z: So you came to an agreement with them?
>
> G: Yeah, we came to an agreement. I told them, "If you guys don't bother me, I'm not going to bother you guys." But, if they do . . . planning to do something, do it good. You know, kill me.
>
> Z: So nothing's happened?
>
> G: No, that's because I don't . . . I'm working. I have my life together. If they know I'm still gangbanging, of course, they could kill me man, you know.
>
> Z: But this is your *barrio*, where you're from?
>
> G: All these guys, they were my friends when I was a little kid, and they get mad because [they say], "Why don't you be jumping in an MS neighborhood?" You know, I told 'em, "Hey, when I went to California I grew up at 6th and Junior." That was PBY territory, now it's 18th Street. You know the hangout for my neighborhood? Of course, they all go in Normandie or Olivar and other streets that was from MS. I would jump in MS because I love my country, but . . . it's not that.

Back in his neighborhood in El Salvador, Gato must now explain why he did not join La Mara Salvatrucha, the gang, at least at its inception, associated with Salvadorans, and which broke away from the Mexican-dominated 18th Street Gang. I look at the *barrio* around us and wonder at how its territorial identifications have been reshaped by the war and by U.S.-bound migration. Gato and his, at least up until then, benevolent enemy hosts grew up together in the same *barrio* in San Salvador—Modelo. But by virtue of their relocation to adjacent inner-city neighborhoods in Los Angeles—Pico-Union versus Korea Town—they are now from different neighborhoods in L.A. and, therefore, inside El Salvador. While they hail from the same home, they are not *homeboys* to one another, but enemies. Salvadoran geography has been rewritten—its political boundaries redistricted, if you will—by this migration, U.S. inner-city politics and deportation.

As Gato explains later, "The problem is that we came deported from the States. Someone . . . they're bringing the neighborhoods down to my country . . . That thing of the neighborhood [is] from California." Gato launches into a critique of the naive transposition of Los Angeles's political terrain onto El Salvador by Salvadoran "wannabes" and poor copies of the real thing in the United States. I have heard this critique from one deported gang member after another.

Whoever brought my neighborhood back here in the 90s, they fucked up, really fucked up my country. Because man, you really see the writing on the walls in the streets. That came in the 90s . . . It's like you're seeing the freeways from L.A., and they don't even know how to write on the walls. They write real stupid, you know. They put "Westside 18th Street" or "Northside MS," and we're not really on the Northside or Westside here. We're in South Central. Or they put area "213." Man, that's a telephone call from downtown California, . . . or put "818." That's El Monte, you know. They get me real mad because they don't even know about the Southside thing, or the Northside thing. They just know enemy 18th Street, or enemy MS.

And so it is to the "real" landscape of California that our conversation wanders. Gato's vivid account of the globalization of his *sureño* (Southside) identity politics demonstrates how deeply linked San Salvador is to the spaces inside Los Angeles and vice versa. As Gato begins to explain the geography and genealogy of his criminalization, he guides us through the familiar landmarks of Pico-Union's built environment. Gato was a student at Belmont High, "right there on Wilmont and Lucas." He jumped into (was initiated into) his neighborhood gang when he was fifteen or so as a means to seek revenge against "a guy from Rockwood" who stole a gold chain. His father, who was killed in El Salvador for his political involvement, had given the chain to Gato before he died. His gang life culminated in an arrest for the attempted murders of two members of Crazy Riders, who had driven into his neighborhood and pulled out an AK-47, hitting his homeboy. "It happened right there by a Jack in the Box, on 6th and Bonnie Brae, by what used to be the Hotel California [infamous first stop for many a newly arrived immigrant], next to a place called La Barata." He was chased down Westlake, close to MacArthur Park—the symbolic center of Pico-Union.

Like so many in his situation, in order to get a lighter sentence, Gato accepted a deal with the judge, and pleaded guilty to the felony counts. Gato begins to talk about the minefield of cultural politics inside the prison, which jump between these scales of identification: neighborhood (the gang), nationality (El Salvador vs. Mexico), geographic orientation (Southsider vs. Northsider), and racial identification (Latino vs. black, white, and Asian).

Every time the door opens and you step out, you don't know if the problem's going to be with a Blood, a white boy, or Japanese, and you got to react because you're Latino man, you are Hispanic. Inside prison, believe it or not, we're united man. We are united as Southsiders, *sureños* . . . It would be cool if . . . neighborhoods could get along like in prison man. Not because you're Mexican, you're from Peru, or you're from El Salvador. No. We're all Hispanic man, we're all brown, we all speak the same language. Just because I'm a Salvadoran, you're going to feel better than me? No. We're all equal, man. Some of my homeboys, and the guys from MS, they don't think that way.

Once inside the prison, the city's geography seems to lose some of its primacy. The relationship between space and identity now transcends the borders of the urban *barrio* that were so crucial to identity formation prior to incarceration. Local *barrio* identities give way to racial, ethnic, regional, and national differences. The prison thus becomes a crucial site for the remediation of urban identities, and deportation takes this reidentification one step further. Gato's discussion concludes with an elaboration of an intricate geography of belonging: a continental American and pan-ethnic identity as Latino. But upon deportation to the streets of San Salvador, this *concientización* (consciousness raising) as Latino and as *sureño*, is more often than not overwhelmed by the reproduction of divisions between *barrios* in San Salvador, reworked as they are by those in Los Angeles.

Gato's words weigh heavily as I write. He was killed not long after this interview by an MS gang member. The burden of representation looms large.

Weasel's Story

You have already been introduced to Weasel briefly in the prologue to this essay, where he describes himself as that "fool banished from the kingdom." Weasel captured my anthropological imagination from the start because, unlike the deportees I had met up to that point, Weasel bore no traces of his Salvadoran identity. I was thrown by Weasel's style and his speech. The latter—filled as it is with the stylistic markers of Chicano and of Californian youth culture, as well as playful appropriations of African American linguistic forms—is unmistakably U.S. English. Indeed, Weasel describes his reencounter with his "native" country as a "complete culture clash."

Nor did Weasel fit into the dominant configuration of gang affiliation among Salvadoran immigrants in Los Angeles: MS or 18th Street. I asked him about his gang.

W: My gang was called the Westside Los Crazies, and we're in Echo Park.

I tell Weasel that I live in Echo Park. His eyes light up, and he jokes about me being his *homegirl*, and from there on out, Weasel always introduces me as

"Elana, she's from my ex-*barrio*."

> W: The members are mostly Chicanos, or if they've got any Salvadoran or Cuban background, Puerto Rican, whatever, you know they're born there, they're born in the States, you know.
>
> Z: So it's not an immigrant gang?
>
> W: No, no, not at all, not at all. I mean, they're all born there. I mean their parents could've been immigrants.
>
> Z: Or you were an immigrant?
>
> W: Yes, but I didn't even recognize that word "immigrant" you know until I got a little older. You know, I just . . . I grew up like, I guess you could say like, naive to the fact that I came from another country and I was living in the States, and I just, I never thought about you know like . . . backgrounds . . . because everybody around like me spoke Spanish or English and you know they were Latino in general, the majority was Mexican, and Chicanos, very few blacks. But I did grow up seeing black people and so it wasn't a total Latino neighborhood.
>
> Z: Do you remember what you said to me the other night over dinner? You said, "I guess you could say, I am, or I was a Salvadoran living in America living a . . ."
>
> W: Living a Chicano lifestyle! Yeah, that's what I said.
>
> . . . [T]he funny thing, is that everyone thought I was Mexican, 'ey. I kept on telling them, "I'm not, you know, I was born in El Salvador, 'ey." You know, every time they would ask me, I'd say, "I'm Salvadoran. I was born in El Salvador." But uh . . . after a while they'd forget about it because they're so used to you and you're so much like them that it doesn't even matter, you know.
>
> . . .[L]ike I was telling you, you know, I had like a Mexican upbringing. And in Los Angeles they have this like, this multicultural uh, uh . . . I guess, they teach you, about other cultures, and since there's a lot of Mexicans there, they teach you a lot about that, you know. They teach you about Cinco de Mayo and stuff like that.

Our conversation turns to the shock of deportation and his complete unpreparedness for such an eventuality. He was, after all, a permanent resident.

> W: [W]ell I thought I was a permanent resident you know . . .
>
> Z: Because you thought permanent resident meant permanent?
>
> W: Yeah, permanent, and plus I never paid much attention to that legal status too much, you know. It was just something that was . . . I mean I thought I was at home you know. I thought . . . that was me forever.
>
> Z: You had no idea that that was a possibility—that you would be deported?
>
> W: I thought that was just for illegals, you know, and since I was legal, you know, I was a resident, and meanwhile my brothers [and sisters] were becoming citizens.

Of course, Weasel couldn't have known that he was vulnerable to deportation because the law—which was applied retroactively—was only put into effect in 1996, once he was already in prison and the year before he was deported.

Z: When did you find out that you were coming back to El Salvador?

W: Well, the first time I went to prison, an immigration guy, agent, came to talk to me, but I was still lost, you know. I was a kid you know.

Z: What did he tell you?

W: He just told me, you know, "Where were you born," and this and that. He goes, "You better be careful, you know messing about. They'll send you back . . ." But I thought he was just, you know, joking or something. I said like, "How're they going to send me back? All my family's here." I didn't even think of anything like that. I'm here growing up thinking I'm this (American) when, in reality, I'm this (Salvadoran) because I was born here, you know . . . When I got out [of prison] the INS agent came to visit me. I didn't think nothing of it. Thought that he just wanted to see my green card and papers. The INS officer was trying to prove that I was a Salvadoran. He kept asking me questions like what was the biggest river in El Salvador. I kept trying to explain that I didn't know nothing about El Salvador. I mean I hadn't been there for twenty years. I mean the biggest river around here is the L.A. River. I grew up in L.A. you know. Anyhow, he said that given my criminal history, he didn't see no chance for me, couldn't see me changing . . . Now I know that the biggest river here [El Salvador] is the Rio Lempa.

Weasel then recounts his arrival scene, an amusing—if not intended—parody of the ethnographer's first encounter with a strange culture.

W: I arrived with a lot of rumors in my mind about there's like this death squad that's going to kill you if you're all tattooed.[10] So I'm a little nervous and scared. Then the police come and snatch you and put you in a little room, and I said, "Oh fuck . . . that's it, forget it. They got me. They're going to kill me." They started asking me like where I live, and where I'm going to live, and took pictures of me, of my tattoos, my fingerprints, looked through my stuff, you know . . .

Z: How did San Salvador feel to you? What were your first impressions?

W: It was like they were sending me to Mars or something. I hadn't been in the country for twenty something, twenty-two years. And then I come back and I'm completely lost, man.

As it turned out, Weasel began his new life in San Salvador in San Jacinto, one *barrio* over from Gato's *barrio*, Modelo. He goes on to describe his shock at his new surroundings.

W: It was like real dirty to me, and I was like, "G-d man, where am I?" you know. "What am I going to do here?" They had trees everywhere and, you know, a lot of shacks. So I was like, "What did I get myself into man. Where am I? . . . Hell no, hell no, I ain't staying here, I ain't staying here. . . . I tried to go get my passport and they, uh, denied me a passport because they didn't think I was from here, coz I couldn't speak Spanish that well. And if I did speak Spanish, I spoke a different Spanish.

Like Modelo, San Jacinto's local geography had also been reinscribed by Los Angeles's territorial conflicts. Unlike Gato, however, Weasel occupied a much different relationship to that geography. Indeed, local gang members, although initially suspicious, did not in the end know where he was from, which is to say, did not recognize his *barrio*. This initially afforded Weasel a modicum of autonomy and space in relationship to Salvadoran gangs, although to Salvadoran society at large, he was just another *marero* (gang member).

In El Salvador, Weasel entered into an identity crisis.

> W: Yeah, I was telling you about the crisis I had. I'd been in a crisis. It goes back to the same thing too. People look down at you because, you know, the way you dress, baggy clothes . . . they call it *marero* here, and that's like something real low to call a person.
> When I first got to San Jacinto, I couldn't really relate to nobody in the house, so I started going out a little bit, hanging out in the front of the house, and the neighborhood kids they would see me. [But t]alking to those people is like, you know, whoever talks to them is part of 'em . . . so you're scum, you're trash, whatever. So I didn't really want to be classified with [gangs], you know, even though I could relate to them.

In an effort to reinvent himself, Weasel started to go to punk concerts.

> Z: This is you moving from your *mara* (gang) to your punk stage?
> W: Gangster.
> Z: *Cholo*? Is that how you would describe your look?
> W: Gangster.
> Z: Is that different from *cholo*?
> W: Not really, but gangster's like, I feel it's a step above *cholo*. *Cholo's* . . . anybody could be *cholo*. Okay, I started going to concerts. I liked it. These guys were cool. . . . I started going out with them. Found a place called La Luna (he laughs), started going there a lot.
> Z: La Luna is a very different scene . . .

I'm astounded at the cultural fusion here. La Luna is a cultural cafe reminiscent of any number of places in, say, Coyocan, Mexico, or Silver Lake in Los Angeles. For me, as a U.S.-based anthropologist, it is one of those places I would retreat to when I needed to escape the assault of being a foreign woman in a conservative society. So I'm curious that Weasel, self-described "gangster" from Echo Park, seeks refuge there too. But there is a spatial logic at work here, which brings both Weasel and me into the same space—globalization. La Luna caters to middle-class leftists, many of whom fled El Salvador as political exiles during the civil war—American, European, and Latin American expatriates working with nongovernmental organizations (NGOs), many of whom forged links to El Salvador through the solidarity movement during the same period. It also attracts unconventional middle-class Salvadoran youth drawn to experimentation with the global cultural flows of punk, rock en español, rap, spoken word, etc. Both Weasel and La Luna are produced and enabled by the spatial logics of globalization—albeit in and through markedly different registers of transnationalism: bohemianism and youth gangs.

Thus, while the focus of this essay is on transnational geographies of violence, the presence of spaces like La Luna in Weasel's narrative demonstrate that these global flows are not simply about violence. If anything, La Luna, which is dedicated to opening up cultural spaces in a socially conservative society, has a utopian dimension. Weasel, who is an accomplished tattoo artist, was able, through contacts made at La Luna, to employ gang expressive culture to build an "art tattoo" business for himself catering to middle- and upper-middle-class Salvadoran youth. Weasel then comes to embody the fusion of both these dimensions of globalization—dystopic and utopian.

Z: You [said you] had a Mohawk?
W: Yeah, I did.
Z: Here in San Salvador?
W: San Salvador. That really tripped people out. Nobody's ever seen stuff like that here. In a way I was . . . I wanted to make a statement . . .
Z: You were still living in San Jacinto at the time?
W: Yeah . . .

The absurdity of a punk rocker with a bright green Mohawk hairdo in a *barrio popular* in post-civil war El Salvador will be lost on those unfamiliar with that landscape. Weasel said being deported to El Salvador felt like being sent to Mars. And once in El Salvador, Weasel refashions himself as the Martian, the alien he is made to feel by the stares, reactions, and disapproval of the people around him. In a follow-up e-mail to me in Los Angeles, Weasel modifies his initial description of himself as "a Salvadoran living a Chicano lifestyle in the United States," to this: "Now [I'm] more like a deported gang member from L.A. living a mixture of a Chicano, Gringo, weirdo lifestyle."

Geographical Disorientations

Contemporary Los Angeles has become intimately associated with Fredric Jameson's essay on the Bonaventure Hotel (or Bonaventura), which Jameson posits as the architectural pronouncement of a depthless postmodern space, and against which he sets the culturally deep "great Chicano markets," located below and just east of that hotel's towering glass surfaces.[11] I began this essay by taking you just west of the Bonaventure to a Central American *barrio*, the Pico-Union district, where—despite their distinct *barrio* identities—both Gato and Weasel were picked up by LAPD officers for the last time before they were pushed through the deportation pipeline. I invoke Jameson here in part to locate and to orient you—although there is a certain irony here since, according to Jameson, spatial orientation is, of course, precisely what we have lost to postmodernism. It is to the latter point that I would now like to turn: Jameson's plea for "new maps" that correspond to this "multi-national global moment,"[12] and to his invocation therein of Kevin Lynch's work on cognitive mapping as a means of way finding.[13]

The cultural history and geography of Weasel's criminalization is different from Gato's. Gato remembers his old *barrio*. Despite his pan-Latino discourse, he retains his identity as Salvadoran. Gato migrated at a different age, a different epoch—at the height of the civil war in the early 1980s—and into a gang politic specific to that era and to that migration. Nonetheless, his geographical knowledge and the old maps no longer work upon his return to El Salvador. The *barrio's* designation, its geography, has changed on him, even as he was by it—both have been transnationalized, and their transnationalization has left them on different sides of the war, a new civil war. Gato's attempt to be from one *barrio* and live in another, to marry across *barrios*, to stake claim to his childhood territory—all proved fatal. His migration story begins and ends in violence. His father was killed in front of him for his political involvement with the FMLN (the then-leftist guerilla force) in the very same spot where Gato was shot and killed in front of his infant son for his past affiliation with the 18th Street Gang.

Weasel, on the other hand, moved to Los Angeles in the mid-1970s, well before the Salvadoran civil war and the attendant massive influx of refugees. As a result, Weasel had no social or geographical memory of El Salvador, no attachment to a *barrio* in San Salvador, or mental maps thereof. He knew nothing of the place from where he came. The test the INS officer gave him on Salvadoran geography is a perfect manifestation of his geographical disorientation—his reference point is the Los Angeles River, not the Rio Lempa. It is only two years after Weasel's return to El Salvador that he can construct the geography of the county. As he put it, "I feel like a tourist, a permanent one."

Gato and Weasel would eventually meet through the Salvadoran branch of Homies Unidos, the transnational youth violence prevention program, which has offices in both Los Angeles and San Salvador. Their different orientations to their Salvadoran identity notwithstanding, both Gato and Weasel found themselves at Homies Unidos precisely for reorientation to their "homeland," and both drew upon the organization to teach them how to navigate hostile and foreign terrain, or to derive a sense of place, a familial bond. While the writing may be on the wall in San Salvador—in the form of gang tagging—the meanings are not the same as they are in Los Angeles. Both deportees depended on Homies Unidos for the translation of these deceptively familiar codes.

As Gato told us:

> For us, it's kind of hard for us to live in our country. Wherever we go, we're always watching our back, our necks. I thank Homies because they showed me my country, man. From them, I learned where my enemies were, because when I came here I didn't really know where I was going. When people would say, "Let's go out, or let's go buy something," shit, I'd only go to the corner and come right back. Magdaleno and Huera [of Homies Unidos] would take me out for coffee, and would tell me [as they drove through the city of San Salvador]: "They are MS, and this corner, this is 18th."

Weasel started coming to the office after he had seen Homies Unidos's rap composer and performer Bullet at concerts. He explains:

> I came down and checked it out. I liked it, you know. I felt like that bond was there again—the one I left in L.A. . . . where I felt comfortable . . . Plus to top it off, I came to the office one day, and I see this guy walking down the street. And I said, "Damn, that guy looks familiar, 'ey." I got closer and closer, and then I said "Damn, I know that fool!" "Hey fool!" I say, "What's up?" And it was Grumpy. And me and Grumpy had been locked up together, so that even . . . so that even made the bond stronger. . . . I ran into other guys I knew from prison . . . Alex, Frank, Rabbit. It was like I'd found my family again.

Homies Unidos is an organization born of and devoted to countering the alienating forces of globalization as they combine with nationalism. In his oft-cited study of cognitive mapping, urban planner Kevin Lynch takes up the problem of spatial alienation wrought by modernization and urbanization.[14] Drawing on this same study, Fredric Jameson suggests that "the alienated city is above all a space in which people are unable to map (in their minds) either their own positions or the urban totality in which they find themselves" and that "[d]isalienation in the traditional city . . . involves the practical reconquest of a sense of place."[15] Certainly Gato's and Weasel's narratives speak to a similar need to mediate a jarring and troubled relationship between space and identity. The spatial alienation and fettered mobility of these deported immigrant gang youth, however, result from very different conditions than those affecting the middle-class city dwellers, tourists, and business travelers in Lynch's and Jameson's respective works. Beyond the generalized destabilizing effects of contemporary urban life, deported gang youth must contend with the effects of zero tolerance policing tactics as they are deployed on the streets of the inner-city immigrant *barrio* and with the subsequent transnationalization of the geographies of gang violence between Los Angeles and San Salvador.[16]

Not unlike the gang itself, Homies Unidos serves a "way-finding" function for these deported gang youth, and provides them with a map of the ways in which Los Angeles's geographies of violence have been rewritten into and altered through their encounters with San Salvador's urban landscape. This geographical reorientation is intended to avert the reproduction of violence itself. Gato's story, alongside the many other deaths within the organization's membership, is, sadly, testimony to just how complex a task this is, and that, in many instances, these navigational maps help to prolong but may not ultimately save lives, stop the violence.

Nonviolence is not simply an individual choice to change one's lifestyle. In San Salvador, Gato is forever marked by "where he is from," which is to say his territorial affiliations in Los Angeles. No longer an active gang member, in El Salvador, Gato remained a target for gang vendettas. Moreover, affiliation with violence and intervention projects like Homies Unidos carries its own dangers. Active gang members might misrecognize or misconstrue the organization as a rival gang and/or view the organization's outreach into their barrios as encroachment and violation of their territory. So, for instance, Weasel, who hailed from territory in Los Angeles unknown in San Salvador, became more vulnerable to gang violence through his subsequent participation in Homies Unidos as a gang peace activist. Beyond gang violence, there have been cases of death squad and police violence directed at gang youth and at deported gang youth in particular.

But the spatial alienation of these Latino others stands outside Jameson's implicitly racialized account of Los Angeles's late capitalist spatiality. In his discussion of the postmodern Mexicano, José Limón argues that Jameson relegates Latino spaces such as the Chicano market to an old modern space, which stands in contrast to the new cultural dominant represented by the Bonaventure Hotel.[17] Similarly, Roger Rouse urges us to look for signs of late-capitalist spatiality beyond architecture and aesthetics in the everyday literal footsteps of Mexican "(im)migrants" and in the emergent transnational space between their hometowns in Mexico and cities such as Redwood, California.[18] Deportation narratives demonstrate how the Latino immigrant *barrio* and the Salvadoran *barrio popular* have both come to occupy what Jameson terms the "global space of the postmodernist or multinational moment."[19] Granted, Weasel may experience El Salvador as the primitive past—a veritable jungle of mud huts. But as a result of his deportation, he in fact becomes an agent in and foil for, and offers an immanent critique of, postmodern spatiality. Indeed, the cognitive mappings of deported immigrant gang youth involves constructing legibility not only within but *between* cities of formerly distinct hemispheres that have, as a result of migration and forced repatriation, become intimately connected, their geographies inextricably linked and complicit.

A Politics of Simultaneity

These narratives of deported immigrant youth speak eloquently to the need for interpretive maps, which interrogate the relationship between space and identity, and the blurred boundaries between the local and the global. They also call into question what constitutes the terrain of study for American, Latino, and Latin American studies at this particular moment in globalization. In this sense, Gato's and Weasel's stories are reminiscent of the texts José David Saldívar draws upon to propose a new continental or pan-American studies. Like the novels of those "other Americanists"—Black, Latino, and Latin American—the deportee's narrative challenges the "limiting set of tacit assumptions that result from perpetual immersion in the study of a single American culture" and demands that we retheorize the very premises upon which the concepts of "American hermeneutics, alterity, history and historiography rests."[20] This need to cross geopolitical lines between the Americas to grasp the blurred cultural zones that people inhabit has been a defining tenet and contribution of borderlands theory.[21] While that literature's primary geographic reference is the U.S.-Mexico border region, Salvadoran transnational migration and community formation allows us to see just how much further south that contact zone between the United States and Latin America extends.

In terms of their immediately experienced scale and size, Latino immigrant *barrios* like Pico-Union are veritable anthropological villages. But the highly localized neighborhood Pico-Union is linked to a complex system of places and politics well beyond the boundaries of the *barrio* and even those of the nation-state. Moreover, the life stories that that emerge from it pose a methodological and representational challenge to the study of culture. They not only require multisited fieldwork, but they also call for a dialogic mode of analysis[22] in order to grasp the shared or contrapuntal histories[23] of these cities—Los Angeles and San Salvador, and these Americas—United States and Central.

In this sense, the identity formation made visible in these deportation narratives bears a relationship to the postcolonial narratives discussed by Edward Said in *Culture and Imperialism*. Said sets out to demonstrate how the imperial power and its colonies were produced in relation, or counterpoint, to each other. He argues that the nineteenth-century British novel, the quintessential genre of British cultural production and expression of British identity, is intimately related to and dependent upon the social space of Empire. National identity is thus worked out through the relationship between home and abroad, the metropole and its colonies. Others have discussed how the postcolonial era has been, in turn, marked by a reversal in this cultural production of identity. The "periphery" emerges at the "center" in the form of the now well-known trope, the *Empire Strikes Back*.[24] I would suggest that these Salvadoran narratives of forcible return reveal a similar structural interdependence and complicity in identity formation between the United States and El Salvador in general and those between Los Angeles and San Salvador in particular. In the north-south relations under consideration here, deported Salvadoran immigrant gang youth oscillate between "home" and "abroad," where both home and abroad are themselves unstable locations. At the same time, Salvadoran gang youth who have never been to the United States construct their identities around imagined urban geographies of cities like Los Angeles.

An examination of the spatial cultural politics behind the expulsion of "fools" like Weasel and Gato "from the kingdom" requires, therefore, a wide-angle lens and a methodology agile enough to jump geographic scales: local, national, and global. Imagine, for instance, riding buses through the streets of San Salvador with two deportees from 18th Street territory in Pico-Union. The stories of these young men and of the geography of their everyday lives in Los Angeles, captured by my tape recorder, are filled with the booming sounds of the street life in San Salvador. Back in Los Angeles, I would drive through Pico-Union and its surrounding *barrios* trying to relocate these narratives in their original geographies of action. Echo Park Lake and its gang-graffiti-covered walls by now had become enlivened by Weasel's stories and disturbed by his absence. As I drove by MacArthur Park, the Hotel California, the corner of Berendo and Eighth, Belmont High, the Jack in the Box, pieces of these narratives would flash into consciousness: This must have been where Gato's friend was shot, this is where Ringo lived, that's where Gato's father's necklace was stolen, and that's where Weasel was last picked up. Los Angeles's urban landscape became saturated with the narratives of these people whom I had encountered in El Salvador, and—even more hauntingly—by those who had since died in the streets of San Salvador. I felt this not just as time warp but also as space warp—the "time-space compression" of simultaneity.[25]

Like nationalism, transnationalism is equally beholden to and built upon what Benedict Anderson terms a grammar of simultaneity.[26] In Gato's and Weasel's transnational narratives, Los Angeles and San Salvador have been compressed into the same field of view, and the chronotope (time and space) of the Latino immigrant *barrio* and the Latin American *barrio popular* now overlap in crucial ways—not only from the privileged perspective of the traveling ethnographer, but from the vantage of Salvadoran immigrants themselves. Indeed, these narratives of forcible return do not simply function as haunting memories or as residues of past lives. They do more than refer back to or recollect their *barrios* in Los Angeles. Banished though these fools may be from the kingdom, they remain linked to that landscape through, among other things, ongoing ties with family—be they actual or fictive kin.

Take for instance Doña Ofelia, who lives in a one-room apartment in the Pico-Union district. I first went to visit Ofelia at the urging of her son Pajaro, a deported member of the MS gang. Pajaro had asked me to look his mother up upon my return to Los Angeles from El Salvador. During our first meeting, Doña Ofelia and I talked as she readied herself for her evening janitorial shift in one of Century City's towering glass executive suites. When our conversation turned to Pajaro, she began to cry, "He can never come back, and now, I cannot go back to El Salvador to retire as I had planned, because I must work to support him there." Ofelia's was just one of many a mournful tale I heard from mothers, who, separated from their children once by civil war, were reunited in Los Angeles only to be separated once again, this time through the forced repatriation of those same children.

Every three weeks or so, Doña Ofelia sets out from her apartment to catch the bus at Pico and Union bound for a neighborhood close to the University of Southern California in South Central Los Angeles. On her way to the bus stop, she traverses a streetscape littered with signs of Central American and Mexican diasporas—the *pupuserias* (restaurants of typical Salvadoran fare), street vendors selling green mango with lime and chile, and the *botanica* windows filled with plaster of paris figurines of saints popular to Central Americans. She continues past Transportes Salvadoreños and Cuscatleco Travel and an array of other delivery and travel services that transport people, goods, money, documents, and letters back and forth along those now well-worn travel routes between Los Angeles, Mexico, and Central America. Doña Ofelia is herself on her way to drop off clothing and money with a personal courier for her deported son. The courier, Doña Leti, who travels back and forth between Los Angeles and cities and towns in El Salvador, navigates this transnational space for those Salvadoran immigrants who cannot themselves travel, but who must find a means to maintain a transnational household.[27]

Deported gang youth are after all the children of immigrant parents, who toil in service to global capitalism as janitors, piece workers in the garment industry, cooks, nannies, gardeners, and day laborers and sometimes against its grain as longtime community organizers and labor activists. Their brothers and sisters—often college students, police officers, or schoolteachers—might well be lauded as exemplars of successful incorporation into the nation-state and its institutions. The banishment of gang-affiliated youth from the United States thus stands in contrast, but in relationship to, their parents' and siblings' naturalization as U.S. citizens. Gang-affiliated young adults also leave U.S.–born children, wives, and girlfriends behind. Moreover, many of these deportees, fearing Gato's fate, reenter the United States illegally even though they risk reimprisonment followed by deportation if caught.[28] Far beyond this literal return of the repressed—the illegal reentry of those excluded from the nation—the absence of the deportee is a strongly felt presence in the neighborhood. Deported gang youth remain an integral part of the "structure of feeling"[29] of the *barrio*, of its internal relations and the everyday practices of its residents.

Toward Transnational Urban Studies

The experiences of forced transnationality presented here have important implications for urban research and point to the need for transnational urban studies as a new domain for research. Clearly, I am not arguing for the declining salience of the nation-state at this juncture in globalization. I am, however, suggesting that the urban scale regains the former importance attributed to the city-state before the rise of the modern nation-state in the exercise of social regulation and the formation of new subjectivities. It is, after all, in the city and through the fabric of its built environment—its streets, intersections, sidewalks, commercial strip malls, parks, and overcrowded apartment buildings— that the boundaries of the nation-state are both regulated and exceeded. The contentious border between the United States and Latin America thus extends into the city and into its immigrant neighborhoods, where it is policed and transgressed. Moreover, a local urban scale of analysis allows us to see that "transnational practices do not take place in an imaginary [deterritorialized or utopian] third space" but are situated in and between specific localities[30]—in this case, between the immigrant *barrios* of Los Angeles and the *barrios populares* in San Salvador. Yet the introduction of the city as a new scale for the analysis of the effects of globalization does not simply serve to reassert the geopolitical scale of the nation. [31] Rather the city, Los Angeles, marks a crucial space of conjunctions and disjunctions between local, national, and global spheres of action and experience.

The experiences of deported Salvadoran immigrant gang youth under consideration here demonstrate the analytical power both transnational and urban studies stand to gain from a mutual engagement with each other, and how both scales of analysis are essential to our understanding of the contemporary form of the nation-state. On the one hand, these stories of forced repatriation and the ongoing criminalization of Salvadoran immigration demonstrate how a transnational perspective can enrich the traditional research domains of urban poverty, racial segregation, ethnic and racial identity formation, and urban youth cultures. On the other hand, they show us that an urban-scale of analysis is essential in our work to unravel the human consequences of globalization.[32] Finally, they reveal that efforts to reassert national sovereignty through zero tolerance policing strategies only, and most ironically, reproduce transnational flows and formations. The complex flows and the multiple geopolitical scales of analysis at work in the urban *barrio* make it impossible to engage with the cultural politics of one side of this social field (Los Angeles) without *simultaneously* accounting for those at play on the other side (San Salvador). Within these politics of simultaneity, the immigrant *barrio* in the north—linked inextricably to those *barrios populares* in the south—serves as a key ethnographic site through which to view the lived and felt effects of urban restructuring as it combines with efforts to manage the dialectical pressures of globalization and nationalism.

Notes

I would like to thank the following people for their thoughtful comments on various versions of this essay: José William Huezo Soriano, Kathleen Stewart, Begoña Aretxaga, James Holston, Vince Rafael, Charles Hale, Marcial Godoy-Anativia, Rossana Reguillo, Raúl Villa, Arlene Dávila, Sonia Baires, and the anonymous reviewers of this article. Thanks also to Silvia Beltrán and Magdaleno Rose-Ávila for their crucial on the ground insights, and to John Ewing, Roy Gary, Orlando Romero, and Martha Henry for their copyediting. Versions of this essay were presented to a workshop on "Translocal Flows: Cities, Inequality, and Subjectivity in the Americas," held at ITESO in Guadalajara, Mexico, in May 2003 during my tenure as fellow with the Global Security and Cooperation Program of the Social Science Research Council. The conference was sponsored by the SSRC's Program on Latin America and the Caribbean with support from the Rockefeller Foundation. A subsequent version of this essay was presented at the Summer Institute on International Migration sponsored by the Center for Comparative Immigration Studies Research at the University of California–San Diego and the Social Science Research Council's International Migration Program, June 2003, San Diego, California.

1. *The Politics and Poetics of Transgression* (Ithaca, N.Y.: Cornell University Press, 1986), 89.
2. See James Holston and Arjun Appadurai, "Cities and Citizenship," *Public Culture* 8.2 (1996): 188–89.
3. For a discussion of the microphysics of policing the space of the *barrio* at the street level, see Elana Zilberg, "A Troubled Corner: The Ruined and Rebuilt Environment of a Central American *Barrio* in Post–Rodney King Riot Los Angeles," *City and Society* IVX.2 (2002): 31–55.

4. Peter Boyer "Bad Cops," *New Yorker*, May 2001, 71.
5. This quote is excerpted from "Radio Diaries," *This American Life*, National Public Radio (May 21, 1999). The show was produced by Joe Richman and narrated by José Huezo Soriano (AKA Weasel).
6. Ibid.
7. By the spatial logic of these cultural politics, I am referring to those politics surrounding the production, representation, use of, and arguments over the space of the *barrio*. My work here draws upon the fruitful and contemporary marriage between geography and anthropology (see A. Gupta and James Ferguson, "Beyond Culture: Space, Identity and the Politics of Difference," *Cultural Anthropology* 7.1 [1992]: 7–23), Henri LeFebrve's notion of the production of space (see Henri LeFebvre, *The Social Production of Space*, trans. Donald Nicholson-Smith [Cambridge, Mass.: Blackwell, 1994], 36–46), and a number of urbanists who focus on Los Angeles's built environment (Margaret Crawford, introduction to *Everyday Urbanism*, ed. J. Chase, M. Crawford, and J. Kaliski [New York: Monacelli Press, 1999]; Mike Davis, *Magical Urbanism: Latinos Reinvent the U.S. City* [London: Verso, 2000]; Dolores Hayden, *The Power of Place: Urban Landscapes as Public History* [Cambridge, Mass.: MIT Press, 1995]; E. W. Soja, *Postmodern Geographies: The Reassertion of Space in Critical Social Theory* [London: Verso, 1989]).
8. For a discussion of the dialectical tension between the *barrio* as a community enabling and disabling space, see Raúl Homero Villa, *Barrio-Logos: Space and Place in Urban Chicano Literature and Culture* (Austin: University of Texas Press, 2000), 1–18.
9. While mine is hardly a linguistic study, I have chosen not to "clean up" the transcription of Gato's English in order to leave these traces in his speech.
10. In El Salvador, the tattoo is taken as a sign of criminality. Those bearing tattoos can be barred from attending school. It has been used as grounds for failing to provide timely medical attention to the wounded in hospital emergency rooms, resulting in unnecessary deaths from bleeding. The discrimination can be so fierce that even the most innocuous tattoos can be misconstrued. For instance, one deportee I knew used to wrap a bandage up the length of his arm before he left for classes in a private college. This, he explained to me, was to avoid conflict with the local gangs and the police and to enable him to enter the college. His tattoo, the source of so much discrimination and danger, was simply the name of his youngest daughter, who lived in Los Angeles. He had tattooed her name into his arm so that "she would always be close" to him. Some gang members try to remove their tattoos, but when I was last in El Salvador, there was still only one laser tattoo removal machine in the whole country, and it was common to be badly scarred and burned by the cruder tattoo removal systems available.
11. See Fredric Jameson, "Postmodernism, or the Cultural Logic of Late Capitalism," *New Left Review* 146 (1984): 62.
12. Ibid., 89–92.
13. See Kevin Lynch, *The Image of the City* (Cambridge, Mass.: MIT Press, 1960).
14. Ibid.
15. See Jameson, "Postmodernism," 89.
16. These U.S.–style zero tolerance policing tactics have, alongside youth gangs, also been successfully exported to El Salvador. In July 2003, the then Salvadoran president, Francisco Flores, launched a "tropicalized" version of U.S. gang abatement strategies in the form of *El Plan Mano Dura* (the Firm Fist/Strong Hand Plan).
17. See José Limón, *Dancing with the Devil* (Madison: University of Wisconsin Press, 1994), 106–7.
18. See Roger Rouse, "Mexican Migration and the Social Space of Postmodernism," *Diaspora* (spring 1991): 8–23.
19. Jameson, 91.
20. See José David Saldívar, *The Dialectics of Our America, Genealogy, Cultural Critique, and Literary History* (Durham, N.C.: Duke University Press, 1991), 3–4.
21. For a discussion of borderlands theory, see, among others, Robert Alvarez, "The Mexican–U.S. Border: The Making of an Anthropology of Borderlands" in *Annual Review of Anthropology* 24 (1995): 447–70; Gloria Anzaldúa, *Borderlands: The New Mestiza=La Frontera* (San Francisco: Spinsters/Aunt Lute, 1987); Michael Kearney, "Borders and Boundaries of State and Self at the End of Empire" in *Journal of Historical Sociology* 4.1 (1991): 52–73; Américo Paredes, *"With a Pistol in His Hands": A Border Ballad and Its Hero* (Austin: University of Texas Press, 1958); and José David Saldívar, *Border Matters: Remapping American Cultural Studies* (Berkeley: University of California Press, 1991).
22. See Saldívar, *The Dialectics of Our America*.
23. Edward Said, *Culture and Imperialism* (New York: Knopf, 1993), 66.

24. Centre for Contemporary Cultural Studies (CCCS), *The Empire Strikes Back: Race and Racism in 70s Britain* (London: CCCS, University of Birmingham, 1983).
25. David Harvey, *The Condition of Postmodernity: An Enquiry into the Origins of Cultural Change* (New York: Blackwell, 1989).
26. Benedict Anderson, *Imagined Communities* (London: Verso, 1991).
27. Elana Zilberg, "*La Viajera*: The Globalization of Face-to-Face Communication across Borders" (presented at the International Communications Association 2003 annual conference, "Communications in Borderlands," San Diego, California, May 23–27, 2003).
28. These return gang members are emerging as a new, albeit controversial, refugee class. See Elana Zilberg, "Traveling Bodies, Traveling Policies: A Cultural Politics of the Forced Repatriation of Salvadoran Immigrant Youth in Post–Civil War El Salvador" (presented to the Youth, Globalization, and the Law project, Social Science Research Council, New York, September 18–19, 2003).
29. Raymond Williams, *Marxism and Literature* (New York: Oxford University Press, 1977), 128–35.
30. Luis Eduardo Guarnizo and Michael Peter Smith, "The Locations of Transnationalism," in *Transnationalism from Below*, ed. Luis Eduardo Guarnizo and Michael Peter Smith (London: Transaction Publishers, 1999), 11. For a discussion of third space as a utopian space of liberation, see Homi Bhabha, *The Location of Culture* (New York: Routledge, 1994), and Edward Soja, *Third Space: Journeys to Los Angeles and Other Real-and-Imagined Places* (Cambridge, Mass.: Blackwell, 1996). Clearly, the third space under consideration in this article is hardly utopian.
31. Holston and Appadurai, "Cities and Citizenship," 189.
32. Zygmunt Bauman, *Globalization: The Human Consequences* (London: Verso, 1998).

Borders and Social Distinction
in the Global Suburb

Kristen Hill Maher

Los Angeles is widely known as a "global city," one of the command-and-control centers for the global economy.[1] However, the urban center is not the only place undergoing transformation. The four counties surrounding Los Angeles have restructured into multicentered metropolitan regions, with centers of commerce and industry interwoven among residential neighborhoods that no longer strongly depend on the urban core.[2] Instead, former bedroom communities have themselves become destinations for commuters, tourists, and international capital. Orange County, in particular, has become one of the main "technopoles" in the larger Los Angeles region.[3] According to the authors of *Postsuburban California*, Orange County's high-tech industrial base and entry into the international economy has made it an increasingly cosmopolitan space.[4] Orange County has become a suburban counterpart to the global city, a "global suburb," if you will.

Like in global cities, economies of service and support have developed alongside transnational commerce in Orange County. Its business and tourist sectors require office cleaning, goods delivery, food preparation, restaurant services, hotels, dry cleaning services, landscaping services, and so on. Service and support industries also operate within residential neighborhoods where home owners' associations hire workers to maintain common amenities such as parks, pools, and tennis courts, and individual households hire housecleaners, nannies, in-home elderly care, and gardeners. Such service positions are one of the fastest growing sectors in the Orange County economy.[5] As in global cities, low-paid service jobs are largely filled by immigrants from less developed states.

These immigrant-based service economies have transformed Orange County's social geography. Whereas many suburban settlements in Orange County developed as white-flight communities intentionally distant from Los Angeles, the current labor market cannot operate within a core-periphery model of segregation. Immigrant service workers cannot be sequestered in Los Angeles enclaves, because they must live close enough to their jobs to facilitate a daily commute. While Orange County remains highly segregated by race and class between residential communities, thriving immigrant enclaves have developed near neighborhoods that are largely white and middle class. In addition, immigrants working in household services have become a significant presence in middle-class homes and communities during the day. In these ways, the transnational household service economy has eroded traditional patterns of segregation in the suburbs.

What happens in historical white-flight suburbs when social hierarchies can no longer be marked easily by physical distance? Is there potential for pluralist integration across divisions of class, race, and migrant status, or do new patterns of segregation emerge? What kinds of anxieties about boundaries and borders are evident, and with what consequences? This study examines these questions through a 1997 ethnographic study of a largely white, middle-class neighborhood in Irvine, California ("Ridgewood") that depended heavily upon service labor by working-class immigrant Latinos. The Ridgewood case suggests that the social landscape of the household service economy is unlikely to usher in a new era of pluralist integration or to promote a cosmopolitan outlook in global suburbs. Instead, it appears to generate anxieties about both physical and social boundaries. The following analysis illustrates how the middle-class residents of Ridgewood marked social distinction through a wide range of everyday practices[6]: through the "talk of crime" and the fortification of physical boundaries,[7] through the legal and informal regulation of aesthetics, and through daily practices that regulated the behavior of service workers within community space. Such practices maintained social distance in circumstances of spatial proximity and even intimacy. These patterns are not entirely new, of course: in many ways they resurrect the dynamics of servitude and social distinction in colonial contexts or in the antebellum American South. However, the Ridgewood case also illustrates what we might expect of emerging global suburbs, and how concerns about local and national border control intersect.

No Place Like Home: The Local Landscape of Irvine, California

Irvine is one of the fastest growing small cities in the United States, part of the mass suburbanization and development of Orange County since the 1950s. Developed from private ranch lands by a single corporation (The Irvine Company), Irvine was centrally planned in the garden city model.[8] Irvine's marketing strategy to potential home buyers historically has resembled what Karen Till has observed among "urban village" developments in Orange County, drawing on the image of "orderly landscapes of a rural small town" in opposition to "Hollywood images of Los Angeles as a dark city on fire, a place where looting, chaos, and violence prevail."[9] That is, its original appeal was as a suburban utopia far from the crowding, poverty, and industrialized aesthetic of urban areas. The Irvine Chamber of Commerce continues to advertise Irvine with images of manicured green landscapes as a place that "has it all": nature, culture, and entertainment.[10] It is an orderly place both physically and socially with very little violent or property crime. Throughout the 1990s, the FBI designated Irvine as one of the safest cities in the United States with a population of more than 100,000. This orderliness has contributed to Irvine's reputation among the cynical as a place lacking soul or spontaneity, inspiring comparisons to "the Stepford Wives—perfect, in a horrifying sort of way."[11]

Significant for the story to come is Irvine's more general location in the Orange County landscape. Within the mental maps of developers and many residents, Orange County divides into a north and a south with a veritable Mason-Dixon line cutting across the middle.[12] South County, where Irvine is located, largely comprises planned developments with a middle-to-upper-class white and Asian population. Given the centrality of high-tech industries in the economic base, the labor market in South County has largely bifurcated into jobs for high-skilled, high-wage professionals and for low-skilled, low-wage workers in the service economy. Latino immigrant labor forms the backbone of the low-skilled service sector; however, high-priced housing and zoning regulations limiting the number of persons per dwelling discourage these workers from local residence. Instead, most service workers in South County commute from Latino residential enclaves such as those in Santa Ana in North County, roughly ten miles away from Irvine.

While North County also includes some planned developments, it is most widely reputed for its older cities like Santa Ana and Anaheim that were incorporated before the turn of the century. In the postwar era, these cities and others in North County grew rapidly as part of Los Angeles' suburban expansion. Starting in the 1970s, Santa Ana's demographics began to shift dramatically; its Latino population went from 15 percent in 1960 to 76 percent in 2000, much as in areas of Los Angeles that have become Latino immigrant enclaves over the past several decades. Raymond Rocco explains how the Latinization of such neighborhoods is rooted in the restructuring of the economy. The loss of blue-collar manufacturing jobs with international capital flight weakened the economic base and spurred former blue-collar workers to move elsewhere. Given relatively low housing costs, Latino immigrants then found this area an attractive point of entry.[13] At the same time, low-paying jobs that remained attractive opportunities for immigrants proliferated nearby, in textile and food production as well as services. There is a complex set of reasons for the growth in Santa Ana's immigrant Latino population, but job growth in the service sector surely has contributed. Demographic changes in Santa Ana are tied to the consumption of services elsewhere in the county such as in Irvine.

Figure 1 shows a concentration of Latinos in North County and their virtual absence in South County, except in a small immigrant enclave in the South near San Juan Capistrano that has developed along with service jobs that are too distant from North County to accommodate a commute. Apart from this one exception, the spatial division between North and South County appears almost as a wall or border demarcating racialized territories. Because household services in South County are performed almost exclusively by Latinos, one might imagine the daily commute for workers from North to South County as a type of "border crossing" that binds North to South in an economic interdependence. Orange County has become another place where "yuppies and poor migrant workers depend upon each other,"[14] living in proximity and yet separately. This study documents interdependencies between the peoples and residential spaces of this bifurcated economy, divisions that largely fall along the lines of class, racial-ethnic identity, and—to some extent—migrant status.

Figure 1.
Percent Hispanic by census tract, Orange County, 1990 (U.S. Census).

The particular site selected for this 1997 study was in many ways a "typical" Irvine neighborhood. A planned community developed in the mid-1970s, Ridgewood comprised 246 single-family homes on a collection of cul-de-sacs connected by three public through streets. On average, residents were highly educated—39 percent had graduate or professional degrees—and most of those who were employed worked in professional, managerial, technical, or sales positions.[15] Fourteen percent of the residents were foreign born, slightly lower than the 22 percent in Irvine more generally. In the racial terms of the census, the residents of this community were Asian (10 percent) and white (90 percent).[16] Ridgewood was not one of Irvine's most elite communities, although its residents were a bit more affluent than the Irvine mean, with a median household income of roughly $100,000 in 1990.[17]

Like most other middle-class neighborhoods in Irvine and in South Orange County, the Ridgewood neighborhood had a steady stream of maintenance and service traffic. Some of these services were hired by the home owners' association via membership dues, such as the pool maintenance and the landscaping work in the park. Individual households also hired service labor: according to those I interviewed, almost every household paid for periodic

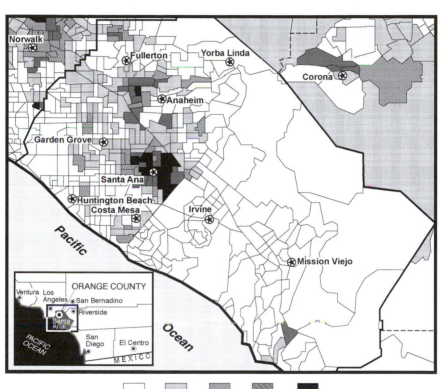

0.0–19.8	19.9–39.7	39.8–59.5	59.6–79.4	79.5–100.0

gardening and housekeeping services. Some households with children employed nannies, most commonly among families without a stay-at-home parent. A small proportion of the housekeepers and nannies in the community lived with their employers from five to seven days per week. In addition to these common services, some households hired home care for the elderly, window washers, and carpet cleaners. As is the pattern in most middle-class neighborhoods in South Orange County, Latinos provided virtually all of these services.

According to reputation and police statistics, Ridgewood was a typically safe neighborhood in Irvine without any significant crime problem. However, its residents had in the previous five years put walls around its perimeter and debated whether to become a gated enclave. The most active period of debate had been in 1994, when the board of the home owners' association announced that it was planning to have the community gated. There was considerable support among some residents for the idea and opposition by a vocal minority. The plan to add entrance gates ran into some legal obstacles, as it would require privatizing the public through streets. After a similar effort in Los Angeles lost a court case,[18] the gating plan in Ridgewood had been postponed. However, the issue of whether to gate was not dead in this community when I conducted the study, nor were the kinds of logics that motivated the desire to gate. The recent debate about gating became the point of departure for interviews, generating a broad set of narratives about how residents of this community made sense of the social and economic transformations around them, and how their anxieties about boundaries and social distinction played out in daily practices.[19]

Talk of Crime and Physical Fortification

One of the main themes of the discussion about gating was the need to increase security. However, the anxieties and narratives about crime in Ridgewood seemed paradoxical since they did not correlate to any empirical reality: there were few personal experiences of crime among those in the neighborhood, and the focus of most anxiety was not about any immediate sense of danger.[20] Indeed, the kinds of added security under debate in this community, such as gated entries, were not even targeted at those persons thought to be the most likely perpetrators of property crimes in the neighborhood. Both the local police and community residents told me that local teenagers had probably been responsible for most crimes that had occurred, and these teens would continue to have access after a gated entrance was installed. Even more puzzling was the fact that a number of those who argued in favor of adding a gated entry for greater security in Ridgewood also claimed that they felt very safe because they *knew* the crime rate locally was very low. One of the strongest advocates for adding a gate to provide more security also told me that "the burglary rate is virtually nil in our neighborhood. We've had a radio or two stolen in the last five or six years." In this regard, the narratives about crime and security in this community did not represent a sense of immediate threat from crime, nor were they simply representative of a "culture of fear" that pervades the middle-class suburban imagination even in places with little risk of crime.[21] Instead, these narratives appeared to have more symbolic purposes.

Teresa Caldeira's study of middle-class residents living in "fortified enclaves" in São Paulo, Brazil offers insight about the potential for crime narratives to have symbolic functions. Caldeira argues that the middle-class people she interviewed engaged in the "talk of crime" to represent the range of local changes they found distressing. She suggests that all sorts of losses and anxieties can be articulated through the language of crime:

> Crime supplies a generative symbolism with which to talk about other things that are perceived as wrong or bad, but for which no consensus of interpretation or vocabulary may exist. It also offers symbolism with which to talk about other kinds of loss, such as downward mobility. Moreover, crime adds drama to the narration of events that themselves may be undramatic—for example, a forty-year process of change in a neighborhood—but whose consequences can be distressing.[22]

The talk of crime reduces a complex, disorderly reality to a few, essentialized categories that "elaborate prejudices" at the same time as they give the narrator a means to organize the world and gain a sense of control.[23]

Examining the talk of crime in Ridgewood helps make sense of residents' discourse about security. Much like in the São Paulo study, the talk of crime in Ridgewood appeared to be a way to articulate fear or unease about a range of local transformations, including gradual urbanization and the shifts in social geographies that had been accompanying macroeconomic change in the region. It also appeared to be a way to articulate social boundaries in an economy in which geographic boundaries less effectively segregated groups by race and class.

Of the various categories of potential criminals discussed in Ridgewood, "strangers" were identified as the primary target of anxiety, defined as nonresidents of a "different element" who were present in the neighborhood without an apparent reason other than to scope it out with criminal intent. For the most part, residents described the strangers they deemed threatening only according to the car they were driving, with particular focus on "bad cars." Talk about cars appeared to be not only the result of a cue-taking about potential criminals, but also a coded language in which people could talk about class and race in a context in which explicit discussion of these topics is widely thought to be impolite. Many of residents' descriptions about what kinds of "cars" made them nervous involved clear class references encoded in the descriptions of cars as "broken down" or not fitting "the Irvine mold." More subtle were the racial overtones of some observations, such as the woman who said she became nervous when drivers were not any of the housekeepers or gardeners she knew personally. Clearly, these drivers were Latinos, since she compared them to service workers rather than to neighbors or others she might have known personally. Others were slightly more obvious about the racial content of their observations about bad cars, identifying the cars that made them most suspicious more specifically as "lowriders," augmented Chevrolets often associated with working-class Chicano culture. Clearly, it was not the cars themselves but the kinds of people driving them that elicited anxiety from Ridgewood residents.

In discussions about where dangerous strangers might come from, some residents remained vague about social geography, suggesting that the danger came from the freeway, where people from all sorts of places drive by in close proximity to Irvine. They apparently imagined the freeway as a connection to the world, and especially to urban areas, that made an otherwise insulated area vulnerable to crime. Others more explicitly identified Santa Ana and other regions north of Irvine as the source of their insecurities. However, the threats that were articulated were not anything immediate, but rather anxieties about an imagined future in which the social geography around Irvine will be transformed by an influx of "urban" minorities and crime. For instance, Cheryl mentioned at the beginning of her interview that she did not fear crime at all and in fact had not had the security system on her house engaged for months. Yet, she wanted to have Ridgewood add gates because of a threat she perceives as spreading soon to Irvine. "They're coming in from Santa Ana," she explained. "In the last two years—I haven't seen it but I hear it from other people, that the gangs are coming down this way. . . . It's something to think about. But you know they're going to be everywhere."

This theme of a dystopic future was a common one in the interviews, particularly among those who supported adding a gated entrance. Jeff presented the problem in terms of population shifts not just in Santa Ana but also over the past century in Los Angeles:

> J: The demographics are changing here. When I moved here back in the early seventies, I was a typical person here in Orange County. And, as you well know, now . . . Costa Mesa and Santa Ana have declined in their social structure. Or, I don't know if that's the proper

terminology, but the bottom line is their crime rates have risen, and that type of person has moved down and started to encroach on Irvine. . . . The best way to look, I guess—go to Los Angeles. Fifty years ago or, you know, ninety years ago, downtown Los Angeles was the place to be. And I guarantee you wouldn't walk there at night now.
Int: So your perception, or people around here perceive, that that's the future for Irvine as well . . .?
J: It's a possibility. . . . I absolutely see change in this neighborhood. I've seen it! Go to the schools and look at the change in where the kids are coming from and what their background is. I mean, what do their parents do? . . . All of a sudden I'm looking around and saying, "Gosh, everything's connected here."

Shifts in the racial composition of the greater Los Angeles area were clearly at the center of Jeff's concerns. While he—as a white man—used to be the "typical person here in Orange County," there had been a "decline" in the "social structure" of Santa Ana and Costa Mesa (the two closest areas experiencing significant Latino in-migration), much like in Los Angeles.

Similarly, in the excerpt below, Tom identifies a rise in crime in Santa Ana and Los Angeles as the primary reason so many communities in South Orange County have been gating:

T: All of the new communities that have opened in Newport [Beach] in the last three or four years, every single one of them has been gated. Because people are seeing crime on the rise. And they perceive that it may eventually get to them, whether it's in the safest city in the U.S., in Irvine, or in the rich city, in Newport Beach.
Int: So the place that they're seeing crime on the rise is not among their own neighbors.
T: No! But it's in *anticipation* of what could happen.
Int: Where do they get it [this idea], do you think?
T: Well, the press. We get a constant diet of it through the press. Christ, turn the six o'clock news on. What is it? Rape, pillage, and plunder. They're not talking about the Boy Scouts having a campout.
Int: But they're talking about Los Angeles most of the time.
T: It doesn't matter. Los Angeles is Orange County. We still have awful things happen here. . . . Listen, we've got a very serious gang problem over in Santa Ana. It's almost out of control; the police there are just—they're beside themselves. And is that going to move our way? I don't know, but people are doing things in anticipation of the fact that maybe it could. And if it is, I want to be behind a gated wall. It's real simple.

Tom emphasized throughout his interview that Irvine was an exceptionally safe city, but here he qualified that observation, representing Los Angeles and Santa Ana as places that for him symbolize the future. He suggested that the "gang problem" in nearby Santa Ana was evidence that the urban ills of Los Angeles were spreading, no longer removed at a safe distance from Irvine.

While Tom identified the media as the source of his anxiety, a few residents instead connected their desire for more secure neighborhood boundaries to more personal experiences amidst economic and demographic transitions in the greater Los Angeles area. For instance, Gerry moved to Ridgewood from Los Angeles in the late 1970s, in the early years of Orange County's economic boom. At that time, he joked with his Los Angeles friends about "living with the Nazis in Irvine . . . It was all blonde hair, blue eyes—everyone looked the same." Despite Gerry's disdain for some aspects of Orange County life, he felt that life in Irvine was getting better and better while "L.A. got worse and worse. . . . There was this invasion of Latinos and . . . the blacks I don't think have increased in numbers, but . . . unfortunately, acting out in senseless violence." Gerry continued to work in the Los Angeles area for a time, and recalled driving home after the Los Angeles riots in 1992. He said, "As I drove from my office in Los Angeles *away from* Los Angeles, the closer I got to Irvine, I felt safer and safer and safer."

In contrast to Gerry, Claire had grown up in Orange County, in an area of South Santa Ana that had seen some major demographic transformations, including an influx of Latino immigrants. Claire described this area now as "a ghetto, or *barrio*," and said that it was too painful and probably unsafe for her even to go back to visit. This experience was how she explained her current stand on wanting the gate: "For me, that's the main thing, to see the property value stay where it is and not decline, not be a declining community. Because I've seen that in Santa Ana. I've lived through watching a community just absolutely go to [pause] . . . somewhere I don't want to be." Both Claire and Gerry saw Los Angeles and Santa Ana as already lost to "decline" and hoped that gating the Ridgewood community would help keep that from happening here.

These observations about the "decline" in Los Angeles and Santa Ana reflect the macroeconomic shifts that have occurred in these cities: the replacement of stable, unionized jobs with "flexible," part-time, and poorly paid jobs; the influx of new immigrants for whom even insecure or poorly compensated jobs remain attractive opportunities; and the heightened poverty among workers earning service wages. But instead of representing these shifts as macroeconomic in nature, Claire and Gerry both seem to represent them as the product of demographics, as if the influx of Latino immigrants or the behavior of blacks had initiated the problems these areas have experienced. This kind of assumption lends itself to anxieties about race more than economic difficulty or crime per se. For instance, in the interview excerpt above, Jeff identified the "encroachment" of "that type of person" (presumably nonwhites) upon Irvine rather than crime itself as the primary issue that concerned him.

The talk of crime represented in these narratives also reflects a common perception of an eroded boundary between urban and suburban spaces. Large

Latino immigrant communities are indeed close to Irvine these days. Insofar as those in Ridgewood view Santa Ana as having been "Los Angelesized" via mobile urban minorities, it is possible for them to perceive the presence of so many immigrant Latinos in and near Irvine as evidence that Irvine may face a similar fate. Whereas physical distance used to secure suburban communities from urban ills, some people like Tom now want to face that future from "behind a gated wall."

There are several ironies in this vision of the future and in the concurrent talk of crime in Ridgewood. One is that the erosion occurring between urban and suburban communities is at least partially attributable to the dependence in Irvine upon "urban" minorities for service labor. Irvine is linked to Santa Ana not just through a network of freeways, but also via economic ties initiated by Irvine consumers. A second irony is that—contrary to the vision of a dystopic future of economic decline in Irvine—this city has in fact benefited a great deal from globalization and the very economic shifts that have devastated Santa Ana and Los Angeles. That is, Irvine has quite effectively attracted transnational capital and high-wage jobs; it is one of the winners in the global economy. It has also benefited from the availability of the nearby low-wage workforce in Santa Ana, a labor relationship that has generated greater wealth in Irvine even as it produces poverty-level incomes in Santa Ana.

Given a tendency toward racialized rather than macroeconomic understandings of the transformations occurring around Irvine, however, connections to Santa Ana appeared as a genuine threat to many of those in Ridgewood. The talk of crime in this community served to "explain" these transformations and to reassert social and geographic distinctions between Irvine and Santa Ana, between white and Latino communities, between the safe and the dangerous, suburban and urban. It also focused attention on the physical boundary of the neighborhood, making it a site of anxiety about control. The following sections address practices of social distinction within Ridgewood community space, practices that—like the talk of crime—articulated difference, status, belonging, and exclusion.

Looking Exclusive: Gating and the Aesthetic of Prestige

A second set of practices within Ridgewood that functioned to establish social distinction involved the regulation of aesthetics within community space. This issue arose strongly within discussions about gating. Besides security, the other explanation most often offered for the drive to add gates to the community was that it would raise property values. The logic of this claim rests on the history of social homogeneity and exclusion in suburban regions. In the first half of the twentieth century, developers used race-specific restrictive deed restrictions and covenants in order to market exclusion, arguing that racial mixing was bad for the stability of real estate values. The Federal Housing Administration adopted these same principles in its policies, given its close ties with real estate interests, and actively promoted suburbanization and seg-regation, insuring home loans for new single-family houses in homogeneous white neighborhoods, to the neglect of multiracial, older, and urban commu-nities.[24] After the Supreme Court outlawed racially exclusive covenants in 1948, residential covenants began using other means to ensure exclusion, shifting the focus to class.[25] Class-targeted restrictions are still common in neighbor-hoods with home owners' associations, such as limiting the number of people per housing unit and forbidding activities that have working-class connota-tions, such as repairing cars in the driveway. The legacy of these historical housing practices is that race and class segregation continue to "seem a mark of social status":[26] the look of a prestigious neighborhood requires exclusivity, as represented in part by gates and walls.

One resident articulated this connection very clearly (though mockingly), suggesting that the image of prestige that accompanies gated communities was related to a vision of "the grand estate":

> You know, you drive up to the estate and there are these *enormous* gates, and there's a man who opens the gate, or electronically the gates open, and you drive up the *long* drive . . . And yet here we all are, sandwiched on these tiny little lots. . . . But if you put the gate there, it's like the whole thing becomes one big estate. (Nancy)

While the grand estate may be part of the cultural repertoire that informed a connection between gated communities and prestige (and hence property val-ues), there were also more immediate cultural references available to residents who made this association. Local real estate publications often represented gated communities as "elite" or "exclusive." And indeed, most new elite hous-ing developments in Orange County in the 1990s were gated, such that a neighborhood without gates or guards such as Ridgewood could be perceived as lacking a key aesthetic signal of prestige. As one resident articulated (lean-ing close and speaking softly as if in confidence), "Even if people may not own up to what their primary motivation was, the primary motivation was—'we're as good as Highland Park [a nearby gated community], and a gate will prove that we are equal.' . . . It was a status thing" (Carolyn).

Of course, the local aesthetic of prestige in suburban housing is not limited to gating, but rather incorporates a wide range of elements—from architectural design to paint color—that all signal a bourgeois standard of living. As Pierre Bourdieu argues, all sorts of ordinary practices and properties can serve as "practical metaphors" for class position.[27] In Ridgewood, the gating debate was perhaps the most overtly discussed element of this elite standard; however, other elements were already a pervasive part of daily life, particularly those that were enforced by the home owner association's Codes, Covenants, and Regulations (CC&Rs). Ridgewood's CC&Rs, which closely resembled those in most Irvine developments, largely functioned to restrict any resemblance to the aesthetic of lower-class or nonwhite neighborhoods, thus enforcing social distinctions of both class and race. Some of these regulations had been instituted as part of the deed contract by the developer; others had been instituted later by the home owners' association.

Some regulations, such as the rule against hanging laundry outdoors on a clothesline, had fairly obvious class content that reflected widespread norms. Outdoor clotheslines are generally circumscribed in suburban areas, given the widespread bourgeois, Anglo reading of such public displays of private items (not to mention the visibility of household labor) as vulgar, Third World, or proletarian. Similarly, pickup trucks that residents used for business could not be parked on the street, as the kinds of occupations that might entail the use of a truck would compromise the professional, white-collar identity of the community. That is, plumbers or carpenters might live in the neighborhood, but their professions should not be visible. Other regulations, like that delimiting the kinds of roofing material allowable, were more local in their meaning. That is, according to one resident, all houses in Ridgewood had to have concrete shake or shake-looking shingles rather than asphalt composite shingles, because asphalt was the material more common in cheaper, less prestigious neighborhoods in Orange County, such as working-class and immigrant communities in Santa Ana. Another resident pointed out that asphalt composite is the city of Irvine's recommended roofing material, because it has high fire retardant properties, is inexpensive, and is relatively light: "Can you imagine having heavy concrete tile roofs and having an earthquake happen?" She concluded that the board's choice was based solely on the criterion that shake roofs "will increase the look and value of our community . . . It's only for the aesthetic" (Marilyn).

Less obvious were regulations aimed at establishing the community's whiteness and eliminating visible associations with nonwhite racial groups. There were rules against visible commerce in the neighborhood, with its connotations of urban centers or the informal economy of immigrant enclaves. Similarly, there was no place to play basketball, a conscious decision that, according to one resident, was made because basketball courts "would attract unsavory people from other places" (Nancy). The sports that could be practiced in the neighborhood included tennis, volleyball, and swimming—sports more appropriate for a mostly white middle-class suburb than basketball, so strongly associated with the inner city.

Finally, there was no formal regulation but certainly informal anxieties about the visible presence of nonwhite people in the neighborhood, insofar as the neighborhood might be assumed to be "salt-and-pepper," one resident's term for a neighborhood in transition to urban decay. This anxiety among white residents did not focus on their Asian neighbors. The Asian residents in the community did not appear to be well integrated socially and were the target of some expressed discomfort about "cultural difference" or aloofness by some of the white residents participating in this study. However, these residents did not identify Asian neighbors as a problem for property values or a sign of a neighborhood in decline, given an apparent assumption of equal class status and that Asian neighbors "keep up their property." In contrast, much anxiety centered on the presence of "darker" people in the neighborhood, presumably Latinos and African Americans. Several residents told me stories about such "incidents." In one case, a visiting relative (described only as "dark") who went to the community pool was approached by a resident and "was not believed" when she explained her connection and where she was staying. Another case involved a resident calling the police in response to a preteen "black kid" simply wandering around the neighborhood. Clearly, race appeared to be a cue for some residents to identify people who were not fellow residents— strangers who lacked legitimate access to the pool or who might be criminally threatening. However, such cue taking also effectively regulated race. It ensured that there were not "darker" people visible in the neighborhood in ways that might indicate that they lived there, compromising the prestige of a "white" neighborhood.

What we see in both the formal and the informal regulations in this community is a pervasive concern with social distinction: the practices and signs that marked its exclusiveness, in terms of both class and race, permeated daily life. It is within this context that the proposal to install gates at the neighborhood perimeter to "boost property values" makes most sense. Gates would have been another marker of exclusiveness and prestige according to local aesthetic standards, a means to position this community as suburban, private, white, and middle class, in opposition to those that are urban, public, minority, or working class. Of course, there is nothing intrinsic to gates that signals prestige. Their meaning—like that of basketball or tennis courts—is constructed within a social context marked by class and racial hierarchies. The range of practices that might affect symbolic status is almost endless, and is a moving target insofar as elite communities continually need to invent new forms of distinction to maintain difference from "less prestigious" communities that might appropriate elite forms.

Despite the local, arbitrary nature of the aesthetic of prestige, it was very real for Ridgewood residents. It was a route to both individual and community status and to the material gains that would result from higher property values. It also manifested itself materially in the walls at the perimeter of Ridgewood, marking its distinction from lower status groups. And finally, this aesthetic had real regulatory effects on all appearances and behavior in the neighborhood, with particular anxiety surrounding the presence of people or signs associated with nonwhite or working-class communities—an issue that had consequences for service workers in the community.

Social Regulation as a Means of Distinction

So far, we have established that Ridgewood residents maintained social distinction through the talk of crime and the regulation of aesthetics. In both cases, the class status of the community, its relative prestige and whiteness, and its social boundaries were defined strongly in relation to those of other racial and class groups. One might imagine that, within this context, the introduction of working-class Latino service workers could inspire considerable anxiety. Instead, Ridgewood residents described service workers in almost entirely positive terms, as "hard-working, sweet people" (Jeff), or "just people who want a better life for themselves" (Jeanne). This kind of positive narrative rested on residents being able to differentiate between service workers and criminally threatening "strangers," both of whom were widely identified by racial and class cues. It also rested upon service workers remaining distinct from residents in terms of their status and role within the community. As explored in this section, workers' distinctions from strangers and from residents were defined and enforced through informal but pervasive social regulations.

Such regulations were most apparent in the kinds of practices service workers engaged in within community space and particularly the circumstances under which they were publicly visible. Remarkably regular patterns emerged that could not have been random. For instance, the interview materials suggest that service workers were visible only when there was some apparent work-related reason. Gardeners stayed close to their trucks and tools. Child-care providers were generally visible only when in the company of their employers' children. Housekeepers were rarely visible. The only instances in which home owners reported seeing female service workers alone was when they were coming to work, walking to the bus stop, or waiting for a ride. Many domestic workers in South Orange County depend upon public transportation, such that suburban neighborhoods tend to have a mass exodus of Latina pedestrians at the end of the workday toward the bus stop. This moment of visibility has come to be part of the expected social landscape and among Ridgewood residents did not seem to incur any anxiety, given that there was a work-related explanation for it.

Given how much anxiety was directed at Latino "strangers," the performance of work must have been necessary to maintain the distinction between workers and strangers, to assure home owners of the benign intentions of the working-class Latino presence in the community. As long as these Latinos were easily legible as service providers, they did not generate anxiety about crime or about Ridgewood looking like a "salt-and-pepper" community. In fact, the approved presence of servants and other service providers had the potential to contribute to the community's aesthetics of prestige, to its whiteness and status.

In addition to establishing distinctions between workers and strangers, informal social regulations also distinguished between workers and home owners. Such regulations came into particularly high relief in relation to live-in domestic workers' use of the private park and pool. In each interview with home owners, I asked whether they recalled seeing live-in nannies taking a walk or swimming on their own during their time off. Virtually no one could recall instances of seeing it happen. Cheryl, who employed Carmen, a domestic worker who had lived with her for the past seven years, said that it would be no problem whatsoever for resident workers to use the pool, but that most of them simply did not choose to go on their own:

> C: Not many of them swim—Carmen does swim, but not many of them do . . . Jeanne's gal does, and her cousin does, across the street. But a lot of them don't swim, so they don't really go "pool it" so much . . .
> Int: So can Carmen just go use the pool any time she wants?
> C: Mm-hm. Well, I always have the key up there.
> Int: Does she go by herself without the kids, or does she always go with the kids?
> C: 99.9 percent of the time she goes with the kids.
> Int: Do you think anyone would have a problem with it if she went just by herself?
> C: No, because they all know her. I mean, she's been here this long—everybody knows her.

Others clearly felt uncomfortable with the idea of resident workers using the park or pool on their own, without being accompanied by their employers' children. For instance, Tom agreed that it might be possible but insisted quite strongly that it doesn't happen:

> Int: In some ways they [the live-in domestic workers] are residents, but . . . according to the neighborhood rules, do they have access to those facilities themselves?
> T: They won't use those facilities only. No, they don't. I mean, clearly they could. We're not going to . . . I mean, I'm not going to be the park cop or the park police and keep them from using it. Certainly, it's discretionary, the judgment of the people that employ them. What you will find is that at noontime or sometime in the morning or the afternoon . . . the domestics will meet in the park with their charges, and of course you'll see that daily. And it's always around the tot lot. So there's six or seven domestics that go in there around 10:00 or 10:30 in the morning, and the kids that they're caring for are there, and all of the Hispanics—only Spanish is spoken so I know they're Hispanic—are there commiserating with one another.
> Int: And in your judgment, that's not a problem in terms of park use?
> T: Oh, hell no, that's not a problem at all, no.
> Int: Do they come to the park on their time off . . .
> T: No.
> Int: . . . I mean like once they've finished?
> T: No, no. [changes the subject]

In this interview excerpt, Tom seemed to want to talk only about the behaviors of the nannies that he felt were appropriate for them, to meet in the park daily "with their charges" and "commiserate" with one another—something he apparently considered a happy neighborhood scene. While he said there was no real rule against them being out in the park alone, he was much less willing to discuss it.

Mary and Harrison, a couple who interviewed together, agreed that nannies shouldn't use facilities alone. The following excerpt raises a number of additional interesting considerations:

> Int: So, in terms of using [common] facilities, can nannies . . .
> M: Oh yeah, the nannies are there. They're there all the time with the kids in the pool, and they have their key and whatever. Not bringing out their, you know, their *families* or whatever, but during the day they're there with the kids.
> Int: That's what I was going to ask. If they're kind of "residents," do they . . . could they use it on their own?
> M: No, I don't think so.
> H: No, that's . . . and they don't do that. They don't abuse it.
> M: They're probably better about not abusing it than some of the residents that used to [live here] . . . legal residents that aren't anymore. . . . They have much more respect for the whole system.

There is a lot here to untangle. First, although the nannies were in the pool "all the time" with the kids during the day, they did not use the pool on their own. That is, "they don't abuse it." In this case, the thing they seemed not to be abusing was the potential to use facilities like the pool even though they obviously had access to keys. In other words, they were not legitimate users of common facilities without being accompanied by someone in their employer's family, part of "the system" of rules and rights in the neighborhood. The contrast that Mary then made between nannies and former home owners in the neighborhood was also very telling. She had earlier complained that people who used to live in the neighborhood kept their pool keys and continued to come back to swim, in blatant disregard for the "home owners only" policy. But here she refers to these people as "legal residents"—in contrast to the domestics, who were evidently "illegal" residents. It is possible that "legal" was not the word she meant, and that she was trying to contrast the nannies with "legitimate" home owners, who properly have rights to common facilities. However, immediately before this excerpt of her interview, Mary had in fact described the nannies in the community as "illegal," meaning that she assumed they were undocumented immigrants. (This assumption may have been true for some of the domestic workers but was certainly incorrect about others.) Here, it appears that she was generalizing their assumed *immigration status* to their status in the neighborhood, as if the reason they were not legitimate users of community facilities was because they were not a legitimate presence in the United States. This assumption arose in one other interview, as well, again in a context in which the home owner said she did not worry about domestic workers "abusing it" (apparently their access to community resources) or inviting in others: "Because most of the workers here are very illegal, they don't want to attract a lot of attention anyway, I don't think. They don't seem to draw people" (Ruth).

The other interesting issue that came up in Mary and Harrison's interview was the question of whether nannies could bring family members to swim in the pool, given that some of the live-in domestic workers in Ridgewood had families living nearby, including their own children. There was nearly complete agreement among all those I interviewed about the taboo against having family members visit or come use the park and pool. When asked whether there was a rule against nannies using the facilities for their own purposes, Claire explained:

> I don't think there's an actual *rule* per se. I think if you're living in the home, that sort of gives you access. I don't know what the feeling of the community would be. It wouldn't bother me personally, unless people were getting out of hand. Or—now this is not very nice—but unless it was attracting some sort of riffraff into the community. You know, that's another issue, too, that had never occurred to me. That if other family members were coming in, then that would be an issue that I think a lot of people would have a hard time with.

Others affirmed this observation about general neighborhood sentiment. One stay-at-home mother reported that she saw nothing wrong if "your live-in [has] her cousin and her cousin's child come and swim who don't have an opportunity in downtown Santa Ana to use a pool," especially if they come during quiet morning hours when the other children are not using it. But, she added, there are "others in the neighborhood who disagree, and I have heard it voiced" (Ruth). Nancy also affirmed that "if they brought their whole family in, I'm not sure that would . . . go over." There are a number of potential reasons that resident workers inviting family members to come swim would not "go over" with many home owners in Ridgewood. On one hand, some like Claire might have suspected these relatives as being "some sort of riffraff" that might constitute a criminal threat. On the other hand, even young children (who would clearly not be suspected criminals) may not have been welcome because they would raise the prospect of a pool full of Latino kids on the weekends, which would then resemble a public pool in Santa Ana much more than the private pool of an elite, mostly white neighborhood.

So far, I have been making inferences about the regulation of resident workers' behavior on the basis of home owners' reports. Conversations with live-in workers in the Ridgewood community confirmed that they did not use common facilities for their own leisure. Resident workers in the neighborhood said that they did not go swimming on their own because they "don't feel comfortable" doing it, and preferred to go swimming elsewhere in apartment complexes. But they did not tend to attribute their discomfort to overt regulation. Instead, for instance, one woman said she did not swim in the neighborhood because she didn't like how her body looked in a swimming suit. In contrast to her employer's confidence that she could freely use the pool, Carmen explained why she did not go on her own:[28]

> C: I do not go there. I am not going to feel comfortable.
> Int: Why?
> C: Because it seems as if I do not belong to the community. . . .
> Int: What gave you that impression—did people look at you? . . . Have you already tried it?
> C: Sometimes I have thought that I would like to go and relax there a little bit, read, be under the sun, but there where everyone already knows who I am, they know me, and they are going to say . . . I think I am not going to feel comfortable (laughs) . . . When I go, sometimes they say to me, "And do you have a key? Do you belong to the club?" They are going to be thinking about whether or not you belong to the community.

Carmen expected to be rebuked for using the pool both by those who did not know her and by those who knew she was a domestic worker.

What started to become evident from these reports about what kinds of things "just did not happen" in the neighborhood were the community's unspoken norms about appropriate behavior for each class of person. The live-in domestic workers in the neighborhood were not making independent claims on neighborhood space or amenities. Their activities in the neighborhood were quite severely constrained. Even Carmen, who had not lived outside this neighborhood for many years, did not feel comfortable going down to the community pool without her employer's children as chaperones to give her legitimacy. There were clearly social regulations at work, even while there was not total agreement about the "rules" or the "system," nor even a formal cognizance among some of the workers that they existed. It appears that the "system" of social distance between home owners and resident workers had been internalized by both groups to the point of being taken for granted, a set of daily practices that (re)produced a highly stratified relationship among people sharing geographic space.[29]

The easiest means to establish social distinction is to have spatial segregation, where borders are geographic as well as social, and certainly there was spatial regulation in this community as well, limiting the extent to which common spaces were truly common. Spatial regulations were not only about where, at what times, and under what conditions domestic workers could be present in visible neighborhood space, but also about where they could be within the houses where they lived and worked. While most houses with live-in workers did not have a formal "servants' quarters" with a separate entrance, domestic workers generally did not have free reign of the house and were expected to retreat and become more or less invisible when they were not working.[30] Another familiar means for distinction when serving and employing classes inhabit the same space has been to have servants wear uniforms. In this circumstance, servant garb seemed to be unnecessary, as the service workers' race served as their uniform in a community with very few Latino home owners.[31] The daily, internalized rules about the kinds of behavior appropriate from each class of person worked in conjunction with these other means of distinction.

Social regulations in Ridgewood helped produce a certain kind of interaction between classes, one in which there was a smooth surface that tamed social distance. With the description of workers as "people who just want a better life for themselves," employers of immigrants could imagine this relationship as a helping hand or an act of benevolence. One employer (Jeanne) actively encouraged her live-in domestic worker to continue her education and supplied birth control to the other nannies on her street. The paternalistic (and historically familiar) fantasy is that workers "choose" to be nannies, house-keepers, and gardeners in order to make something better of their lives, and their employers give them a leg up on the ladder of economic opportunity.[32] One might imagine that this fantasy is most effective in masking relations of power when the interactions between workers and those who hire their services are virtually scripted and the "rules" for what behaviors are appropriate for each class are not experienced as coercive.

The limits of this smooth interaction were apparent, however, in the anxieties Ridgewood home owners had regarding the friends and families of workers. Unlike service workers, who were assumed to be "good people," workers' social networks were not safely regulated within the neighborhood social system and hence were not welcome. The dichotomy between workers and "strangers"—between employees and their spouses, siblings, children, and parents—appeared to rest solely on the extent to which these groups were obligated to behave within the subordinated and limited role of service. Indeed, this was the only identifiable difference between workers and strangers: some of those who performed service labor in Ridgewood lived in Santa Ana in the same households as "strangers" assumed to be potential criminals. At the end of their workday and at the end of their employment in the neighborhood, workers hypothetically rejoined the ranks of the "urban" minorities that Ridgewood residents feared would someday invade Irvine, bringing crime and economic malaise.

Borders in the Global Suburb

Parts of Irvine still feel suburban, but its economy and social geography have been reshaped by transnational capital and a growing reliance upon transnational labor in the service economy. This economic structure has eroded historical, core-periphery patterns of racial and class segregation, as immigrant enclaves develop in and around former bedroom communities and immigrant workers become a pervasive presence in middle-class homes. However, the proximity between groups has not resulted in the erosion of social hierarchies or the bridging of social distance. Instead, the shifting social geography in and around Irvine is laced with tensions about social distinction that were expressed in three types of practices that we have considered. First, the "talk of crime" articulated differences between urban and suburban, Latino and white, and manifested itself in anxiety about neighborhood borders as a site for control. Second, legal and informal regulations of aesthetics within Ridgewood delimited the range of appearances appropriate to maintain a white, middle-class community identity. Third, the immigrant Latinos working in Ridgewood were subject to pervasive social regulations that defined their social place within the community, as people who were welcome while working but otherwise illegitimate. These practices each contributed to the maintenance of social stratification and social distance when these could no longer be established through geographic distance.

While the social regulation of service workers did leave most residents of Ridgewood feeling comfortable with the presence of working-class Latinos in community space, they did not mollify more general anxieties about the proximity of Latino immigrant enclaves or the social networks in which workers were embedded. The relations of the transnational service economy in this community had a relatively smooth surface at the interpersonal level, but also produced significant, diffuse fears about the future—about impending urbanity, crime, and economic decline. Even while Irvine itself remains a very orderly place, most Ridgewood residents held the view that mayhem might soon erupt or that their quality of life and the security of their status would soon take a turn for the worse. The popular impulse to fortify the neighborhood perimeters with gates and walls appeared to relate to this sense of a loss of control.

We might speculate that the experienced loss of control and border fortressing in Ridgewood reflects a sense that social and political borders more generally are becoming porous. I have focused above on the erosion between "the suburban" and "the urban" that has taken place in a globalizing economy, as well as the interdependent relationship between immigrant workers and suburban consumers. However, a transnational labor force also entails a porous border at the perimeter of the nation-state, and it is very possible that the widespread sense in California that immigration at the border is out of control informs some of the efforts to fortress at a local level. Undocumented immigration had been a major focus of political mobilization in California during the years prior to this study, even after the highly visible border control measures of Operation Gatekeeper (including a double fence, spotlights at night, new detection technologies, and a larger Border Patrol force) had been implemented in 1994. Although I did not direct conversation toward the topic of immigration during interviews, one might imagine that the narrative of immigrant invasion resonated strongly among Ridgewood residents who watched the growth of immigrant populations in Santa Ana with a wary eye.

The patterns of anxiety in Ridgewood suggest that, although global suburbs are reliant upon immigrant labor, they may be fertile ground for anti-immigrant politics. It seems no coincidence that California's Proposition 187 denying social services to the undocumented in 1994 had its origins among Orange County suburbs that already depended strongly upon an immigrant labor force. Such policies are aimed primarily at regulating the status of certain groups of immigrants, trying to ensure that these workers and their families would remain contained within a service relationship and not make independent claims to common resources and "amenities" like education or health care. It would make sense that people who live in neighborhoods like Ridgewood might want to extend the subordinated role of Latino immigrants in their community to the polity more broadly.

Ridgewood's debate about whether to add security gates also has potential to lend some insight to national immigration politics. Recall that it was not immediately apparent how further fortressing at the Ridgewood perimeter would address anyone's security concerns. Even Ridgewood residents who supported installing gates for security acknowledged that they would be unlikely to keep criminals out, as there would still be unhindered pedestrian access. Like the talk of crime, security gates appeared to have largely symbolic functions, marking a line in the sand beyond which urban ills were not welcome. As the preceding analysis suggests, the other potential function for gates would be to enforce social distinctions and differences in status. The gates certainly would not be intended to keep immigrants or working-class minorities out, given that large numbers of service workers were invited to enter the neighborhood on a daily basis. Instead, gates would serve to reinforce the social position of workers that was already informally institutionalized in social regulations—workers were to remain strictly in a service capacity and could make no claims as social equals. This kind of logic is also evident in the efforts to control the U.S.–Mexico border, where the fortification of the border is not intended to keep immigrants out so much as to control the status of various groups once they enter. Control at the border preserves legal hierarchies between citizens, permanent residents, aliens, and the undocumented; it is the basis for the unequal distribution of rights and social standing within the United States.

The production of "illegality" through border control has become a critical part of immigration politics in Southern California, where Latino immigrants—particularly those who work in "immigrant jobs"—are widely assumed to be illegal even when they are permanent residents or citizens. Stories about "illegal immigrants" crowding hospital emergency rooms abound, for instance, based solely on the observation of people who speak Spanish and who very likely lack health insurance. The assumption that immigrants are illegal serves to justify discrimination against them and to legitimate claims that they are not entitled to rights. In a liberal society in which discrimination based solely on race is no longer tolerated by law, discrimination based on legal status is still widely seen as legitimate. Evidence of this kind of thinking arose in the Ridgewood case, where the "illegality" of immigrant workers was at times used to justify their relative invisibility, subordination, and lack of rights. Several interviews included phrasing that suggested that immigrants were not social equals within Ridgewood because their presence in the United States was not legitimate. Border control at the neighborhood level works in conjunction with that at the national level to regulate status by marking populations as legitimate or illegitimate claimants of rights.

Finally, the Ridgewood case begins to illustrate what we might expect of global suburbs. The literature tends to celebrate the cosmopolitanism of such places as evidenced in their growing foreign populations and their consumer tastes that reflect an appreciation for other parts of the world. Certainly, Irvine does have a significant international population as well as cultural and economic ties. But its international character is also about the global hierarchies that structure its labor markets and social relations. Global suburbs are marked not just by high-tech professionals, an arts and culture scene, and ethnic restaurants; they also incorporate economies of service and support inhabited by immigrant workers from less-developed states. In some ways, such regions embody the global economy come home, a postcolonial "reverse invasion" of the most insular and provincial cultural outposts in America. The Ridgewood case suggests that immigrant-based service economies will involve significant social stratification as well as elaborate and multiple practices of social distinction. Contact and physical proximity across social divisions certainly does not ensure social leveling or even mutual understanding. Instead, the social relations of global suburbs reinforce many of the same inequalities as in the traditionally segregated city.

Notes

1. Saskia Sassen, *The Global City* (Princeton: Princeton University Press, 1991).
2. William R. Barnes and Larry C. Ledebur, "The Regional Economic Commons," in *The Politics of Urban America*, ed. Dennis R. Judd and Paul Kantor (New York: Longman, 2002), 380–93; Rob Kling, Spencer Olin, and Mark Poster, eds., *Postsuburban California: The Transformation of Orange County since World War II* (Berkeley: University of California Press, 1991); Joel Garreau, *Edge City: Life on the New Frontier* (New York: Anchor Books, 1992).
3. Alan J. Scott and Edward W. Soja, eds., *The City: Los Angeles and Urban Theory at the End of the Twentieth Century* (Berkeley: University of California Press, 1996).

4. Kling, Olin, and Poster, *Postsuburban California*, 20–22.

5. The State of California's Labor Market Information Division, "Orange MSA Annual Average Labor Force and Industry Employment" (available on the World Wide Web at http://www.calmis.ca.gov/) documents that service sector jobs more than doubled in Orange County from 1983 to 1999.

6. My use of the concept "social distinction" draws from Pierre Bourdieu, *Distinction: A Social Critique of the Judgment of Taste* (Cambridge: Harvard University Press, 1984); Pierre Bourdieu, "Social Space and Symbolic Power," *Sociological Theory* 7.1 (1989): 14–25; and David Swartz, *Culture and Power: The Sociology of Pierre Bourdieu* (Chicago: University of Chicago Press, 1997).

7. Teresa P. R. Caldeira, *City of Walls: Crime, Segregation, and Citizenship in São Paulo* (Berkeley: University of California Press, 2000).

8. Martin J. Schiesl, "Designing the Model Community: The Irvine Company and Suburban Development, 1950–88," in Kling, Olin, and Poster, *Postsuburban California*, 55–91.

9. Karen Till, "Neotraditional Towns and Urban Villages: The Cultural Production of a Geography of 'Otherness.'" *Environment and Planning D: Society and Space* 11 (1994), 709–32.

10. Master Planned Community Video, available at www.destinationirvine.com.

11. Garreau, *Edge City*, 271.

12. M. Dodson, "Where Is the County's 'Mason-Dixon' Line? Start at Costa Mesa Freeway and Meander South," *Los Angeles Times*, Orange County edition, August 27, 1989, Metro 2:1.

13. Raymond A. Rocco, "Latino Los Angeles: Reframing Boundaries/Borders," in *The City: Los Angeles and Urban Theory at the End of the Twentieth Century*, ed. Allen J. Scott and Edward W. Soja (Berkeley: University of California Press, 1996), 365–89.

14. Teresa P. R. Caldeira, "Fortified Enclaves: The New Urban Segregation" in *Public Culture* 8.2 (1996): 310.

15. The number of advanced degrees in both Ridgewood and in Irvine was relatively high in part because of the high-tech economic base, but also because of the colleges and university located in Irvine.

16. Four percent of those identifying as white reported a Hispanic origin, all of Peruvian descent. The category of "white" also included several Persian families, who were identified as nonwhite by some residents during interviews.

17. U.S. Census of Population and Housing (block level), 1990.

18. For discussions of this case: *Citizens Against Gated Enclaves (CAGE) v. Whitley Heights*, see David J. Kennedy, "Residential Associations as State Actors: Regulating the Impact of Gated Communities on Nonmembers," in *Yale Law Journal* 105.3 (1995), 761–93; and Edward J. Blakely and Mary Gail Snyder, *Fortress America: Gated Communities in the United States* (Washington, D.C.: Brookings Institution Press; Cambridge, Mass.: Lincoln Institute of Land Policy, 1997), 106.

19. I located respondents through referrals that led me to some of the activists in the neighborhood both for and against gating, as well as to some whose opinions were less polarized. The resulting sample of eighteen residents was socially diverse in terms of age, occupation, educational attainment, and nativity, but not fully representative of the demographics of the neighborhood. I supplemented the interviews with materials from participant observation, the census, the Irvine police department, local real estate publications, and secondary academic sources. I also worked with a bilingual research assistant to gain access to and interview some of the live-in domestic workers in the neighborhood.

20. The already low crime rate in Irvine had been in decline since the early 1990s, much like the rates of property and violent crime in Santa Ana, Orange County, and Los Angeles County (California Crime Index, Rand California Community Statistics).

21. Barry Glassner, *The Culture of Fear* (New York: Basic Books, 1999); Mike Davis, *City of Quartz: Excavating the Future in Los Angeles* (New York: Vintage Books, 1992).

22. Calderia, *City of Walls*, 34.

23. Ibid., 19–41.

24. Evan McKenzie, *Privatopia: Homeowner Associations and the Rise of Residential Private Government* (New Haven: Yale University Press, 1994), 60–67; Douglas S. Massey and Nancy A. Denton, *American Apartheid: Segregation and the Making of the Underclass* (Cambridge: Harvard University Press, 1993).

25. McKenzie, *Privatopia*, 75–78.

26. Ibid., 72.

27. Bourdieu, *Distinction*, 173.

28. Interview originally in Spanish.

29. This interpretation draws strongly on Bourdieu, coming very close to what he calls "habitus," which Rogers Brubaker defines as "the system of internalized dispositions that mediates between social struc-

tures and practical activity, being shaped by the former and regulating the latter." Rogers Brubaker, "Rethinking Classical Theory: The Sociological Vision of Pierre Bourdieu," in *Theory and Society* 14.6 (1985), 758.

30. Regarding the household relations of domestic service in Southern California, see Pierrette Hondagneu-Sotelo, *Doméstica: Immigrant Workers Cleaning and Caring in the Shadows of Affluence* (Berkeley: University of California Press, 2001); Doreen Jeanette Mattingly, "The Home and the World: Domestic Service and International Networks of Caring Labor," *Annals of the Association of American Geographers* 91.2 (2001): 370–86.

31. Block-level Census data from 1990 documented 4 percent of the Ridgewood population reporting Peruvian descent. Regarding the notion of race as a uniform, see Hilda Kuper, *The Uniform of Colour: A Study of White-Black Relationships in Swaziland* (Johannesburg: Witwatersrand University Press, 1947).

32. The literature on domestic work is rife with stories about the dynamics of paternalism (perhaps more properly identified as maternalism). See Hondagneu-Sotelo, *Doméstica*; Leslie Gill, *Precarious Dependencies: Gender, Class, and Domestic Service in Bolivia* (New York: Columbia University Press, 1994); Nicky Gregson and Michelle Lowe, *Servicing the Middle Classes: Class, Gender, and Waged Domestic Labor in Contemporary Britain* (New York: Routledge, 1994); and Mary Romero, *Maid in the U.S.A.* (New York: Routledge, 1992).

Nuestra Los Angeles

Michael Nevin Willard

In his 1949 book *North from Mexico: The Spanish Speaking People of the United States,* Carey McWilliams notes that the "settlers" who established Los Angeles in 1781, and whom city elites would later celebrate as "Spanish," were, in fact, two Indians, two mulattos, two Spaniards (each married to an Indian), a Negro, an Indian married to a mulatto, an Indian married to an Indian, a mestizo married to a mulatto, and "'a Chino' . . . probably of Chinese descent" (36).[1] Rather than assimilate (or whitewash) Los Angeles's multiracial founders within a Spanish fantasy heritage, as had become common by the time *North from Mexico* was published, McWilliams notes the racial categories used to classify them. Highlighting their marital status to evoke a doubly *mestizo* history of Los Angeles, he counteracts the national/racial purity in Spanish origin narratives of the city. From the standpoint of current American studies scholarship, McWilliams's counternarrative of Los Angeles's origins relocates the city's beginnings to an intersection of the Spanish Borderlands, the Black Atlantic, and the Pacific Rim. In all of his writings, McWilliams sought to convey the complexities of the West, California, Southern California, and especially Los Angeles. The range of issues to which he turned his pen remain central to Los Angeles scholars today.

"Titles have always bothered me and never more so than in selecting a title for this book. How is one to characterize, in a phrase, a people so diverse in origin?" McWilliams declares in the first sentences of *North from Mexico.* "I was told that 'Americans from Mexico' would be an appropriate title. . . . [B]ut, strictly speaking, the Spanish-language minority did not come from Spain and Mexico," he continues. "They were already very much a part of the landscape when the Anglo-Americans came to the Southwest. . . . [I]n the end, I was driven to the conclusion that the title would have to refer to a process, a movement, a point on the compass" (7–9). McWilliams would ultimately reconcile the paradoxes of identity inherent to Mexican migration by emphasizing culture as a whole way of life: "For it is the direction in which the people have moved that has given unity to their lives. . . . 'North from Mexico' . . . implies the extension of a way of life rather than a crossing or a jumping of barriers" (10).

McWilliams's solution to the contradiction of a singular national identity that belies great heterogeneity is a useful starting point for a review essay on recent Los Angeles scholarship, for it historicizes key aspects of the city itself, then and now. Additionally, his early attention to the centrality of race— Michael Denning and Nikhil Pal Singh best explain the underappreciated significance of his writing/activism in the history of twentieth-century American pluralism and racial thought—is an enduring issue explored in a great deal of recent L.A. studies scholarship. McWilliams's adroit dismantling of the racial-national assumptions underlying L.A.'s Spanish origin myth offers a glimpse of his constant attention to negative racial signification in order to emphasize systematic racial exclusion *and* class exploitation as the defining factors in the development of California society. Such historical observations were reconfirmed by his personal experiences. During the early 1930s he wrote articles for national magazines and traveled the state delivering speeches to labor organizations in an effort to stop xenophobic Mexican repatriation campaigns and exploitation in farm labor. As California's chief of the Division of Immigration and Housing from 1939 to 1943, he devised means to hold farmers and growers accountable for their treatment of laborers by increasing labor camp inspections and holding wage-rate hearings (Sachs, 239). In 1943 he used his skills as a lawyer and writer to chair the Sleepy Lagoon Defense Committee. During the early 1940s he also wrote condemnations of the Japanese internment and the zoot suit riots as incidents that scapegoated Japanese Americans and race-baited Mexican Americans.[2]

Although McWilliams cited Chicago School figures such as Robert Park or Chicago-trained U.S.C. sociologist Emory Bogardus when it suited his purposes, his observations about California's multiracial demography and cultural heterogeneity often differed from prevailing academic models of individualist ethnic succession and assimilation. In *North from Mexico*, he implicitly rejects the Chicago School's model of linear progression from contact through conflict, and accommodation to assimilation, when he asserts that "it is . . . misleading . . . to assume that . . . [Mexicans] occupy a relation to the majority element which is like that, say of Poles in Detroit or Italians in New York. . . . Mexicans have never emigrated to the Southwest: they have returned" (58). For McWilliams an adequate explanation of human movement that populated Los Angeles (whether from Sinaloa or Iowa) required overlapping scales from the regional (the Southwest and Midwest) to the hemispheric, and attention to multivectored causality.

North from Mexico anticipated diasporic or transnational models of migration and cultural exchange. Chapter titles such as "The Fan of Settlement" and "Heart of the Borderlands" reveal a spatial approach. In McWilliams's view, the extensive history of social interactions along the two-thousand-mile border from Matamoros/Brownsville to Tijuana/San Diego, but also extending north to Los Angeles, inextricably bound Mexico and the United States, Hispanic and Anglo, together. He understood the borderlands as a place determined by cultural combination and intermediate identity rather than a rigid boundary creating polarities of nation that required homogeneous, assimilated, indeterminate identity *and* hierarchies of race. In this regard McWilliams's attention to the diversity of peoples in California places him in a tradition of others who critiqued racial hierarchy and embraced their multiracial circumstances, such as Cuban poet/journalist/essayist José Martí. His famous 1891 essay "Nuestra América" (Our America) called attention to a hemispheric pattern of racial-colonial rule common to North and South American nations, and championed a multiracial ideal that would acknowledge the diversity, intersections, and divergences between and among the many peoples and nations of North, Central and South America.

Virtually all of Carey McWilliams's writings have become a touchstone, because they prefigure key aspects of current work in L.A. studies. Contemporary L.A. scholars have mined his near-universally cited study of greater Los Angeles, *Southern California Country, an Island on the Land,* for his analysis of topics ranging from planning, housing, and industrial location (Hise), to the Hollywood film industry (Moran), and religious diversity (Peter). Similarly, Aaron Sachs singles out McWilliams's 1939 book *Factories in the Field: The Story of Migratory Farm Labor in California* as anticipating central concerns of the environmental justice movement, which argues that in places where environmental damage occurs it is often simultaneous with the suppression of local workers' and residents' civil liberties (220–21, 244). Laura Pulido's work on environmental racism in Los Angeles (and Arizona) develops and extends such insights today. Recent/forthcoming books on the myths and symbols of Spanish "fantasy heritage"—a term that McWilliams coined in *North from Mexico*—by Kate Phillips, William Deverell, Matthew Bokovoy, and Phoebe Kropp chronicle the influence of Southern California's first culture industry. Virginia Marie Bouvier in *Women and the Conquest of California, 1542–1840* has since explained in greater detail the relationships "between and among men and women . . . Europeans and Indians" (xv) that McWilliams highlighted in his description of L.A.'s first settlers that opens this essay. Drawn to the example of L.A.'s first settlers, like McWilliams, in order to note L.A.'s "segregated diversity," Philip Ethington asserts that "Los Angeles has two parallel traditions: the earliest being diversity and the most dominant being segregation." Ethington continues, "These contradictory traditions begin with the multiracial and mostly nonwhite founders of the city in 1781, and with the self-consciously racist dreams of a white metropolis voiced by many Anglo leaders in the 1920s" (2000a, 7).

Some L.A. scholars echo McWilliams's argument that Los Angeles is exceptional when they claim that the city is now a paradigmatic example of contemporary urbanism. In his book *Postmetropolis: Critical Studies of Cities and Regions*, Edward Soja more subtly differentiates Los Angeles, claiming that it indexes all other places when he emphasizes the city's "generalizable particularities, the degree to which one can use the specific case of Los Angeles to learn more about the new urbanization processes that are affecting, with varying degrees of intensity, all other cityspaces in the world" (154). Janet Abu-Lughod, author of *New York, Chicago, Los Angeles: America's Global Cities*, points out (and Soja would agree) that the economic, social, and spatial effects of global-economic restructuring are different in these three cities because "common forces originating at the level of the global economy operate always through local political structures and interact with inherited spatial forms" (417). As the essays in this special issue of *American Quarterly* demonstrate, Los Angeles embodies American studies' ongoing exploration of racial/gender formation, hybridity and cultural exchange, and counterhegemonic expressive cultural practices. Similar in cosmopolitan diversity to, yet different in specific demographic composition from, New York, New Orleans, Miami, Chicago, Detroit, Houston, Seattle, and many other cities that have distinct histories of multi- and interracialism, Los Angeles exceeds the white/nonwhite or biracial common sense that so dominates mass media and public policy debate.[3] Whether exceptional or paradigmatic, as we learn from L.A.'s founders, from Carey McWilliams, and the books reviewed in this essay, learning from Los Angeles, past or present, is important for illuminating and attaining "Our America" today.

The L.A. School and Los Angeles Urbanism: From Anomaly to Paradigm

This essay surveys key scholarship on Los Angeles published since 1997. That year represents a breakthrough for L.A. studies. In 1996 the critical mass of scholars published in two collections, *Rethinking Los Angeles*, edited by Michael Dear, H. Eric Shockman, and Greg Hise, and *The City: Los Angeles and Urban Theory at the End of the Twentieth Century*, edited by Allen Scott and Edward Soja, announced a discernable "L.A. School" of urban studies.[4] Prior to these books, Mike Davis's 1990 book *City of Quartz: Excavating the Future in Los Angeles* almost single-handedly brought L.A. School ideas, but not an awareness of the combined scholarly efforts of other L.A. School urbanists, to a broader audience.[5] Davis was one of a group of twenty-some geographers, urban planners, architects, labor historians, and economists at Southern California universities who, in the middle 1980s, convened a meeting to consider the possibility that their common research interests constituted an L.A. School. Geographer Michael Dear, a member of this group, explains that they "became convinced that what was happening in the region was somehow symptomatic of a broader socio-geographic transformation taking place within the United States as a whole" (2002a, 10–14).[6]

To explain the changes they observed in Southern California, the L.A. School consistently emphasized what Edward Soja calls "crisis-generated restructuring" (2000, 96). This explanation of urban-economic change, though not invented by the L.A. School, is one of the hallmarks of L.A. School urban theory. It has been taken up by subsequent L.A. scholars who have extended its explanatory power to make sense of social, political, and cultural processes. Soja argues that urban/spatial development makes economic transformation possible. He details a well-rehearsed history of the shift from the Fordist city of large-scale manufacturing for a national economy (the L.A. region was home to major rubber, auto, steel, and aircraft plants) to the de- and reindustrialized post-Fordist city characterized by small-scale, less-unionized manufacturing (textiles, furniture, light metals), flexibly adapted to production for rapidly changing, global markets. In this regard, as Soja, Allen Scott, and Janet Abu Lughod point out, Los Angeles differs from "global" cities that have lost industry over the last twenty to thirty years.[7] Los Angeles today is a city with an hour-glass class profile polarized between the predominantly white affluent and the predominantly nonwhite disadvantaged. The affluent are members of a growing corporate service sector. The disadvantaged, largely immigrant (Asian and Central American through the portal of 1965 immigration reforms) are members of the manufacturing/service (janitorial, gardening, domestic) sector.

In the collection edited by Michael Dear, *From Chicago to L.A.: Making Sense of Urban Theory*, Dear and Steven Flusty usefully schematize the contradictory conditions resulting from economic restructuring and globalization that Mike Davis first narrated in *City of Quartz*. Diversity and hybrid cultures exist concurrently with political/economic polarization. Urban space becomes increasingly mono-functional and exclusive. Amusement/consumer zones, privately governed and gated communities, and single-use, membership communities defined by wealth, age, or leisure, constitute the insular spaces of

privilege. For the poor and working classes, urban space is increasingly secured, policed, and defensively fortified. Recapitulating the concerns of Davis's
1999 book *Ecology of Fear: Los Angeles and the Imagination of Disaster*, as well
as those of other L.A. environmentalists, Dear and Flusty outline L.A.'s urban-environmental contradictions. Southern California's unpredictable, often
extreme weather combines with poorly regulated development to ensure damage from earthquakes, fires, and floods of apocalyptic proportions. As an urban ecosystem, Los Angeles abuts precipitous mountains and canyons, leading to "habitat loss" and a wild edge of urbanization where "encounters between
humans and . . . animals" (63–71) have become increasingly frequent and
deadly. In *Ecology of Fear*, Davis details the racialization of L.A.'s environmental extremes: wildfires are attributed to gangs and the homeless, and terrified
residents blame the victims of their encroachment into mountain foothills
when they compare marauding mountain lions to gangbangers. Throughout
his tour of the "literary destruction of Los Angeles," in which L.A.'s demise
has been imagined through invasion, disaster, and nuclear war, Davis uncovers the xenophobic and supremacist fantasies of Los Angeles's white racial
unconscious.

Like McWilliams, L.A. School proponents have countered the Chicago
School of urban sociology that dominated urban studies for most of the twentieth century. The authors in *From Chicago to L.A.* critique the Chicago School
on several counts: for the naively modernist assertion of a city as a "unified
whole" whose areas are oriented to its center; for an overemphasis on the individual whose "personal choices ultimately explain . . . the overall urban condition, including spatial structure, crime, poverty and racism"; and for the too
linear assertion of an "evolutionist paradigm" of ethnic succession and accul-
turation into modern society (vii–ix).

Rather than the Chicago School concentric circle model of organic urban
growth and development oriented toward a city's center, Dear and Flusty liken
recent urban growth to a game of keno. In their model, urbanization resembles
a checkerboard pattern made up of rapidly built, single-use parcels dropped
willy nilly into the city, in which the periphery organizes the center. Here, the
presence of postnational, global entities (e.g., transnational corporations, migrant networks, or networks of terrorism) influence urban planning priorities
and the allocation of municipal resources (71–80).

While such conceptual models usefully condense processes of urbanization, cities are not organisms or gaming boards. In the final analysis, they are
lived in and built by people who carry out their urban lives interacting with
fantasies, myths, images, symbols, and structures over which they have vary-

ing degrees of control. As Raymond Rocco puts it, "We need to view each 'Los Angeles' as constituting a particular, specific, and concrete way of living in and through the city that is both bounded and linked to other sectors by its particular configuration of factors such as race, class, gender, immigrant status, political access, and economic resources" (366). Recent L.A. studies both following and diverging from the L.A. School conceive of the city in such a way as to reveal such contingent qualities: social constructions of the urban and spatial constructions of the social.

Yesterday's Tomorrowlands:
Historical Geography of Land Use and the Built Environment

Apocryphally, if inaccurately, described as any number of "suburbs in search of a city," Los Angeles, in its diffuse sprawl, is not the antithesis of planned urban development as such core-periphery phrases imply. Rather, planning led to the multicentric city of nodes and parcels condensed in Dear and Flusty's "keno board" metaphor. Recent studies of public housing and community-scale suburban development help to revise the misconception that L.A.'s urban form is the result of only housing development. L.A. city builders pursued and implemented divergent, and thus highly political, "master plans" for urban Southern California. Beginning in the 1930s, and becoming more controversial during the late 1940s and early 1950s, public housing in Los Angeles became an obstacle to pro-business growth coalitions who advocated for federal assistance to private development, namely central-city urban renewal.

In *The Provisional City: Los Angeles Stories of Architecture and Urbanism*, Dana Cuff uses L.A. City Housing Authority photos to show how housing officials, prevented from building on open sites, "constructed" the housing crisis in working-class neighborhoods in order to legitimate their plans for removal of old stock housing. Though housing authority officials were well intentioned, their visual justification for new housing racialized and pathologized East L.A. residents. Housing removal ruined coherent neighborhoods and dislocated hundreds of predominantly Mexican American families. *The Provisional City* affirms cultural studies theories that representation is not secondary to economic, material (and in this case architectural) reality, but is constitutive of it.

That said, during the 1940s and 1950s the community-scale, superblock, self-contained public housing developments that the L.A. Housing Authority built presented new political opportunities for their occupants and residents from surrounding neighborhoods. Prior to Cuff's book, L.A. scholars have long relied on a series of superb articles by Don Parson as almost the only recent scholarship on urban redevelopment in central city Los Angeles. In *Making a Better World: Public Housing, the Red Scare, and the Direction of Modern Los Angeles*, Parson contrasts the community modernism of public housing advocates and the corporate modernism of urban renewal advocates. One of the many strengths of Parson's book is his emphasis on the agency of housing directors and residents who used tenant organizations and the physical space of public housing itself as important platforms for labor and civil rights struggles. Public housing developments were important places for mid-twentieth-century interracial alliance and political activism. For example, the Aliso Village housing development became a place of temporary protection for Mexican American youth fleeing vigilante violence during the 1943 zoot suit riots. After the riots, housing directors formed organizations that provided local youth with important social capital (social and political skills, recreational opportunities) that was otherwise severely limited in the working-class neighborhoods of East Los Angeles. During the 1940s, L.A. public housing was a place where *pachucos* were not draft dodgers but, in Parson's estimation, "colorful revolutionists."

The community builders Greg Hise studies in *Magnetic Los Angeles: Planning the Twentieth-Century Metropolis* are the corporate modernists from Parson's account of the battle for affordable housing in 1940s and 1950s Los Angeles. *Magnetic Los Angeles* opens a window onto the parcelization of the Los Angeles urban landscape and is a major revision of American suburban history. Hise argues that the history of mid-twentieth-century neighborhood development in Los Angeles forces a reconsideration of the city's dispersed urban form. He corrects the common misperception that it was housing and suburbs that lead to L.A.'s sprawl. Sprawl was intentional, carried out by city planners and companies such as Kaiser Community Homes, who built community-scale housing developments according to regional master plans that advocated balanced decentralization. While superblock housing developments were to be self-contained, with space for recreation, schools, churches, and retail consumerism, their builders also believed that they should be laid out in coordinated proximity to local industries. It was industry as much as housing that produced L.A.'s urban form, Hise argues. In countering misperceptions about L.A. sprawl, Hise leads us to a better understanding of L.A. as a polynucleated, multicentric city.

Cuff and Parson lead us to a better understanding of the development of areas within central city Los Angeles as a history of its transformation from an urban core to "discrete land use parcels" (Dear 2002b, 88) occupying partitioned squares on the L.A. keno-scape. Originally planned for central city sites, public housing projects were pushed to the industrial districts on the eastern periphery of downtown from original sites at Bunker Hill and Chávez Ravine. Where affordable housing would have been built on Bunker Hill, downtown growth coalitions initiated plans for office buildings barricaded by freeways from inner-city, working-class neighborhoods. Where affordable housing would have been built in Chávez Ravine, Dodger Stadium, surrounded by a sea of parking lots, was erected as a replacement for an older Wrigley Field located in South Central. To extend Cuff's and Parson's analyses, unlike Dodger Stadium but like its Chicago namesake, L.A.'s Wrigley Field—as a venue for other uses such as outdoor pro wrestling and boxing matches, and especially rhythm-and-blues concerts featuring performers from nearby Central Avenue like Johnny Otis, Dinah Washington, Big Jay McNeely, and Roy Milton— was closely linked to its surrounding neighborhoods and the mixed-use urban fabric of early-twentieth-century Los Angeles.

Zoöpolis

While L.A. decentralization was planned on a regional scale, Hise notes in *Magnetic Los Angeles* that it was not as balanced as it should have been.[8] Profit-driven community builders could not or would not adequately integrate agriculture or green space into their residential-industrial vision of land use. In *Eden by Design: The 1930 Olmsted-Bartholomew Plan for the Los Angeles Region*, Hise and coeditor William Deverell have reissued, with an extensive introduction and an interview with a former Olmsted firm planner, a regional master plan for L.A. parks that was never implemented. The plan, *Parks, Playgrounds, and Beaches for the Los Angeles Region*, is an example of decentralized planning informed by a vision of integrated land use. The highlight of the plan for 70,000 acres of park space was to have been a 440-mile system of "continuous parks and parkways interpenetrating the region and connecting it with the countryside" (95). Locating greenbelts of parks and open space within easy travel distance of any Los Angeles resident by following the river channels and streambeds that cross the L.A. basin would have served the double purpose of providing both recreation and flood control.

 Eden by Design also contributes to a growing body of urban-environmental work on Los Angeles that includes important recent essays by Jennifer Wolch, Stephanie Pincetl, and Laura Pulido, and two books, Blake Gumprecht's *The Los Angeles River: Its Life, Death and Possible Rebirth* and Jared Orsi's *Hazardous Metropolis: Flooding and Urban Ecology in Los Angeles*, which recount the massive public works projects that straightened L.A.'s rivers and creeks, lined them with concrete and consigned them to the single use of flood control. Los Angeles decentralized even further when suburban development of flood plains became possible, adding more streets, parking lots, and runoff, requiring more flood control (Orsi, 178). Rapid delivery of untreated sewage, grease, oil, chemicals, and refuse to Southern California beaches when major storm runoff overtaxed the flood control/sewer systems compromised public health (Gumprecht, 123–29). Admittedly, single-use flood control also contributed to the local economy, youth subcultures, and the housing crisis in unplanned ways when movie makers, performance artists, drag racers, skateboarders, and the homeless recognized the opportunities to be had in the empty, paved space of these often-dry urban arroyos. Orsi notes the ways that racialization led to environmentally unsound urban development. During the first decades of the twentieth century, before L.A.'s rivers were turned into flood control channels, Anglo Angelenos contributed to flood disasters. Because they accepted L.A.'s Spanish fantasy and discounted Mexican residents' memories of unpredictable weather as the product of an archaic culture, they built where they shouldn't. City boosters ignored generations of accumulated knowledge about drought, flooding, and erratic rivers in favor of another myth they held dear: that of Southern California having an idyllic climate free from natural disasters, favorable to health, agriculture, and industry (13–16).

White Houses

William Fredericks's study of one of Los Angeles's most influential, early-twentieth-century real estate developers, *Henry E. Huntington and the Creation of Southern California,* shows how Los Angeles grew. Huntington's practice of buying land and building homes along his Pacific Electric streetcar lines, the largest electric interurban system in the United States, demonstrates that when Southern California became suburban throughout the first half of the twentieth century, far-flung residential nodes were positioned to become insular in ways that either foreshadowed or contributed to the current city of parcels. Similarly Clark Davis's book on corporate culture in the early twentieth century, *Company Men: White Collar Life and Corporate Cultures in Los Angeles, 1892–1941,* shows that moving up at work and attaining solid middle-class status also meant moving up and out of the wrong kind of white neighborhoods (mixed-class and mixed-ethnicity) to more class and ethnically homogenous tracts that matched prevailing ideals of Anglo Saxon homogeneity. In *Popular Culture in the Age of White Flight: Fear and Fantasy in Suburban Los Angeles,* Eric Avila shows how popular culture institutions contributed to postwar suburban whiteness. Finally, as of 1990, more than 54 percent of whites, nearly 40 percent of African Americans, 37 percent of Latinos, and 17 percent of Asians lived in census tracts dominated by their ethnic group (Soja 2000, 291–94).

Two recent books about mid-twentieth-century suburbanization reveal the social logic of white Los Angeles's most pronounced mono-racial group. In *My Blue Heaven: Life and Politics in the Working Class Suburbs of Los Angeles, 1920–1965*, a community-labor history of the Southeast L.A. County working-class suburb of South Gate, Becky Nicolaides locates workers' construction of white identity in the social-material fact of suburbanization itself: the realization and then defense of their material dreams. In the 1920s, white migrants from the South and Midwest came to South Gate to work in L.A. industries. They moved to homes built explicitly to support and attract local manufacturing industry. Using their homes as a hedge against unemployment, they supplemented factory incomes in rural terms with backyards devoted to self-sufficient activities such as gardening and auto repair. Continuing into the postwar period, relative affluence from stable jobs in the booming Southern California auto and rubber industries allowed South Gate residents to transform their yards into spaces of privacy that signaled middle-class status. Predominantly white throughout the forty-five years Nicolaides covers, South Gate differed from more racially diverse working-class districts such as Watts on its western border. Nicolaides's attention to city politics in South Gate and social strife with black residents of nearby Watts shows that, like working-class white home owners in Detroit or Chicago, South Gate residents defended their property values (by ballot and violence) and actively maintained the white homogeneity of their community by segregating schools. *My Blue Heaven* is significant for Nicolaides's attention to the history of the "possessive investment in whiteness."[9] More often told as the story of white working-class ethnics in northeastern cities, the history of the silent majority revealed in *My Blue Heaven* shows that such racial *resentment* was well-established in the West. For these blue-collar workers, who supported unions but also voted for Barry Goldwater, home ownership, as much as work, defined class and racial identity.

Similar to working-class residents of South Gate, middle-class residents of Orange County explained and defended their affluence in individualist terms. Lisa McGirr's *Suburban Warriors: The Origins of the New American Right* focuses on the suburban, middle-class roots of the New Right in postwar Orange County.[10] Although they benefited directly or indirectly from the fact that Southern California enjoyed the highest level of federal defense funding for any region in the United States, these conservatives attributed their success and relative affluence to hard work, not government defense funding. Like

South Gate residents, many among Orange County's first suburban residents were recent arrivals from the Midwest. They experienced homogenous housing developments as devoid of the traditional values of church and community they had left behind. Political activism as a means of reinventing their sense of community helped to resolve the contradictions they felt between their affluent "modern" consumer lifestyles and their traditionalist, individualist, antimodern beliefs. Through John Birch Society meetings held in their homes, church organizations, and grassroots Republican Party organizations, Orange County's politically conservative residents worked against communism, liberalism, and cultural relativism, which they identified as threats to American society. Honing their beliefs and strengthening their sense of community in local battles over education, conservative Orange Countians would fashion the political ideology at the grass roots that would eventually take over the California Republican Party, deliver the governorship of California to Ronald Reagan in 1966, and give the presidency to Richard Nixon in 1968 and Reagan in 1980.

Shades of L.A.

There are two sides to the coin of whiteness. Nicolaides's and McGirr's studies of working- and middle-class suburbs are examples of defensive and exclusionary attempts to secure white privilege, submerged under class and conservative political ideologies in the case of McGirr's middle-class Orange County residents. The other side of the white coin is offensive, imprinted by police, media, and legal tactics of repression and segregation. Edward Escobar's comprehensive study of Mexican Americans and the L.A. Police Department, *Race, Police, and the Making of a Political Identity*, expands our knowledge of the extent of the repression the police carried out against Mexican Americans throughout the first four decades of the twentieth century. João Costa Vargas's forthcoming *Blackness as Blueprint: Resistance and Social Transformation in Los Angeles* similarly illuminates police brutality in African American South Central. Three books by Eduardo Obregón Pagán, Ian Haney-López, and Josh Sides chronicle the political/spatial struggles for inclusion and community self-determination that challenged white repression (Pagán, Sides) and the collective logic of whiteness (Haney-López).

In *Murder at the Sleepy Lagoon: Zoot Suits, Race, and Riot in Wartime L.A.* Eduardo Pagán places a dual emphasis on urban imaginaries and spatial location to provide new insight into the Sleepy Lagoon murder case and the zoot suit riots. Whereas previous studies of these events—Carey McWilliams's *North from Mexico* and Mauricio Mazón's *The Zoot-Suit Riots*—established the extent of racial animosity directed toward Mexican American, African American, and Filipino youth, Pagán contextualizes these two Los Angeles wartime events socially and geographically, providing greater insight into dynamics of identity formation among Los Angeles Mexican Americans.

Effectively contrasting productions of "Mexicanism," Pagán shows how the meaning of the city and Mexican presence in it were contested. During the interwar period Mexican expatriates and Mexican Americans expressed a "Mexico Lindo" nostalgia for a lost homeland through mutual aid societies, social clubs, and community service organizations. Influenced by Roosevelt's Office of the Coordinator of Inter American affairs, Mexican American community leaders such as Manuel Ruíz claimed Latin American identity and promoted "a Pan Americanism founded on a common western heritage" (33) as a wartime solution to L.A. racial strife. Pagán reveals the deeper geographical factors and expressions of place commitment that were at issue during the events leading to the death of José Díaz at the Sleepy Lagoon and the events of the zoot suit riots. In the face of anti-Mexican sentiment, Mexican American youth asserted their presence in public places through distinctive hair and clothing styles, and in L.A.'s parks, streets, movie theaters, and nightclubs. Claims to public places, such as city streets or the Venice beach boardwalk, were linked to neighborhood social networks, established through weekly dances sponsored by neighborhood associations, "home parties," and at school or church. Pagán carefully maps the Williams Ranch area to reconstruct the coincidence of events that led to José Díaz's death, providing a perspective on the Sleepy Lagoon defendants that had previously been buried in court records, overshadowed in historical memory by police brutality and racism (police, judicial) and by the political advocacy conducted by the Sleepy Lagoon Defense Committee, who countered portrayals of the 38th Street youth as a gang by portraying them as wholesome innocents. Similarly, Pagán recovers a history of clashes over control of public space that preceded and was the opposite of the vigilantism, neighborhood invasion, and spatial repression of the zoot suit riots. He shows that the provocations Mexican American youth directed at servicemen on Figueroa Boulevard—misperceived as unpatriotic acts of juvenile delinquency—were really attempts to defend their neighborhoods from insensitive outsiders. The young men from these neighborhoods who skirmished with sailors and other men on downtown streets, Pagán emphasizes, felt downtown to be an adjunct to their neighborhoods worth defending.

A few years later in 1949, just before the Bishop, La Loma, and Palo Verde neighborhoods commonly known as Chávez Ravine would be bulldozed to make way for Dodger Stadium, photographer Don Normark conducted a year-long visual study of this semirural Mexican American community tucked into the hills in the center of urban Los Angeles. Finally published in 1999 as *Chávez Ravine, 1949: A Los Angeles Story*, Normark's ethnographic social realism recovers the now-lost community's sense of coherent place. The networks of sociability rooted in homes, yards, storefronts, and street corners documented in Normark's photos and interviews, vividly echo Pagán's careful reconstruction of 38th Street youths' neighborhood life. Normark's photos and testimonies render zoot-suiters' resistance as part of larger, more complex lives. Like Carolyn Kozo Cole and Kathy Kobayashi's *Shades of L.A.: Pictures from Ethnic Family Albums*, a selection from the extraordinary archive of family snapshots compiled at Los Angeles Public Library, Normark's and Pagán's books show that the Mexican American identity that was politicized in moments of repression and asserted/claimed in moments of resistance was inseparable from social worlds of neighborhood, friends, and family.

Josh Sides documents another history of commitment to place in *L.A. City Limits: African American Los Angeles from the Great Depression to the Present*. In this labor-community study of black L.A., one of the most important but understudied postwar African American cities, Sides traces the history of shifts in geography and class within South Central Los Angeles's African American community as it grew from its original location in Watts to adjacent communities like West Adams, Compton, Leimert Park, and Ladera Heights. As black workers' labor struggles secured gains in the war/postwar defense and heavy manufacturing industries, and successful court battles began to open up formerly segregated neighborhoods, some African Americans left Watts to purchase homes in adjacent, all-white Compton. For the time during the 1950s that defense plants remained open near Compton, the city was a blue-collar, middle-class community of blacks and whites. Heavy industry (steel, auto, rubber) shut down or suburbanized from the 1960s through the 1980s, and defense manufacturing converted to high-tech electronics and aerospace and moved to suburban locations like Orange County. Compton's remaining white residents, who had initially stayed when black families began to buy houses, followed industry to neighborhoods closed to blacks. Inadequate education and training made it difficult for many African Americans to gain high-tech jobs. With no jobs, no industrial tax base, and rising crime, new businesses were reluctant to locate in all-black Compton and the city spiraled into decline. When Los Angeles's urban crisis led to rebellion in 1965, Compton, like Watts, came to be associated in the popular imagination with poverty and urban disorder. Throughout *L.A. City Limits*, Sides details civil rights struggles against workplace discrimination, housing segregation, industrial relocation, and white flight. Sides points out that many whites erroneously believed that black civil rights struggles were motivated by a desire to "intermingle with whites" (132) when in reality they were motivated by the desire for total access to public institutions. Where African Americans did settle, the community was often biracial or multiracial. Watts residents were black, Mexican American, Japanese American, and white during the 1940s and 1950s, and the black middle-class neighborhoods of Baldwin Hills and Inglewood formed organizations to preserve the integrated character of their black/white neighborhoods. Douglas Flamming's *Bound for Freedom*, on early-twentieth-century African American Los Angeles, contributes further to this underpublished area of L.A. history.

While Sides emphasizes racial discrimination as the ultimate barrier to greater African American spatial/economic mobility, in *Racism on Trial: The Chicano Fight for Justice*, Ian Haney-López analyzes the logic that informed such discrimination. He brings a critical legal studies and racial formation analysis to key trials generated by police repression of Chicano movement protest. In both the trial of the East L.A. Thirteen (members of the Brown Berets as well as other Chicano activists arrested after more than five thousand high school students walked out of Wilson, Garfield, Roosevelt, and Lincoln High Schools in East Los Angeles in March 1968 to protest terrible educational conditions) and the trial of the Biltmore Six (arrested after a demonstration and fire disrupted a speech by Governor Ronald Reagan at the downtown Biltmore Hotel in 1969), Haney-López identifies a pattern of beliefs and assumptions about nonwhites that informed judges' and grand jurors' conclusions. He analyzes trial transcripts and defense lawyer Oscar Acosta's strategies to expose grand jury members' "unconscious racism." In so doing, Haney-López shows the active production of white racial ideologies as part of the processes of unconscious and institutional racism/segregation in Los Angeles.[11] *Racism on Trial* is complemented by Burton Moore and Allesandra Cabello's *Love and Riot: Oscar Zeta Acosta and the Great Mexican American Revolt*, a recent biography of Oscar Acosta, and Ernesto Chávez's "*¡Mi Raza Primero!*": *Nationalism, Identity, and Insurgency in the Chicano Movement in Los Angeles, 1966–1978*, which is an exceptional historical overview of the Chicano movement.

Mestizo City

If Los Angeles has dense nodes of racial aversion and conservatism, its development has also led to equally dense sites of diversity and interethnic contact.

As a result of immigration law reforms in 1965, Los Angeles is now one of thirty-seven multiethnic metropolitan areas "where at least two of three minority groups exceed their percentage in the U.S. population as a whole" (Bobo et al., 11). Indeed, the two most diverse cities in the United States are the South L.A. County cities of Carson and Gardena, with an almost "perfect quartering of the population into white, black, Asian, and Latino" (Soja, 2000, 295–96).[12] Studies of racial interaction in Carson and Gardena have yet to be written; however, Monterey Park, a middle-class suburb inhabited by Japanese American, Chinese American, Chinese, Mexican American, and white residents has been the subject of monographs by Timothy Fong, John Horton, and Mary Pardo. One of eighty-four incorporated cities within Los Angeles County, it "has the particular distinction of being the only city in the continental United States with a majority Asian population: some 56% of its 60,000 inhabitants are of Asian origin" (Palumbo-Liu 2003, 260).

Leland Saito, author of *Race and Politics: Asian Americans, Latinos, and Whites in a Los Angeles Suburb*, explains that as part of the longer history of collaboration between Latinos and Asians in California from "agricultural struggles to urban politics," political alliances developed in contexts of similar class and racial positions where Asian Americans and Latinos held shared interests (126–27). Monterey Park became multiracial during the 1950s and 1960s when Japanese Americans and Mexican Americans moved from nearby East Los Angeles and, despite illegal restrictive covenants, purchased homes. Although they had experienced white opposition when they first moved to Monterey Park, Asian American (Japanese and Chinese) and Mexican American residents in turn became alarmed at the increasing presence of Chinese immigrants and businesses in Monterey Park during the early 1980s, but then found common cause with Chinese residents when white, slow-growth leaders backed city council candidates who espoused anti-immigrant rhetoric. Saito argues that class and ethnicity can be understood only in the context of the specific "conditions that create different interests and conflicts between groups" (122–23).

If San Gabriel Valley cities like Monterey Park remained segregated in housing well into the 1960s, Matt Garcia's analysis of San Gabriel Valley popular culture shows that cultural production and popular consumption comprised a differently inflected landscape of race, beyond segregated entertainments within L.A. city limits. *A World of Its Own: Race, Labor, and Citrus in the Making of Greater Los Angeles, 1900–1970* is a history of Mexican American citrus workers in the *colonias* and suburbs of the San Gabriel Valley, an agricultural hinterland east of the Los Angeles metropolis. Garcia addresses the relationship between the form/creation of the landscape and the social relations that occur in it. Two of the most innovative chapters in the book are his studies of the Padua Hills Theater during the 1930s, and the rock-and-roll dance halls of El Monte during the 1950s. Through negotiation with the white owners and theatergoers, Mexican American actors at the Padua Hills Theater not only helped create the plays they performed, but they also used their participation as a means to make money for school or future careers. Similarly, El Monte dance halls became for Mexican Americans, whites, African Americans, and Asian American/Pacific Island youth important nodes of cultural intersection within a suburbanizing Southern California landscape increasingly partitioned by freeways. Exploiting new opportunities of greater mobility afforded by freeways, youth came from many parts of greater L.A. to El Monte Legion Stadium and Rainbow Gardens, which were located in L.A. County beyond the more restrictive laws of Los Angeles City that prohibited racial mixing. They traveled across zones of residential segregation to listen to rock and roll performed by multiracial bands such as the Mixtures. If Los Angeles was the metropolis to the San Gabriel Valley citrus hinterland, the L.A. County city of El Monte was Los Angeles's suburban rock-and-roll borderland. *A World of Its Own* is one among many books on Southern California music by Sherrie Tucker, Clora Bryant, Josh Kun, Anthony Macías, Philip Pastras, Deborah Wong, Eric Porter, Horace Tapscott, David Reyes and Tom Waldman, and Jacqueline Cogdell DjeDje and Eddie S. Meadows. Garcia's study is also part of a growing body of literature on Los Angeles's multiracial past and present by scholars such as Scott Kurashige, Kevin Allen Leonard, Natalia Molina, Daniel Widener, Brian McGuire and Duncan Scrymgeour, and Mark Wild.

While these works have examined L.A.'s multiracial complexity from a cultural and historical perspective, *Prismatic Metropolis: Inequality in Los Angeles*, edited by Lawrence Bobo, Melvin L. Oliver, James H. Johnson Jr., and Abel Valenzuela Jr., deploys social science to focus on the effects of economic restructuring on racial and ethnic groups in the present. The essays in the collection are the distillation of 4,025 survey questionnaires administered in 1994 to a multiracial sample of adults in order to document the "social processes and interactions among and between recent arrivals and more established ethnic and minority groups" (5). The book covers three aspects of inequality: "labor market processes, residential segregation, and intergroup attitudes and relations" (6). Bobo and his coauthors assert that the totality of their research "implies that urban inequality is heavily racialized" (7). Most significant, the book's fifteen essays confirm the L.A. School's refutation of Chicago School explanations of urban poverty within an individualist framework. These neo–Chicago School scholars dismiss spatial mismatch and racial discrimination explanations of urban poverty in Los Angeles, citing instead statistics of upward mobility as proof that cities need only make human capital investments, such as education and public health, so that people can lift themselves out of poverty.[13]

If *Prismatic Metropolis* provides a statistical snapshot of interracial attitudes/tensions, the ethnographic picture Nora Hamilton and Norma Stoltz Chinchilla present in *Seeking Community in a Global City: Guatemalans and Salvadorans in Los Angeles* shows those attitudes in practice. Noting that many migrants maintain bicultural identities and transnational ties to their homelands, Hamilton and Chinchilla document the history of the economic institutions (restaurants, travel agencies, and financial and legal services), and labor, refugee assistance, political, and community organizations through which Guatemalans and Salvadorans have shaped their neighborhoods and influenced metropolitan/state policy. Many Central Americans live in mixed Latino-Korean neighborhoods in Westlake and Pico Union, mixed Latino–African American neighborhoods in South Central, and mixed Mexican, Mexican American, and Central American neighborhoods in East Los Angeles. While there have been tensions, living in multiethnic/racial proximity has also led to cooperation, mutual recognition, and cultural exchange. The Korean Immigrant Workers Association organizes Koreans and Latinos who work for Korean firms (187). As part of the Multiethnic Youth Leadership Collaborative, the Central American Refugee/Resource Center works with agencies that serve Koreans and African Americans to "provide leadership training in interethnic relations for youth from Pico Union, South Central, and Mid Wilshire" (187). Some Central American youth living in mixed Latino–African American neighborhoods in South Central Los Angeles identify with African American culture and see figures like Martin Luther King and Malcolm X as role models (199). One central-city Guatemalan youth from Belmont High School, who encountered assumptions that he was Chicano, used Cuban poet José Martí's concept of "Nuestra América" as the organizing principle for Unión para Nuestra América, a pan-Latino organization that works with Chicano students and others in a third world/Native American coalition (201–2). For indigenous Guatemalans who feel isolated from Latinos and their ladino (Spanish-Indian) compatriots, affirmation of Mayan identity is important. Conversely, Guatemalan ladino youth are inspired by both Mayan culture and *roc en español* (204). If diversity in Los Angeles is distinct in its demographic composition from other multiracial cities, that diversity is also influenced by the history of L.A.'s dispersed communities. Borders and border crossings within the L.A. metropolis occur between both neighborhoods and cities within this vast conurbation.

Taking Place and Making Space

Throughout this essay I have followed the L.A. School's emphasis on spatiality. Central to this aspect of L.A. School urban theory is the idea that space is not a container for social and political action, that places are not merely backdrops to the dramas that unfold within them. Three books in particular demonstrate the relationship of identity and space in Los Angeles studies. Rick Bonus, in *Locating Filipino Americans: Ethnicity and the Cultural Politics of Space*, Raúl Villa, in *Barrio-Logos: Space and Place in Urban Chicano Literature and Culture*, and Moira Rachel Kenney, in *Mapping Gay L.A.: The Intersection of Place and Politics*, posit the concrete and geographical materiality of the city itself as an agent of sociopolitical and cultural struggles. In different ways, these studies delineate the lines of connection between distinct places and their location within larger areal networks of identity. Los Angeles residents' active *use* of space as a resource for negotiating the circumstances of their daily lives is foregrounded in these books to show identity being made.

Locating Filipino Americans explores the social and spatial meaning of Filipino identity created in "Oriental stores" that sell diverse Asian products, community center politics, beauty pageants, and newspapers in Los Angeles and San Diego. Serving as the portal to a transnational connection to their Philippine homeland, Oriental stores sell familiar products that "market difference." Frequenting these consumer spaces is an expression of Filipino identity within the largely hostile anti-Asian landscape of Southern California. Bonus analyzes the give-and-take of "Palengke"-style politics at community center meetings. When understood in the context of such community activity, pageants take on political significance beyond ideals of beauty. Newspapers foster identity through their presentation of news not covered in the mainstream press, information about events in the Philippines, and Filipino advertising. These community newspapers also allow for a delineation of differences within the Filipino community or among Filipino Americans.

Place making is also key to the historical and spatial sweep of Chicano cultural production in greater East Los Angeles that Raúl Villa presents in *Barrio-Logos*, including place-representing expressive practices ranging from newspapers to poetry, punk rock, and murals. Villa highlights social networks and place attachment in *Mexicano* and Mexican American communities. He traces the persistent emphasis on social location that Chicano/a writers, artists, and musicians foreground in their cultural expressions. Dramatizing the dynamic, dialectic interplay between "barrioization" (the combined use of the law, the media, and the built environment in sociospatial repression) and "barriology" (the culturally affirming, place-specific, hybrid knowledges and practices that result from interaction with destructive urbanization that form the basis of Chicano sociospatial opposition),Villa's study shows that cultural work not only produces counternarratives and knowledges to challenge and reframe urban growth and racial segregation, but in so doing produces alternate places that form a resource for identity formation and community politics. In Villa's rereading of popular institutions, cultural associations, and "small scale networks of support" that provide self-help, or the exchange of goods, services, and information, traditional aspects of community studies are reconsidered for the paths of connection people traverse between them.

Similar to the Chicano urban experience analyzed by Villa, urban places have been integral to gay and lesbian community and identity since the early twentieth century. Moira Kenney's attention to the influence of L.A.'s vast and diffuse urban form on gay and lesbian community activism in *Mapping Gay L.A.* shows the relationship between spatiality and social movement politics. Unlike enclaves in more geographically compact cities like Manhattan or San Francisco, Los Angeles's multicentered gay and lesbian communities follow its centerless urban form. Kenney's four case studies—West Hollywood as a symbolic location of gay and lesbian Los Angeles, AIDS service organizations and the redevelopment of Hollywood Boulevard, the downtown art space Women's House and the Connexxus lesbian community center, ACT UP and Gay Liberation Front street protests—show that mapping social space and politicizing public places result in the creation of spatial networks and lived geographies of a gay and lesbian city. In all these case studies, the assertion of a public presence within the spatial landscapes of the city is central to political practice.

Bonus's, Villa's, and Kenney's emphasis on the processes that turn places into connected networks (real or imagined) offers a rich way to think about questions of exclusion and segregation. Identity in actual practice, as the product of spatial network creation, is different from identity theorized as a response to alienation or marginalization. It is more grounded in social structure, and perhaps less open to criticism from opponents of multiculturalism who would dismiss "identity politics" as arbitrary expressions of symbolic ideals.

Expressive Cultural Practice: Los Angeles Performed

Disseminating spectacular images of the city as exotic, or undifferentiated images of the city as anyplace U.S.A., Los Angeles's entertainment industries and institutions of high culture reinforce the misperception of L.A. as placeless: all spectacle or all suburb. Recent and forthcoming studies of Hollywood by Saverio Giovacchini and Philip Ethington are significant for their authors' efforts to ground this global culture industry in its urban location. Equally important are recent books that consider non–mass cultural efforts to produce culture in Los Angeles.

The commodified myths and images of Los Angeles overshadow a history of expressive cultural practices. In contrast to the commercial dissemination of L.A. imagery, the intent of expressive cultural practice is to produce collective representational aesthetics (iconographies, formal techniques), contingent identities, and enacted place simultaneously. The place-based cultural production that results from such expressive cultural practices has been documented in a number of recent books. Taken as a whole, these books trace the history of changing emphases in processes of identity formation: from emphasis on group identity through the 1970s (Lon Kurashige and James), to explorations of hybridity, situational, and contingent identity during the 1980s (James and Cheng), to explorations of location, spatial networks, and place consciousness from the 1990s to the present (Leclerc, Villa, Dear; and Leclerc and Dear). Recent scholarship recognizes the importance of the intracommunity negotiations, municipal political interventions, and institutional organization that occur prior to a final cultural product. The value of expressive cultural practice, whether intentionally performative or not, lies in its social, political, educational, and psychological transformative power.

In *Japanese American Celebration and Conflict: A History of Ethnic Identity and Festival, 1934–1990*, Lon Kurashige traces competing notions of group identity from integration to radical cosmopolitanism *within* the community of Little Tokyo as Japanese Americans sought wider "acceptance, legitimacy, and class status" (6) in relation to anti-Japanese racism. As the face of the community, Nisei Week festivals presented an idealized and unified version of Japanese/Japanese American culture and history to the broader public. Nisei Week began in the 1930s when first-generation Issei sought to regain the ethnic and consumer allegiance of second-generation Nisei, whose bicultural knowledge of English and familiarity with American mass culture drew them away from Little Tokyo businesses that were the vital center of the Japantown enclave. Issei and Nisei leaders came up with a final roster of promotions and events that balanced community economics with expressions of Japanese ethnic tradition and expressions of Americanism. Emphasizing cultural adaptation and employing the concept of racial rearticulation—the process by which racially subordinated groups reinterpret racist discourse—Kurashige shows how parades, beauty pageants, talent shows, and cultural exhibitions challenged stereotypes. Always the product of compromise, public festivities often left the concerns of women, blue-collar workers, disadvantaged youth, and those with less education unaddressed. As a result—unresolved youth violence and "gang" activity during the 1930s, 1940s, and 1950s, student radicalism during the 1960s and 1970s, car cruisers (from Gardena) during the 1980s, women's critiques of beauty pageants during the 1980s, Sansei activists opposed to Japanese foreign investment and redevelopment of Little Tokyo in the 1980s and 1990s—those whose concerns were not adequately addressed took to the streets of Little Tokyo, disrupting and challenging official proceedings. The concept of community and Little Tokyo itself have thus always been contested.

In *The Sons and Daughters of Los: Culture and Community in L.A.*, editor David E. James and his fellow contributors document the formation of a different kind of community. Focusing on institutional histories of art communities, James and his coauthors provide numerous examples of the differences between community-based art making and art-based community making. Each chapter is a snapshot of the development of one of L.A.'s most durable/successful community cultural institutions: Self Help Graphics, Highways, LACE, and lesser known places such as the African American cultural district of shops, galleries, jazz clubs, and restaurants in Leimert Park, the Foundation for Art Resources, the Vedanta Society of Southern California, and L.A.'s popular cinemas. These institutions had greater and lesser degrees of engagement with the exploration/definition of formal aesthetics, political intervention, and community service. In its early years Beyond Baroque promoted an aesthetic-based but open-ended definition of poetry that generated multiple poet communities.[14] The L.A. Women's Building encouraged feminist explorations of identity that merged art and politics, such as Suzanne Lacy's late 1970s public performances about rape and violence against women. Her collaborations with artists and city officials resulted in "public policy changes, including city sponsorship of free self-defense training for women and the publication of rape hotline numbers by the telephone company" (48). Primarily emphasizing professional art, the Korean Cultural Center (KCC), run by the Korean government, combined commercial motives, orientation to the L.A. Korean immigrant community, and the promotion of Korean culture to greater Los Angeles. In every case these institutions made room for art as expressive cultural practices that linked aesthetics to identity and place. As a result they had to adapt their artistic vision and organizational purpose through interaction with the diversity of L.A.'s residents who made claims to their resources. The KCC is a case in point. In the late 1990s the KCC began to mount cross-cultural exhibitions as a means to form social and cultural alliances with Mexican American and African American communities.

In her analysis of L.A. performance art, *In Other Los Angeleses: Multicentric Performance Art*, Meiling Cheng foregrounds the particular relationship between geography, identity, and aesthetics that performance art enacts. Developing case studies of Suzanne Lacy, Elia Arce, the Highways performance space, the Sacred Naked Nature Girls, and "art performance," Cheng follows the development of the feminist and multicultural ideals that animate the majority of such expressive culture in L.A. She employs an analytical framework that allows her to consider the reflective function of performance art (its multiple/dispersed development mirrors L.A.'s multiple/dispersed geography), its redressive function (as a response to social/political inequalities), and generative function (creation of aesthetic properties and communities of expressive practitioners). While conceptual and process-oriented performance art occurred in other cities as well, Cheng makes a strong case that it is especially appropriate to Los Angeles. Her reconceptualization of multiculturalism as multicentricity provides a theoretical framework for cultural analysis that departs from a center/margin model of identity formation in the same way that L.A. School urban theory departs from a core/periphery model of urbanism. In form—a "flexible mode of expression" (18)—and content, performance art "is most directly linked with [L.A.'s] other cultures" (19).

Postborder Metropolis

While all of these books on expressive cultural practices foreground issues of place and space, two edited collections explicitly take up the relationship between art and urban knowledge as it reveals an increasing emphasis on place and spatial networks in expressive cultural practice. *Urban Latino Cultures: La Vida Latina en L.A*, edited by Gustavo Leclerc, Raúl Villa, and Michael Dear, and *Postborder City: Cultural Spaces of Bajalta California*, edited by Gustavo Leclerc and Michael Dear, are notable for their efforts to integrate two forms of urban knowledge: the more abstract knowledge of academics and planners and the everyday, experiential knowledge that comes from living in L.A.'s neighborhoods and moving through its multiple nodes of activity.[15]

The expressive practices of cartoonists, artists, photographers, filmmakers, musicologists, architects, poets, performance artists, and literary scholars that Leclerc, Villa, and Dear have collected in *Urban Latino Cultures* display an explicit spatial aesthetic/ethos common to all genres of Latino artistic cultural production *and* modes of daily life. Latino art in Los Angeles displays a distinct attachment to place that spans personal experience, collective memory, and modifications of the built environment. Spoken word/ performance artist Teresa Chavez recounts her personal connections to the history of Southern California. Through her family genealogy, Chavez traces her connection to Southern California, not to claim priority of place (as say, the Daughters of the American Revolution would, or promoters of anti-immigrant ballot referendums like proposition 187 would) but to explore the way her mestizo history links her to conflicting visions of Los Angeles. Chavez returns to 1781, as McWilliams and others have done, but looks farther back to Jewish and Moorish, Middle Eastern peoples of Spain to understand the ways in which Los Angeles's history makes us multiple in the present. Carlos Avila and Harry Gamboa draw on the popularity and spatial ubiquity of *fotonovela* comic books—they are for sale everywhere in L.A.'s Latino retail districts. Avila uses *fotonovelas* as a vehicle for urban stories that repopulate L.A.'s mass-media landscape with figures other than stereotypical gangbangers, gardeners, household maids, and supervixens. In "Acid Reign," one of Gamboa's photographic tableaux, he draws connections between urban decline, environmental pollution, and indifference to Latinos. Everyday Latino urbanism produces a Latinization of the city itself. From Spanish language signage, gang *placas* (graffiti), and murals, to *palateros* (drivers of ice cream trucks), the conversion of gas stations to taco stands, and home modifications, urban space is literally rewritten according to a distinct Latino urbanism. Homes are altered according to a Latino spatial sensibility: stucco laid over clapboards, columns replaced with wrought iron or stuccoed arches. When carried out on early-twentieth-century Craftsman bungalows, such alterations alarm Anglo preservationists. *Urban Latino Cultures* maps the nodes of activity and representational practices that constitute the spatial networks of contemporary Latino urban identity.

In *Postborder City: Cultural Spaces of Bajalta California*, editors Gustavo Leclerc and Michael Dear characterize the Los Angeles–San Diego–Tijuana–Mexicali metropolis as an urban and cultural borderlands of global significance, a contemporary continuation of the Spanish borderlands, but the first time "Bajalta California" has been an "integrated region" (2). They assemble essays on the parallel histories of settlement and development of Baja and Alta California, the distinct nodes of globalization that mark a city like Tijuana, art history essays on Mexican/Chicano border films and visual/performance art, and representative examples of multimedia art itself. Historians, urban theorists, artists, and literary and media critics together document the ways in which border representations and simultaneous experiences of multiple places generate a postborder aesthetic that emphasizes bodily performance, resistance, memory, hybrid identity, and creation of structured places (institutions). In his contribution to the volume, "Hybridities and Histories: Imagining the Rim," David Palumbo-Liu argues that art and literature are places that first articulate such new historical moments and conditions. Analyzing Vietnamese artist Dinh Q. Lê's digital montage *Self Portrait 15*, in which Dinh stands as a scrambled but distinguishable composite image woven from the interpixelation of the Buddhist icon on his right and the Christian icon on his left, Palumbo-Liu points out that such mestizo identity is not simply a matter of the juxtaposition of two distinct entities to produce a third entity that replaces the originals, but rather a process through which the distinct entities from which a third entity is derived remain distinct *and* also change in meaning.

The Bus Stops Here: Nuevo L.A. and Areal Worlds

In 1997/1998 Sergio Arau and Yareli Arizmendi released their short film, *A Day Without a Mexican*, a "mockumentary" about the economic and social consequences when all "Mexicans" (American and undocumented transnationals) suddenly disappear from the state of California: in brief, the state shuts down, highlighting Latino presence at every societal level. Through counterintuitive logic, Arau and Arizmendi *place* Latino California in bold relief. Similarly in *Banda: Mexican Musical Life across Borders*, Helena Simonett outlines the broad spatial dispersion of Latino newcomers in Los Angeles beyond historic East L.A. into "the San Gabriel Valley in the east, San Fernando in the north . . . San Pedro in the south . . . into African American South Central, Watts, Compton, and Inglewood . . . [and] in the industrial heartland of the county: Huntington Park, South Gate, Bell Gardens, Cudahay, and Maywood" (33). Among the Latinos who live there but also in their home countries, which they return to frequently, this city within a city is known as "Nuevo L.A." Such spatial extension and invisibility is a defining condition of Los Angeles, for immigrant workers, or performance artists—engaged in cultural work throughout the city yet rendered invisible by entertainment culture industries—or labor organizers.

At the beginning of her book, *Doméstica: Immigrant Workers Cleaning and Caring in the Shadows of Affluence*, about Mexican, Salvadoran, and Guatemalan women who work as domestics and nannies in middle-class and upper-middle-class homes throughout Los Angeles, Pierrette Hondagneu-Sotelo poses the question put to us by Arau and Arizmendi's film: "Can we conceive of a Los Angeles where . . . there is 'A Day Without a Mexican'?" (ix). Hondagneu-Sotelo makes visible the work performed by immigrant women. Faced with the impossibility of meeting domestic workers at their places of work, homes scattered throughout Los Angeles, Hondagneu-Sotelo and her fellow researchers conducted interviews and handed out questionnaires at parks and bus stops, nodes in the spatial networks of domestic workers' daily lives. Rather than approach these women's invisibility as a problem of "academic" research, Hondagneu-Sotelo approaches her academic work through social justice.

Prior to beginning her research, she helped start, with immigrant rights attorneys and community organizers, the Coalition for Humane Immigrant Rights of Los Angeles (CHIRLA), an organization to inform domestic workers (especially live-in workers) about their rights. Under the auspices of CHIRLA, Latina immigrant workers for the Domestic Worker's Association visited parks and rode buses handing out *novelas*. One novela features "Super Doméstica," a comic superhero who defends the rights of immigrant workers, informs readers about legal issues, and refers them to appropriate agencies for legal aid. As an advocate and organizer for the women she writes about, Hondagneu-Sotello does not conceive of her work as only producing verifiable research for a professional community of scholars or policy makers, but as a partnership with people who can benefit from her expertise and access to resources and institutions.

Nora Hamilton and Norma Stoltz Chinchilla, in *Seeking Community in a Global City*, explain similar circumstances and solutions for Central American men. To organize day laborers who congregate on street corners near hardware stores or in vacant lots in the hopes of being hired for a day's work in light construction, gardening, home repair/maintenance, it became necessary to create formal hiring sites. Pablo Alvarado, a Salvadoran organizer, created soccer teams at new hiring sites to encourage cooperation among workers who were placed in unregulated situations of intense competition by employers. Organizers at another site included a cabbage and onion garden maintained by workers.

These examples are significant for the ways in which academics, labor organizers, cultural producers, and workers come together to form networks that allow them to solve problems of work and civil rights compounded by spatial invisibility. More often these groups are separated, moving within their own networks. Arjun Appadurai notes that academic knowledge about globalization is one of the many products that moves in the circuits of global capital but that it is separated by languages of social science from people who could use it. For Appadurai the solution to this problem is spatial. Academics must translate their knowledge into a form that allows them to work with artists and workers to establish what he calls "areal worlds," networks that, through their creation, bridge diverse ways of knowing and worldviews.[16] This process of translation is fundamentally cultural by any definition of the term, and it suggests that forms of already existing culture, from novelas to soccer teams and gardens may serve as a conduit to bring academics, workers, and artists together.

Carey McWilliams faced similar issues of invisibility in his efforts to publicize major issues of work and civil rights. His writings on Los Angeles, Mexican migration, and California agriculture anticipated American studies' attention to racialized representation, cultural exchange, and hybrid identity in national and transnational contexts, but his work was not part of American studies. McWilliams was part of what Michael Denning calls "the Cultural Front" a loosely associated, broadly coherent, multiracial movement of 1930s and 1940s writers, musicians, artists, and political progressives. Despite the extensive appeal of the Cultural Front, by the early 1950s McWilliams's writings were, writes Denning, "overshadowed by the explosion of studies of the *national* culture and 'character' of the United States." They were not part of a "new field of 'American Studies'" that, during the 1950s, would take "shape in the rapidly expanding universities."[17]

At the time when Carey McWilliams published, his attention to racism *and* class exploitation made even sympathetic readers uncomfortable, for he departed from the racial common sense espoused by most social scientists, intellectuals, and others in American society at large.[18] Then as now, even to pose the question of whether racial oppression was an independent causal factor or whether it could be attributed to some more fundamental determinant such as ethnicity or class required vigorous debate. As Nikhil Singh points out, McWilliams not only posed but decisively answered the question (473–79). For most, however, the significance of race was easily rejected or downplayed. Dominant thinking (ultimately leading back to the Chicago School cycle of race relations) held that race was a subset of ethnicity and that racial inequality was a version of ethnic inequality, attributable to individual prejudice and/or the incompatibility of ethnic culture with modern "American" society.

Attention to place requires a corresponding attention to social structure. American studies' theoretical analysis of the relationship between culture and identity (but relative lack of attention to social structure) is more vital now that the structures of the state that protected civil rights and made affirmations of racial and gender identity more possible have been dismantled and taken apart to create a state that serves the interests of corporations and global markets. Channels and formal mechanisms of political redress have been eroded and dissolved in favor of economic policy. Cultural commodities now conform to the logic of this new market-state. Yet, the means for producing and analyzing culture have become opportunities for engaging with people working in other realms of civil society to secure those political gains that are still achievable.

To research his study of farm labor, Carey McWilliams traveled around California in a convertible Dodge Roadster with L.A. schoolteacher Herb Klein to document labor conflicts (Sachs, 237). McWilliams's travels also established connections with farm laborers. At the same time he was reading social science and translating it into a journalistic prose style that would reach a broader audience. McWilliams did this to show the relationship between racial discrimination and exploitation. What is striking about the greater part, if not the majority, of scholars currently researching and writing about Los Angeles, as almost all of the works surveyed in this review essay demonstrate, is their emphasis on Los Angeles as a place formed by race, a place of racial formation. Likewise, the greater part of Los Angeles studies work surveyed in this essay considers culture as emanating from and engaged with social structure, showing the importance of establishing networks and engagements with place through culture to enable the affirmation of diverse identities. Now politicians from George W. Bush to Joe Lieberman, following the logic of Samuel Huntington's *The Clash of Civilizations*, would return us to the "American" identity that overshadowed McWilliams's insights in order to dismiss current multiculturalism as unpatriotic.[19] It is tempting to overstate that scholarship on Los Angeles has caught up to Carey McWilliams. A better way to put it would be that McWilliams's engagement with a specific place, Los Angeles and the state of California, led him to ways of explaining race, culture, and identity that are important for American studies.

Notes

1. Thank you to family and friends for their help with this essay. Mary Kay Van Sistine, Sophie and Sam Willard-Van Sistine, David and Janet Van Sistine, the Mahers, the Van Sistines, and the Van Sistine-Yosts gave me time to write. A conversation with George Lipsitz and a reading of his essay were very helpful. Matthew Bokovoy, *American Quarterly* editors Marita Sturken and Raúl Villa, and an anonymous reader commented on drafts to help me get the writing right. *AQ* staff members Hillary Jenks and Cynthia Willis helped to compile the bibliography. Any errors that remain are mine.
2. Geary discusses the nuances of McWilliams's opposition to the Japanese evacuation. McWilliams also prepared the report for Governor Earl Warren's Committee on the zoot suit riots. See McGucken.
3. In their important study of the 1992 riots, Abelmann and Lie point out that L.A. media persistently portrayed these events that involved Korean, Mexican American, Mexican, Central American, African American, and white L.A. residents as a black-Korean conflict.

4. In response to the publication of *The City*, review essays marking its importance surveyed key works in L.A. studies from the late 1980s to the mid-1990s. See the essays by Schneider, Engh, Coquery-Vidrovitch, and Ethington in a special Los Angeles issue of the *American Historical Review* 105.5 (December 2000). See also Monahan (2003), Dear (2002a), Keil (1998), Abu-Lughod (1999), and Soja (2000), which are the most comprehensive single-source descriptions and syntheses of scholarship on L.A. published up to 1997.
5. Davis mentions the nascent L.A. School in *City of Quartz* (83–88). The book was one of many published during the 1980s and early 1990s by members of the L.A. School such as Edward Soja, Michael Dear and Jennifer Wolch, and non L.A. School authors such as George Lipsitz, Vicki Ruíz, George Sánchez, and Kevin Starr. Lipsitz's influential L.A. writings are published as journal articles or book chapters.
6. Some original members include Dana Cuff, Mike Davis, Michael Dear, Margaret FitzSimmons, Rebecca Morales, Allen Scott, Edward Soja, Michael Storper, and Jennifer Wolch (Dear 2003a, 493–509). See Monahan (2003) and Dear (2002a) for further discussion of factors that define a "school."
7. Other studies of Los Angeles and globalization include Keil (1998) and Smith (2001).
8. The word *zoöpolis* is found in Dear (2002b), 367.
9. George Lipsitz, *The Posessive Investment in Whiteness: How White People Profit from Identity Politics* (Philadelphia, Penn.: Temple University Press, 1998).
10. See also Schuparra (1998).
11. Other important studies of Los Angeles 1960s social movements include McBride (2003) and Espinoza (2003).
12. Of the hundred most diverse urban areas in the United States in 1980, more than half were in California, and of those, twenty were in Los Angeles County (Soja 2000, 295, citing Allen and Turner 1997).
13. See Gordon and Richardson (1999), who critique the L.A. School.
14. For more on the history of artistic communities formed in pursuit of poetic/literary aesthetics, see Novak (2003). For further history of L.A. art, see Barron (2000).
15. Ethington and Meeker (2002b) distinguish between abstract and experiential urban knowledges.
16. Arjun Appadurai, "Grassroots Globalization and the Research Imagination," *Public Culture* 12.1 (2000): 2.
17. Denning, 445–46.
18. Sachs, 245.
19. David Palumbo-Liu, "Multiculturalism Now: Civilization, National Identity, and Difference Before and After September 11th," *Boundary 2* 29.2 (2002): 109–27.

Bibliography

Abelmann, Nancy, and John Lie. *Blue Dreams: Korean Americans and the Los Angeles Riots.* Cambridge: Harvard University Press, 1995.

Abu-Lughod, Janet. *New York, Chicago, Los Angeles: America's Global Cities.* Minneapolis: University of Minnesota Press, 1999.

Alcaraz, Lalo. *Cartoonista. http://www.cartoonista.com/* (accessed July 14, 2004).

Allen, James Paul, and Eugene Turner. *The Ethnic Quilt: Population Diversity in Southern California.* Northridge: The Center for Geographical Studies, California State University, Northridge, 1997.

Alamillo, José Manuel. "Bitter-Sweet Communities: Mexican Workers and Citrus Growers on the California Landscape, 1880–1941." Ph.D. dissertation, University of California, Irvine, 2000.

———. "*Peloteros* in Paradise: Mexican American Baseball and Oppositional Politics in Southern California, 1930–1950." *Western Historical Quarterly* 34.2 (Summer 2003): 191–211.

Apostol, Jane. *Painting with Light: A Centennial History of Judson Studios.* Los Angeles: Historical Society of Southern California, 1997.

Appier, Janis. *The Sexual Politics of Law Enforcement and the LAPD.* Philadelphia: Temple University Press, 1998.

Arau, Sergio, and Yareli Arizmendi. *A Day Without a Mexican.* Los Angeles: Produced by AraU-AriZmendi, 1997. 30 min., 24 sec.

Avila, Eric. *Popular Culture in the Age of White Flight: Fear and Fantasy in Suburban Los Angeles.* Berkeley: University of California Press, 2004.

Barron, Stephanie, Sheri Bernstein, and Ilene Susan Fort. *Reading California: Art, Image, and Identity, 1900–2000.* Berkeley: University of California Press, 2000.

Bengston, John. *Silent Echoes: Discovering Early Hollywood through the Films of Buster Keaton.* Santa Monica, Calif.: Santa Monica Press, 2000.

Bobo, Lawrence, Melvyn L. Oliver, James H. Johnson Jr., and Abel Valenzuela Jr. "Analyzing Inequality in Los Angeles." In *Prismatic Metropolis: Inequality in Los Angeles,* ed. Lawrence Bobo, Melvyn L. Oliver, James H. Johnson Jr., and Abel Valenzuela Jr., 3–50. New York: Russell Sage Foundation, 2000.

Bobo, Lawrence, Melvyn L. Oliver, James H. Johnson Jr., and Abel Valenzuela Jr., eds. *Prismatic Metropolis: Inequality in Los Angeles.* New York: Russell Sage Foundation, 2000.

Bokovoy, Matthew. *The Peers of Their White Conquerors: The San Diego Expositions and the Heritage Crusade in the Southwest, 1880–1940.* Albuquerque: University of New Mexico Press, forthcoming.

Bonacich, Edna, and Richard P. Appelbaum. *Behind the Label: Inequality in the Los Angeles Apparel Industry.* Berkeley: University of California Press, 2000.

Bonus, Rick. *Locating Filipino Americans: Ethnicity and the Cultural Politics of Space.* Philadelphia: Temple University Press, 2000.

Bouvier, Virginia Marie. *Women and the Conquest of California, 1542–1840.* Tucson: University of Arizona Press, 2001.

Brown, Scot. *Fighting for US: Maulana Karenga, the US Organization, and Black Cultural Nationalism.* New York: New York University Press, 2003.

Bryant, Clora, et al. *Central Avenue Sounds: Jazz in Los Angeles.* Berkeley: University of California Press, 1998.

Burgos, Rita, and Laura Pulido. "The Politics of Gender in the Los Angeles Bus Riders' Union/Sindicato De Pasajeros." *Capital, Nature, Socialism* 9.3 (September 1998): 75–82.

Carby, Hazel V. "Figuring the Future in Los(t) Angeles." *Comparative American Studies* 1.1 (March 2003): 19–34.

Chang, Edward T., and Jeannette Diaz-Veizades. *Ethnic Peace in the American City: Building Community in Los Angeles and Beyond.* New York: New York University Press, 1999.

Chávez, Ernesto. "¡*Mi Raza Primero!*" *Nationalism, Identity, and Insurgency in the Chicano Movement in Los Angeles, 1966–1978.* Berkeley: University of California Press, 2002.

Chávez, John R. *Eastside Landmark: A History of the East Los Angeles Community Union, 1968–1998.* Stanford, Calif.: Stanford University Press, 2000.

Cheng, Meiling. *In Other Los Angeleses: Multicentric Performance Art.* Berkeley: University of California Press, 2002.

Clark, David. *A History of the California Club, 1887–1997.* Los Angeles: The Club, 1997.

Cole, Carolyn Kozo, and Kathy Kobayashi. *Shades of L.A.: Pictures from Ethnic Family Albums*. New York: New Press, 1996.

Coquery-Vidrovitch, Catherine. "Is L.A. a Model or a Mess?" *American Historical Review* 105.5 (2000): 1683–91.

Corwin, Miles. *The Killing Season: A Summer Inside an LAPD Homicide Division*. New York: Simon & Schuster, 1997.

Cuff, Dana. *The Provisional City: Los Angeles Stories of Architecture and Urbanism*. Cambridge: Massachusetts Institute of Technology, 2000.

Curry, James, and Martin Kenney. "The Paradigmatic City: Postindustrial Illusion and the Los Angeles School." *Antipode* 31.1 (1999): 1–28.

Davis, Clark. *Company Men: White Collar Life and Corporate Cultures in Los Angeles, 1892–1941*. Baltimore: Johns Hopkins University Press, 2000.

Davis, Mike. *City of Quartz: Excavating the Future in Los Angeles*. New York: Verso, 1990.

———. *Ecology of Fear: Los Angeles and the Imagination of Disaster*. New York: Vintage Books, 1999.

———. *Magical Urbanism: Latinos Reinvent the U.S. City*. New York: Verso, 2000.

Davis, Mike, Jim Miller, Kelly Mayhew, and Fred Lonidier. *Under the Perfect Sun: the San Diego Tourists Never See*. New York: New Press, 2003.

Davis, Margaret Leslie. *Dark Side of Fortune: Triumph and Scandal in the Life of Oil Tycoon Edward L. Doheny*. Berkeley: University of California Press, 1998.

———. *The Los Angeles Biltmore: The Host of the Coast*. Los Angeles: Regal Biltmore Hotel, 1998.

Dawes, Amy, and Michael Diehl et al. *Imagining Los Angeles: Photographs of a 20th Century City*. Los Angeles: Los Angeles Times Books, 2000.

Dear, Michael J. "Los Angeles and the Chicago School: Invitation to a Debate." *City and Community* 1.1 (2002a): 5–32.

———. "Imagining Postmodern Urbanism." In *From Chicago to L.A.: Making Sense of Urban Theory*, ed. Michael Dear, 85–92. Thousand Oaks, Calif.: Sage Publications, 2002b.

———. "The Los Angeles School of Urbanism: An Intellectual History." *Urban Geography* 24.6 (2003a): 493–509.

Dear, Michael J., ed. *From Chicago to L.A.: Making Sense of Urban Theory*. Thousand Oaks, Calif.: Sage Publications, 2002b.

Dear Michael J., and Jennifer R. Wolch. *Landscapes of Despair : From Deinstitutionalization to Homelessness*. Princeton, N.J.: Princeton University Press, 1987.

Dear, Michael J., H. Eric Shockman, and Greg Hise, eds. *Rethinking Los Angeles*. Thousand Oaks, Calif.: Sage Publications, 1996.

Dear, Michael, and Gustavo Leclerc. *Postborder City: Cultural Spaces of Bajalta California*. New York: Routledge, 2003b.

Dear, Michael J., and Steven Flusty. "The Resistable Rise of the L.A. School." In *From Chicago to L.A.: Making Sense of Urban Theory*, ed. Michael Dear, 3–16. Thousand Oaks, Calif.: Sage Publications, 2002b.

de Graaf, Lawrence B. "African American Suburbanization in California, 1960 through 1990." In *Seeking El Dorado: African Americans in California*, ed. Lawrence de Graaf, Kevin Mulroy, and Quintard Taylor, 405–49. Seattle: University of Washington Press, 2001.

de Graaf Lawrence, Kevin Mulroy, and Quintard Taylor, eds. *Seeking El Dorado: African Americans in California*. Seattle: University of Washington Press, 2001.

Denning, Michael. *The Cultural Front: the Laboring of American Culture in the Twentieth Century*. New York: Verso, 1996.

Deverell, William. *Whitewashed Adobe: The Rise of Los Angeles and the Remaking of Its Mexican Past*. Berkeley: University of California Press, 2004.

DjeDje, Jacqueline Cogdell, and Eddie S. Meadows. *California Soul: Music of African Americans in the West*. Berkeley: University of California Press, 1998.

Duke, Donald. *Incline Railways of Los Angeles and Southern California*. San Marino, Calif.: Golden West Books, 1998.

Engh, Michael E. "At Home in Heteropolis: Understanding Postmodern L.A." *American Historical Review* 105.5 (December 2000): 1676–82.

Escobar, Edward. *Race, Police, and the Making of a Political Identity: Mexican Americans and the Los Angeles Police Department, 1900–1945*. Berkeley: University of California Press, 1999.

Espinoza, Dionne. "Tanto Tiempo Disfrutamos . . .: Revisiting the Gender and Sexual Politics of Chicana/o Youth Culture in East Los Angeles in the 1960s." In *Velvet Barrios: Popular Culture and Chicana/o Sexualities*, ed. Alicia Gaspar de Alba, 89–106. New York: Palgrave/Macmillan, 2003.

Ethington, Philip J. *The Challenge of Intergroup Relations in Los Angeles: An Historical and Comparative Evaluation of the Los Angeles City Human Relations Commission, 1966–1998*. Los Angeles: Southern California Studies Center of the University of Southern California, 1998.

———. *Segregated Diversity: Race-Ethnicity, Space, and Political Fragmentation in Los Angeles County, 1940–1994*. Los Angeles: John Randolph Haynes and Dora Haynes Foundation, 2000a.

———. "Los Angeles and the Problem of Urban Historical Knowledge," *e-AHR* multimedia article. *American Historical Review* 105.5 (December 2000b). *http://cwis.usc.edu/dept/LAS/history/historylab/LAPUHK/index.html* (accessed July 13, 2004).

———. *Ghost Metropolis: Los Angeles and the Cartography of Time, 1921–2001*. Forthcoming.

Ethington, Philip, and Martin Meeker. "*Saber y Conocer*: The Metropolis of Urban Inquiry." In *From Chicago to L.A.: Making Sense of Urban Theory*, ed. Michael Dear, 403–20. Thousand Oaks, Calif.: Sage Publications, 2002b.

Fine, David. *Imagining Los Angeles: A City in Fiction*. Albuquerque: University of New Mexico Press, 2000.

Fulton, William. *The Reluctant Metropolis: The Politics of Urban Growth in Los Angeles*. Baltimore: Johns Hopkins University Press, 1997.

Flamming, Douglas. "A Westerner in Search of Negroness: Region and Race in the Writing of Arna Bontemps." In *Over the Edge: Remapping the American West*, ed. Valerie J. Matsumoto and Blake Almendinger, 85–106. Berkeley: University of California Press, 1999.

———. "The Star of Ethiopia and the NAACP: Pageantry, Politics, and the Los Angeles African American Community." In *Metropolis in the Making: Los Angeles in the 1920s*, ed. Tom Sitton and William Francis Deverell, 145–60. Berkeley: University of California Press, 2001.

———. "Becoming Democrats: Liberal Politics and the African American Community in Los Angeles, 1930–1965." In *Seeking El Dorado: African Americans in California*, ed. Lawrence de Graaf, Kevin Mulroy, and Quintard Taylor, 279–308. Seattle: University of Washington Press, 2001.

———. *Bound for Freedom: Black Los Angeles in Jim Crow America*. Berkeley: University of California Press, forthcoming.

Flory, Richard W., and Donald E. Miller. *Gen X Religion*. New York: Routledge, 2000.

Fong, Timothy. *The First Suburban Chinatown: The Remaking of Monterey Park, California*. Philadelphia: Temple University Press, 1994.

Fredericks, William. "Henry E. Huntington and Real Estate Development in Southern California, 1898–1917." *Southern California Quarterly* 71 (Winter 1989): 327–40.

———. *Henry E. Huntington and the Creation of Southern California*. Columbus: Ohio State University Press, 1992.

Gabler, Neal. *An Empire of Their Own: How the Jews Invented Hollywood*. New York: Anchor Press, 1998.

Garcia, Matt. *A World of Its Own: Race, Labor, and Citrus in the Making of Greater Los Angeles, 1900–1970*. Chapel Hill: University of North Carolina Press, 2001.

Geary, Daniel. "Carey McWilliams and Antifascism, 1934–1943." *The Journal of American History* 90.3 (December 2003): 912–34.

Getty Research Institute. *Cultural Inheritance/L.A.: A Directory of Less-Visible Archives and Collections in the Los Angeles Region*. Los Angeles: Getty Research Institute for the History of Art and the Humanities, 1999.

Gilfoyle, Thomas. "White Cities, Linguistic Turns, and Disneylands: Recent Paradigms in Urban History." *Reviews in American History* 26.1 (March 1998): 175–203.

Gilmore, Ruth Wilson. "'You Have Dislodged a Boulder': Mothers and Prisoners in the Post Keynesian California Landscape." *Transforming Anthropology* 8.1/2 (1999): 12–38.

———. *Golden Gulag: Labor, Land, State, and Opposition in Globalizing California*. Berkeley: University of California Press, forthcoming.

Giovacchini, Saverio. *Hollywood Modernism: Film and Politics in the Age of the New Deal*. Philadelphia: Temple University Press, 2001.

Gordon, Peter, and Harry Richardson. "Los Angeles, City of Angels? No, City of Angles." *Urban Studies* 36.3 (1999): 575–91.

Gumprecht, Blake. *The Los Angeles River: Its Life, Death and Possible Rebirth*. Baltimore: Johns Hopkins University Press, 1999.

Halle, David, ed. *New York and Los Angeles: Politics, Society, and Culture—A Comparative View.* Chicago: University of Chicago Press, 2003.

Hamilton, Nora, and Norma Stoltz Chinchilla. *Seeking Community in a Global City: Guatemalans and Salvadorans in Los Angeles.* Philadelphia: Temple University Press, 2001.

Haney-López, Ian. *Racism on Trial: The Chicano Fight for Justice.* Cambridge: Harvard University Press, 2003.

Hines, Thomas S. *Irving Gill and the Architecture of Reform.* New York: Monacelli Press, 2000.

Hise, Greg. *Magnetic Los Angeles: Planning the Twentieth-Century Metropolis.* Baltimore: Johns Hopkins University Press, 1997.

Hise, Greg, and William Deverell. *Eden by Design. The 1930 Olmstead Bartholomew Plan for the Los Angeles Region.* Berkeley: University of California Press, 2000.

Hoover, Stewart M., and Lynn Schofield Clark, eds. *Practicing Religion in the Age of Media: Explorations in Media, Religion, and Culture.* New York: Columbia University Press, 2002.

Hondagneu-Sotelo, Pierrette. *Doméstica: Immigrant Workers Cleaning and Caring in the Shadows of Affluence.* Berkeley: University of California Press, 2001.

Horne, Gerald. *Fire This Time: The Watts Uprising and the 1960s.* Charlottesville: University Press of Virginia, 1995.

Horton, John. *The Politics of Diversity: Immigration, Resistance, and Change in Monterey Park, California.* Philadelphia: Temple University Press, 1995.

Hunt, Darnell M. *Screening the Los Angeles 'Riots': Race, Seeing, and Resistance.* Cambridge: Cambridge University Press, 1997.

Iwamura, Jane Naomi, and Paul Spickard, eds. *Revealing the Sacred in Asian and Pacific America.* New York: Routledge, 2003.

James, David E., ed. *The Sons and Daughters of Los: Culture and Community in L.A.* Philadelphia: Temple University Press, 2003.

Jurca, Catherine. *White Diaspora: The Suburb and the Twentieth-Century American Novel.* Princeton, N.J.: Princeton University Press, 2001.

Keane, James Thomas. *Fritz B. Burns and The Development of Los Angeles: The Biography of a Community Developer and Philanthropist.* Los Angeles: Thomas and Dorothy Leavey Center for the Study of Los Angeles, Loyola Marymount University, 2001.

Keil, Roger. *Los Angeles: Globalization, Urbanization, and Social Struggles.* New York: J. Wiley and Sons, 1998.

Kenney, Moira Rachel. *Mapping Gay L.A.: The Intersection of Place and Politics.* Philadelphia: Temple University Press, 2001.

Kielbasa, John R. *Historic Adobes of Los Angeles County.* Pittsburgh: Dorrance Publishing, 1997.

Klein, Norman M. *The History of Forgetting: Los Angeles and the Erasure of Memory.* New York: Verso, 1997.

Kropp, Phoebe S. "'All Our Yesterdays': The Spanish Fantasy Past and the Politics of Public Memory in Southern California, 1884–1939." Ph.D. dissertation, University of California, San Diego, 1999.

———. "Citizens of the Past?: Olvera Street and the Construction of Race and Memory in 1930s Los Angeles." *Radical History Review* 81 (Fall 2001): 35–60.

Kun, Josh. *Strangers among Sounds: Music, Race, and America.* Berkeley: University of California Press, forthcoming.

Kurashige, Lon. *Japanese American Celebration and Conflict: A History of Ethnic Identity and Festival, 1934–1990.* Berkeley: University of California Press, 2002.

Kurashige, Scott. "Transforming Los Angeles: Black and Japanese Struggles for Racial Equality in the 20th Century." Ph.D. dissertation, University of California, Los Angeles, 2000.

———. "The Many Facets of Brown: Integration in a Multiracial Society." *Journal of American History* 91.1 (June 2004): 56–68.

Landres, J. Shawn. "Public Art as Sacred Space: Asian American Community Murals in Los Angeles." In *Practicing Religion in the Age of Media: Explorations in Media, Religion, and Culture,* ed. Stewart M. Hoover and Lynn Schofield Clark, 91–112. New York: Columbia University Press, 2002.

LeClerc, Gustavo, Raúl Villa, and Michael J. Dear. *Urban Latino Cultures: La Vida Latina en L.A.* Thousand Oaks, Calif.: Sage Publications, 1999.

León, Luis. "Born Again in East L.A.: The Congregation as Border Space." In *Gatherings in Diaspora,* ed. R. Steven Warner and Judith G. Wittner, 163–97. Philadelphia: Temple University Press, 1998.

Leonard, Kevin Allen. "'Is That What We Fought For?' Japanese Americans and Racism in California: The Impact of World War II." *Western Historical Quarterly* 21 (1990): 463–82.

————. "'Brothers under the Skin'? African Americans, Mexican Americans, and World War II in California." In *The Way We Really Were: The Golden State in the Second Great War*, ed. Roger W. Lotchin, 187–214. Urbana: University of Illinois Press, 2000.

————. "'In the Interest of All Races': African Americans and Interracial Cooperation in Los Angeles during and after World War II." In *Seeking El Dorado: African Americans in California*, ed. Lawrence de Graaf, Kevin Mulroy, and Quintard Taylor, 309–40. Seattle: University of Washington Press, 2001.

Lipsitz, George. "World Cities and World Beat: Low-Wage Labor and Transnational Culture." *Pacific Historical Review* 68 (May 1999): 213–31.

Longstreth, Richard. *City Center to Regional Mall: Architecture, the Automobile, and Retailing in Los Angeles, 1920–1950*. Cambridge: Massachusetts Institute of Technology Press, 1997.

————. *The Drive-In, the Supermarket, and the Transformation of Commercial Space in Los Angeles, 1914–1941*. Cambridge: Massachusetts Institute of Technology Press, 1999.

Loukaitou-Sideris, Anastasia, and Tridib Banerjee. *Urban Design Downtown: Poetics and Politics of Form*. Berkeley: University of California Press, 1998.

López-Garza, Marta Christina, and David R. Diaz, *Asian and Latino Immigrants in a Restructuring Economy: the Metamorphosis of Southern California*. Stanford, Calif.: Stanford University Press, 2001.

Macías, Anthony. "From Pachuco Boogie to Latin Jazz: Mexican Americans, Popular Music, and Urban Culture in Los Angeles, 1940–1965." Ph.D. dissertation, University of Michigan, 2001.

————. "Raza Con Jazz, Rock Con Raza: Latinos/as and Post–World War II Popular American Music." In *Musical Migrations: Transnationalism and Cultural Hybridity in Latin/o America*, ed. Frances R. Aparicio, and Cándida F Jáquez, 183–98. New York: Palgrave/MacMillan, 2003.

May, Kirse Granat. *Golden State, Golden Youth: the California Image in Popular Culture, 1955–1966*. Chapel Hill: University of North Carolina Press, 2002.

May, Lary. *The Big Tomorrow: Hollywood and the Politics of the American Way*. Chicago: University of Chicago Press, 2000.

McBride, David. "Death City Radicals: The Counterculture in Los Angeles." In *The New Left Revisited*, ed. John Campbell McMillian and Paul Buhle, 110–38. Philadelphia: Temple University Press, 2003.

McGirr, Lisa. *Suburban Warriors: The Origins of the New American Right*. Princeton, N.J.: Princeton University Press, 2001.

McGuire, Brian, and Duncan Scrymgeour. "Santería and Curanderismo in Los Angeles." In *New Trends and Developments in African Religions*, ed. Peter B. Clarke, 211–22. Westport, Conn.: Greenwood Press, 1998.

McClung, William Alexander. *Landscapes of Desire: Anglo Mythologies of Los Angeles*. Berkeley: University of California Press, 2000.

McGucken, Joseph T., et al., "Report and Recommendations of the Citizens Committee, Los Angeles, June 12, 1943." In *Readings on La Raza: The Twentieth Century*. ed. Matt S. Meier and Feliciano Rivera, 138–44. New York: Hill and Wang, 1974.

McWilliams, Carey. "Getting Rid of the Mexican." *American Mercury* 28 (March 1933): 322–24.

————. *Factories in the Field: The Story of Migratory Farm Labor in California*. Boston: Little Brown, 1939.

————. *Japanese Evacuation: Interim Report*. New York: Institute of Pacific Relations, 1942.

————. "The Zoot-Suit Riots." *New Republic* 108 (June 21, 1943): 818–20.

————. *What about Our Japanese Americans?*. New York: Public Affairs Committee, 1944a.

————. *Prejudice: Japanese-Americans, Symbol of Racial Intolerance*. Boston: Little Brown, 1944b.

————. *Southern California Country, An Island on the Land*. New York: Duell, Sloan, and Pearce, 1946.

————. *North from Mexico: The Spanish-Speaking People of the United States*. Philadelphia: Lippincott, 1949.

Milkman, Ruth. *Organizing Immigrants: The Challenge for Unions in Contemporary California*. Ithaca, N.Y.: Cornell University Press, 2000.

Molina, Natalia. "Contested Bodies and Cultures: The Politics of Public Health and Race within Mexican, Japanese, and Chinese Communities in Los Angeles, 1879–1939." Ph.D. dissertation, University of Michigan, 2001.

————. "Illustrating Cultural Authority: Medicalized Representations of Mexican Communities in Early-Twentieth-Century Los Angeles." *Aztlan* 28.1 (Spring 2003): 129–44.

Monahan, Torin. "Los Angeles Studies: The Emergence of a Specialty Field." *City and Society* 14.2 (2003): 155–84.

Monroy, Douglas. *Rebirth: Mexican Los Angeles from the Great Migration to the Great Depression*. Berkeley: University of California Press, 1999.

Moore, Burton M., and Andrea Alessandra Cabello. *Love and Riot: Oscar Zeta Acosta and the Great Mexican American Revolt.* Mountain View, Calif.: Floricanto Press, 2003.

Moran, James M. "All Over the Map: A History of L.A. Freewaves." In *The Sons and Daughters of Los: Culture and Community in L.A.*, ed. David E. James, 174–94. Philadelphia: Temple University Press, 2003.

Mullholland, Catherine. *William Mulholland and the Rise of Los Angeles.* Berkeley: University of California Press, 2000.

Murphet, Julian. *Literature and Race in Los Angeles.* Cambridge: Cambridge University Press, 2001.

Nicolaides, Becky M. *My Blue Heaven: Life and Politics in the Working-Class Suburbs of Los Angeles, 1920–1965.* Chicago: University of Chicago Press, 2002.

Normark, Don. *Chavez Ravine, 1949: A Los Angeles Story.* San Francisco: Chronicle Books, 1999.

Novak, Estelle Gershgoren. *Poets of the Non-Existent City : Los Angeles in the McCarthy Era.* Albuquerque: University of New Mexico Press, 2003.

Nunis, Doyce B., Jr., ed. *The Founding Documents of Los Angeles: A Bilingual Edition.* Los Angeles: Historical Society of Southern California, 2004.

Ono, Kent, and John Sloop. *Shifting Borders: Rhetoric, Immigration, and California's Proposition 187.* Philadelphia: Temple University Press, 2002.

Orsi, Jared. *Hazardous Metropolis : Flooding and Urban Ecology in Los Angeles.* Berkeley: University of California Press, 2004.

Pagán, Eduardo Obregón. *Murder at the Sleepy Lagoon: Zoot Suits, Race, and Riot in Wartime L.A.* Chapel Hill: University of North Carolina Press, 2003.

Palumbo-Liu, David. "Hybridities and Histories: Imaging the Rim." In *Postborder City: Cultural Spaces of Bajalta California*, ed. Michael Dear and Gustavo Leclerc, 249–76. New York: Routledge, 2003.

Pardo, Mary. *Mexican American Women Activists: Identity and Resistance in Two Los Angeles Communities.* Philadelphia: Temple University Press, 1998.

Parson, Don. *Making a Better World: Public Housing, the Red Scare, and the Direction of Modern Los Angeles.* Minneapolis: University of Minnesota Press, forthcoming.

Pastras, Philip. *Dead Man Blues: Jelly Roll Morton Way Out West.* Berkeley/Chicago: University of California Press/Center for Black Music Research, 2001.

Peter, Nithila. "Unorthodox Mystics: Swans that Flock to the Vedanta Society of Southern California." In *The Sons and Daughters of Los: Culture and Community in L.A.*, ed. David E. James, 211–30. Philadelphia: Temple University Press, 2003.

Phillips, Kate. *Helen Hunt Jackson: A Literary Life.* Berkeley: University of California Press, 2003.

Phillips, Susan. *Wallbangin': Graffiti and Gangs in L.A.* Chicago: University of Chicago Press, 1999.

Pitt, Leonard, and Dale Pitt. *Los Angeles A to Z: An Encyclopedia of the City and County.* Berkeley: University of California Press, 1997.

Poole, Jean Bruce, and Tevvy Ball, eds. *El Pueblo: The Historic Heart of Los Angeles.* Los Angeles: The Getty Conservation Institute and the J. Paul Getty Museum, 2002.

Porter, Eric. *What Is This Thing Called Jazz? African American Musicians as Artists, Critics, and Activists.* Berkeley: University of California Press, 2002.

Pulido, Laura. "Multiracial Organizing among Environmental Justice Activists in Los Angeles." In *Rethinking Los Angeles*, ed. Michael Dear, H. Eric Shockman, and Greg Hise, 171–89. Thousand Oaks, Calif.: Sage Publications, 1996.

———. "Race, Class, and Political Activism: Black, Chicano, and Japanese American Activists in Southern California, 1968–1978." *Antipode* 34.4 (September 2002): 762–88.

Reyes, Adelaida. *Songs of the Caged, Songs of the Free: Music and the Vietnamese Refugee Experience.* Philadelphia: Temple University Press, 1999.

Reyes, David, and Tom Waldman. *Land of a Thousand Dances: Chicano Rock n Roll from Southern California.* Albuquerque: University of New Mexico Press, 1998.

Rocco, Raymond. "Latino Los Angeles: Reframing Boundaries/Borders." In *The City: Los Angeles and Urban Theory at the End of the Twentieth Century*, ed. Allen J. Scott and Edward Soja, 365–38. Berkeley: University of California Press, 1996.

Rasmussen, Cecilia. *L.A. Unconventional: The Men and Women Who Did L.A. Their Way.* Los Angeles: Los Angeles Times Books, 1998.

Rodríguez, Gregory S. "Palaces of Pain, Arenas of Mexican American Dreams: Boxing and the Formation of Ethnic Mexican Identities in Twentieth-Century Los Angeles." Ph.D. dissertation, University of California San Diego, 1999.

Rolfe, Lionel. *Literary L.A.: Expanded from the Original Classic & Featuring the Coffeehouse Scene Then and Now.* Los Angeles: California Classics Books, 2002.

Ross, Steven J. *Working-Class Hollywood: Silent Film and the Shaping of Class in America.* Princeton, N.J.: Princeton University Press, 1998.

Rudd, Hynda, ed. *Los Angeles and Its Environs in the Twentieth Century: A Bibliography of a Metropolis.* Los Angeles: Los Angeles City Historical Society, 1996.

Ruíz, Vicki. *Cannery Women, Cannery Lives: Mexican Women, Unionization, and the California Food Processing Industry, 1930–1950.* Albuquerque: University of New Mexico Press, 1987.

Sachs, Aaron. "Civil Rights in the Field: Carey McWilliams as a Public-Interest Historian and Social Ecologist." *Pacific Historical Review* 73.2 (2004): 215–248.

Salas, Charles, and Michael S. Ross, eds. *Looking for Los Angeles: Architecture, Film, Photography and the Urban Landscape.* Los Angeles: Getty Research Institute, 2001.

Saito, Leland. *Race and Politics: Asian Americans, Latinos, and Whites in a Los Angeles Suburb.* Urbana: University of Illinois Press, 1998.

Sánchez, George J. *Becoming Mexican American : Ethnicity, Culture, and Identity in Chicano Los Angeles, 1900–1945.* New York: Oxford University Press, 1993.

Sawhney, Deepak, ed. *Unmasking L.A.: Third Worlds and the City.* New York: Palgrave/MacMillan, 2002.

Schneider, Robert A. "The Postmodern City from an Early Modern Perspective." *American Historical Review* 105.5 (2000): 1668–75.

Scott, Allen J. "High Technology Industrial Development in the San Fernando Valley and Ventura County." In *The City: Los Angeles and Urban Theory at the End of the Twentieth Century,* ed. Allen J. Scott and Edward Soja, 276–31. Berkeley: University of California Press, 1996.

Scott, Allen J., and Edward Soja, eds. *The City: Los Angeles and Urban Theory at the End of the Twentieth Century.* Berkeley: University of California Press, 1996.

Schuparra, Kurt. *Triumph of the Right: The Rise of the California Conservative Movement, 1945–1966.* Armonk, N.Y.: M. E. Sharpe, 1998.

Sides, Josh. *L.A. City Limits : African American Los Angeles from the Great Depression to the Present.* Berkeley: University of California Press, 2003.

Singh, Nikhil Pal. "Culture/Wars: Recoding Empire in an Age of Democracy." *American Quarterly* 50.3 (1998): 471–522.

Simonett, Helena. *Banda: Mexican Musical Life Across Borders.* Middletown, Conn.: Wesleyan University Press, 2001.

Sitton, Tom. *The Haynes Foundation and Urban Reform Philanthropy in Los Angeles: A History of the John Randolph Haynes and Dora Haynes Foundation.* Los Angeles: Historical Society of Southern California, 1999.

Sitton, Tom, and William Francis Deverell, eds. *Metropolis in the Making: Los Angeles in the 1920s.* Berkeley: University of California Press, 2001.

Smith, Michael Peter. *Transnational Urbanism: Locating Globalization.* London: Blackwell, 2001.

Soja, Edward. *Postmodern Geographies: The Reassertion of Space in Critical Theory.* London: Verso, 1989.

———. *Thirdspace: Journeys to Los Angeles and other Real-and-Imagined Places.* Cambridge, Mass.: Blackwell, 1996.

———. *Postmetropolis: Critical Studies of Cities and Regions.* Malden, Mass.: Blackwell, 2000.

Stanic, Borislav. *Museum Companion to Los Angeles.* 2d ed. Beverly Hills, Calif.: Museon Publishing, 1998.

Starr, Kevin. *Material Dreams: Southern California through the 1920s.* New York: Oxford University Press, 1990.

———. *The Dream Endures: California Enters the 1940s.* New York: Oxford University Press, 1997.

———. *Embattled Dreams: California in War and Peace, 1940–1950.* New York: Oxford University Press, 2002.

Tapscott, Horace, and Steven Louis Isoardi. *Songs of the Unsung: The Musical and Social Journey of Horace Tapscott.* Durham, N.C.: Duke University Press, 2001.

Timberg, Scott, and Dana Gioia, eds. *The Misread City: New Literary Los Angeles.* Granada Hills, Calif.: Red Hen Press, 2003.

Tucker, Sherrie. "West Coast Women: A Jazz Genealogy." *Pacific Review of Ethno Musicology* 8.1 (Winter 1996/1997): 5–22.

Ulin, David L. *Writing Los Angeles: A Literary Anthology.* New York: The Library of America, 2002.

Valle, Victor M., and Rodolfo Torres. *Latino Metropolis.* Minneapolis: University of Minnesota Press, 2000.

Valenzuela, Abel, Jr. "Day Labor Work." *Annual Review of Sociology* 29 (2003): 307–33.

Vargas, João H. Costa. "Blacks in the City of Angels' Dust." Ph.D. dissertation, University of California, San Diego, 1999.

———. "The Inner City and the Favela: Transnational Black Politics." *Race and Class* 44.4 (2003): 19–40.

———. *Blackness as Blueprint: Resistance and Social Transformation in Los Angeles.* Minneapolis: University of Minnesota Press, forthcoming.

Villa, Raúl Homero. *Barrio-Logos: Space and Place in Urban Chicano Literature and Culture.* Austin: University of Texas Press, 2000.

Wacker, Grant. *Heaven Below: Early Pentecostals and American Culture.* Cambridge: Harvard University Press, 2003.

Warner, R. Stephen, and Judith G. Wittner, eds. *Gatherings in Diaspora: Religious Communities and the New Immigration.* Philadelphia: Temple University Press, 1998.

Weibel-Orlando, Joan. *Indian Country, L.A.: Maintaining Ethnic Community in a Complex Society.* Rev. ed. Urbana: University of Illinois Press, 1999.

Widener, Daniel. "Something Else: Creative Community and Black Liberation in Postwar Los Angeles." Ph.D. dissertation, New York University, 2003a.

———. "'Perhaps the Japanese Are to Be Thanked?' Asia, Asian America, and the Construction of Black California." *The Afro-Asian Century,* a special issue of *Positions: East Asia Cultures Critique* 11.1 (2003b): 135–81.

Wild, Mark. "Red Light Kaleidoscope: Prostitution and the Politics of Cross-Cultural Sex in Los Angeles, 1880–1940." *Journal of Urban History* 28 (2002a): 720–41.

———. "'So Many Children at Once and So Many Kinds': Schools and Ethno-Racial Boundaries in Early-Twentieth-Century Los Angeles." *Western Historical Quarterly* 33.4 (2002b): 453–76.

———. *Rumored Congregation: Confronting Multiethnic Neighborhoods in Early-Twentieth-Century Los Angeles.* Berkeley: University of California Press, forthcoming.

Wolch, Jennifer, Stephanie Pincetl, and Laura Pulido. "Urban Nature and the Nature of Urbanism." In *From Chicago to L.A.: Making Sense of Urban Theory,* ed. Michael Dear, 367–402. Thousand Oaks, Calif.: Sage Publications, 2002.

Wong, Deborah, *Speak It Louder: Asian Americans Making Music.* New York: Routledge, 2004.

Zilberg, Elana Jean. "From Riots to Rampart: A Spatial Cultural Politics of Salvadoran Migration to and from Los Angeles." Ph.D. dissertation, University of Texas, 2002.

Contributors

Dana Cuff

Dana Cuff is professor of architecture and urban design at the University of California, Los Angeles, where she also holds a joint appointment with the Urban Planning Department. She received her Ph.D. in architecture from the University of California, Berkeley, and has since published and lectured widely about postwar American urbanism, the modern evolution of Los Angeles, the architectural profession, and affordable housing. Her most recent book, *The Provisional City* (2000), analyzes urban transformation through a number of private and public housing projects in Los Angeles, from their initial design to their eventual demolition. She is currently working on a book concerning the architectural, social, and technological transformation of the contemporary neighborhood.

Regina Freer

Regina Freer is an associate professor and chair of the Politics Department at Occidental College in Los Angeles. She recently completed her term as a 2003–04 Institute for American Cultures postdoctoral fellow in the Ralph J. Bunche Center for African American Studies at the University of California, Los Angeles. She is a co-author of the forthcoming book, *The Next Los Angeles: The Struggle for a Livable City* (2004), which examines connections between historical and contemporary progressive social justice organizing in Los Angeles. She also authored "Black Korean Conflict," a chapter in the edited volume, *The Los Angeles Riots*. Her current project is a political biography of Charlotta Bass.

Greg Hise

Greg Hise is associate professor of urban history in the School of Policy, Planning, and Development at the University of Southern California, where he holds joint appointments in the departments of history and geography. He is co-author (with William Deverell) of *Eden by Design: The 1930 Olmsted-Bartholomew Plan for the Los Angeles Region* (2000), the author of *Magnetic Los Angeles: Planning the Twentieth-Century Metropolis* (1997), a co-editor of *Rethinking Los Angeles* (1996) and of the forthcoming *Land of Sunshine: An Environmental History of Greater Los Angeles*. This essay is drawn from a work-in-progress, *Ciudad to City*, a history of property, social distance, and the local state that focuses on the ways Angelenos came to know race-ethnicity through architecture and landscape.

Josh Kun

Josh Kun is assistant professor of English at the University of California, Riverside and an arts columnist for the *San Francisco Bay Guardian* and *Boston Phoenix*. His writings on music have appeared in numerous scholarly books and journals, as well as in the *New York Times*, the *Los Angeles Times*, *Los Angeles Magazine*, the *Village Voice*, *SPIN*, and *Rolling Stone*. He is the author of *Strangers Among Sounds: Music, Race, America* (forthcoming, 2005), and is currently co-editing a book about David Mamet and writing a book on Tijuana.

George Lipsitz

George Lipsitz is the author of *American Studies in a Moment of Danger* (2001) and editor of the Critical American Studies series at the University of Minnesota Press. His publications include *The Possessive Investment in Whiteness* (1998), *Dangerous Crossroads* (1997), *Rainbow at Midnight* (1994), *Time Passages* (1990), *The Sidewalks of St. Louis* (1991), and *A Life in the Struggle* (1988). He also serves as co-editor of the American Crossroads series at the University of California Press. Lipsitz has been active in fights for fair housing and educational equity at the local and national levels, and is currently working on a book about social movements and historical change.

Anthony Macías

Anthony Macías is an assistant professor in the Department of Ethnic Studies at the University of California, Riverside, where he teaches Chicano studies. His research interests include twentieth-century American cultural history, comparative race and ethnicity, and popular cultural production, circulation, and reception. He is currently writing a book, titled *Mexican American Mojo: Popular Music, Dance, and Urban Culture in Los Angeles, 1935–1968*.

Kristen Hill Maher

Kristen Hill Maher is an assistant professor of political science at San Diego State University. She writes on women's labor migration, immigrant rights, and anti-immigrant politics, based on fieldwork in Southern California and Santiago, Chile.

Marisela Norte

Marisela Norte is considered one of the most important literary voices to come out of East Los Angeles. Her work has appeared in *Rolling Stone*, *Interview*, *Elle*, *Option*, *Venice*, the *Los Angeles Weekly*, *Buzz*, the *LA Opinion*, and the anthologies *Microphone Fiends*, *Bordered Sexualities: Bodies on the Verge of a Nation*, *The Geography of Home: California's Poetry of Place*, and *Rolling*

Stone's Women of Rock. Norte lives in East Los Angeles, is a member of PEN West, the Bus Riders Union, and the Progressive Jewish Alliance as well as a long-time volunteer at the East Los Angeles Women's Center. Her latest works include *East L.A. Days/Fellini Nights* and the upcoming *Scenes From the Dining Room.*

George J. Sánchez

George J. Sánchez is an associate professor of history and director of the Program in American Studies and Ethnicity at the University of Southern California, as well as a former president of the American Studies Association. His work focuses on Los Angeles, Mexican American history, and the intersection of race and ethnicity with urban space. He is the author of the award-winning *Becoming Mexican American: Ethnicity, Culture, and Identity in Chicano Los Angeles, 1900–1945* (1993), and is currently at work on a book manuscript about race and community in Boyle Heights.

Sarah Schrank

Sarah Schrank received her Ph.D. in history from the University of California, San Diego. She is assistant professor of United States urban and cultural history at California State University, Long Beach and the author of "Picturing the Watts Towers: The Art and Politics of an Urban Landmark," in Stephanie Barron, Ilene Fort, and Sheri Bernstein, eds., *Reading California: Art, Image, and Identity, 1900–2000* (2000). Schrank is the recipient of Haynes research grants from the Huntington Library and the Historical Society of Southern California and currently holds a year-long fellowship at the Shelby Cullom Davis Center at Princeton University, where she will complete her forthcoming book on Los Angeles spatial politics and art communities.

Josh Sides

Josh Sides is assistant professor of history at Cal Poly Pomona. He is the author of *L.A. City Limits: African American Los Angeles from the Great Depression to the Present* (2004).

Victor Hugo Viesca

Victor Hugo Viesca is an assistant professor in the Liberal Studies Department at California State University, Los Angeles. He teaches courses on popular culture, race and ethnicity, and twentieth-century urbanism.

Raúl Homero Villa

Raúl Homero Villa is an associate professor in English and comparative literary studies at Occidental College. His work focuses on urban studies, Chicano and U.S. literature and popular culture, and Southwest/Borderlands culture.

He is the author of *Barrio-Logos: Space and Place in Urban Chicano Literature and Culture* (2000) and co-editor of *Urban Latino Cultures: La Vida Latina en L.A.* (1999). He is an associate editor of *American Quarterly.*

Michael Nevin Willard

Michael Nevin Willard is assistant professor of history and director of the American Studies Program at Oklahoma State University. He will join the faculty at California State University, Los Angeles as an assistant professor of Liberal Studies in the fall of 2005. His most recent publication on Los Angeles appears in *America in the Seventies* (2004).

Henry Yu

Henry Yu is associate professor in the departments of history at the University of British Columbia in Vancouver, Canada, and at the University of California, Los Angeles, where he is also a faculty member at the Asian American Studies Center. Currently, he is working on developing collaborative research and teaching on trans-Pacific migration, as well as a book entitled *How Tiger Woods Lost His Stripes.* His book, *Thinking Orientals: Migration, Contact, and Exoticism in Modern America* (2001), focuses on the importance of migration and Asian Americans in the social scientific production of ideas about race and culture, and received the Norris and Carol Hundley Prize for Most Distinguished Book from the American Historical Association, Pacific Coast Branch.

Elana Zilberg

Elana Zilberg is an assistant professor in the Communication Department at the University of California, San Diego, where she writes and teaches on the contentious spatial and cultural politics surrounding the uneven flows of people, money, commodities, and ideas between Los Angeles and Central America. She has published in *Wide Angle* and *City and Society,* and is currently completing a book manuscript entitled *From Riots to Rampart: Culture, Mobility and the Politics of Simultaneity between Los Angeles and El Salvador.* The book is based on a dissertation completed in the Department of Anthropology at the University of Texas, Austin in 2002, and on postdoctoral research conducted in 2002–03 through a fellowship with the Social Science Research Council's Global Security and Cooperation Program.

Index

Abu-Lughod, Janet, 312–13
Acosta, Oscar, 323
Actors Laboratory Theatre, 149
Adams, Robert, 103
Adorno, Theodor, 245
African Americans, 4, 22, 41, 53, 57, 65, 85–104, 109–31, 136–37, 140–41, 155, 168–69, 195–215, 225, 247, 250, 252, 257, 266, 296, 323
Aguilar, Pepe, 255
Akwid, 244–47, 249, 253–54, 256
Aliso Village, 66–70
All City Art Show, 169, 172, 182
Altoon, John, 183
Alvarez, Carmelo, 234
American Civil Liberties Union (ACLU), 128, 213
American Federation of Musicians Union, 201
Anderson, Benedict, 276
Anti-Defamation League, 141
Appadurai, Arjun, 261
Asian Americans, 22, 126, 141, 209, 212, 214, 225, 324
Associacion Nacional de Mexico-Americanos (ANMA), 146
Avila, Eric, 318
Aztlán Cultural Arts Foundation, 224
Aztlán Underground, 221, 226–31, 237

Banda music, 225, 229
Barela, Alfred, 197
Barnsdall Park, 182
Barrows v. Jackson, 88–89
Bass, Charlotta, 109–31
Bass, Joseph Blackburn (J. B.), 111
Bates, Sam, 150

Beat generation, 175–81
Bell, Larry, 165–66
Bell Gardens, 55, 86, 208
Belvedere, 53, 55, 150
Bengston, Billy Al, 183, 185
Benny Goodman Orchestra, 195
Berman, Wallace, 183–85
Birth of a Nation, 110
Black Panthers, 125
Bloods, 95
Blue, Julius, 140
Blues Experiment, 221, 226, 229–30, 235
Blum, Irving, 185–86
Bogardus, Emory, 55
Bojorquez, Chaz, 232
Bokovoy, Matthew, 311
Bonaventure Hotel, 271, 274
Bonus, Rick, 327–28
Borek, Catherine, 104
Bouvier, Virginia Marie, 311
Bowron, Fletcher, 56, 146, 172, 195, 199, 204
Boyer, Peter, 262
Boyle Heights, 4, 15, 55–58, 64–69, 112, 135–59, 197–98, 201, 224
Boym, Svetlana, 246
Boy Scouts of Los Angeles, 205
Boyz in the 'Hood, 100–101
Bradley, Tom, 92
Brandt, Rex, 170
Bring Your Love Records, 221
Brittin, Charles, 185
Brown, James, 258
Brown Berets, 125
Browne, Samuel, 202
Bunche, Lonnie, 110
Bunker Hill, 56, 317
Bus Riders Union (BRU), 26–29

Cabello, Allesandra, 323
Cacho, Lisa, 226
Caldeira, Teresa, 289
California Art Club, 167
California Eagle, 109–14, 117–29, 155, 170, 195, 199
California State Board of Health, 55
California's Un-American Activities Committee, 149
California Watercolor Society, 174
Californios, 50, 57
Campbell, Gerald, 157
Cano, Eddie, 200
Carter, Artie Mason, 199
Carter, Edward, 187
Cassady, Richard, 174
Ceeje Gallery, 181
Central Americans, 58, 224, 261–64, 266, 271, 276–77
Central Avenue, 25, 53, 89, 112–13, 118–19, 195, 206, 210, 252
Centro de Regeneracion, 237
Chambers, Iain, 248
Chandler, Harry, 167
Chavez Ravine, 55–56, 198, 317, 321
Cheng, Meiling, 331
Chernin, Rose, 148
Cherry, Herman, 176
Chessman, Caryl, 180
Chicana/os, 5, 205, 211, 221–36, 246, 326
Chinatown, 58, 198
Chinese, 35–38, 48, 54–55, 57, 124, 199, 324
Chinese Exclusion Act of 1882, 35–36, 38
Church Federation of Los Angeles, 198
Churchill, Ward, 21
City of Quartz, 1, 188, 313
Civic Light Opera, 203
Civil Rights Congress (CRC), 126, 128
Coalition Against Police Abuse, 15
Coalition for Humane Immigrant Rights of Los Angeles (CHIRLA), 334
Cobb, Jelani, 128
Cohen, Herb, 177

Cole, Carolyn Kozo, 322
Comara Gallery, 181
Combs, R. E., 149
Communist Party, 126, 128–29, 147–48, 151
Community Redevelopment Agency (CRA), 56
Community Relations Committee, 145–46
Community Service Organization (CSO), 135, 145–46, 148, 158
Compton, 4, 85–104
Congress of Industrial Organizations, 122–23
Conley, Leroy, 93
Coordinating Committee for Traditional Art, 170
Coplans, John, 165
Corral, Jaime, 200
CRASH (Community Resources Against Street Hoodlums), 261
Crenshaw, 88–89, 170
Crips, 95
Crow, Thomas, 183
Cuadros, Gil, 15
Cuff, Dana, 315
Curtis, Maurice, 141
Cuthbertson, Mary, 91

Davis, Clark, 318
Davis, Doris, 98
Davis, Mike, 1, 93, 149, 188, 313
Day Without a Mexican, A, 333
Dear, Michael, 247, 312–13
Defense Advanced Research Projects Agency (DARPA), 19
De Graaf, Lawrence, 110
De la Rocha, Roberto "Beto," 237
De la Rocha, Zach, 236–37
De Neve, Felipe, 55
Denning, Michael, 310
Department of Housing and Urban Development (HUD), 96
Deverell, William, 311
De Volada Records, 221
Dolan, Harry, 97
Dollarhide, Douglas, 92–93, 98

Dolphin, John, 209–10
Donahue, Kenneth, 187
Dones, Sidney, 117
Dorn, Warren M., 187
Du Bois, W. E. B., 22
Dwan Gallery, 181

East Compton, 103
East Los Angeles, 53, 135, 197, 201, 204, 222–37
Eastside Committee for the Protection of the Foreign Born, 152
Eastside Jewish Community Center, 156
Easy E (Eric Wright), 99
18th Street Gang, 262, 265, 272
Ejercito Nacional de Liberacion Nacional (EZLN), 232–33
Elman, Richard M., 90, 96
El Monte, 26, 212–13
Escobar, Edward, 320
Esquith, Joseph, 146, 149
Ethington, Phil, 190, 311
Everett, Elin, 181

Fair Employment Practices Commission, 198
Family, The, 174–76, 180
FBI (Federal Bureau of Investigation), 99
Ferlinghetti, Lawrence, 176
Ferus Gallery, 175–76, 181–88
FHA (Federal Housing Authority), 87, 294
Fiering, Ida, 148, 156
Filipinos, 38, 57, 195, 327
Flamming, Douglas, 110, 323
Flores, Quetzal, 230, 232
Fong, Timothy, 324
Ford, John Anson, 203–4, 211–12
Franklin, H. Bruce, 21
Frederick, William, 318
Freer, Regina, 103
Fregoso, Rosa Linda, 205
Frias, Ed, 206–7
Friendship Festival, 144
Frumkin, Leo, 143

Gabriel, Juan, 251, 253, 259
Galerie de Ville, 181
Galleria Gianni, 181
Gangs, 95–99, 266. See also Bloods, Crips, 18th Street Gang, La Mara Salvatrucha
Garcia, Matt, 26
Garvey, Marcus, 114
Gas House coffeehouse, 176, 180–81
Getty Museum, 185, 188
Gibbs, Marla, 17
Ginsberg, Allen, 176
Goldberg, David Theo, 199
Gomez, Francisco, 249
Gomez, Sergio, 245, 249–50
Gonzales, Martha, 228
Gottlieb, Dahlia, 97
Gray Conservatory of Music, 202
Green, Bill, 202
Griffith Park, 72, 169
Guerrero, Chico, 200
Guild Opera, 203
Gumprecht, Blake, 317
Gustafson, Cloyd, 55–56

Hancock, Hunter, 206, 213
Haney-López, Ian, 320, 323
Harby, Harold, 172, 175, 180
Harris, Wynonie, 208
Haynes Foundation, 55
Healey, Dorothy, 148
Herms, George, 183
Hersford, Miss Edgar, 180
Hidalgo, David, 228
Higgins, Chuck, 206
Highland Park Art Guild, 174–75
Hip-hop music, 244–45, 256
Hise, Greg, 312, 316–17
Hoffman, Harry and Hilda, 157
Hollenbeck, 55–56, 135, 143
Hollywood Bowl, 199, 203
Holston, James, 261
Holy Barbarians, The, 176–79
Home Owners Loan Corporation (HOLC), 56

Homies Unidos, 272–74
Hondagneu-Sotello, Pierrette, 333–34
Hopkins, Henry, 187
Hopps, Walter, 181–82
Horne, Gerald, 110
Horton, John, 324
Houston, Joe, 206
Hugg, Dick "Huggy Boy," 207–9
Huntington Park, 57, 86, 88

Ice Cube (O'Shea Jackson), 99, 250
Immigration and Naturalization Service
    (INS), 152, 262
Infante, Pedro, 201
International Workers Order, 149, 151
Irvine, 6, 283–308
Irwin, Robert, 165–66

Jackson, Alfred and Luquella, 85, 89, 104
Jacobs, Arthur Leslie, 198
Jacobson, Matthew, 138
Jae-P, 254–56
Jameson, Fredric, 271, 274
Janapol, Mel, 144–46, 158
Japanese American National Museum, 15
Japanese Americans, 15, 112, 139, 147, 153,
    186, 199, 310, 323–24
Jarvis, Al, 213
Jeffords, Susan, 21
Jews, 15, 22, 40, 135–59
Jones, Isabel Morse, 199

Kanemitsu, Marsumi, 186
Kauffman, Craig, 183, 185
Kaufman & Broad, 102
Keats, Mark, 144
Keep America Committee, 175
Keil, Roger, 248
Keinholz, Edward, 181–85
Kelley, Robin, 22, 205
Kenney, Moira Rachel, 14, 327–28
Kerouac, Jack, 176
King, Rodney, 130, 262
Kinney, Abbot, 176

Kirk, Rahsaan Roland, 17
Knights of Columbus, 72
Kobayashi, Kathy, 322
Korean Americans, 15, 326, 330
Ku Klux Klan, 113, 121

Laboe, Art, 211–12
Labor Community Strategy Center (LCSC),
    26, 28–29
Lacy, Suzanne, 330
La Fiesta Club, 195
La Mara Salvatrucha, 264–67, 273
Lance, Philip, 80
L.A. School, 1, 7, 325–27
Latina/os, 15, 22, 103–4, 212, 222, 224–25,
    229, 243–45, 252, 267–68, 274, 285–86,
    288, 292–93, 296, 303, 305, 324
LeClerc, Gustavo, 247
Lichtenstein, Roy, 185
Limón, José, 274
Lipsitz, George, 251, 258
Lipton, Lawrence, 176–81
Lizarraga, Don Cruz, 250
Long Beach, 93, 102, 203
Lopez, Paul, 197
Los Angeles All-City High School Symphony
    Orchestra, 200
Los Angeles City: Board of Public Works,
    173, 175; Bureau of Music, 198–203, 213;
    Council, 92, 199; Cultural Affairs
    Department, 188; Health Department, 55;
    Housing Authority, 56, 67; Metropolitan
    Recreation and Youth Services Council,
    204; Municipal Art Department, 169–70,
    172–74, 182, 198; Police Department,
    177, 184, 195,198, 262
Los Angeles County, 90; Board of Supervisors,
    179, 211; Local Area Formation Commis-
    sion, 93; Museum of Art, 183, 187;
    Sheriff's Department, 179
Los Angeles Mirror News, 179
Los Angeles Negro Art Association, 169
Los Angeles Philharmonic Orchestra, 200–
    201, 203

Los Angeles Sentinel, 210
Los Angeles Times, 53, 98–99, 177, 179, 187
Los Angeles Urban League, 88
Los Lobos, 228
Lummis, Charles, 167
Lunceford, Jimmie, 195
Lydy, F. A., 174
Lynch, Kevin, 272–73

MacArthur Park, 79–80, 196
Maki, Val, 244
Marshall, William, 17
Martí, José, 311
Martinez, Matthew, 159
Martinez, Rubin, 252–53, 255
Massa Gallery, 181
Matthews, Al, 180
McCarren-Walter Act of 1952, 151–53
McGirr, Lisa, 319–20
McNeely, Cecil "Big Jay," 206–7
MC Ren, 98–99
McWilliams, Carey, 7, 48, 197, 309, 311–12,
     314, 320, 335–36
Menace II Society, 100–101
Mendez, Rafael, 200
Meredith, Julie, 180
Mexican Americans, 57, 65, 87, 122, 126,
     135, 141, 144, 157, 196–215, 225, 246,
     254, 264, 310, 315–16, 320–36
Mexicans, 38, 48–50, 52, 54–55, 58, 65, 87,
     112, 118, 124–25, 137, 140, 142–44,
     152–53, 156, 168, 195–215, 222–24,
     227–28, 243, 249, 252, 254, 256–57, 264,
     268, 277, 309, 318
Mexican Tipica Orchestra, 201
Miller, Loren, 90
Milton, Roy, 317
Monroy, Douglas, 50
Monroy, Jaime Gonzalez, 204
Montalvo, Joseph "NUKE," 232
Mooney, Tom, 168
Moore, Burton, 323
Moses, Ed, 183

Mulherin, Thomas, 180
Municipal Art Patrons, 172

NAACP, 114, 116, 125, 128, 213
National Civic League, 86
National Sculpture Society, 175
Native Daughters of the Golden West, 175
Negrete, Jorge, 201
New Jack City, 101
Newman, Charles, 176
Nicolaides, Becky, 86, 319
Noble, David W., 20
Nord, Eric "Big Daddy," 180
Norman, Gene, 208
Normark, Don, 322
Norte, Marisela, 23
Norwood-Brown, Ebony Starr, 104
Now Gallery, 181
NWA, 98–102, 249, 256

Ofelia, Doña, 277
Ollin, 221, 226, 229–30
O'Malley, Walter, 155
Orange County, 283, 286, 290–91, 294, 305,
     320
Orsi, Jared, 317–18
Otis, Harrison Gray, 167
Otis, Johnny, 25, 206–11, 317
OT: Our Town, 104
Ovando, Javier, 262
Ozomatli, 221, 226–27

Pacheco, Raul, 228
Pagán, Eduardo Obregón, 320, 322
Pardo, Mary, 324
Parker, William H., 209
Parson, Don, 315
Peace and Justice Center, 234–35
People's Educational Center, 149
People's Resource Center, 237
Perez, Rafael, 262
Perkoff, Stuart, 176
Phillips, Kate, 311

Phillips, William, 146
Pincetl, Stephanie, 317
Pitt, Leonard, 50
Plagens, Peter, 184
Plaza de la Raza, 224
Poulson, Norris, 172
Powell, Clifton, 100
Powell, Noah, 188
Price, Ken, 165–66
Primus Gallery, 181
Priority Records, 98, 101
Proposition 187, 225–26, 243, 304
Proposition 209, 225
Pueblo Nuevo, 80–81
Pulido, Laura, 311, 317
Purifoy, Noah, 188

Quetzal, 221, 227, 229
Quiñones, Sam, 256
Quinto Sol, 221, 226, 229–31

Ramirez, Lilia, 234
Randolph, A. Phillip, 123
Restovich, George, 210
Rexroth, Kenneth, 176
Reyes, Tony, 200
Richter, Arthur, 176
Ridgewood, 284, 286–90, 292–93, 297–98,
    301–6
Rivera-Salgado, Gaspar, 58
Roberts, Alfred S., 177, 180
Robeson, Paul, 111
Rocco, Raymond, 285, 315
Rodart, Scott and Randy, 227
Rodger Young Village, 72–75
Rodriguez, Luis, 222
Rodriguez, Richard T., 231
Rojas, James, 57
Rose, Tricia, 101
Rosenthal, Bernard, 173, 175, 180
Ross, Kenneth, 172–73, 181
Rouse, Roger, 274
Roybal, Ed, 173
Rubio, Jess, 207

Ruíz, Manuel, 321
Ruscha, Ed, 183, 185

Sachs, Aaron, 311
Said, Edward, 275
Saito, Leland, 324
Saldívar, José David, 275
Sánchez, George, 15, 58
San Fernando Valley, 140, 201
San Salvador, 267, 272–73, 275
Saxton, Alexander, 50
Schwarzenegger, Arnold, 243
Scott, Allen, 312–13
Self-Help Graphics, 224
Semina, 184
Sesma, Chico, 201
Shakur, Tupac, 15
Shelley v. Kramer, 88–89
Shipey, Lee, 199
Shockman, H. Eric, 312
Sides, Josh, 110, 320, 322
Singh, Nikhil Pal, 310
Singleton, John, 100
Slotkin, Richard, 21
Smith, Richard Cándida, 185
Snoop Dogg, 250
Sobel, Mechal, 48
Soja, Edward, 312–13
Solnit, Rebecca, 184
Sonoratown, 50, 53–54, 58
Source magazine, 101
South Central Los Angeles, 88–90, 93, 95,
    100–101, 188, 197, 200–201, 225, 249,
    252–54, 257, 277, 317
Southern California Country, an Island on the
    Land, 48, 311
Spivak, Gayatri, 246
Srole, Leo, 40
Sterry, Nora, 54
Stockwell, Dean, 184
Stone, Irving, 174
Suburbs, 25, 86, 90, 96–98, 279–302
Sweet Sweetback's Baadasss Song, 101
Syndell Studio, 182

Taft-Hartley Act of 1947, 151
Takaki, Walter, 213
Taniguchi, Kenji, 147
Tapscott, Horace, 15–17
Tatum, Art, 25
Tenney, Jack, 149
Tenney Committee, 150, 158, 170
Terminal Island, 55
Terrorism Information and Prevention System
    (TIPS), 19
Torres, Rodolfo, 222
Tostado, Edmund "Don Tosti," 200
Tovar, Robert, 230
Treaty of Guadalupe, 47
Turnbull, Betty, 184

Umeda, Kiyo, 204
University of California, Los Angeles, 90, 93
University of Southern California, 53, 55
U.S. v. Wong Kim Ark, 39

Valens, Ritchie, 213
Valle, Victor, 222
Van Peebles, Melvin, 101
Vargas, João Costa, 320
Venice Beach, 165–66, 175–88
Venice Civic Union, 177, 180
Venice West Café, 176, 181
Villa, Raúl, 327–28
Village Callers, 222

Warhol, Andy, 185
Warner, W. Lloyd, 40

War Production Board, 198
Warren, Earl, 88
Washington, Dinah, 317
Watts, 87, 90–95, 100, 109–10, 119, 130,
    198; riots, 92–93, 188, 205; Towers Art
    Center, 188
Waxman, Al, 150
Welfare Federation of Los Angeles, 150
West Adams, 88
Western School of Music, 202
West Hollywood, 175, 181
Westwood, 201
Williams, Michael, 34
Willowbrook, 87, 92–93, 95
Wilson, Gerald, 195
Wilson, Pete, 226
Wolch, Jennifer, 317
Women's Civic Club of Venice, 177, 180
Women's Club of Hollywood, 174
Works Progress Administration, 56
Wyman, Rosalind, 155

Xicano Records and Film, 221

Yanex, Josefina, 152
Yee, Lee Choi, 36
Yorty, Sam, 111
Yousman, Bill, 101

Zapatistas, 233, 237
Zeiger, Hal, 211
Zinzun, Michael, 15
Zoot-suit riots, 198